The Frederick J. Miller family and its brewery

THE MILLER BEER BARONS

Tim John

Badger Books Inc.
Oregon, Wis.

© Copyright 2005 by Timothy John
All Rights Reserved.
Published by Badger Books Inc.
Edited by Pat Reardon
Cover design by George McCue
Cover photo by John Maniaci of the Wisconsin State Journal
Printed in the U.S.A.

ISBN+10 1-932542-16-7
ISBN+13 978-1-932542-16-5

Badger Books Inc./Waubesa Press
P.O. Box 192
Oregon, WI 53575
Toll-free phone: (800) 928-2372
Fax: (608) 835-3638
Email: books@badgerbooks.com
Web site: www.badgerbooks.com

Library of Congress Cataloging-in-Publication Data

John, Tim.
     The Miller beer barons : the Frederick J. Miller family and its brewery / Tim John.
        p. cm.
     Includes bibliographical references and index.
     ISBN 1-932542-16-7
     1. Miller, Frederick J. (Frederick Johnas), 1824-1888. 2. Miller, Frederick J. (Frederick Johnas), 1824-1888--Family. 3. Miller Brewing Company--History. 4. Brewers--Wisconsin--Milwaukee--Biography. 5. Breweries--Wisconsin--Milwaukee--History. 6. Beer industry--Wisconsin--Milwaukee--History. I. Title.

     HD9397.U52M555 2005
     338.7'64123'0922--dc22

                              2005017387

I dedicate this book to my family.

CONTENTS

INTRODUCTION

Tim John takes us back to a time where our modern-day expression of "Miller Time" commenced. Tim, a great-grandson of the founder of Miller Brewing Company, Frederick J. Miller, takes on the distinctly onerous task of charting a history of a brewing dynasty — the Millers. In 1855, Fred Miller, a dapper German immigrant with an unusual flair for beer, brewing, and branding roamed the streets of Milwaukee determined to distinguish his fine, noble malt beverages by their quality. Fred became known for his "confoundedly good taste of beer" and the expression "Quality Uncompromising" - a mandate that still stands as a cornerstone of the Miller Brewing Company today.

Of course, there have been other brewing dynasties in the Cream City. Many began around the time that Fred started his brewery on Milwaukee's Plank Road, utilizing the abundance of pure water in Milwaukee, the limestone hills that were excavated to become naturally cool cellars, and the abundance of ice from nearby lakes to ensure the limestone caves remained cold for the successful fermentation and conditioning of beer. Famous names and obvious competitors, but also collaborators, from this time stand out as evidence of what was to make Milwaukee famous. Jacob, Charles, Lorenz and Phillip Best; Captain Fred Pabst; Valentine Blatz; and Joseph Schlitz were all noted personalities, entrepreneurs, and icons to a beer industry that was to be revered worldwide.

But it was Fred J. Miller who initiated and leveraged brewing innovation. He introduced the beer garden to Milwaukee and beer style after beer style and perfected the rich-colored, light-flavored American lager style that has became the mainstream beer of today and is copied worldwide. Fred relentlessly challenged the status quo. The legacy is the foundation of Miller's continuing success today. The Miller Brewing Company's 150-year history has survived on the premise of "delighting the consumer." Whether it is such innovations as Miller High Life, Miller Light, Miller Genuine Draft, or whatever new brand fashion we will experience in the future, it all started with one man's dream and pursuit of traditionally brewing excellent beer to be enjoyed responsibly with family and friends.

Tim John takes us through a journey of ambition, of persistence and determination, of intrigue, of happiness and sadness, and of history as we follow the Millers from Fred J. to Fred C. and beyond over 100 years of traditional brewing. Cheers!

— David S. Ryder, PhD.
Vice President
Brewing, Research and Quality Assurance
Miller Brewing Company

FOREWORD

This project grew out of my interest in the year that my dad, Harry G. John, Jr. (1919 to 1992), was president of the Miller Brewing Company, 1946 to 1947. It is the event in my family's history that has most intrigued me; that I most brag about. Primarily, I set out to write an analytical book about my dad's tenure as the brewery's chief executive officer. In a nutshell, in May 1946, he was unanimously elected president and, one year later, removed by his mother, sister, and most of his extended family. As I delved into the documentation, I discovered that there was inadequate material for an article let alone a book, so I enlarged its scope to its current theme, the entire period that the Miller family owned the brewery.

Regardless of the change in scope, my dad's presidency held my interest. This unpleasant period in his life determined his future and, in many ways, mine. My father was unable to forgive or forget any perceived malefaction against him, remaining paranoid toward those closest to him. My sister Emily was born in 1957, ten years after his dismissal and, soon after, I followed. He proceeded to have nine children with my mother, Erica P. John, (who happens to be the last surviving member of the Miller family's third generation). While raising us, he maintained his distrust of his extended family, often unfairly denigrating them. As adults, it was the responsibility of us children to discover the kernels of truth in his personal perceptions.

After my dad was banished from its presidency in 1947, the Miller Brewing Company diminished in his awareness, even though he remained a minority stockholder until 1970. As the years passed, he spoke so little about it that my mother did not know of his association with it when they married in 1956. Until I was in my mid-teens, I understood little about his connection with the brewery, even though, in 1970 when I was eleven years old, he took me to various brewery meetings as he finalized the sale of de Rancé, Inc.'s stock. De Rancé was a private Catholic foundation that my father created with his stock from the Miller Brewing Company, which eventually totaled 47% of the outstanding shares. During the lengthy meetings, a kindly brewery employee would give me private brewery tours, terminating with an orange soda at the Miller Inn.

As I unraveled and then reconstructed the lives of my relatives who were involved with the Miller Brewing Company, I determined to give them equal and fair footing. Although, due to the large collection of material that I received from my father and his immediate ancestors, I over-represented the interests of my grandmother Elise K. John's family. Much of the documentation from her four siblings is either lost or inaccessible in private hands. Regardless, I used the Millers' relationship with the Miller Brewing Company as the standard against which I measured their success. The book is a treatment of the Miller family's management of the brewery and the brewery's financial importance to them. I was cautious in my treatment of relatives whose children are still living, except my father, who I have earned the right to review critically. Otherwise, I did not withhold any pertinent information regarding my relatives.

Even though the vast majority of this book was written about the Miller family, some of whom added very little to the brewery, I provided information on as many early non-family employees as reasonable. Though the Millers owned and controlled the brewery, thousands of workers; men and women, white and black, straight and gay, German and American, determined and continue to determine the brewery's success. I doff my hat to every past and current employee of the Miller Brewing Company, and its associated concerns, who daily, regardless of any personal difficulties, brewed and sold beer to millions of the world's inhabitants. They improved the world by providing a clean, socially lubricating, healthful, and tasty drink.

My mother, Erica P. John, was my primary cheerleader as

I researched and wrote this book. She filled me with fascinating stories, while helping me to discover connections between seemingly unrelated historical events. She also corrected many grammatical mistakes, even explaining to me that finches do not eat sunflower seeds but rather thistle seeds, thus repairing one of my similes. My sister Paula provided me with hundreds of old photos and a considerable amount of historical research that she had accomplished.

Over the past five years, Miller Brewing Company employee and historian Tice Nichols selflessly reached out to the Miller family, including us in ceremonial events at the brewery. Since 1970, there had been no such connection between the brewery and the family. At the brewery's founder's day celebration in September 2003, the corporate employees stood and cheered for five family members as we were introduced; it sent chills up my spine. My gratitude also goes to Miller contract archivist David Herrewig for his intellectual and practical assistance, immeasurably improving this book. This book would have been incomplete without the help of the brewery's archives. Dave assisted in editing numerous drafts of the manuscript and writing some of the captions for the photographs, especially ones relating to the brewery. Mary Weishan Maruszewski read every chapter several times and, with her considerable knowledge of the English language, smoothed out many sentences. Dr. David S. Ryder, Miller Brewing Company's brewmaster, patiently explained the intricacies of brewing history to this neophyte. Thomas Cannon, de Rancé's long-time attorney, read the manuscript, improving it with his legal experience, knowledge of history, and grammatical expertise.

The late Dr. Frederick I. Olson, the one-time luminary of Milwaukee history, was my "secret weapon." When I began this project, my paucity of knowledge of local history had me searching in myriad directions for assistance. During hours of phone calls and personal visits, this esteemed gentleman, who was always gracious with his time and knowledge, filled me in on many areas of local history.

My relatives were generally helpful in my research. Especially, I wish to acknowledge my second cousin Charles "Chuck" Bransfield, who was born in 1918 and brought me stories from the 1800s that he had heard as a boy. Additionally, he lived with his grandparents Clara and Carl Miller off and on from his childhood, giving him experiences spanning three generations. At times, I thought that this book was merely my transcribing Chuck's stories, instead of researching my own project. I cannot overestimate how much my beloved cousin Chuck has aided this project.

My first cousin Karen Mulberger Swanson helped me understand our common grandparents, Harry and Elise John. She had the enviable experience of knowing them both, (they had died before my birth), and kindly shared her knowledge, papers, and photos with me. Her husband Jack gave me some colorful stories. My second cousin, Frederick McCahey, generously plied me with stories and allowed me to borrow his mother's (Claire Miller McCahey) scrapbooks, illuminating a branch of my family of whom I knew little. Another cousin, Elizabeth Blommer, shared her knowledge and photographs, while her sisters, Marguerite "Margo" Saule and Mary DuFon recounted stories. Additionally, besides Frederick McCahey, his sisters Anita Gray, Claire O'Neil, and Carol O'Neil and his sister-in-law Mary Lou McCahey helped me with their stories. Rose Mary Bradford Hewlett was generous with stories, papers, and photos. Frederick C. Miller's daughters, Gail Wray, Kate Kanaley Miller, Adele Miller, Clair Krause, and Carlotta Johnson were generous with their stories. Siblings, Joan and Frederick Miller Bransfield filled in niches with valuable information.

My wife, Martha, and children, Joseph, Brandon, and Isabel supported me in this project, often nodding glassy-eyed at me as I prattled on about some recently discovered minutia. This four-year project took me away from my family, for which I apologize. I explained to them that the sacrifice will be worthwhile, as the book would give subsequent generations of our family a clear understanding of their heritage.

Some of the many people who helped me write this book

include;

Robert Abraham (Harry G. John, Sr.'s hunting guide), George Archibald (Pilot), Donna Brandt and her late husband John (John was the premier Miller Brewing Company private collector. Since his death, Donna has kindly allowed me to review the collection). Timothy Cary (Milwaukee Archdiocesan archivist), John C. Eastberg (Pabst family historian), Guenther Eisenmann (Rose Eisenmann's nephew), Rose Marie & the late Norbert Falkenstein and my maternal aunt Margarete Bernava (German-language translators), Dr. Michael Gordon (professor of history at the University of Wisconsin-Milwaukee), Dr. Tom Moore (teacher of sociology at the University of Wisconsin-Milwaukee), John Gurda (Milwaukee historian), Michael Hansen (businessman and Certified Public Accountant), Dr. Dean Klinger (Milwaukee surgeon), Wayne L. Kroll (Wisconsin brewery historian), John Lang (Phyllis Engelhardt's great nephew), Dorothy Lechtenberg (John Wittig's sister), Brother Leo Gregory (former Trappist fundraiser), Rev. Msgr. Richard McCabe and Dr. Robert McCabe (former neighbors of Elise and Harry John in the Washington Highlands), the late Frank McDonough (Harry G. John, Jr.'s friend at the University of Notre Dame), Joyce Meinicke (an employee of Fred A. Miller, Elise K. John, and Harry G. John, Jr.), John P. Miller (attorney for de Rancé, Inc. and Harry G. John, Jr.), the late William "Bill" Miller, Peter Sanfilippo, and Paul Wolf (Harry G. John, Jr.'s childhood friends), John Steiner (Pabst Brewery collector and historian), and Joan and Gabriel Szekely (residents of Elise and Harry John, Jr.'s Washington Highlands home, who have enthusiastically shown their home to me and my relatives). Here are the institutions at which I did research for this book:

Archdiocese of Milwaukee Archives
Concordia University Archives in Mequon, Wisconsin (by phone)
Divine Savior Holy Angels High School (by phone)
Franklin, Wisconsin City Library
Marquette University Library Archives

Mead Public Library in Sheboygan, Wisconsin
Miller Brewing Company Archives
City of Milwaukee Public Library
Milwaukee County Historical Society
Milwaukee Journal Sentinel Archives
Mormon Church Family Resource Center in Greenfield, Wisconsin
Newberry Library in Chicago
North Dakota State Historical Society (by mail)
Rutherford B. Hayes Presidential Center in Fremont, Ohio (over the internet)
The Milwaukee Catholic parishes of St. Joseph, St. Rose and St. Sebastian
Sheboygan County in Wisconsin Historical Research Center
Woodlands Academy of the Sacred Heart in Lake Forest, Ill.
University of Wisconsin – Milwaukee Archives
Waseca, Minnesota County Historical Society

— *Tim John*
March 2005

1.
Coming to America

By early 1888, the Miller Brewing Company in Milwaukee was a spectacular enterprise with numerous specialized buildings annually producing tens of thousands of barrels of refreshing beer. The headquarters and brewhouse were constructed of brick. The other buildings, built of lumber, held men that manufactured wooden barrels (coopers), stored ice, stabled horses, repaired wagons, and made malt from barley, boiled water, malt, and hops and then added yeast to make beer, and bottled the finished product. There also was an extensive system of caverns in a limestone cliff that protected thousands of barrels of the fermented malt beverage. Additionally, there were many small homes to house the workers. Frederick J. Miller, whose life began on November 24, 1824, orchestrated this enterprise with a rare talent.

Frederick's father, Thaddeus Edward Miller (born on October 14, 1771), hailed from southern Germany. Thaddeus Miller served as mayor of Riedlingen, in the present day German state of Baden-Wurttemberg, from 1820 to 1826. The city's marketplace had a gothic fountain and old frame houses that demonstrated a culture of many hundred years. Thaddeus came from a comfortable merchant family and raised his children in an attractive three-story stone house in the center of town. Frederick's parents, along with many of their regional countrymen, were devout Catholics. "On both his father's and mother's side, there was ancestral lineage bright with scholarly, political, and commercial accomplishments."[1] His paternal uncle, van Kolb, was the Oberamsrichter (high judge) of Baden. His father and his first wife, Anna Zeller, had two children who survived childhood; Maria Anna born on

July 19, 1798, and Anton Adrian born on September 8, 1802.
Anna died on May 26, 1812. One year later on June 24, 1813,
Thaddeus married Maria Ludowika Zepfel, who was born in
1792 in nearby Constance, Switzerland on the south shore of
Lake Constance.

Thaddeus and Maria had six children: Maria Katharina
Antonia in 1814; Maria Josefa Karoline in 1816; Thaddae
Eduard in 1819; Maria Sophia in 1821; Maria Luise in 1822;
Friedrich Eduard (our future brewer), born November 24, 1824;
and Wilhelm Gottlieb Bonifacius in 1826.[2]

At some point Friedrich Eduard Miller, the future beer
baron, Anglicized his name to Frederick Johnas Miller. Possibly
Johnas was Fred's 1838 confirmation name, which he preferred over Eduard. There is no record extant regarding Fred's
schooling, but his handwriting style and clear ideas showed
that he enjoyed a solid education. In 1837, when Frederick
was 12 years old, his father died and, thereafter, Maria reared
the brood. Thaddeus was an affluent man who, by one report,
left an estate valued at $75,000 to $100,000. To reinforce this
point, for many years after coming to Milwaukee, Fred received
a $3,000 annual stipend from the estate.[3]

Most widows, due to their diminished household income,
become more pragmatic after their husband's funeral. No doubt
if Thaddeus Miller had lived twenty more years, his children
would have enjoyed more vocational opportunities, but Maria
Miller promoted careers that included a practical education and
immediate earnings. Owing to their straitened circumstances,
the Miller children were precluded from pursuing jobs requiring years of education that would delay their earning potential.
Maria persuaded young Frederick to enter an apprenticeship at
a brewery in Riedlingen, beginning a series of events that led
ultimately to the creation of the Miller Brewing Company.[4] If
Frederick is the father of the Miller Brewing Company, then
the farsighted Maria is its mother.

At age 17, after three years of brewery apprenticeship, Fred
left home and began seven years of travel and study in Germany, France, and Algeria. Along the way, he learned seven

languages, including Latin, all of which were important for the future beer baron to become, as his ancestors, a great merchant. During this period he worked in various breweries in France and Bavaria (southern Germany) improving his beer-making knowledge and skills.

Excellent apprenticeships require generous masters who share their knowledge instead of merely extracting cheap labor, and Frederick learned under just such a *mensch*. Certainly, this apprenticeship taught Fred the inner workings of a brewery. The master brewers measured, timed, managed, and tasted, leaving the odious work to the underlings. Becoming a brewmaster was a demanding assignment. To succeed, one needed to be a chemist, an engineer, an agronomist, and a purchasing agent, all rolled into one. And then add a perfectionist with a determination to maintain an unvarying quality and taste to his brew. During the hectic winter and spring brewing period, workers put in 15- to 17-hour days hauling, dipping, pumping, breaking, stirring, and boiling.[5] Since cleanliness was vital to brewing, scrubbing floors, walls, and equipment, surely, was integral to Fred's daily routine. Fortunately besides a keen mind, Fred was blessed with a strong back, giving him a natural inclination for the strain of a busy brewing season.

This apprenticeship lasted approximately three years until 1841, at which time Frederick decided to train at other breweries in Bavaria, and in France. Bavaria was the natural choice, especially Munich — the Mecca of beer making. In all likelihood, Fred's knowledgeable friends and relatives recommended well-run breweries to him. From 1841 to 1848, Frederick improved his familiarity with making fermented barley extract but more importantly, increased his comprehension of managing a brewery. If this young man had remained at one brewery, he would have obtained an intimate knowledge of how to operate one brewery but, by traveling and serving apprenticeships at various facilities, he learned failures and successes on a broader scale. At this time, Fred Miller was likely unaware that he was preparing to become a brewery manager or beer baron rather than a master brewer. Diverse training, whether self-initiated or promoted by others, was the most important tool, besides money, that Frederick brought to Wisconsin to create the Miller Brewing Company.

In the fall of 1849, at age 25, Frederick applied for the lease of a brewery owned by Prince Karl of Hohenzollern-Sigmaringen, a sovereignty in what is now southern Germany, twenty-seven kilometers from Riedlingen. The town featured the magnificent Hohenzollern Castle on a bluff overlooking the storied Danube River. This palace was constructed more for residency than defense, and today it is a museum with an eclectic collection of armaments and stuffed animals. On September 7, 1849, the *Sigmaringen Official Gazette* proclaimed that on the 27th of that month the prince's brewery, together with the licensed premises for selling beer, would be leased, by public auction.[6] Ten years of brewery training, along with Fred's mother's ongoing support, provided him with the confidence to attempt such a significant leap in social status.

Winning this lease would be a substantial enterprise requiring extensive brewing knowledge, a stellar reputation, and considerable financial backing. Fred had ample brewing experience and good standing that he demonstrated through letters of recommendation from his previous employers. An October 13, 1849 missive, issued by the municipality of Riedlingen, remarked, "that during eight years in Germany and France but especially in Bavaria, he reached in this profession [brewing] such a perfection that his personal qualification for the independent operation of this profession cannot be doubted." Lastly, Frederick fulfilled the financial commitment with a combination of his own money and funds from his sister, Maria Sophia, but most notably, his mother conveyed to the royal administration that, if necessary, she would double the security deposit.[7]

On October 21, 1849, to augment ongoing negotiations, Frederick J. Miller declared his intent to rent the brewery if the princely administration made specific repairs to the premises and provided him with a livery stable. Finally, the entrepreneur captured the lease by outpacing two other applicants, including the gentleman who previously had held it. Frederick gave the princely administration a sizeable security deposit and made plans to pay the rent in the regional currency of Florians and Kreutzers on the first day of February, May, August, and November. The ten-year lease, set to commence on November 11, 1849, also stated that the lessee had to pay 5 percent interest on the brewery inventory and to remunerate the chimney sweeper. The rented business included a 375-gallon brew kettle, and cellars (below the brewery, under the castle, and in the town of Hedingen, Switzerland). Before the widespread use of ice and mechanized refrigeration, brewers aged and then stored beer in nearby and distant cool cellars until its sale.[8]

On October 24, Prince Karl, who was serving the last days of his reign, approved the contract. Germany was unifying, and regional sovereigns such as Prince Karl were abdicating their thrones to larger political entities. In April 1850, Prince Karl relinquished his sovereignty of Hohenzollern-Sigmaringen to the ruling family of Prussia, but the castle and lease remained under his family's dominion.[9]

Fred Miller had mustered his resources to procure a tenancy brewing various varieties of beer and brandy. The work was demanding, but if he performed it well he was assured of an excellent income in the regulated economy of 19th Century Western Europe. No doubt he had substantial help, both familial and professional, in securing the lease. We do not know of his professional backers, but we do know that he was abetted by his mother and sister, Maria Sophia.

Frederick Miller announced his new status as lessee of the Royal Brewery in a November 12, 1849, newspaper ad, promising to put, "every effort to please our regular guests and any travelers stopping in."[10] The new businessman brewed lower alcoholic content beer for everyday consumption and concocted products with more alcohol for special occasions such as *Oktoberfest*. The bottom fermenting beer, common in southern Germany, was lagered (aged) for several months before sale. Its cousin, ale, popular in the British Isles and 18th Century America, employed yeast, which rose to the top after fermentation and had an abbreviated aging — or maturation — period. Due to the lack of artificial refrigeration, brewers made beer only during the cold season, from October until the middle of April. Southern Germanic people and lager beer were inseparable providing Fred with a stable and substantial market for his product. Besides supplying the royal family and the State of Hohenzollern-Sigmaringen with the product of fermented barley, the future Milwaukee brewmaster may have had some opportunity to sell it elsewhere. Due to the difficulty in procuring this brewing lease, certainly, the prince enforced a limited regional monopoly allowing Fred to sell his product at elevated prices, providing him with a tidy profit.[11]

In all likelihood, Fred spent more of his energy managing the business and promoting its products than brewing beer. His sanguine personality lent itself to oversight and promotion rather than brewing, which may have been done by a lower-paid worker with a keen palate. The fact that he paid a fifth more than the other lease applicants, including the man who had previously owned the lease, demonstrated his understanding of investment and return. He gained this insight at other breweries or was given valid advice at the time of the lease negotiations perhaps by his mother. An unsubstantiated theory states that Fred won the lease due to his sister's supposed employment at the castle. At any rate, the young man aggressively pursued a goal and was willing to risk his and his family's finances to achieve it.[12]

Fred Miller provided product for the residents in and around Sigmaringen according to the Reinheitsgebot Purity Law, introduced in 1516, by Duke Wilhelm IV of Bavaria, dictating that beer could be brewed only with pure water, barley and hops. This narrow list of ingredients and "Germanic" attention to detail provided most Teutonic brewers a repeatable formula for success. These products give current German beer its robust taste and color in comparison to America's lighter taste and clearer cast. In the mid to late 19th Century, many brewers emigrated from southern Germany and created successful breweries from Chile to Canada using locally grown barley and hops.

In June 1851, Fred Miller requested that his landlord reduce the value of the kiln-dryer, mash vat, and oak cooler, which would allow him to pay lower property taxes. He blamed, "this circumstance the most for the fact that my lager-beer turned sour last fall." He asked them to lower the established value of these items that he had spent a considerable amount of money to repair, due to their poor condition. He also explained that it was in, "the interest of both the esteemed owner and the tenant that the Lordly Brewhouse be able to compete in the vicinity with Strodorf, especially, which has expanded in the last years." When necessary, Frederick confronted his superiors and provided logical arguments to bolster his position. If not a brewer, Frederick would have been a competent barrister.[13]

On June 7, 1853, Fred, then settled and financially successful, married Josephine Miller, who was no relation. On January 25 of the succeeding year, their son Joseph Edward was born. Fred and Josephine, apparently with little disagreement, accomplished meaningful goals on two continents. It is difficult to discern Josephine's role in the family's business endeavors, so I interchange the names "Frederick Miller" and the "Millers" indicating that, lacking contrary evidence, they cooperated in their familial and financial dealings.

Apparently, at the time that Fred Miller married Josephine, he began to consider leaving southern Germany for America where he would be less constrained by economic laws and tradition. In fact, he may have discussed emigrating with Josephine before their marriage to avoid her possible future intransigence. Fred may have been apprehensive of the increasing political turmoil in Sigmaringen, and he may also have been drawn to America by stories of potential riches. The four-and-a-half years that the future beer baron brewed beer in Sigmaringen gave him the money and confidence to explore opportunities in America. The only noteworthy obstacle to his emigration would be the 1849 ten-year lease, which he needed to legally terminate, or the municipality of Riedlingen would have denied him permission to leave.[14]

In time, Fred Miller found master brewer Joseph Vierthaler, an acceptable replacement, thus satisfying the prince. On April 28, Fred was determined to tie up the loose ends of his business by placing a local advertisement listing for sale the amount of various malts, seed barley, quarts of brandy, pigeon fodder, and fine hops. He also warned his lagging debtors that if they have not settled with him by May 7, he would sue them. On May 21, 1854, the royal administration released Frederick from the remaining 5 1/2 years of his lease permitting him to continue preparations for immigrating to America. Nevertheless, they kept Miller's security deposit until the lease ended on November 11, 1859.[15]

As all emigrants, Fred converted most of his assets into cash, then gold, for surviving in the New World and, in the Millers' case, purchasing a brewery. He, along with two other men, auctioned their worldly goods on May 9, 10, and June 12, and, due to the large number of departing emigrants, they probably received low bids. After converting their estate into $8,000 in gold, they sailed from La Havre, France, on the ship Connecticut and on August 23, 1854, they arrived in New York City.[16]

In late 1854, 29-year-old Fred and 24-year-old Josephine, with seven-month-old Joseph Edward in tow, visited George Ehret, a fellow countryman living in New York City whose son, in 1866, founded the famous Hell Gate Brewery. Fred sought advice from Ehret who said, "Take your time, look the country over before you settle down." Milwaukee was likely on their short list before the Millers left Sigmaringen. In the 1840s and 1850s, multitudes of Germans had been coming to America and settling primarily in what was known as the German Triangle — Milwaukee, Cincinnati, and St. Louis. So before departing, Fred must have known about Milwaukee from previous emigrants.[17]

The Millers spent some months in New York City, and on November 15, 1854, Fred declared his intent there to become an American citizen. In March 1855, Fred and Josephine left

America's pre-eminent city on a steamship for New Orleans and then traveled up the Mississippi River past St. Louis. The boat was filled with immigrants, which made dormitory arrangements scarce. Some unlikely lore reports that Fred had been sleeping on the deck when a vacant space opened up on a sack of corn meal, where he dozed soundly. The next day the future beer baron discovered that the slot had been cleared by the death of a man from cholera. "Miller rushed to the steward; got a bottle of whiskey, and swallowed it in a single tilt. He lived in fear for a week but he didn't get the cholera." The Millers disembarked at La Crosse, Wisconsin, and traveled to Milwaukee, where they most likely arrived in the spring of 1855. When the immigrant saw the city's grand lakefront, he remarked to Josephine in German, "A town with a magnificent harbor like that has a great future in store." They rented a hotel room until a house became available.[18]

2.
PLANK ROAD
BREWERY

Milwaukee grew from the confluence of three rivers: the Milwaukee, the Menomonee, and the Kinnickinnic. In the late 1600s and early 1700s, the Fox, Mascouten, and Potawatomi Indian tribes lived in the area. The Potawatomi became dominant by 1700 and remained so until the 1830s when the entire region was ceded to the United States. In the 1830s, after treaties were signed and the U.S. promoted the land for American development, Yankees and Yorkers (Easterners) began to stream into the area. Land speculators, Solomon Juneau, Byron Kilbourn, and George H. Walker, who each had a distinct village site, promoted settlement. Milwaukee, which received its state charter on January 31, 1846, competed with Chicago as an important destination until the railroad arrived, giving Chicago a tremendous boost. By 1850, Milwaukee had 20,000 residents, by 1860 – 45,000, and, by 1870, a little over 70,000.[19]

Milwaukee's personality started to change in October 1839 when German immigrants began to arrive. By the 1840s and 1850s Germans were flowing into the area and remaking the city in their own image. By 1860 half of Milwaukee's residents were immigrants with 35% of those being of German descent. At that time, Germany did not exist as a separate political entity but many ethnic and national groups claimed the German language as their own. Eventually, Milwaukee and its state, Wisconsin, became dominated by Teutonic people. Many of them came from the southern region of what is now Germany with a tradition of beer drinking that greatly exceeded that of northern Germany.[20]

Fred and Josephine arrived in Milwaukee, to an improving
transportation system. According to the 1855 City Directory horse drawn stagecoaches were still popular means of
conveyance, especially to less populous destinations. Where
large waterways existed, steamboats were an easy means of
moving people, animals, and goods, for instance between the
growing municipalities on Lake Michigan. Rivers and canals
were pathways for smaller boats. Finally, the railroad was approaching from the East. The north and south running Green
Bay, Milwaukee & Chicago Rail Line, and, therefore to all
points east, was completed in early 1855. At this same time,
the Milwaukee and Mississippi Railroad, which began in 1850,
was operable to Madison.

Fred probably deposited his gold in a bank while searching
for a suitable brewery to purchase. In 1855, Milwaukee had 25
breweries serving its citizens, with more opening all the time.
Total Milwaukee beer production then was 50,000 barrels,
enough to make it the second ranking product behind manufacturing of all types. Saloons paid $5 a barrel for their beer and
sold it for 3 to 5 cents a glass. Periodically, the breweries would
wage price wars driving the price for four mugs of beer to five
cents. In all probability, Fred would have had to pay a premium
for an established brewery due to the growth in beer sales. Daily,
there were many Germans arriving from the East Coast, which
boosted the beer market in southeastern Wisconsin. Business
efficiency was unimportant in a rapidly expanding market so,
at that time, it was doubtful that there were many distressed
breweries for sale. Milwaukee beer and ale production increased
from about 20,000 barrels of beer in 1850 to over 100,000
barrels in 1857. Certainly, Fred reviewed various lease and sale
opportunities before discovering the Charles Best Plank Road
Brewery, situated approximately three miles west of Milwaukee
in the Township of Wauwatosa. (The Township of Wauwatosa
was not the current City of Wauwatosa that is centered three
miles west of Miller Brewery. The Town of Wauwatosa was a

thirty-six square mile locale immediately west of the City of Milwaukee that has since been completely eliminated by the annexations of surrounding cities.) The only local municipality, besides Milwaukee, was the Village of Wauwatosa, two miles west of the brewery.

The Best family played an important role in the brewery Frederick Miller purchased.[21]

Jacob Best, Sr. and his four sons, who were the founders of the Empire Brewery in Milwaukee, had owned a brewhouse and winery in Mettenheim on the Rhine River, (in present day Germany). In 1842, his second oldest son Friederich Karl "Charles" Best immigrated to Milwaukee and opened a vinegar factory that flourished, so he returned two years later to persuade his father and brothers to relocate the whole Best family to Milwaukee. In 1844 after immigrating, the five Best males, Jacob, Sr.; Jacob, Jr.; Charles; Phillip; and Lorenz "Lawrence" began the Best Company Empire Brewery, which became the Phillip Best Brewing Company and then the Pabst Brewing Company. In July 1845, due to a schism among the sons, Charles left the Empire Brewery and, in 1849, created the Plank Road Brewery in the Town of Wauwatosa.[22]

The 37-year-old Charles and his partner Gustovus Fine (probably an investment partner) founded the Plank Road Brewery, which at different times was named "Best & Fine" and "Charles Best and Company." On April 30, 1849, Best and Fine purchased two acres of land from James Holton and his wife, in the Menomonee River Valley along side the Milwaukee Watertown Plank Road.[23] The area was surrounded with heavy woods on the hillsides and swampland in the valley. Many of the brewery's buildings were constructed with wooden pilings to keep them from sinking. The nearby Menomonee River was rife with curves and wider than today's straightened riverbed in its concrete jacket. In the spring, the melting snow would swell the river and, occasionally, it would almost reach the brewery.[24]

There were only remnant bands of Indians since most of them had been moved westward or killed. Frederick Miller's daughter, Clara, remembered stories of Indians camping beside the brewery in its early days. She noted a story from her parents that there was, "a little bridge on the street with a brook running under it where the Indians used to sit and fish." She recalled that her father told her about the "trouble" the "Indians made coming over to the brewery for firewater and drinks. This happened so frequently that it was necessary for father to report them and they were forced to move on." Clara's son, Frederick C. Miller, remembered a family story that originated with Frederick J. and Lisette Miller in which members of the Menomonee Nation used to camp in the region and smoke fish, from the river for winter sustenance.

Wayne Kroll, the foremost expert on historical Wisconsin breweries, who has explored the sites of numerous defunct breweries, explained that Best and Fine sought a location with three factors, a clean water supply (an artesian well), limestone cliffs into which they could excavate caverns, and lastly a nearby source of ice, (in most cases a pond, lake, or slow-moving river). He remarked that this locality had all three features. The Menomonee River, which runs alongside the original brewery site, flows south from the northern portion of Milwaukee County before turning east in the City of Wauwatosa and then emptying into Lake Michigan. Kroll explained that the Menomonee River, although close at hand, was a poor source of brewing water because, by the 1850s, it was already too polluted for beer production by municipalities and farms upriver. Mucky or polluted water could lead to spoiled batches of beer, as brewery filtering systems were insufficient to remove particulate matter. Brewers preferred springs and wells to rivers and streams because their water was naturally cleaner, due to the filtering process of percolating water. Springs also emitted colder water than brewers could acquire from rivers. Kroll remarked that an added benefit of the nearby limestone was that the water naturally was more alkaline than acidic, improving the beer's flavor.

Best and Fine placed their brewery on the Watertown Plank Road, which was begun in 1847 and completed in 1855. During the 1840s, many privately capitalized plank roads were built in Milwaukee under franchise from the state, with tolls charged for their use. They looked like wheel spokes emanating from downtown. Their paved offspring exist today named for their destinations; Beloit, Appleton, Lisbon, Chicago, and Fond du Lac. The Watertown Plank Road was built to facilitate travel between Milwaukee and Madison, the state's new capital. Previously, it could take up to ten days to travel to Madison depending on weather and road upkeep. The builders placed traverse planks on the ground where poor drainage and soft ground impeded movement. Unfortunately, soon after its completion, railroads made this road obsolete. Watertown Plank Road's eastern stretch, which bisects the Miller Brewery has been renamed State Street.[25]

In locating their brewery, Best and Fine likely considered the approaching rail service between Milwaukee and the growing town of Waukesha, fifteen miles west of Milwaukee. Beginning in 1847, Wisconsinites began building a railroad line between the two cities and, in 1851, train service reached Wauwatosa and then extended to Waukesha. For much of its early westward course, the railroad ran alongside the Menomonee River. It was not until 1886 that the railroad added a spur directly to the brewery but, nevertheless, nearby access to the railroad reduced shipping costs of raw materials and product. In 1855, Milwaukee was connected to Chicago and, therefore, all points east by rail.[26]

In 1849, Charles and Lawrence Best created a brewery that continues unabated at that exact site, as the Miller Brewing Company. Since Charles was a savvy brewer there is no reason why, with sufficient capital, his new venture would not have been operational in a matter of months. In short order, he contracted for the construction of wooden buildings, such as a residence, icehouse, malt house, brewhouse, and small barn. He also purchased brewing equipment, delivery wagons, and repair tools. Except for the brewing equipment, which took some time to construct, everything else was immediately available locally.

On October 14, 1850, Gustovus Fine sold his share of the land, (and probably the brewery), to Charles' youngest brother, Lawrence, who earlier that year had left the Empire Brewery, giving the brothers complete control of the Plank Road Brewery. At that time, they owned two acres that, on January 1, 1851, they increased to four acres of $138.60 equalized value. The Plank Road Brewery's equalized property value grew from $138.60 in 1850, to $300 in 1851, and to $855 in 1852. (Milwaukee County utilized "equalized value" to adjust the worth of properties among its municipalities that they assessed at different rates.)[27]

The following two years were a halcyon period for Charles and Lawrence as they expanded their fledging business. Certainly, some of their momentum came from competing against their brothers at the Empire Brewery. Charles and Lawrence, the oldest and youngest of the Best Brothers, must have been emotionally close and fed off each other's enthusiasm. The 1850 U.S. census showed that the Best and Company Empire Brewery (the original Best Brewery) had $7,400 in capital, brewed 2,500 barrels, had four employees, and paid an average monthly payroll of $62. On the other hand, the Plank Road Brewery had $4,200 in capital, brewed 1,200 barrels of beer, had two employees, and an average monthly payroll of $200.[28]

As with all brewers, certainly the Bests had cash-consuming failures; batches of fouled beer, uncollectible invoices, and lame horses. It took years to streamline their systems and create a successful business; even, if beginning in 1849, they regularly brewed beer. It was at this time that an ample amount of cash was necessary to survive. Along with the difficulty of operating a successful brewery, the Bests excavated substantial caverns from the northeast corner of the limestone cliffs that rose above a bend of the Menomonee River Valley. To stabilize the tunnels, the workers lined them with brick and stone. One can imagine the difficulties involved with this undertaking before the availability of electrical and gasoline-powered excavation machinery.

In the mid to late 1800s, American brewers created proprietary saloons also known as "tied houses" that were "tied" to individual breweries. The breweries leased these saloons to entrepreneurs who exclusively sold their landlord's labels. These attractive establishments were outfitted with furniture and bric-a-brac sporting the name of their tied brewery. (Currently tied houses are illegal in the U.S. but remain popular in England.) At this time, almost all beer was sold at saloons instead of, as today, at liquor and grocery stores. Brewers developed these saloons out of fear that, under certain circumstances, independent outlets might cease carrying their product. There was intense competition to place "barley pop" in independent saloons, especially popular ones, and a brewery with no outlets to sell its beer would soon close. Therefore, fear motivated brewers to open tied houses to ensure that their customers had access to their product. Once one brewery began buying up popular street corners, others followed suit. Before 1920, major American breweries had thousands of tied houses. On April 27, 1851, the Bests opened a Milwaukee beer hall at 427 East Water Street, at Market Square. (This site is at present-day North Water Street just south of Milwaukee's City Hall.)[29] This undertaking required money, time, employees, and fresh product in a city flush with saloons. The Bests advertised that their bar was also furnished with the best wines, liquors, and segars (ceramic containers).

In 1853, the Bests suffered anguish when 27-year-old Lawrence Best died, leaving a widow. His family buried him in the storied Milwaukee Forest Home Cemetery; currently there is no marker for Lawrence's grave in a Best family plot. This passing had a deleterious effect on the Best Brewery, if for no other reason than Charles losing his preeminent friend and business partner. After Lawrence's death on December 29, 1853, Charles sold one-half interest in his land and probably one-half interest in his business to Frederick Tobler, who doubtless was a financier like Gustovus Fine. Charles might have sold it to raise cash to compensate Lawrence's widow for his share. Two days later, Tobler sold this same interest to Henry Wild, another financier interested in the brewery business.[30]

On Tuesday April 25th, 1854, Charles Best opened a second saloon on East Water Street. (It is unknown what happened to the first one.) He bought the store, formally owned by John Hickey, and converted it to a "magnificently fitted" beer hall. On May 27, Charles Best and Henry Wild bought 3.5 acres from a Mr. Holton to build a deluxe beer garden at the top of the limestone bluff behind his brewery while his employees continued to dig storage cellars into it. The beer garden copied similar venues in Milwaukee, whose design origin lay in Bavaria. Beer gardens were endemic to southern Germany's heritage giving its citizens a place to dance, eat, drink, bowl, and share *gemuetlichkeit*, a feeling of friendliness and contentment. In 1879, one frequent guest at Milwaukee's beer gardens noted that these beautiful places were equipped with bowling alleys, gymnasiums, gymnastic apparatus, springs, summer theaters, music halls, and clubrooms. The gentleman relished visiting Ludemann's Garden on the Lake, Ludemann's Garden on the River, Omentius Park, and the famous Milwaukee Gardens. In the days before electricity and its related entertainment gadgets, beer gardens provided amusement locales where families could, for a fee, listen to bands and dance. Food and drink were extra.[31]

With high-minded notions, Charles Best planned a "summer retreat" on the bluff overlooking his brewery, as the beer gardens were generally open only during summer and fall weekends. The architect, Otto Schwartz, by combining beauty and utility, designed an airy structure supported by light columns, in the form of a cross, and surmounted by an observatory thirty-five feet above the ground. From this vantage, a guest could overlook the City of Milwaukee and Lake Michigan. Best bragged that he would spare no cost in fulfilling this dream. Charles did not complete his beer garden but in 1858, the Millers did, adding gazebos, stone paths, and wooden staircases. They also landscaped the bluffs, creating terraces.[32]

On November 29, 1854, Charles Best and Henry Wild obtained a mortgage from George Papendick, owner of the

Milwaukee Germania Bank. Charles' aggressive expansion of his brewery, combined with Lawrence's death, may have caused a severe cash shortage leading to the loss of his business. In January 1855, in an action unrelated to the status of the Best Brewery, the Germania Bank declared bankruptcy and transferred its assets, including the Best & Wild Brewery mortgage, to a court-appointed receiver, James H. Rogers. The bank stockholders had a vested interest in keeping the brewery operational because it would garner a greater price for an ongoing business than a shuttered one.[33]

Meanwhile, in early 1855 the Millers arrived in Milwaukee with funds and a desire to procure a brewery. It is unknown how Frederick discovered the Plank Road Brewery and whether Charles Best ever met Frederick Miller. At any rate, on July 30, 1855 the Millers purchased the operational Plank Road Brewery's mortgage from Rogers for $8,000. Part of the basis for the sale price came from the knowledge that, if the Millers could sell all of the brewery's 1,200-barrel capacity at $5 a barrel, yearly, they could gross $6,000. Capacity aside, the Miller Brewery sold 300 barrels in its inaugural season. The Millers escaped considerable difficulties by purchasing an ongoing business, whereas Charles Best had had the unenviable task of creating a successful enterprise from an undeveloped piece of Wisconsin soil. A year later on June 11, 1856, the Millers purchased the brewery's land for $2,070 from Rogers and his wife, Emily.[34]

After September 1855, there was no mention of Charles Best's Milwaukee beer hall; either he closed it or sold it to someone other than Fred Miller. After Charles left the brewery business, he lost most of his money in the financial panic of 1857 before moving to Chicago. After some years, he returned and served three terms as Milwaukee County's register of deeds. In 1871 his son Charles reentered the brewery business to become a bookkeeper and then corporate secretary, until 1890, under Captain Frederick Pabst at the Phillip Best Brewing Company (which later became the Pabst Brewing Company). Charles

Best, a man who played the major role in founding two of the world's greatest breweries, died at age 64 in 1877 and was buried at Milwaukee's Forest Home Cemetery.[35]

Upon purchasing the business, the Millers changed the brewery's name to Frederick Miller's Plank Road Brewery or in Fred's broken English "Miller – Milwaukee – Plank's brewery." The immigrant Miller was exhilarated to market a beer keg upon which his name was branded. The first part of the business's name honored its new owner and the second part described its location. Often, an entrepreneur will name his company after himself with the belief that he is its primary asset. Through production quality or marketing expertise, these owners trust that customers, more often than not, will buy their product if their moniker is attached to it. Due to the local nature of most mid-19th century breweries, it was essential that customers went to the site and bought the product. Fred wanted Milwaukeeans to travel to the Watertown Plank Road in order to buy his beer, although, as he developed more sales outlets, the importance of the brewery's location lessened. (To minimize confusion, I always refer to the Plank Road Brewery by its current name, the Miller Brewing Company, despite its varied appellations.)

Between July 30, 1855, when the Millers purchased the brewery and September 25, 1855, when they assumed control, Fred and Josephine Miller surveyed their new holdings. After completing the financial transactions, Frederick developed a plan to improve the business. He must have made several inspections of the facilities and then traveled to Chicago and maybe New York City to cement Charles Best's marketing contacts. Besides the brewery and land, these sales connections constituted much of the value of the Plank Road Brewery. In his own hand, Fred carefully noted all of the brewing equipment, conveyances, livestock, and tools that he had purchased. Oil cans, pumps, a pitchfork, three iron shovels, four wooden tubs, wooden baskets, drills, a whip, a horse cart, several fattened pigs, a cow, and a horse were among the sundry articles that the Millers procured. The brewmaster was especially proud of his three irons for branding beer barrels with the brewery's new name. Pigs were practical to raise because the Millers could fatten them for free with their spent, yet nutritious, barley malt.[36]

Thanks to the Charles Best Brewery workers, brewing continued throughout the business's permutations. Some of Miller's employees including, Katharina Marst (age 20); George Scheuring (age 31); Karl Balluff (age 23) from Riedlingen, Wurtemberg — Fred's hometown; Joseph Pichel (age 21); Eva Winterling (age 20); and Gastil Vuschger (age 23) apparently had worked for Charles Best. These immigrant employees eased the transition during a difficult time in the company's history. In all likelihood they lived on the brewery property rather than commuting from Milwaukee. In the first days, they were without the means to obtain necessities, so Fred extended credit to them for boots, food, gloves, trousers, and doctor bills. Commonly, the Millers sent their employees to shop at Julius Goll's "Goll and Frank" dry goods and notions store, at 267 East Water Street in Milwaukee. In all likelihood, Fred subtracted these expenses from their wages. The Millers paid these employees varying amounts depending on their jobs. Some of the men with brewing experience received $12 to $14 a month whereas others, mainly women, got half of that.[37]

At this same time, the Millers sold a Woerst whiskey distillery that the Best Brewery had employed. It was common for early brewers to also distill whiskey that was the liquor of choice in early America. The early immigrants from the British Isles drank whiskey, and it was not until Germans began populating America, in large numbers, that beer grew in popularity. No doubt, the Bests had also created and sold whiskey to supplement their beer sales. Fortunately, Fred Miller decided to concentrate solely on beer.[38]

At Miller Brewery's inception, besides selling beer locally, Fred Miller shipped it to distributors in New York City and Chicago. (Breweries that sold beer outside of their region were known as shippers.) Much of Miller Brewery's long-term success was due to Fred shipping his product to the large markets of New York City and Chicago. Among all local breweries, only a handful were successful shippers, such as the Milwaukee breweries Blatz, Melms, and Phillip Best [Pabst] that had been doing so since 1852. In fact various breweries, including Miller, developed brands, called Export for shipping afar, with a four or five per cent higher alcohol content than usual, to withstand the transport without becoming soured or losing their transparency. After 1855, when the Chicago and North Western Railway connected Chicago to Milwaukee, shipping became more efficient. Selling barrels of beer to distributors in New York City and Chicago was more complicated than marketing it at a local Wauwatosa or Waukesha tavern where collections usually were made upon delivery. Besides differentiated brewing to give it a greater alcoholic content, railroad schedules, reliable contacts, collections, and tolls were complicating factors in shipping to distant markets versus local ones. It was the courageous brewer who struggled to master these complexities. By 1872, the relatively small city of Milwaukee had overtaken such great brewing centers as New York, Philadelphia, and St. Louis as the largest beer-exporting center in the nation. From the beginning, the Millers sold most of their beer to L. Weis in Chicago with proceeds equaling $100 a month. Conversely, Miller's early local sales were pitiful, with a few quarter barrels marketed monthly at $1.75 each.[39]

The Millers sacrificed at this early stage in the brewery's history. They lived in a Spartan way to conserve capital, reinvesting the money in the business. Fred kept only one overworked stallion the first four winters that he owned the brewery and, to save horsepower, walked the three miles to Milwaukee. With experienced brewers in place, Fred probably put his energy into increasing sales and upgrading the facilities. Part of his weekly routine included personally paying his employees and making deposits at the People's Bank in downtown Milwaukee. Fred used this bank, in part, because it could transfer money with all of the major European cities, helping the brewer receive German funds from his family. It is conceivable that Fred never personally brewed a batch of beer but, rather, made suggestions to his brewers and searched for the best barley and hops available.[40]

Fred's thriftiness and sales acumen increased the value of his holdings. The Millers needed to economize because, two years after purchasing their brewery, a depression hit Milwaukee and did not release its grip until 1863. Between 1857 and 1859, Milwaukee breweries' overall sales decreased by two thirds and did not return to 1857 levels until after the Civil War. Nevertheless, by July 1860, Fred's brewery real estate was worth $10,000 and his personal property was valued at $2,000. By 1870, the brewery's land was worth $50,000 and Fred's personal estate was worth $20,000.[41]

3.
THE BREWERY'S
DAILY OPERATION

L ike all beer producers, Frederick Miller obtained raw materials, (water, barley, yeast, and hops), processed them,
and sold the result. In the early years, well water was free and
plentiful on the property. Wisconsin farmers grew barley and
hops for the sizeable brewing industry. Fred purchased barley
crops that suited his taste, as there were various strains of the
grass and each one gave the beer a unique flavor. Barley is an
ancient and hardy cereal grass that was a staple of the human
diet, though it is now mainly consumed in malt products.
Through a chemical change, barley is converted into malt, the
foundation of most lager beers. Beginning on October 1, 1855,
Fred bought 155 bushels of barley from local farmers for $1.08
to $1.12 each. He liked "Farmer Biehl's" produce and, later
that month, bought many more bushels from him at increasing
prices. After Mr. Biehl delivered the barley crop, the Miller
Brewery employees began to convert it into malt.[42]

Malting involved washing and then soaking the shucked
barley kernels in clean water in a steeping tub, for about two
days. Afterward, the moist barley kernels were spread over the
stone or cement floor of the malthouse. During this stage, to
achieve uniform results, occasionally the brewers would gently
flip the barley. It germinated for anywhere between three-and-
one-half to twenty-one days, depending on the brewer. Germi-
nation converted the insoluble starch of the barley into soluble
sugars for brewing by the action of natural barley enzymes. The
process was complete when a little sprout in each barley grain
grew to about the length of the barley kernel itself. Then the

brewers used the dry heat of a kiln to stop barley growth, thus producing malt. The rootlets from the barley malt were then separated from the kernel and fed to livestock. The dry, brown malt kernels were the foundation of the brewing process. The brewers could control the color of their beer by varying the length of time and conditions that they kilned or roasted the barley kernels; the longer the kilning time, the browner the kernels became and the darker the beer would be.[43]

The brewers then ground the malt, often using horsepower, before pouring it into a mash tub to be heated with water. Mashing completed the conversion of starch in the barley malt to malt sugar, which then dissolved in the hot water. The brewers used long paddles and rakes to stir this syrupy liquid called wort. After the sugars were sufficiently dissolved, the spent barley kernels were removed and warm water was added to dilute the wort. At this phase, the brewers boiled the wort in large kettles while occasionally adding hops, which are the green flowers of a vine and give beer its bitter taste while providing preservative qualities. For several hours, the employees boiled the wort after which the hops were removed.[44]

When the wort cooled to about 45 degrees Fahrenheit, the brewers added yeast, which is a unicellular fungus that, while multiplying, secretes enzymes that convert the malt sugars into alcohol, also known as fermentation. It tastes good, clean, and pungent. "Seen in a tumbler, yeast looks like smooth prune whip; ready for the day's brew of beer, it resembles a lot of brown foam cast upon the beach on a windy day."[45] Obtaining and preserving a pure yeast culture was problematic for the brewers, as it was easy for sundry airborne yeast varieties to enter the wort and multiply along with the original strain. Wild yeast might prevent the beer from fermenting properly or could ruin its flavor.

Every generation (batch) of yeast increased the chances that the vital yeast culture would become adulterated. Originally, the brewers brought yeast from Germany and later purchased pure batches of it from the old country, which were then shipped to them. After 1883 or so, brewers could buy pure brewers' yeast from Denmark. Yeast's importance cannot be overstated. Wisconsin's foremost rural brewery historian Wayne Kroll added that the rural breweries' inability to keep their yeast pure, compared to the large technologically advanced Milwaukee breweries, helped lead to their demise. The rural breweries' beer batches probably varied in flavor, whereas, the large shippers had better control over their products' consistency.[46]

Ice was vital to fermentation because, except for winter and cool spring seasons, brewers could not sufficiently reduce the wort's temperature without it. During this first stage of fermentation of lager beer, a white froth appeared on the surface of the fermenting tub, covering the entire surface by the end of the second day. A few hours after covering the entire surface, it disappeared, signaling the end of the first stage of fermentation.[47]

The brewers then strained off the lager beer just above the yeast, which had settled to the bottom. They kept some of the yeast from the previous fermentation for their next brew. They poured the beer into casks to *ruh* (rest) in the coldest part of the caverns, with the ideal temperature just a degree or two above freezing. The *ruh* fermentation lasted from ten days to several weeks, with more substances settling out of the beer and the alcohol content rising slightly. After completing the *ruh* process, they put the beer into storage barrels and tightly sealed them with bungs (cork seals) to retain the carbonation. After a period, they poured the beer into 31-gallon barrels or fractional barrels for sale. Until the beer was removed for sale, the brewers stored it in the coldest part of the cellars. By necessity, brewery cellars were large because they stored great quantities of beer for the high volume summer sales period.[48]

Following the pattern Fred Miller learned in Sigmaringen, on June 1, 1856, he procured a license from the Town of Wauwatosa to operate a saloon on his premises. Also in that same year, Fred installed horse-watering troughs for travelers using the Watertown Plank Road so that, while the horses were drinking, the drivers and passengers could eat lunch while enjoying a glass of cool Miller beer.[49]

Along with the Millers' business progress, their family increased. In December 1856, the Millers baptized their second child, Mary Margaret, at the Catholic St. Joseph Parish at 11th and Cherry Streets in Milwaukee. Following Mary Margaret, on February 16, 1858, the Millers baptized Louisa, and then finally, the Millers' last child, Anna Maria, was born on September 25, 1859.[50]

In 1857, to compensate for hiring many more employees, Fred and Josephine increased the number of on-site residences for them. Miller Brewery workers of this period included Fred's nephew Louis Borcher (brewer), 19; Christian Foltz (brewer), 29; and George Denpledine (teamster), 26.[51] Also in 1857, the Millers built a hotel, tavern, and personal home on their property greatly expanding the number of customers who could use their property. Along with this aboveground construction, the brewery workers continued to enlarge the system of limestone caverns begun by the Bests.

Besides building employee housing, the Millers improved their beer garden by adding bowling alleys, a pigeon house, and bakery ovens. Due to the competition among Milwaukee's beer gardens, the Millers searched for attractive ways to encourage Milwaukeeans to make the 3 to 5 mile trip to their beer garden. It was necessary for Miller's Garden in Wauwatosa to be better promoted than Milwaukee's beer gardens in order to attract clients to its more distant location. A newspaper reporter of that vintage noted that Miller's garden remained one of the most native and cozy excursion centers of any in the Milwaukee area. There was so much traffic on those summer Sundays and holidays that Fred and Josephine kept their young children in the house for fear of traffic hurting them. The five-cent omnibus, a horse drawn public conveyance and precursor to the streetcar, which began at Third and Chestnut (now Juneau) Streets in Milwaukee, could transport them through some lovely woods west of Milwaukee and to the garden. Despite the distance, many clients walked from Milwaukee. Miller also announced that he would open the northern Spring Street gate so those who rode buggies could avoid the Watertown Plank

Road toll.[52] It was later remembered that, daily, Fred would sell as many as 60 barrels, glass by glass. In 1861 the entrepreneur advertised the garden season's opening, trumpeting the news that the Union Band would provide a grand concert for all the nature-loving public. He bragged that if people came to the Menomonee Valley, which he compared to the Valley of Nectar, they could savor wine or beer while smoking one of his cigars. Also attentive waiters would be awaiting the nods of guests, to serve Westfahlen ham, famous headcheese, cold cuts, and other delicacies. Also, they would serve mocha coffee to the women.[53]

The Millers' first expansion beyond the Menomonee Valley site was in downtown Milwaukee where, on April 24, 1857, they opened a beer hall at 222 East Water Street. It is likely that the beer hall was located on what is now North Water Street between Wisconsin Avenue and Mason Street. David Herrewig, a Milwaukee historical researcher and contract archivist for the Miller Brewery, explained the difficulty in discovering its exact current location because, at that time, addresses were more haphazard than today and, often, did not regularly progress up and down the street. In opening this Miller Beer outlet, the Millers copied what many Milwaukee brewers had done; they publicized the saloon's opening in the *Milwaukee Sentinel*. Owning a business site in downtown Milwaukee brought risks and, on Saturday night February 1, 1858, an unknown burglar broke into the rear of his establishment stealing $30 worth of items including a little money.[54] It is unknown how long the saloon operated, but it was less vital to the business than the beer garden and brewery.

Since his marriage to Josephine in Friedrichshafen, Frederick Miller's personal and financial life had thrived. Unfortunately it changed on April 21, 1860, when Josephine died of a common disease, possibly tuberculosis. At about this time, the Millers had four children and, soon, the two oldest, Joseph Edward and Mary Margaret also succumbed to disease, leaving Fred to raise Louisa and Anna Maria. The beer baron interred

Josephine alongside her children in the Catholic Calvary Cemetery, thousands of miles from her German birthplace. These deaths motivated Fred to establish a family cemetery plot that still receives his descendants.

Seventeen years later Frederick Miller wrote, "Whenever I think of all of them, how they were taken from me so quickly and unexpectedly, then I become sad and melancholy." He continued, "So I bow in humility and thank the Lord that He has given and also taken away." Despite these deaths, the beer baron demonstrated that he could overcome tragedy while remaining focused on his long-term goals. In 1879, he bragged that in spite of his misfortunes and fateful blows he never lost his head. After every blow, just as a bull, he jumped back higher and higher.[55]

Throughout this difficult period in Fred's life, Rev. Hermann Joseph Holzhauer, St. Joseph Catholic Parish's founder and pastor, buttressed him. The Millers attended this German-language parish, which has now relocated to the City of Wauwatosa. Father Holzhauer's facial features were both noble and pleasant; his manner cultured yet simple. He was somewhat serious by nature yet, despite his heavy cares and duties, frustrations and disappointments, he always wore a smile when in contact with others. Fred had a remarkable relationship with Rev. Holzhauer, who presided over the brewer's spiritual triumphs and disappointments. Their relationship strengthened as the pastor officiated at the Millers' baptisms, confessions, first communions, confirmations and funerals. Fred was a devout Catholic and, no doubt, made good use of the priest's counsel.[56]

After Josephine died on April 21, 1860, Fred searched for another young German-American woman with whom to share his life and provide him with heirs. Soon enough, he met young Lisette Engelhardt Gross of St. Martins, in Franklin Township, the only daughter of a brewing and farming family. John Steiner, the Wisconsin brewery historian, surmised that due to Lisette's father's brewery and their probable common involvement in Milwaukee's German societies, her family came to know the urbane Wauwatosa Millers. Also, both brewers had the common goal of striving to survive in a rural area.

The Grosses could not match the education, finances, and sophistication of Frederick Miller but had a pleasing earthiness born of their hard work and patience. Some months after Josephine's funeral, Frederick received permission from the Grosses to woo Lisette. After a brief courtship the couple married on October 25, 1860, six months after Josephine's death.

Lisette was 19 years old and Fred was 36 at their nuptials at the Catholic Parish of the Sacred Hearts of Jesus and Mary, (now St. Martin of Tours), in St. Martins, of which, Lisette's father, Gottfried, was a founding member. This delightful church, built in 1859, with an onion-steeple and field-stone and cement-coated outer walls, provided the setting for the gala affair. Guests probably included Fred's two children, his business associates, Lisette's parents, brother Philipp, her aunt Anna Mary Gross, her aunt and uncle, (the Engelhardts), and their friends from Wauwatosa and Harrisburgh. Rev. Hubert Jansen, the 32-year-old Prussian pastor and friend of the Engelhardts, celebrated the sacrament.

In Bavaria, Josephine's parents, Gottfried and Agnes Gross (nee Engelhardt), bore three children, Philipp George, born in 1834, Peter born in 1835, and Lisette born on May 31, 1841. (It is unclear what happened to Peter as he was unlisted in the 1850 and later United States' Censuses and, also, there are no known documents denoting his death.) In 1846, the Grosses and Agnes's brother and sister-in-law, George Henry and Elizabeth Engelhardt, immigrated to Wisconsin. The two couples, likely, were invited by Agnes and George's brother, John Philip Engelhardt, who in 1838, had immigrated to Milwaukee, opened a brewery, and was raising his family. John Engelhardt had arrived in Milwaukee in its earliest days, as the city did not receive its charter from the state until 1846.

The Grosses and Engelhardts settled in Harrisburgh, which was immediately north of St. Martins, (a German farming community approximately twelve miles southwest of downtown Milwaukee.) This scenic area was in the northwestern corner of the Township of Franklin, with its wooded rolling hills and wandering stream. Currently, Harrisburgh and St. Martins are wholly within the City of Franklin, ceasing to exist as independent towns.

The Grosses and Engelhardts, on November 12, 1846, shortly after their arrival in Milwaukee, purchased 145 acres of land for $1,625 from John Everts, who on March 13, 1839, had bought it from the U.S. Government. In all likelihood, the Grosses and Engelhardts cleared their land of trees, a grueling and time-consuming task, to prepare it for planting. In the 1850s and 1860s, the Grosses continued to buy farmland and, by 1875, owned a sizeable portion of the northwestern Franklin Township.

To augment their farm income, the Grosses built a brewery that was well suited to the villages of Harrisburgh and St. Martins. The Grosses and Engelhardts likely had beer-brewing experience in Germany and wanted to continue this trade in the New World. Wisconsin breweries were common, though not omnipresent, in the 1860s through the 1880s because the entrepreneurs needed brewing expertise, often obtained in Germany; funding, which was beyond the average farmer's means; an ability to work intensely; and the willingness to accept substantial risk. Wayne Kroll explained that in the area there were numerous German residents whose culture prominently included beer, and there were low-lying hills into which the brewers could excavate caverns to lager (store) it. Additionally, there was plenty of cheap ice from lakes and streams near Harrisburgh that was necessary to keep the beer cool during lagering.

The Gross Brewery, located at what is now 11765 West St. Martins Road, was similar to many Wisconsin rural breweries, lucrative but physically taxing. Brewers toiled in hot steamy rooms boiling a mash of water, malt, and hops, then toting heavy barrels in and out of cold caverns. Kroll wonders why more of these workers did not die of pneumonia. In winter, a slow time for farmers, the Grosses brewed their product in a thick-walled building before filling quarter or half barrels for lagering in three limestone and mortar-lined caves with red brick floors, packed with ice, to keep it from spoiling until the beer-quaffing summer. The three caverns, with vaulted ceilings, were approximately thirty feet long by fifteen feet wide. The Grosses, Engelhardts, Matthew Pilmiro, who was a 50-year-old experienced brewer, and laborers brought ice to a hole above the caverns to lower into the cool dark abyss. As the ice melted, it drained into a dry well toward one end of the brick floor.

As with most breweries at that time, the Grosses marketed their beer locally, often selling it at a tavern on the premises. Wayne Kroll noted that, based on federal tax records, the Grosses and Engelhardts probably brewed and sold between 200 and 400 barrels at $8 or $9 each. Their brewery revenue, taken with their farm earnings, provided the Grosses with an upper-middle class lifestyle in comparison with their neighbors, who were merely farmers. With these proceeds, they built a home, brewery, barn, and donated money to their Catholic parish, Sacred Hearts of Jesus and Mary, now St. Martin of Tours, for construction projects.

Living approximately twelve miles from Milwaukee and being part of one of Harrisburgh's founding families, Lisette had a constricted childhood that featured a strong reliance on family and communal cooperation. The Grosses and Engelhardts came upon virgin land and, within a few years, created a home, a farm, and a brewery. Surely, in Lisette's early years, she had precious little playtime. The Grosses expected their two surviving children, Philipp and Josephine, to cooperate in the farming and brewing operations. Young Lisette likely cooked for the employees and cleaned the brewing equipment. In 1860, a census worker noted "house servant" near Lisette's name, a designation with which the 18-year-old young woman probably heartily agreed. Miss Gross attended a one-room schoolhouse in St. Martins with a teacher who boarded, in a revolving fashion, with his pupils' families.

The Gross Brewery, though a modest enterprise, benefited through its connection with the Town of Wauwatosa Miller Brewery and, after Lisette's marriage to its founder Frederick

Miller, began to sell its brew to the larger Wauwatosa company. Eventually, Lisette's brother Philipp assumed ownership of the farm and brewery. The researcher/writer Jan Kowalski, in the March 17, 1976, *Franklin Hub*, speculated that Frederick Miller's brewery was significantly larger than the Gross Brewery and, by the late 1800s, bought all of the beer that the smaller brewery could produce.

Kowalski reported that in 1894, the Grosses shuttered their brewery and gave the Miller Brewery its recipes. Also at this future date, Ernest and Frederick "Fritz" Miller, Lisette's grown sons, were intimately involved with the Gross Brewery in its last days and, after its cessation, came to Harrisburgh to remove any useable assets. A recurring rumor, among some St. Martins residents, states that the Millers garnered the recipe of their flagship brand, High Life, from a product at the Gross Brewery. The brewery historian Kroll mentioned that, in all probability, Miller Brewery continued to use the Gross Brewery caverns to warehouse beer for transport to Illinois and points south until gasoline trucks made such storage facilities obsolete, due to their ability to quickly cover vast distances. After the brewery closed, the Grosses' descendants continued to farm for many more decades. As with most defunct Wisconsin breweries, one cavern is all that remains of the Gross Brewery, although, St. Martins has retained its historic charm.

After the wedding, Lisette moved into Fred's modest wooden house on the brewery grounds replete with Fred's two children, baby Anna Maria, who died soon after, and 2-year old Louisa who lived until her sixteenth year in 1875. Lisette's Aunt Anna Mary "Bebe" Gross, her father's sister and a life-long spinster, supported her. Bebe lived with the Millers until her death on September 26, 1899.

Miller Family member Gail Wray related that from early on, in order to establish a role for herself in Fred Miller's life, Lisette busied herself in the brewery kitchen preparing meals for the brewery workers, labor she was accustomed to doing at her parents' farm and brewery. Frederick wanted heirs; unfortunately, he and Lisette had several miscarriages before a successful pregnancy five years into their marriage. On July 12, 1865, seventeen months after Fred became a naturalized citizen on February 23, 1864, Lisette, with her doctor present, delivered a healthy boy in her bedroom. Following Ernest George, Frederick Andrew "Fritz" was born on April 17, 1867; Clara Anna on February 8, 1870; Edward "Eddie" in May 1874, unfortunately, on January 14, 1877, the Millers buried Eddie at Calvary Cemetery; Emil Paul on August 7, 1878; and on March 21, 1880, when Lisette was thirty-eight years old, Elise Katherine. Of the five children who reached adulthood, Fred Miller received three boys to prepare to run the brewery and Lisette Miller two girls to help her with housework.

Lisette enjoyed buying fashionable clothing and finery with brewery proceeds. She had many beautiful long dresses and adorned her children with the finest clothes available. She was determined to put her Spartan childhood behind her and enjoy the lifestyle of a financially successful matron. Throughout her lifetime, Lisette had long luxurious hair that she braided and then wound around her head. As a young woman she was quite thin and fine boned with taut facial skin that gave her a gaunt appearance. As she aged, she gained weight, ultimately becoming portly. One can discern from her numerous photos that often Lisette was a rather unhappy person; possibly depressed. Beyond the socially accepted somber expressions in photographs, one can observe a life-long sadness in her eyes. Conversely, her husband Fred had a sanguine personality exuding an energetic air. Their children had problems with depression so, theoretically, she also possessed this inheritable trait.

In November 1870, while Lisette was experiencing long-sought success in bearing children, her six-years older brother, Philipp Gross, and his New York City born wife, Mary Gross (nee McAneny), lost all four of their children, within three weeks, to an epidemic. At that time, Philipp and Mary were living, with his father, on the Gross homestead in Harrisburgh managing the farm and brewery. Mary's parents lived within blocks of their home creating a close-knit community. After this disaster Philipp and Mary regrouped giving birth to George,

Emma, Anna, and Elizabeth. Their children had no progeny who survived past 1920, so Lisette became the sole member of the Gottfried and Agnes Gross family whose offspring carried forward.

Fred and Lisette Miller raised their children akin to others of their era and social group. They tried to safeguard them from deadly diseases that had ravaged Fred's first family, while imbuing them with German culture and lessons in morality. Despite the Millers' efforts, they lost two children, including 2 1/2-year-old Edward. In later years, Lisette had noted in the census forms that she had borne nine children of which five survived. By the children's birth, the Millers were earning enough money to afford the best medical care. They also employed house servants to help attend to the young ones. In southeastern Wisconsin, most children were not as fortunate as the Miller offspring and matured with less food, educational opportunities, and freedom; they were often forced to work industrial or rural jobs to help support their families.

The Millers insisted on Catholic schooling for their offspring and sent them to St. Joseph Parish, at 11th and Cherry Streets, where Rev. Joseph Holzhauer was the shepherd. While in the early grades, the Miller children were driven the two miles to school by a brewery teamster, and years later, they likely independently took a horse-drawn omnibus. In her later years, Lisette's daughter Clara remembered that her mother put hot bricks near her children's feet in the sleigh in the wintertime. At St. Joseph, the Millers received conventional instruction, along with a dose of catechism and the German language. After grade school, the children, who were generally intelligent, matriculated at local single-sex secondary institutions. The boys attended Marquette College that later divided into Marquette High School and Marquette University, Clara attended the now defunct St. Mary's Institute, and Elise attended Holy Angels Academy that has since become Divine Savior Holy Angels High School.

In 1881 when Ernest was 16 years old, he attended the

inaugural year of the Jesuit-run Marquette College, at 10th and State Streets. In 1906, Marquette College became Marquette University that is currently at 16th and Wisconsin Avenue. Fritz entered this same school in 1882 and Emil began in 1889. Ernest and Emil attended for two years and Fritz for three. Marquette College consisted of a grade school or preparatory program, a high school program consisting of a classical and commercial course, and a college program. The Miller boys enrolled in Marquette's high-school commercial course that was longer and easier than the classical course and concentrated on business-related subjects. In 1881, Ernest obtained a distinguished award for German penmanship and a 2nd premium for his German classes. In January 1882, his semiannual examinations were, with 20 being the highest possible score; Latin 16.5, English 15.25, arithmetic 16. In June, his achievements were; English 14 and arithmetic 15. In his second year, Fritz was awarded for his diligence and deportment, and also won second premium for arithmetic. Fritz finished two years of class work in the three years that he attended. Likely, his illnesses caused him to repeat his first year. In both years, Marquette College awarded Emil for excellent deportment. He also garnered 2nd Commercial distinguished awards in math, history, geography, and penmanship. In 1891, with a score of 85%, Emil landed on the honor roll.[57]

After leaving Marquette, Ernest and Fritz studied at the Milwaukee Spencerian Business College and were enrolled in, but never attended, a nine-month program at the Brewing College of Herr Schwartz in New York City. Clearly, Fred Miller wanted his sons to complete their formal education in order to commence their *practicum* at the brewery.

Upon graduating from St. Joseph's School at fourteen years of age, Clara attended St. Mary's Institute, which took up the entire block of Milwaukee, Jefferson, Knapp, and Ogden Streets. Founded in 1850, this now defunct all-girls high school, with its $28 yearly tuition, was staffed by the School Sisters of Notre Dame. The school's system was designed to develop the mental, moral, and physical powers of the pupils; to make them useful women of refined tastes and cultivated manners. They offered classes in mathematics, composition, German, natural science, and history; also, penmanship, drawing, needlework (both plain and fancy), lace work, hair braiding, and music. Upon finishing at St. Mary's, Miss Miller was satisfactorily versed in the fundamentals of liberal arts and upper-class comportment.

In 1892, at age 12, Elise was in the inaugural class of Holy Angels Academy at 12th and Kilbourn Streets. From its inception, Holy Angels' Sisters of Charity of the Blessed Virgin Mary catered to Milwaukee's upper echelon and, along with its demanding curriculum, taught social graces to its girls. Still today, Divine Savior Holy Angels, one of two remaining Milwaukee-area Catholic all-girl schools, graduates its students in white formal gowns and elbow-length white gloves.

William George Bruce, a Milwaukee civic hero, who among his many accomplishments, founded the Bruce Publishing Company, in 1937 wrote *I Was Born in America*. His book describes his life growing up in German Milwaukee, and his experiences surely mirrored those of the Miller children. He was born on March 17, 1856 in Milwaukee, ten years before Ernest Miller. Bruce was of Teutonic extraction and knew many of the same streets as the Millers. Although the Miller children were born and raised in the Town of Wauwatosa, then three miles west of Milwaukee, they attended school, shopped and socialized in the larger burg.

Bruce mentioned that the German language was dominant on Milwaukee's north side, to the extent that the non-German residents had to learn a smattering of it to conduct business there. The "butcher and the baker, the tailor and the carpenter, the saloonkeeper and the owner of the tavern, the tax assessor and the policeman, all spoke German." There were so many thriving Teutonic activities in Milwaukee that it became widely known as the "German Athens of America." In the late 1800s, boys and girls played in the Milwaukee area's rivers and creeks, such as the Milwaukee, Kinnickinnic, and Miller Brewery's nearby waterway, the Menomonee. The children would splash in the water with or without suits and, in the wintertime, would skate or simply slide on the ice. Milwaukee's youth also played with skiffs and yawls in the rivers, mimicking the large schooners that plied Lake Michigan and its inlets.

Besides the wintertime activities of ice skating and sledding, Bruce recalled that football and baseball were popular summertime boys' games. He remembered the noises of his childhood such as horse hooves regularly click-clacking up the street, the creaking of wagon wheels, the tooting of steamboat whistles, the ringing of the bridge bell, the voices of women gossiping over the fences, and the yelling of children playing. Throughout the year, the neighborhoods also resounded with noises of roosters and live music, usually German. Independence Day produced pranksters with explosive powder who created bangs and pops with any handy container. Frederick Miller's work-related trips, the family's vacations, Milwaukee's plays, dances, and circuses were all part of their social upbringing. Certainly, the Miller offspring partook in many of these experiences.

The Millers raised their children in the midst of a burgeoning brewery; any child's dream. Daily, the Watertown Plank Road, which bisected the brewery, was busy with horse-drawn wagons hauling produce to the City of Milwaukee and then returning with finished goods for outlying towns and farms. The frenetic activity level in early spring made the brewery look like a beehive. On a whim, any of the Miller children could dash into the brewhouse where black-booted German-speaking workers washed and scrubbed, or stirred and then emptied large vats of hot brew. Their mustaches and facial hair accented their stolid appearance complete with heavy-duty shirts and pants, knee-high black leather boots, and wool hats of all shapes.

The Miller children at times behaved badly but usually were compliant. For example, Chuck Bransfield, a Miller family member, related that, as a youth, Ernest lined up the neighborhood boys and then, oddly, punched each of them in the nose. Another time, 10-year old Fritz, while at Martino's, a saloon in which his father likely supplied beer, won a $60 gold watch from a drawing. His father may have colluded with the owner to provide his son with a substantial gift for his good behavior or to boost his spirits after a long illness.[58] In 1886, Fred wrote that, "For the past week Emil has taken up violin lessons and is very diligent." Probably he was a Mass acolyte, as were many Catholic boys, and was awarded a merit card by his baptiser and St. Joseph Rector, Rev. Holzhauer.

In an 1879 letter Frederick mentioned that Ernest had a good head. He was healthy, quick, and spirited and he spoke English, German, and Latin well. He also studied piano. Fritz was neither bodily nor spiritually as lucky as Ernest, and their doctor had cautioned them not to pressure him. They warned the Millers to be very patient with Fritz for another two or three years, at which time he should be out of danger. For this reason they allowed their ailing son to behave as he wished. Frederick concluded that after Fritz became stronger, he could pick up where he left off, presumably, in reference to his studies. Fred Miller wrote that Fritz's passion was the animal world; he raised sheep, cats, dogs, chickens, ducks, and birds of all kinds. He added that Fritz had at least a dozen birdhouses on top of their home. Inside, Fritz tended to good singers such as canaries, cardinals, and mocking birds. The boy overcame his illnesses, but not his weak constitution, and struggled for his lifetime to be healthy. Not everybody was convinced of Fritz's adult maladies and his great nephew, Chuck Bransfield, believed that he had the tendencies of a hypochondriac.

Other stories increase our understanding of the Miller children. As Emil reached his mid-teen years, his older siblings pressed him into collecting and delivering their mail and messages and picking up and dropping off guests at the Milwaukee train depot. No doubt, feeling grown up, he relished taking out the horses and buggies to perform these tasks.

Clara embodied her father's spirit and best personified his drive, energy, and can-do attitude. Fred described Clara as spirited and energetic but sometimes too wild. The beer baron also noted that he and Lisette were sending Clara to a high school where she could learn music and obedience. Clara Miller overcame most roadblocks to achieve her goals, which was also true of her father, who surmounted many personal tragedies; turning despair into energy in order to achieve more objectives. In Fred's lifetime, he lost a wife and seven children to disease. In Clara's lifetime, she lost two adult children, a husband, and a grandson.

The exotic-looking Clara did not resemble her fair-skinned, plain-faced siblings. Her olive-toned skin and dark, deeply-set shadowed eyes gave her a gypsy-like appearance. Chuck Bransfield wrote that she resembled a typical German-Jewish mother; a group with whom she felt a kinship. She also had a delightful oval face and a pronounced aquiline nose. As the 7-year-old Clara sat for a formal portrait, she was exquisite, sporting pulled-back hair, sparkly earrings, and piercing eyes that accentuated a determined countenance.

Elise, who as a child was called Lizzy, may have been named for her mother Lisette, whose moniker was a derivative of the name Elizabeth. Elise, whose nature resembled her mother's reticent character, was a pensive child who preferred to remain in the background and observe.

The night of January 29, 1872, found Frederick and his friends at a dance at the German Turner Hall, quaffing beer and other alcoholic libations until well after midnight. After a last gulp from their private steins, they extinguished their cigarettes, cigars, and emptied their pipes in preparation of returning home. As Fred was walking down the stairs on this cold night, he slipped on a patch of ice. The nasty spill left him unable to rise due to a badly broken leg. He must have let out a string of German epithets before calling his friends. The *Milwaukee Sentinel* noted that Milwaukee police officers Danenfelser and Weber carried him back inside where he was cared for by his friends.

Frederick J. Miller had various publicity-producing events, such as in September 1873, when his horse bolted from its hitching post to gallop along Reed Street (currently South 2nd Street). Fortunately, it was captured without harm to himself, the buggy, or pedestrians.[59] In August 1877, the *Milwaukee Sentinel* reported that Fred entered a St. Patrick Parish Fair fundraiser where attendees could vote on the more popular beer baron, Frederick Miller or Franz Falk of the Falk Brewery. The winning brewer would garner a $50 meerschaum (white clay) tobacco pipe. At close of the first day Fred was winning 255-210. On the second day the tide turned; Brewer Falk earned 4,510 and Fred won 1,320 votes. All had a good laugh.

Fred also dealt with journalistic misinformation, such as an article that appeared in the mid-to-late 1870s noting that his youngest child had recently died. He had missed the article that ran in a local German-language newspaper but was astonished when friends expressed their sympathy to him. Ironically, one year previously, this same newspaper had erroneously reported Fred's death.[60]

Currently, it is difficult to determine what role Fred's first wife, Josephine, played in the development of Miller Brewery. On the other hand, Lisette and her relatives substantially influenced it. Besides Lisette's corporate responsibilities, family lore relates, she cooked meals for the workers, although it is doubtful that she toiled at the brewery after her children arrived. Lisette also brought to Miller Brewery an understanding of the brewing process from her family's business, the Gross Brewery. Another connection that Lisette's family had with the Miller Brewery was a long-running relationship between her mother's family, the Engelhardts, and the Millers.

By 1881, Henry Anthony Engelhardt, Lisette's cousin, who was born on in 1846, had become an important and well-paid employee of Miller Brewery. No doubt, Mrs. Miller was proud to have her kin, who lived next to her on brewery property, achieve such an exalted position at her business. In 1850, Henry Engelhardt's father, who was Lisette's maternal uncle, John Philip Engelhardt, of Bavaria, and his wife, Elizabeth, of Cincinnati, established the Main Street Brewery at Main (now Broadway) and Chicago Streets in downtown Milwaukee, which in 1860 was valued at $5,000. John and Mary Elizabeth, who had come to Milwaukee in 1838, were two of the city's early settlers and, besides Henry, had six other children. No doubt the Engelhardts came from a Bavarian brewing family as they created two Milwaukee-area breweries, the Main Street Brewery and the Gross Engelhardt Brewery. The Main Street Brewery prospered and soon outgrew its facilities. The Engelhardts decided to buy another piece of property at 1150 West Windlake Avenue, on Milwaukee's near South Side. Construction began immediately, and by 1857 the brewery's storage vaults were completed. Beer was brewed on Main Street and stored on Windlake Avenue.[61]

In early September of 1860, John Engelhardt traveled to Chicago to purchase a new vat for his brewery. At 11:30 p.m. on September 7, 1860 after finishing his business in Chicago, he departed for Milwaukee on the Lady Elgin, which was the finest large side-wheel steamer to ply the Great Lakes. At 2:30 a.m., about seven miles off Winnetka, Illinois, the 129-foot schooner Augusta plowed into her side and, twenty minutes later, the Lady Elgin sank. Approximately 150 of the 500 passengers drowned, including John Engelhardt. The brewery continued operating for two more years, then Phillip Best of the Best Empire Brewery purchased it from Mary Elizabeth, John's widow. There is an Engelhardt family story that the Best Brewery, which became the Pabst Brewery, obtained the hop-leaf part of their trademark from the Main Street Brewery that had originally used it. Subsequently, Phillip Best put a "B", representing their brewery, in the middle of the leaf design and then later added the blue ribbon representation.[62]

When John's son, Henry Engelhardt, reached working age, he gained employment at the Miller Brewing Company. After some time at Miller Brewery and then Blatz Brewery, Henry left for Cincinnati, Ohio where he worked as a first kettle boy at the Eagle Brewery. Cincinnati was also a center of German settlement and a brewing hotbed. On May 20, 1874, Henry married Elizabeth Anna Grobe at the Catholic St. Peter in Chains Cathedral in Cincinnati. Their children followed, Angeline in 1875 and Alvena in 1877. In 1879, the Engelhardts returned to Milwaukee where Henry began working at Miller Brewery, primarily, as first foreman and then brew master. Fred paid this "reliable and thorough brewer" $1,300 yearly plus free-living quarters, wood, and electricity. In Milwaukee, the Engelhardts had two more children; Philomena "Phyllis" in 1879 and Frederick Henry in 1881, who probably was named after Fred Miller.[63]

On October 29, 1881, Fred Miller signed Henry Engelhardt to a two-year employment contract, beginning January 8, 1882, codifying his responsibilities. Engelhardt agreed to perform his regular duties besides Frederick Miller's special requests. Fred expected Henry to perform his job in a, "good workmanlike manner becoming a first class brewer and first class foreman of a first class brewery." Miller Brewery was to compensate him $1,800 yearly, payable in equal monthly installments, except $300, which the brewery would pay him, at the end of the term, guaranteeing his faithful performance of the contract. Engelhardt could continue to live in his house, owned by the Miller Brewery, free of charge and, also, receive complimentary firewood.[64]

Unfortunately, in 1882 or early 1883, Henry reportedly developed a severe thyroid condition for which he sought medical treatment. The local doctors were unable to cure his ailment so he, at Fred Miller's urging, sought a remedy in Vienna, Austria, which was known worldwide as having superior doctors. Soon enough, Henry made plans to take a steamship to Europe. On April 4, 1883, he signed his will, which, in the event of his death, gave his wife and four children each one fifth of his estate.

One can imagine the family's melancholy on the day that Henry left Elizabeth, Angeline, 8, Alvena, 6, Phyllis, 4, and Freddy, 2, at the Milwaukee train station for parts east. Subsequently, he took a steamship to Europe. On July 19, 1883, Henry died of his illness and was buried in Vienna. Elizabeth then raised four young children, depending on a $4,500 estate. Until the probate court settled the estate, it ordered a $140 monthly stipend to Mrs. Engelhardt.[65] The Millers helped Elizabeth financially for some period after Henry's death, including free board at her Miller Brewery house and complimentary firewood. Henry's descendants say that Fred Miller promised Henry's son, Frederick, life-long employment at their brewery.

In the 1890s, Angeline and Alvena sought work as dressmakers and stenographers. By 1900, Fred Engelhardt was employed as a drug store clerk at 30th and Lisbon Avenue. For long forgotten reasons, Fred Engelhardt never worked at Miller Brewery and instead, in 1903, commenced an over fifty-year term of employment as a bookkeeper with the Gettelman Brewing Company, which was mere blocks west of Miller Brewery. Alvena and Frederick married while Angeline and Phyllis remained single, living with their mother until her death. Phyllis became the Millers' daughter, Elise's, lifelong best friend and, after Elise's death in 1952, continued a friendship with Elise's children, Lorraine and Harry. Phyllis even came to know some of Lorraine and Harry's children, giving her the unprecedented opportunity to be acquainted with four generations of the Miller family.

4.

EXPANSION, UNIONS
AND THE BISMARCK
EXPERIMENT

By 1867, Milwaukee had become a brewing capital that exported thousands of barrels to many states and sundry foreign countries. The top Milwaukee-area breweries were among the world's largest. Lager beer was bringing Milwaukee almost as much national recognition as its yellowish, fired cream city bricks. A popular story explains that in approximately 1863, during the American Civil War, Fred Miller shipped a load of beer to St. Louis, Missouri where he rented a wagon and sold it "under the noses" of the local brewers.

In 1867, Miller Brewery, which was in seventh place locally, sold just over 3,200 barrels at $12 each, grossing $38,400. In comparison, the Blatz, Best, and Melms breweries, all modern marvels, each were selling over 18,000 barrels and occupying nearly one city block. Miller's success gave Fred the opportunity to build additional structures on his property. In 1867, he constructed his second home, a two-story dwelling on the top of the bluff opposite of North 39th Street on the south side of the brewery's property. Fred had more time for volunteer efforts and, in March of 1869, joined his fellow brewers Frederick Pabst and Valentine Blatz on the executive committee of the Brewer's Protection Insurance Company. In June of 1878, he traveled to Baltimore to represent the Milwaukee-area brewers at the National Brewers' Congress, where he was elected one of the secretaries. The beer baron also took an active interest in the Milwaukee Brewers' Association, serving as its chairman for many years and, several times, saving it from going out of existence.[66]

In 1870, Frederick J. Miller built a large brewhouse, which provided him with a significantly increased capacity and added a room to house a steam driven engine to power the machinery. When feasible, he utilized new technology to remain competitive. Miller Brewery's management could not match the largest breweries' expenditures on technology; nevertheless, they wisely continued to purchase new equipment. His new steam-powered generator allowed him to sell a forty and a thirty-barrel capacity brewing kettle, one practically new 100-barrel fermenting tank with a floating bottom and discharge tubes, two copper spray machines, one heavy masher, one wort pump, and one malt mill all with horsepower. He also replaced a 2,500 pound Fairbanks scale and two iron cooling kettles.[67]

In May 1873, Fred changed his brewery's name from Fred Miller's Plank Road Brewery to Fred Miller's Menomonee Valley Brewery. Recently, he had opened an agency in Chicago, following the lead of the Best and Schlitz Breweries, to which he shipped beer and stored it in an icehouse. This small beginning in developing distributors grew steadily and, by 1884, the brewery had twenty distributors east of the Mississippi River. The beer baron may have wanted the new name to represent the brewery's burgeoning status. Fred Miller's moniker remained the first element of both names demonstrating his importance to the business. This name change also reflected the usurpation of the Plank Road by the railroad, whereas, the Menomonee Valley was a booming area made possible by the iron horse. The name change caused confusion among Milwaukee beer drinkers as Adam Gettelman's brewery, merely two blocks west, was known as the Menomonee Brewery. An 1880 print ad displayed the words "Fred. Miller – Brewer and Maltster" in large curved type, bracketing a cut of the brewery, and the words "Menomonee Valley Brewery" in tiny curved type below the picture. In a manner, the words "Menomonee Valley Brewery" were a description of the brewery rather than its title. Fred's brewery's name was always the Fred Miller Brewing Company except that, at times, the description of its location changed and later the word "Fred." was eliminated.[68]

In May 1873, Miller Brewery was in fifth place locally. That month, it produced 1,091 barrels, sold 1,194 barrels, and stored 4,348 barrels in its caverns. At the end of 1874, its production surpassed the 10,000-barrel mark for the first time (11,647). The 1875 sales were virtually the same as 1874. In fact, total beer sales, among Milwaukee brewers, fell between 1874 and 1875. In 1876, Miller was in fifth place among Milwaukee brewers while brewing 9,480 barrels, selling 10,057 barrels, and having 3,044 in storage. In comparison, the Pabst Brewery brewed 128,427 barrels, sold 122,563 barrels, and stored 26,620 barrels. Miller Brewery's sales spurred the need for more ice storage space, as there was a ratio between barrel production and ice usage. Fortunately, ice was easy to obtain and store in Wisconsin due to its cold winters and over 10,000 lakes. On September 20, 1875, Fred Miller announced plans to build a $7,000 icehouse on his property using architect Henry Messmer. The wooden structure would be fifty feet wide, eighty-five feet long, and thirty feet high. In approximately 1877, the Millers opened a storage and sales depot on the south side of the Menomonee Valley on South 6th Street to service Milwaukee's bourgeoning South Side.[69]

One method that Fred Miller used to fund his building projects was to mortgage his properties and business. On October 13, 1877, Fred and Lisette Miller obtained a $30,000 mortgage from Milwaukee's Northwestern Mutual Insurance Company. Currently, it is an immensely successful insurance company anchoring the eastern stretch of Wisconsin Avenue in downtown Milwaukee. The Millers satisfied this mortgage on October 13, 1884.[70]

Over the years as the brewery prospered, the indefatigable Fred returned to the comfortable standard of living he had known in Germany. His growing income allowed him to eat and dress well, while traveling extensively in the United States. He arose at 3:00 a.m., after which, he reviewed his employees, who had started employment at 4 a.m. They rested from noon to 1 p.m. and finished at 6 p.m., their routine year in and year out. After his tour, he wrote a few letters. He would eat breakfast at 7 a.m., then attend to his business correspondence. In the afternoons, he made trips to the bank, post office, and railroad station where he would either collect or ship produce and equipment. At times, he would purchase some of the brewery's materials.[71]

In July 1879, Miller Brewery weekly collected approximately $2,000 from large customers and daily about $100 from small clients. In September of that same year, Miller Brewery contracted exclusively with Charles C. Henning, who owned the Milwaukee Bottling Company, at 58 Oneida Street (now Wells Street), beside the opera house, to bottle some of their beer. The brewery delivered kegs of beer to Henning, who pumped the product by hand into the bottles that were then capped with cork and wires to prevent the stoppers from popping. Henning then distributed the pint and quart glass bottles of Fred. Miller's Celebrated Export Lager Beer and Fred. Miller's Bavarian Beer. He advertised Miller beer in the *Milwaukee Sentinel* and other local papers noting that Miller beer was, "brewed from carefully selected materials by the most approved processes which science and experience can suggest. Guaranteed to be absolutely free from deleterious adulterations. It possesses appetizing and nourishing qualities, which have made it a prime favorite with consumers." Bottling began hesitantly with few barrels sold this way.

On the morning of December 10, 1885, the Millers' second-oldest son, Fritz, approaching his eighteenth birthday and friends, Frank Barwart and Jacob Schukaski, rode horses downtown to the area near the Milwaukee Grand Opera House, at Oneida and East Water Streets. While visiting a now unknown place, their horses came untethered and fled creating a dangerous state of affairs for pedestrians. In early Milwaukee, citizens were scared, seriously hurt, or killed by horses or their wagons speeding down its streets. Officer William Schilke caught the horses and then arrested the sheepish young men. Fritz was fined $5 plus court costs for his absentmindedness.[72]

Consumer demand grew for bottled beer and Fred Miller sought more of the bottling profits. By 1883, he terminated his partnership with Henning and created a new relationship with John Fellenz, Jr., to bottle his Export beer at 15th and State Streets. This venture was short-lived, and soon after the Millers built their own bottling plant on the brewery's property. Meanwhile, Henning went to work for the Pabst Brewing Company eventually becoming a shareholder and corporate officer and Fellenz, in 1884, became an agent for the Jung and Borchert Brewery.[73]

As an adult, Fred maintained a deep respect and interest in German-language poetry and, one can presume, that he found solace while reading and re-reading his favorite verses. When entertaining at his house, he occasionally employed zither players to fill the air with sweet notes. He also had a penchant for traveling and, in mid-May 18, 1866, returned from an extended visit to Germany, (that may have been his first since emigrating in 1854), with six exquisite clocks. The beer baron did not buy the clocks for speculation and, to that end, showed each purchaser the invoice, freight, and import duty documents to verify the costs. Instead, he was promoting German culture and artistry, a matter close to his heart.[74]

This collection attracted many visitors to his Wauwatosa brewery to see the intricate mechanisms hand-crafted by the artisans of Baden with wood from the famous Black Forest. These delicately carved clocks displayed German ingenuity. One clock featured a tiny wooden quail that would, at each quarter hour, appear at a door and call out four times for four quarters, and then a cuckoo would appear at a different door to announce the hours. Another clock featured a little Swiss shepherd that, each half hour, stepped forward through a set of doors to blow a bugle.

Fred was sufficiently pleased with this undertaking that he ordered another batch of clocks that arrived one year later in June 1867, in time to create added attention to the opening of the beer-garden season. The second collection of clocks was more numerous and demonstrated myriad curious mechanical devices. Many pieces were of large desk-top display size but others were no larger than a wrist watch.[75]

In 1869, Fred Miller hired William Marx for a $200 to $300 yearly salary. The young man, with his untiring devotion and clear thinking, became the brewery's bookkeeper. Fred trained Marx in the German language to enable him to help Fred with his correspondence. By 1879, Marx was receiving a yearly salary of $1,200, which allowed him to marry and build a beautiful house near work at 261 North 36th Street. When the beer baron traveled, which he often did, even returning to Germany several times, William managed the business in his stead. This honorable clerk handled much if not all of the brewery's cash. From Thursday to Saturday he spelled Fred, visiting the bank, post office, and telegraph bureau to communicate with the brewery's agents. He also visited saloons and, when necessary, settled accounts with them. On April 2, 1883, Fred Miller and William Marx signed an employment contract, which would keep the gentleman, who was then second in command at the brewery, for two years and seven months beginning February 1, 1883. The brewery was to pay Marx $700 in seven equal installments and deed to the clerk a small parcel of the company's land adjoining Marx's house, which was on the bluff near the beer garden. The $700 salary terminated on September 1, 1883, at which time, F. Miller was to pay Marx 10% of the brewery's net profit to be computed on September 1, 1884 and 1885. Marx could make $100 monthly draws against his annual salary. Fred Miller retained the first right to purchase Marx's property. Since 1877, William Marx supervised William Prege, a reliable, hard-working, single clerk from Bremen, Germany, who received $400 yearly, along with free room and board.[76]

The multi-talented Marx handled Fred's taxes, which, as the brewery expanded, became increasingly complicated. He also oversaw the brewery's municipal and circuit court affairs, such as suing John Radinger, a saloon owner, for nonpayment of bills. William handled a more serious affair on August 2, 1884, when Marie Mullen filed suit against Fred Miller because a heavy Miller delivery wagon, driven by Fritz Bones, ran over her, breaking her thighbone and causing other injuries. The seven-year-old Marie, through her guardian ad litem, sought $10,000 in damages and $600 in doctor's bills. This accident occurred the previous October while Marie was crossing Chicago Street in Milwaukee's Third Ward. The case's resolution is unknown but, likely, Fred paid for her pain and suffering.[77]

William Marx handled another legal matter on Saturday February 12, 1876, when Fred Miller appeared before U.S. Tax Commissioner Bloodgood and posted a $500 bond guaranteeing his appearance at a hearing the following Monday. He was accused of removing beer from kegs without destroying the tax stamps. Beginning in 1862, as a way to help finance the Civil War, the federal government placed a $1 per barrel tax on all beer sales. The breweries purchased tax stamps and then placed them over the bungs immediately after the barrel was filled. Brewery historian Wayne Kroll noted that when the saloon operators tapped the barrel through the bunghole, they effectively destroyed the large stamp. A federal tax agent had discovered that Miller Brewery was storing full barrels without stamps, thus saving $1 per barrel. Conceivably, this "crime" was the result of oversight, with the brewery planning to impose the stamps later before transporting them, rather than malfeasance. Nevertheless, the brewery pleaded guilty paying the taxes and court costs.[78]

In 1879, other Miller Brewery employees included Jacob Thomas, 40, a hard working, first kettle boy who earned $700 yearly. Louis Blum, 40, the first cooperage boy (barrel maker) who earned $650, had been with the brewery for five years. Wendel Volz, 35, also a first kettle boy, had an annual salary of $540 and a five-year tenure. There was also a second kettle boy and a first wash houseboy who each received $540 yearly. There were four or five washhouse boys and a barrel washer who each received a salary of $480, which was the least of any brewery worker. (At this time, Fred provided no information on any female employees.) The cellar and washhouse boys came from North and South Germany, Bohemia, Switzerland, Tyrol, Alsace, Poland, and Scandinavia, while others were native born. The six peddlers and teamsters, who were all German, received annual salaries between $480 and $540. The maltsters received $600 annually. Altogether, there were 25 men in addition to 16 horses in Wauwatosa. The branch office in Chicago had three men and four horses. Most of the brewery's employees lived at or near the business and paid $15 a month for bed and lodging. Breakfast for the single men, as the married men ate with their families, was at 6 a.m. and consisted of coffee, bread, butter, potatoes, eggs, and beefsteak or some other roasted meat. Lunch at 9 a.m. consisted of a meat portion, cheese, bread, and pickles. The twelve o'clock midday meal was made up of soup, a choice of two meats, vegetables, and cakes. The 6 p.m. evening meal consisted of meat, salad, eggs, tea, and cakes.[79]

At 3:40 p.m. on Thursday November 18, 1880, a Miller Brewery employee summoned the fire department by telephone to battle a fire on its premises. The blaze started when a wooden barrel that a worker was "pitching" caught fire and spread to other kegs. Breweries exclusively used barrels (kegs) to distribute beer and employed coopers to fabricate and repair them. The coopers branded each keg, with the brewery's name, in the hope that saloon owners would return them. After receiving the empty barrels, the coopers cleaned them with an automatic machine that sprayed hot soapy water into the bunghole. After they dried, if necessary, they sprayed hot liquid pitch (tar) into them to seal them. It was here that many fires started because, in performing this task, the coopers used an open flame near pitch and wooden staves, both flammable materials. Since coopers were always surrounded with numerous barrels, these fires could spread quickly causing quite a blaze. Two days later, the grateful Fred Miller donated $25 to the Fireman's Relief Fund for their assistance.[80]

Miller Brewery experienced many noteworthy fires during its history and fellow brewers, including the Gettelman and Blatz, had massive blazes that nearly ruined them. In the 1880s possibly due to this latest blaze, Miller Brewery built a firehouse to more quickly bring water to infernos on its property. The other large brewers also had their own firehouses. It is unknown whether Miller's firefighters fought neighbors' fires. While building a firehouse, the brewery also constructed a pitch house, cooperage, and washhouse.[81]

In 1881, Miller Brewery sold 30,000 barrels of beer and employed 30 men who, while at work, weekly consumed fifteen barrels of beer, an amazing quantity. Today, the thought of brewery workers drinking an intoxicant at work seems peculiar but, until recently, it was a valuable employee perk and reportedly did not hurt production. At that time, the brewery's two labels were F. Miller's Celebrated Export Lager Beer and F. Miller's Lager Beer. In 1881, Miller Brewery, while being valued at $200,000, had an annual storage capacity of 12,000 barrels and used 6,000 tons of ice. Breweries purchased the frozen water as soon at it was thick enough to cut into blocks, which often was in December. Ice cutting, transportation, and storage were a massive undertaking for the large brewers. Moderate winters could be disastrous for these businesses that then paid a premium for ice to be brought from further north or delayed their brewing season. In 1879, the nearby Gettelman Brewery diverted water from the Menomonee River into a field, to create ice, and Miller Brewery may have done likewise. Otherwise, the breweries cut their own ice or purchased it from ice-cutting contractors. Miller stored the cold substance in its icehouses sandwiched between layers of insulating sawdust that kept it frozen throughout the warm months. By 1881, Miller had seven icehouses; some of which were in Milwaukee, Waukesha, and Chicago. The brewery placed ice in rail cars to transport beer and filled storehouses in their larger marketing areas to protect the product for sale.[82]

For the first twenty years after Frederick purchased the Plank Road Brewery, the beer garden was vital to his financial empire. Early in its history, the garden provided a considerable profit for the brewery, but as time passed, its financial importance to the enterprise declined. In February 1880, Karl Kron, a former magazine editor, leased the garden until October 1883, at which time he sold the lease to a Mr. Walden. One reason that Fred may have relinquished control over the pleasure garden was that independent managers could hire non-brewery employees at lower rates.

Each warm spring, summer, and fall weekend, hundreds of guests arrived on foot, horseback, buggy, and streetcar at Miller's Garden to drink their Lager Beer. A newspaper observed that the rear platform of the Wells Street horse-drawn omnibus often was so crowded with passengers bound for Miller's Beer Garden that its front wheels teetered inches off the track. In 1861 the season opening was on Sunday, June 16, but in 1871 its first weekend was on Pentecost Sunday and Monday (May 28 and 29) and featured a famous Vienna Beer and home-baked, strong rye bread. At that time, Fred noted that he had just added new plants and garden houses to beautify the establishment. In April 1880, a warm spring encouraged the owners of Milwaukee's pleasure parks to open earlier than usual to satisfy the hot and thirsty crowds. In February 1878, the brewery paid Otto Osthoff to plank the two blocks from the Wells Street streetcar terminus to their beer garden, improving the trip from Milwaukee after a rain. Thereafter, female patrons were assured that their ankle-length dresses would not get muddy or dusty. The planked walkway helped increase attendance. For example, on Saturday May 17, 1878, two hundred employees of the E. Anderson Company visited the garden, filling twelve streetcars to get there. Besides the general public, various societies, schools, and Milwaukee private clubs used the garden for picnics and socials. On July 4, 1881, the mixed choruses of the Trinity Lutheran Church and the male chorus of the Gemuethlichkeit Society picnicked at Miller's Garden. At 3 p.m., the Heine Quartette joined with them for a rousing Independence Day concert. By the early 1880s, the whole side of the bluff was laid out with winding paths, rustic benches, level lawns, and high swings. Beautiful shade trees covered the garden making it delightfully cool during the hot and sultry summer days. Because Fred lived alongside the garden, he assured that it closed by 8 p.m. In July 1880, the *Milwaukee Sentinel*, in a persnickety moment, reported that Miller's Garden attendance and beer sales were scanty, paralleling its amount of advertising.[83]

In the summer of 1881, Frederick Miller built a handsome cream brick office building on the north side of State Street opposite his brewery. Until this time, the brewery restricted itself to the south side of State Street but, as its need for space grew, the entrepreneur bought land immediately north of the street. Previously, the brewer lacked the money to build a brick building, so his sprawling operation was composed of wood. This new headquarters was modest by Pabst Brewery's standards, but to Miller it was grand. Its handsome façade, featuring large picture windows, survived upgrades largely intact until 1949, when it was razed to make way for a brewhouse.[84]

On April 30, 1885, Lisette and Fred were shocked when in the wee hours of Thursday morning, Fritz, then 18, ran into their bedroom to arouse them. After pausing to compose himself, he stammered that someone had just robbed the house. The May 1, 1885, *Milwaukee Sentinel* reported that, while rummaging through their rooms, a masked burglar inadvertently had awakened Fritz and, when he brandished a gun, Lisette's sensible son retreated. Fritz waited for the prowler to depart before running to awaken his parents. Presently, Lisette calmed down, relieved that even though the thief stole two-dozen silver spoons, nobody had been injured.

In 1887, Fred and Lisette built and moved into their third home on brewery property, which had few luxuries. (This wooden house still stands, in an altered state, near Miller Brewery nestled among newer homes.) Clearly, the beer baron built this home at his wife's urging, using his resources sparingly to barely appease her. Frederick was more interested in investing the family's resources into the brewery's expansion than in his living quarters. This home was notable compared to Wauwatosa's simple houses but it fell short when balanced against Milwaukee's finest brick and stone mansions. Claire Miller McCahey, who knew her grandmother, Lisette, remembered that the Miller house was built before electricity was available, and used gas to light the rooms and hallways. She noted that there was a coal boiler in the basement and fireplaces in most of the rooms. The Millers used an outside pump for water and, also in the back yard, there was a summer kitchen to keep the house cool in the warm-weather months. Lisette kept an English garden for vegetables and flowers. There was a substantial front yard, a white wooden fence around the property, and storage rooms in the basement for apples, butter, and potatoes.

By 1886, the brewery sat on 11 acres and the cellars, which were some of the finest in the country, had been expanded to store 15,000 barrels. Each cavern was lined with brick and featured a drainage system for the melting ice blocks. At this time, the newly constructed railroad spur to the brewery saved it numerous labor hours as, at night, the workers could load the railroad cars directly from the docks. Miller Brewery had 15 icehouses scattered about, and sales had grown from 300 barrels in 1855 to 60,000 barrels by 1884. By 1886, the brewery used 150,000 bushels of barley and 125,000 pounds of hops. It bottled over 5,000 barrels annually and there were over 20 agencies, spread throughout the United States, with beer shipped directly to them. Almost 100 people worked at the brewery, which also had 40 wagons and 50 horses.[85]

In 1883 and 1884 Fred Miller searched for opportunities to diversify his holdings, since all of his assets were invested in the Miller Brewing Company. Fred relished challenges. With William Marx entrenched as his capable number two man at the Wauwatosa brewery, in 1884 Fred decided to build a brewery in Bismarck, North Dakota, which at that time was the Dakota Territory. Bismarck was the territorial capital and a rapidly growing town as Midwesterners flocked there by steamboat and train. Besides wanting to earn more money by tapping into the growing Dakota and Montana markets, Frederick feared the growing union and prohibition movements. The beer baron believed that unions would cause him to lose partial control of his employees. He also feared the occasional violence, economic disruption, and increased production costs that accompanied unionization efforts. In part, Fred left Germany to escape the political turmoil in Sigmaringen, and now he believed that the same trouble might occur at his plant.

Throughout America's history, the alcohol prohibition movement progressed in fits and starts. The brewers, distillers, and vintners were all well aware of its potential and, at times, actual damage to their business. During the 1850s this movement led to thirteen states adopting some form of prohibitory legislation. From 1860 to 1880, three states were continuously dry. The Wisconsin rural Protestant order, known as the Grand Lodge of the Good Templars, prompted the passage of the Graham Law of 1872 that required a $2,000 bond from licensed liquor sellers, on which they could be sued for any of a long list of possible civil offenses. Frequently, Wisconsin's prohibition movement was quashed by its large German-American population. Fred may have desired two distant breweries to diminish the risk of having a business in a state that might outlaw its existence.[86]

In June 1884, Fred Miller purchased two acres of land on a bluff near the Missouri River immediately west of Bismarck and made plans to begin construction of a $30,000 brewery. Some of the money may have come from the April 21, 1884 sale of 84.5 acres of farmland to Jacob Wellauer, for $10,000, at what is now the land surrounding 72nd Street and Grand Parkway in the City of Wauwatosa. Fred may have used this farmland to grow barley or hops.[87] The beer baron failed to anticipate the personal and financial demands of the Bismarck project. This new brewery, along with a major expansion at his Wauwatosa brewery, eventually would cause Fred serious health problems. In all likelihood, Fred's family and close friends fruitlessly counseled against this distant undertaking, instead, beseeching him to reduce his work load and spend more time at home. At age 61, Fred's physical, high-energy years were behind him but his restive character pushed him forward. Surely, he exhausted people around him.

On February 7, 1885, Fred Miller incorporated the Milwaukee Brewing Company of Bismarck, Dakota Territory,
with 750 shares, at $100 each, totaling $75,000. Fred Miller's
attorney, Thomas Jefferson Pereles, must have demanded that
Fred incorporate this new venture to save his personal assets
should it collapse. Interestingly at this time, the Town of Wauwatosa Miller Brewing Company was not incorporated. Fred's
associates and former St. Cloud, Minnesota, residents George
Eckhardt and John Legler, and Fred's wife Lisette Miller each
owned 50 shares of the Bismarck corporation's stock, with
Fred holding the residue. The brewery's name demonstrated
Milwaukee's reputation as a nationally respected brewing
center. It is unclear why Fred did not name this new brewery
after himself; possibly, his new partners wanted a neutral title.
The directors were Frederick Miller, George Eckhardt (brew
master), and John Legler (management). The corporate officers
were Fred Miller, president; John Legler, secretary; and George
Eckhardt, treasurer.[88]

As the sole underwriter of this substantial endeavor, the
Wauwatosa beer baron believed that he had sufficient resources to launch it. The late 1870s and early 1880s saw a
large growth in Miller's sales. The accompanying profits gave
him the confidence to fund the distant new brewery, along
with the improvements at his Milwaukee plant, including his
new home. For instance, the brewery posted a $97,000 net
profit on September 1, 1884, that was the end of their fiscal
year. Previously, on June 20, 1884, in Milwaukee, the directors
were engaged with their architect, a Mr. Heinze, to make the
final plans for their new brewery before breaking ground. After
celebrating Independence Day at his Milwaukee brewery, Fred
traveled to Bismarck where George Eckhardt had just arrived
with his family to make a new home.[89]

In late July 1884, construction commenced on the Bismarck
facility, and by August 8 the foundation was nearly excavated.
By August 22, the basement walls were nearly complete and
ready to accept the upcoming brickwork, but a delay in the
arrival of lumber kept the architect from beginning the super-

structure. The plans called for a residence, and brewing, ice storage, and malting buildings. Fred had ordered Mr. Heinze to construct the brewery with all due haste, and to that end the architect had seventy bricklayers and assistants along with twelve carpenters working many hours. By September 5, some of the 100 construction workers finished painting the Eckhardt residence, while the remaining men worked on the ever-rising edifice.[90]

By October 10, 1884, with George Eckhardt present to inspect the work, the malt house was nearly complete and carpenters were at work on the tower of the malt kiln. The architect promised that, by November 15, the six-story brick brewhouse would be ready for machinery that was en route, as was Frederick Miller who was expected to arrive by October 13. The buildings were built in the same style as Miller's Milwaukee brewery, with elegant, tall, arched windows gracing the walls. With much local fanfare the brewery began operations and, presumably, sold beer in the spring of 1885. A year later on May 7, 1886, it bragged that its bock beer, a strong-tasting specialty product, would soon be ready for Bismarck residents.[91]

From the day it opened, the Milwaukee Brewing Company in Dakota was bedeviled with production and marketing problems. Fred Miller, who had traveled to Bismarck eight times by early 1886, grew increasingly frustrated with Eckhardt and Legler's lack of management expertise. The beer baron could not dedicate enough of his time, while remaining a father and husband and managing his Wauwatosa construction projects. Eventually, he realized that the Plains States' market was small and not growing quickly. People were just passing through them on the way to the more lush Pacific states. Also, other Milwaukee brewers such as Falk and Schlitz were establishing agencies in Bismarck to serve the local market.

In addition, on October 12, 1886, Fred announced plans to begin building a $130,000 brick and iron brewhouse at his Town of Wauwatosa property. The new building featured two brew kettles of 250 and 175-barrel capacity. It was completed in the fall of 1888, along with a condenser building. This handsome brewhouse still stands, sandwiched between the old refrigeration building and the old wash house in "Miller Valley" along the south side of State Street. The second and third floors held the brew kettles and lauter tubs (straining tanks) heated with exhaust steam, which were amply ventilated with special well openings. The brewmaster's office that was located at a stair landing, between the ground floor and the kettle floor, permitted good supervision of all the brewing operations.[92]

Some of Fred's frustration regarding the Bismarck brewery may have come from distribution problems. Customarily, the brewery used steamships to send bottles and kegs to the Dakota and Minnesota towns of La Grace, Fort Yates, Winona, Pierre, and Fort Sully; otherwise railroad cars moved the product. For reasons that are obscure, the Milwaukee Brewery was incapable of reaching the growing West Coast or southern markets. Fred's desire to create a large shipping operation at Bismarck may have overreached his financial and personal resources. Also there may have been insufficient ice along the railroad route or, rather, Fred may have lacked confidence in his Bismarck product, and wanted to eliminate the brewery's quality-control problems before shipping it to the larger southern or West-Coast cities.

Fred mistakenly thought that if he built a state-of-the-art brewery in Bismarck, any problems would be easily ameliorated. He ignored the fact that Milwaukee had a forty-five year brewing culture that could solve an array of brewing-related problems. For instance, in July 1887 the Bismarck brewers were unable to bottle beer while keeping its effervescence and they wrote to Fred for advice. Conversely, Milwaukee was rife with brewing experts, often meeting in professional or social clubs, and helping to resolve each other's problems. The proud Milwaukee worker, who often was the second or third generation member in this same type of job, was specifically trained to provide the world's best beer. Coopers, brewers, teamsters, and brewery owners socialized with members of their own profession forming strong bonds. Additionally, brewery workers moved between the breweries, often bringing fresh ideas to their new employer. Highly skilled workers at cooperages, railroads, ice storage companies, malting businesses, livery services, and contractor operations kept the massive brewing industry flourishing. At this time, Bismarck, in comparison, had precious few of these resources.[93]

Fred Miller's frustration increased as he sent more of his personal capital to Bismarck, putting more stress on the Miller Brewery resources. The Milwaukee Brewery in the Dakota Territory was like a demanding adolescent, to which the beer baron acquiesced, while receiving little in return. Fred continued to underwrite the brewery in Bismarck. By 1886, it was two months in arrears to its employees. Frederick waited in vain for the Bismarck brewery to repay the interest on his loans, the principal notwithstanding. In early 1886, the annoyed beer baron was still personally guaranteeing invoices to contractors who supplied goods and services to the Milwaukee Brewing Company. He worried that a financial disaster in Bismarck would have a negative impact on his Wauwatosa brewery.[94]

Frederick Miller blamed the Bismarck brewery's shortcomings on everyone except himself. He overlooked his own complicity in not sufficiently researching the potential pitfalls of this new venture. Fred complained that various Bismarck employees would not perform duties apart from their daily role. He bragged that nobody in Wauwatosa shirked his duty when there was unscheduled work to do. Fred was livid that the Bismarck management utilized three horses whereas, if the men walked into town, they could make do with two horses. Miller asked rhetorically how was it possible that he, a practical and experienced brewer, could keep the Bismarck brewery that sold only 100 to 200 barrels a month while employing eleven men at $700 to $800 a month. He proclaimed that, "I am truly ashamed of myself for all the worry, regrets, and work the business has caused me."[95]

Also in 1886, Fred chastised the Bismarck management team for selling full kegs at approximately $7 each when the barrel, with the $1 federal tax included, cost $6 to produce. He fumed that no brewery in the world could survive while realizing only $1 to $2 in profit per barrel and claimed that its liquidation was only a matter of time. "I would be an irresponsible and unconscionable husband and father if I did not care for my wife and children." He threatened to close one of his two breweries and since he had toiled for 30 years on his Wauwatosa brewery, it was obvious which one would remain open.[96]

Fred struggled to provide sufficient oversight to his new far-flung enterprise. In the space of a few months in 1886, he had traveled five to six thousand miles. Twice, he took 1,000 mile round trips to Lake Superior to visit and monitor several agencies, which stored, marketed, and then delivered Miller beer to the surrounding area. Two times he traveled to Bismarck and Sioux Falls, each excursion being 1,500 miles. His trips, often lasting ten to fourteen days, exhausted him and put him a week behind in paperwork. He made frequent excursions to Bismarck because, as president, he was entrusted to assure the business's proper operation. To help him on site, at first he used Eckhardt and Legler, and by early 1886 he had given Legler the power of attorney to act on his behalf. Finally, the beer baron, at his wits' end, eliminated this original management team. On October 23, 1886, before firing Eckhardt, he purchased the employee's 50 shares of the Milwaukee Brewery stock for $1,000 cash and interest-free notes totaling $4,000 of varying lengths. Then he bought Legler's 50 shares for $6,000, notes included, while demanding that he remain to train Anton Mauer, or anyone else Fred would soon hire, in the art of brewing, bottling, and sales. The men then agreed, on ten days notice, to vacate their living quarters on the brewery property. Fred then bestowed more authority on his 21-year-old son, Ernest George, who was already helping at the Bismarck brewery. Later on, Fred relied on master brewer Louis Hirsch to improve the business.[97]

At this time, Frederick Miller was training Ernest to assume the brewery empire that he had created. Fred trusted his son Ernest implicitly and had equally high expectations of him as he did of himself. Occasionally, Fred would write to his son in Bismarck, encouraging him to complete the corporation's monthly trial balance and send it to him for review. Fred also asked Ernest, who was a bright young man, to monitor Bismarck's financial records and find the best barley at the best prices. The Milwaukee brewer wanted his son to discover whether there was good barley in St. Paul. At one point Fred, who was angry at the Bismarck brewery's inability to buy and malt barley, fumed that if they did not improve their operations, he would do all of the malting in Wauwatosa and then ship it to Bismarck.[98] While there, Fred Miller chastised Ernest for not writing his mother more often and said that she inquired about him "one hundred times" a day. Fred asked Ernest if it was too much for him to send his mother a brief monthly letter. He wrote that it would be unforgivable, after Lisette's faithful eyes are closed in eternal rest, then, "you will bitterly regret that you loved her so little in life."

To ease Ernest's loneliness, Fred sent his second oldest son Fritz to Bismarck for short periods. Fritz, on one occasion, drank too much beer, which along with stomach troubles saw him ill for three days. Years later, Fritz remembered that the famous Sioux chief Sitting Bull frequently camped with many of his band at the edge of the brewery's property. "Sitting Bull had returned in 1881 from Canada, where he had fled in 1876 after the Indians were defeated in the campaign which was marked by the massacre of General George Custer and his men." Fritz recalled the mercury plunging to 30 below zero in the winter and to stifling heights in the summer, creating a considerable demand for the Millers' beer at the U.S. forts along the Missouri River.[99]

By July 15, 1887, the Milwaukee brewery was running day and night, producing some large shipments. The local newspaper trumpeted that the Milwaukee brewery's beer was equal to any in the land. The brewery featured the newest technology available, imported from the East. On August 26 of that same year, Fred was visiting the Bismarck brewery while announcing plans to construct icehouses in the Montana territory towns of Miles City, Billings, Livingston, Helena, and Butte. These icehouses, which were to be built alongside the railroad, allowed the railroad cars to replenish their ice supply. This route headed west toward Washington State, and Fred may have had plans, eventually, to build icehouses all the way there. His proposed outlay for the icehouses brought his total investment in the Milwaukee brewery to $200,000. Later he made plans to build a two-story brick 72 x 60 foot bottling plant in Bismarck.[100]

The May 6, 1888, *Bismarck Daily Tribune* remarked that the brewery was doing a "big business." The manager, Louis Hirsch had just employed two new brewers to fill the large orders shipped every day. The brewery pumped water from the Missouri River for cleaning their equipment, while using well water for brewing their beer. The workers labored around the clock to brew enough beer, and Hirsh was close to hiring many more employees. At this time, the Milwaukee Brewery was at its apex with two large edifices and seven outbuildings. One large building had an icehouse, beer storage facilities, aging cellars, and a brew house. The other sizeable one had a cooperage, malt kiln, malt cellar, and employee sleeping quarters. Previous to June 1890, due to the federal government's $1 per keg beer tax, new breweries were constructed with their brewhouses across a public street from the bottling facility so that all beer had to be put in barrels with a stamp tax before bottling. Since the federal government did not tax bottles, they feared that the brewers would surreptitiously fill bottles, with beer from kegs without stamps if both operations were under one roof. After mid-1890, due to Captain Fred Pabst's efforts, the Internal Revenue Act was amended to allow the construction of pipe-lines with locked gauges from storage to bottling facilities to measure the quantity of beer for tax purposes. The bottling and storage facilities still had to remain separate but the pipelines reduced costs dramatically for the breweries.[101]

Meanwhile, on June 14, 1886, Carl Miller, a nephew of Josephine Miller, Fred's first wife, wrote to Fred from Germany requesting employment at one of his breweries. Fred responded that the employment picture was not positive at that time. Carl wrote to Fred again on February 27, 1887, requesting help in finding a job. The beer baron responded that he would employ

Carl at his Wauwatosa business if the emigrant could not find work elsewhere. In September 1887, Carl arrived and lived with the Millers until finding his own residence. After Carl settled in, the Milwaukee businessman gave him a bookkeeping job at the Wauwatosa brewery. Within a few months, the new immigrant took a liking to the Millers' oldest daughter, Clara, and they began dating. Eventually, they married.[102]

On February 7, 1863, Carl Miller was born in Friedrichshafen, Wurttemberg, on the northeastern shore of Lake Constance, in southern Germany; seven years and one day before Clara was born. Carl was unrelated to Clara but was the nephew of Frederick J. Miller's first wife, Josephine.

Claire McCahey noted that her father Carl, as was the German custom, was required to repay his father for his education and asked him if he could work in France and, while earning money, could learn French. Before he left Germany, Carl served a year in his country's army. A friend of Carl's father, in Lyon, France, owned a printing company and agreed to board and employ the 17-year-old Carl. For a year, Carl Miller lived at this home in Lyon and worked in the first-floor print shop, speaking no German, while learning to read and write French. After this period, Carl, content with his knowledge of the new language, asked his father for a contact in England to learn English. His father recommended a commercial shipper in London where the young Mr. Miller traveled next. After learning English, Carl, against his parents' wishes, boarded one of his boss's ships bound for the then German colony of South West Africa (now Namibia). He was fascinated with Victoria Falls, on the current border of Zambia and Zimbabwe, and wanted to experience it personally. This spectacular world-famous remote site, named for England's Queen Victoria, is formed by the powerful Zambezi River plummeting into a narrow chasm, creating mountainous clouds of mist.[103]

Claire McCahey noted that, on arrival in Africa, her father experienced difficulties that, one can imagine, mostly consisted of a Western European encountering a lesser-developed region for the first time. For instance, Carl Miller was frustrated by the lack of horses and was averse to traveling on a donkey or a camel. Soon enough, he learned that he would travel with 90 to 100 black Namibians, some of whom would carry him and his luggage from Namibia to Johannesburg, currently in South Africa (then an English colony). After the voyage and a two-week vacation in Johannesburg, he and two guides mounted horses and trekked to Victoria Falls; his dream destination. This voyage occurred in 1885 or 1886, and the distance is approximately 700 miles one direction, a considerable trip at that time in southern Africa. Carl had a wonderfully active mind, and as an amateur biologist he studied Africa's flora and fauna, sketching flowers in the letters that he sent home. After his return to Johannesburg, the young German continued to fulfill his responsibilities to his employer, purchasing elephant ivory and raw rubber to transport overland to Namibia and then, by ship, to England. Carl also worked for a while in West Africa in the Gold Coast (now Ghana). While on this trip, he also hunted big game, bagging a dozen trophies that were later displayed in the Milwaukee County Museum.

One difficulty that Europeans experienced in much of sub-Saharan Africa was the mosquito-borne malaria disease, whose name is derived from the misconception that victims contracted it at night from bad (mal) air (aria). Carl Miller contracted a serious case of this illness. Most of the native inhabitants in infested areas also got malaria, but due to their multigenerational contact, they did not suffer the same mortality from the common strain of the disease. Their suffering was similar to an American's experience with a moderate cold virus, while visitors such as Carl could become very ill and possibly die. Carl suffered from a painful cycle of fevers and chills until a doctor's quinine treatment relieved the symptoms. He continued to suffer stomach problems and finally his doctor suggested that he return to Germany to recover. Upon his return to Germany, a doctor recommended a lifelong treatment of hot baths and a strict diet of bland food, like rice, while skipping potatoes and cabbage. He was also charged to reduce his intake of alcohol, which may have been due to the malaria damaging his liver.

Henceforth, he eliminated beer consumption but continued to enjoy his favorite wine; Haut Sauterne. Throughout his days, Carl suffered recurrent attacks of malaria's ill effects.

In September 1887, the 23-year old Carl Miller arrived on a sailing ship in New York. He took a train to Milwaukee to begin working at Fred Miller's brewery. Loretta Miller Kopmeier, Carl's oldest daughter, remarked that her father arrived at the Milwaukee train station during a political convention. As Frederick collected him in his horse-drawn carriage the established brewer cautioned Carl to keep his distance from the placard carrying crowds, especially the Democrats. Carl learned quickly, and his grandson, Charles "Chuck" Bransfield, said that Carl became a life-long Republican, and reveled when the long-serving Democratic President Franklin Roosevelt died. Certainly Carl was warmly welcomed as a countryman from Fred's home region. Loretta Kopmeier recalled that Frederick enjoyed Carl's company and, periodically, took him along in his open horse-drawn carriage and, to keep his hat from flying off of his head, would hand it to Carl to hold. Soon, Frederick obtained an apartment for Carl at 1816 Cedar Street (which today is 1824 West Juneau Avenue) in Milwaukee, although, within a year, the young man had moved to a home at 36th and Juneau Streets, a residence near and probably owned by Miller Brewery.

Soon after coming to Milwaukee in late 1887, Carl began to substitute "Charles" for his given name. The 1889 Wright's Milwaukee City Directory found Carl using the name "Charles" for the first time in that year. In all likelihood, he changed it to Americanize more quickly because he may have viewed the name "Carl" as being overly Germanic, although, his family and friends continued to refer to our world traveler by his birth name. This duality continued past his death, as his probate records are listed under both Carl A. Miller and Charles A. Miller.

After he had been in Milwaukee awhile, Carl became romantically interested in Clara Anna Miller, then 17 and Fred and Lisette's third oldest child. Carl, then 24, waited for Clara to reach age 18 on February 8, 1888, before asking her father if she could accompany him to a social event; their first date. Fred and Lisette must have been thrilled to have this cultured, Catholic, educated, and handsome German take an interest in their vivacious daughter. Surely, this date included a chaperone, such as Lisette's aunt, Anna Maria Gross, because Milwaukee's high-society social strictures demanded it.

Between 1879 and 1881 in Cincinnati, and then in New York City, brewery workers began to organize in pursuit of a shorter workday. At that time, Miller employees were working six fourteen-hour days with two hours of break time included. These hours were compensated at straight time. The early unions failed to organize but brewery managements generally met their demands. Afterwards, hours customarily were set at twelve to thirteen hours daily with breaks for two meals, leaving a ten-to-twelve hour workday. Two or more hours were usually required on Sundays, but with overtime pay. In the mid-1880s, the Knights of Labor, a trade union including all types of skilled and unskilled workers, quickly rose to national prominence. The Knights was one large union divided into trade assemblies representing the major types of industry, one being brewing. Activity leading to the formation of Brewers Union Number 1, Local Assembly 1672, of the Knights of Labor, began in New York late in 1884, and reached Milwaukee in the spring of 1886.[104]

The year 1886 was pivotal for the Knights of Labor and their ranks had grown within a year. The eight-hour workday movement was their rallying cry. The maltsters at the Best Brewery were the first to unionize in March of 1886. Captain Frederick Pabst acceded to their demands of recognition and abolition of Sunday work; the other breweries followed suit. For a long period in Milwaukee's history, Captain Frederick Pabst, the president of Pabst Brewery, was the de facto leader of Milwaukee's brewery owners due to his company's industry preeminence and his own persuasive personality.

The remainder of the brewery workers joined with the

maltsters in organizing Local 7953 of the Gambrinus Assembly of the Knights of Labor. On April 21, 1886, they sent a letter to the nine Milwaukee brewers asking for an eight-hour day, maintenance of the current wage scale with the full wage paid on the first Monday of each month, time-and-a-half pay for overtime, and that all employees be forced to join the union within one month of beginning employment. The unions knew that their demands, if accepted, would dramatically increase brewery costs. But, they also knew that the brewery-owners' profits had been significant for many years. The nine breweries, including Miller, rejected most of the demands except for paying 150% for work performed on Sundays. The closed shop was the biggest sticking point for the brewers and the issue against which they struggled the hardest. The brewers were adamant that they should have final say, not the unions, over who worked in their buildings.[105]

The union rejected the brewers' association counteroffer and negotiations ensued. Finally, the union terminated the talks and began striking on May 1 at all the Milwaukee-area breweries except the Falk Brewery. The union chose the period of peak production, causing the brewers the maximum harm by ceasing brewing. Miller Brewery lost eighty workers to the strike. At any rate, its owner was undeterred and advertised the availability of draught Bock Beer at his brewery on Saturday April 30 and Sunday May 1. The largest brewers kept the ice machines running to keep the thousands of barrels of beer from spoiling. The workers, dressed in their finest clothes, patrolled their employers' gates guarding against scabs. It was unnecessary because the brewers had decided against hiring replacement workers. On the day the work stoppage began, the striking brewery workers marched with banners proclaiming that they were kept as slaves and were compensated less than other Milwaukee workers. Miller's owner was convinced that the Milwaukee worker was already compensated from "fair to very good." He was baffled how workers, many of whom owned at least one house, would consider themselves underpaid. The beer baron was appalled that his employees, who he had supervised for so many years, were breaking their figurative shackles. Of course, he never believed that these men were restricted. He figured that "demagogues and troublemakers" had caught their ear and were giving them bad advice. Fred naively believed that unions were unnecessary. He trusted in the social contract that provided for moral business owners who employed loyal workers; under those conditions, unions were "superfluous."[106]

The brewery workers were elated with their newfound strength and independence. The brewery work stoppage overall was peaceful, unlike some of the other numerous local strikes. A general strike throughout the city was in progress at that same time, and on May 5 the Wisconsin State Militia fired upon thousands of marching strikers at the North Chicago Rolling Mills Company in the southeastern Milwaukee suburb of Bay View, killing six and wounding three of the crowd. The brewery strike ended on May 7, with the workers victorious in their wage demands but losing on their claims for the eight-hour day and the closed shop. Frederick Miller winced, upon discovering that the new wage scale would cost his business an additional $9,000.[107]

In the fall of 1887, the workers at independent malthouses looked to strike in order to raise their wage scale to that of the brewery maltsters. On November 24, 1887, the maltster workers intended to strike Milwaukee's three smallest breweries, Gettelman, Miller and Cream City for buying product from non-union malters. Fred Miller's dear friend, Adolph C. Zinn, owned one of the affected malting companies, so the beer baron had a personal and professional interest in this strike. In a show of fraternal spirit, the brewers' union boycotted these three breweries for doing business with the non-union malthouses. The remainder of the breweries supported the boycotted breweries and severed their relations with the brewery workers' union, who then falsely advertised that the three breweries produced non-union malt beer. The union also distributed slanderous pamphlets to its members reporting that beer purchased from these "non-union brewers" was poorly made and might make them sick. The boycott failed, and in January 1888 all of the Milwaukee brewery owners canceled the unions that operated in their plants. They fired the few employees that did not comply. Nevertheless, the brewery owners maintained the benefits for their non-unionized workforce.[108]

In 1887 the Miller Brewery, thanks to their new brewhouse, was capable of producing 82,000 barrels of beer annually. Also that year, the brewery installed a coal-fed, steam-driven, mechanical refrigeration machine that immediately reduced the need for ice. Artificial refrigeration slowly brought an end to the ice cutting, storage, and delivery business, which in the mid 1800s was a substantial Wisconsin industry. For instance, in 1888 the Pabst Brewery stopped buying ice due to the installation of refrigerating machinery. The advent of artificial refrigeration also amended the lagering process. No longer were brewers tied to large underground caverns. They could now lager beer above ground allowing for more efficient horizontal production lines. Currently, old storage cellars are novelties harking back to the early hardships of brewing, while, overhead, newer buildings send beer rushing through pipes to tanks and then cans, bottles, and barrels.[109]

Fred Miller, who had overcome many obstacles, encountered an insoluble one in the first months of 1887; he discovered a cancerous lump in his right breast. In the middle of February it was removed. The brewer realized that he might not survive into his seventies or eighties, so he quickly began to finalize plans for his succession. Over the past few years, he had been training his sons Ernest, and to a lesser extent Fritz, to assume the mantle after his passing. He noted, "I desire my sons to take proper care of my business, so it will not suffer by reason of my death."[110] Before sending Ernest to Bismarck, Fred personally trained him at the Miller Brewing Company.

Fred's cancer forced him to complete his estate planning. His friend and noted attorney Thomas Jefferson Pereles advocated that Fred incorporate the Miller Brewing Company, which would facilitate its transfer to the next generation. The Miller Brewing Company was incorporated on April 27, 1887, with 2,000 shares priced at $100 each. Fred Miller possessed 1,940 shares, Lisette — 50 shares, and Ernest — 10 shares. The company's fiscal year began on September 1. The ailing beer baron opened the first stockholders' meeting on April 27 at 9 a.m. and immediately asked Ernest, as secretary *pro tem*, to read the names of the proposed directors; Frederick, Lisette, and Ernest. At 10 a.m. the directors met and Lisette then made a motion to elect her husband as president and Ernest as secretary/treasurer. After the motion passed, the directors purchased all of Frederick Miller's brewery assets, including the real estate, buildings, machinery and fixtures, horses, cooperage, and personal property, on May 3 of that year.[111]

At the time of the incorporation, Fred Miller changed the brewery's name from the Fred Miller's Menomonee Valley Brewery to the Fred. Miller Brewery. Seeing that the business had been known informally as Frederick Miller's Brewery since its inception, this change was perfunctory. It also signaled an era when the public's knowledge of a brewery's location was lessening. Miller Brewery shipped beer around the U.S., dramatically overshadowing any product that it sold at its Wauwatosa brewery tavern and beer garden.[112]

Other unfinished business for Fred included his Bismarck brewery, so he traveled there in August 1887 to discern how another season of brewing and sales had progressed. Afterward, he returned to Milwaukee for the September 5 annual corporation meeting. On February 8, 1888, due to Pereles's urging, the brewer completed his last will and testament. He named his wife, Lisette, and sons, Ernest and Fritz as executors, with the famous brewer Captain Fred Pabst, the maltster Adolph C. Zinn, his doctor Dr. Jacob Lang, and friend John H. French as alternatives. Fred instructed Ernest to care for his mother Lisette, after Fred's death, and instructed Fritz to support Ernest in his endeavors.[113]

Frederick Miller had intended to send his sons to the Herr Schwartz Brewery Academy in New York City but his declining condition precluded it. Ernest and Fritz unpacked their valises and assumed enlarged roles at the brewery. Over the past few years, Fred had inculcated his sons on the importance of the beer's quality. To reinforce his point, Frederick told them of his father Thaddeus Miller's experience in Germany a half-century earlier. Thaddeus had contracted for a ship full of coffee from Java to his Wurtemburg warehouse. Within sight of land, it sprang a leak, dampening the coffee beans. Thaddeus might have dried and then sold them but, instead, to maintain his reputation, he dumped the whole batch into the Danube River.[114]

In 1888, Fred Miller's cancer recurred and he tried various unsuccessful treatments. On June 2 at 3:30 p.m., Surgeons Jacob Lang and Nicholas Senn, along with other doctors, operated on him, removing a cancerous growth under his right arm. Some weeks previous they had performed a minor operation on their patient. The doctors gave the latest surgery little chance for success, but due to Lisette's urging, performed it. After Dr. Lang finished the recent exploratory procedure and related his distressing news to Lisette, all turned their attention to comforting Fred in his final days.[115] On the morning of his final surgery, Fred penned a heartfelt letter in German to his children in which he noted that he might die during the upcoming operation. In all likelihood, depending upon the intensity of Fred's pain, Dr. Lang provided him with morphine to ease his suffering, which may have induced some mental confusion and put him into a semi-conscious state.

At 11 a.m. on June 11, 1888, Fred lost his battle with cancer, leaving a wife and five children to carry on his traditions. The brewery suffered the loss of its founder and thirty-three year leader. At that moment, Ernest and Fritz were at the Bismarck brewery and hurried home for the funeral. Some days before his death, Frederick penned a generally addressed missive spelling out his wishes. He beseeched Ernest, who was scheduled to assume the family's financial empire, to retain the employees who had been so loyal over the years. Frederick Miller remarked that his employees liked working with him because he treated them as friends and coworkers rather than subordinates. He asked for his employees' forgiveness for his occasional harshness or unpleasantness. Finally, the beer baron bid farewell to the workers who toiled in his brewery and others who were carpenters, common laborers, and engineers. "I say farewell and thank them all for all of their love and loyalty."[116]

Lisette contracted with the undertaker, Fredrick Zander, of 495 East Water Street, to handle the burial preparations. On Wednesday June 13, at 9 a.m. at the family home, Fred's friend, Father Hermann Joseph Holzhauer, who had shared so many of Fred's familial joys and tragedies, conducted the funeral service. Today, Fred "sleeps" between his two wives, Josephine and Lisette, at the Catholic Calvary Cemetery, in the plot accented by an impressive obelisk engraved with the Miller name.

5.
A New Generation
Takes Over

After Frederick J. Miller's death in 1888 the brewery confronted four key problems: (1) finding a suitable successor to its dynamic founder; (2) stemming the financial losses sustained by its subsidiary, the Milwaukee Brewery in Bismarck; (3) confronting the growth and eventual success of the Prohibition movement; (4) expanding brewery operations to deal with the growing concentration in the industry.

Frederick Miller had propelled the Miller Brewing Company, from its purchase until his death at age 63. Possessing intelligence, foresight, ambition, courage, resilience, loyalty, and trust, he created a financial empire and left a family to run it after his death. Lisette Miller, 46, and her five children, Ernest, 22, Frederick "Fritz," 19, Clara, 17, Emil, 12, and Elise, 7, carried on in his stead. After his death, the brewery operated seamlessly, largely due to his employees who efficiently performed their jobs. Fred traveled extensively, until his last few months, when he became a virtual invalid. Due to his many absences and foresight, he had established a management team that, following his death, functioned well.

Soon after Fred Miller's funeral, the family's attorney, Thomas Jefferson Pereles, began processing the will. As Lisette was named primary executor and had little formal education, she delegated her fiduciary duties to Pereles and Ernest. A hand-written note that Lisette sent to her son Fritz in about 1889, demonstrated her rudimentary education and German grammar. "Fred! Sent [send] us horse and buggy at 9 o'clock. to go to Salvey's [Salbey's] and you and Salbey be there too at his house half past nine. [signed] Lisette Miller." On the day the brewery's founder died, one report valued his estate at over $500,000, but within a month another appraised it at $800,000.[117] The estate's gem was the "colossal manufactory" in Wauwatosa, which, at its inception, daily were selling three barrels and, at his death, this number had grown to five hundred a day or 82,000 per year. The remaining real estate included the Miller Brewery's subsidiary, the Milwaukee Brewery in Bismarck, Dakota Territory, numerous ice and beer storage facilities outside Milwaukee, and several valuable pieces of city property.[118]

On July 7, 1888, Pereles filed Fred Miller's will for probate at the Milwaukee County Courthouse. Afterwards, the attorney, as dictated in the will, put the estate into a trust, called Fred Miller Heirs, with Lisette, Ernest, and Fritz Miller as trustees. This trust provided Lisette with all of Fred's household goods, furniture, wearing apparel, and personal ornaments. Additionally, she received $36,000 from his life insurance proceeds and the net income from his property and estate for her support and that of her children under age 21. Within a year of his death, of the 2,000 outstanding shares of the Miller Brewing Company, Ernest and Fritz each were to receive 50 shares or $5,000. These shares would immediately establish the young men's role as brewery leaders. The remaining children would receive 50 shares each upon their twenty-first birthday or, in his daughters' case, earlier if they wed. Upon Lisette's death, the residue of the estate would be divided among the surviving children. If his children did not survive their mother, then their children would inherit their parent's share and, if Fred's children died without issue (children), then their spouses would receive one-third, and two-thirds would pass to their surviving siblings.

A June 2, 1888 codicil to the will bequeathed $1,000 each to Fred's sister, Josephine Borcher, and Julia Miller, the widow of his deceased brother in Germany. He also left $5,000 to be divided among Marquette University, St. Joseph Parish (his home parish), St. Michael Parish, the Capuchin Catholic

Religious Order, the Milwaukee Orphan Home, Frudelhaus, Taubstum (Deaf and Dumb) Institute, among other benevolent institutions; these donations were to be paid before January 1, 1890. In mid-December, the Milwaukee Emergency Hospital received $100 from Fred's estate. On December 17, 1889, the management of the Milwaukee Infants' Home accepted a $100 check from the estate, which was the first bequest they had ever received.[119]

Fred Miller bequeathed some of his brewery stock to his children but much of it, along with his life insurance proceeds, went into a trust, called Fred Miller Estate, for Lisette's life estate. On May 23, 1899, this trust valued at $1 million was derived from Miller Brewery stock and its substantial dividends that accrued faster than Lisette's living expenses. On May 5, 1905, Lisette Miller assigned $2 million of the Trust's assets to her children in equal shares and, on January 7, 1909, she transferred an additional $1.8 million. By December 31, 1910, these gifts reduced the value of Frederick J. Miller's Estate to $1.025 million; still enough to provide a satisfying living for Lisette in her final years.[120]

Fred determined that his life's work, the Wauwatosa brewery, would remain under the Millers' dominion. He knew that family cohesiveness was the primary ingredient for generations of his heirs to fulfill this task. Therefore, days before his death, he beseeched his children and future grandchildren to: "Be considerate and kind to each other and remain in peace and unity." Time would determine whether Fred's wish was followed.[121]

Lisette and Ernest Miller held a special Miller Brewery stockholders' meeting on June 14, 1888, during which Lisette successfully made a motion to elect her son, Fritz, to the board of directors in place of his father. Thereafter, the directors met and Lisette successfully moved the election of Ernest as president and Fritz as secretary/treasurer. Lisette, Ernest, and Fritz continued as directors until the annual stockholders' meeting on November 6, 1899, at which time Emil replaced Lisette as director. Corporate directors represent the will of the stockholders and elect the officers who conduct the daily operations. In closely held corporations such as was Miller Brewing Company, the same people are often stockholders, directors, and officers. Corporations with diverse stock ownership often hire professional managers to serve as officers; therefore, these stockholders and directors perform a more supervisory than managerial role.[122]

Through correspondence, incorporation, and his last will and testament, Fred established that, upon his death, his oldest son, Ernest, would assume management of the family's financial empire. Ernest was as adequately prepared to assume this undertaking as anyone could be at almost age 23. At that time, Ernest had the added responsibility of helping his mother, Lisette, care for his four younger siblings. Methodically, Fred had taught his son about life and business. The young Miller had not studied at one of the new brewmaster schools, as had some of his contemporaries, but throughout his life was involved with his family's business. It is unclear what brewing tasks the serious-minded Ernest performed as an adolescent, but at age 18 he became involved with the bookkeeping and material purchasing at the Wauwatosa and then the Bismarck plants. Ernest's secondary education included two years of high school at Marquette College (now Marquette University) and evening courses at Milwaukee's Spencerian Business College.[123]

Ernest's personality was poles apart from Fred's, leading to a different leadership style at the brewery. Gone from the president's chair was the intelligent, ebullient risk-taker with indomitable drive. By contrast, his son led with cleverness, steadiness, and earnestness. Frederick Miller was best suited to create and develop the early brewery, while Ernest could patiently manage its increasing complications. He did not dominate a room as his father had, but in order to solve a problem, he could out-work and out-think others. Ernest was an intelligent and studious man, who thoroughly consulted with professionals before instituting a solution to any problem. The young man also lacked his father's impulsive tendencies. Unlike his socially oriented father, the young Miller stayed home after work and read, listened to music or played pool. Ernest had various male friends from youth and adulthood. Throughout his life, he seemed to have minimal or no interest in pursuing relationships with women and remained single while living with his mother until her death in 1920.

Ernest had a magnificent organization to support him as he assumed the president's chair. Louis Hirsch was progressing at the Bismarck plant while Albert A. Sims, Eugene Salbey, and Carl Miller oversaw Miller Brewery's assets. The esteemed Pereles provided Ernest with sound legal advice, both business and personal. Demonstrating his fiduciary responsibility, years earlier, Pereles on occasion angrily confronted Fred Miller about his profligate spending on the Bismarck brewery. Ernest also had a panoply of mature advisors who were friends of his father, such as Captain Frederick Pabst of the Pabst Brewery, Franz Falk of the Falk Brewery, and Adolph Zinn of the Zinn Malting Company. Ernest needed only to inquire in order to obtain an abundance of valuable advice. Fred Miller was loyal to his friends and, following his funeral, they repaid him by helping his son.

Since its inception, the Miller Brewing Company had struggled against various temperance movements, but they did not seriously affect beer sales in its early history. The brewery sold the majority of its beer in cities that remained "wet" due to their large, Catholic, immigrant population that considered moderate alcohol consumption a natural part of everyday life. The temperance movement garnered much of its strength from small towns and rural areas that were dominated by Americans from the British Isles, who often were members of traditional Protestant denominations. Years later, however, Ernest, Fritz, and their youngest brother, Emil, unsuccessfully confronted those who would abolish their livelihood. As the years passed, Ernest must have thought that he was living out a nightmare, because his tenure was blessed with a massive growth in sales and brewery improvements, despite being stalked by a burgeoning movement determined to destroy his efforts.

Nevertheless, the youthful Ernest and Fritz had a business

to manage and by 1888, the efficiency of sales and consistent outcome, from large breweries able to ship their product, led to the demise or takeover of hundreds of smaller breweries. The shipping breweries actively transported and sold beer over a large geographical region in comparison to locally based breweries. Miller Brewery survived due to its strong leadership, its location near the large and growing population centers of Milwaukee and Chicago, and the stockholders' desire to remain independent. Every year after Fred's death, Fred Miller's family determined whether or not to sell their business, as surely they had numerous opportunities. Selling their stock would bring immediate wealth, a diminution of stressful duties, and increased time for frivolity. Conversely, selling the stock would eliminate the opportunity to reap future large profits that shipping brewers traditionally provided to their stockholders. Furthermore, the brewery gave the Millers a relatively high local social profile that would have begun to diminish if they had dispensed with the stock. Lastly, selling their shares would have been disloyal to Fred Miller's wishes. For many decades, the Miller family's faithfulness to Fred's wishes was the deciding factor in retaining their brewery.

Beginning in 1889 and throughout the 1890s, several financial groups became interested in forming a trust to hold the stock of a number of medium and large-sized brewers. They believed that a trust would give them control of the price of beer in many markets, therefore securing them enormous profits. They were moderately successful in the brewing centers of Cincinnati and St. Louis. There is evidence that a syndicate made a serious effort to purchase Miller Brewery stock. Of the three large Milwaukee breweries, Pabst, Joseph Schlitz, and Valentine Blatz, an English syndicate purchased the Blatz Brewery. The financial panic of 1893 finished their acquisitions. They were unable to acquire enough of the market share to control beer prices. The marketplace had not changed much for Miller Brewery, as most of the large breweries, such as St. Louis's Lemp and Anheuser-Busch and Milwaukee's Pabst and Schlitz remained family owned.[124]

One of Ernest's pressing concerns was re-establishing financial control over the Milwaukee Brewery in Bismarck. Mere weeks after Fred's death, Miller Brewery sent its accountant, Albert Sims, to Dakota to review the finances. To further evaluate their enterprise, on September 30, 1888, Ernest and the family's trusted friend, Adolph Zinn, owner of the Zinn Malting Company, traveled by train to Bismarck. Fred praised Zinn in his final missive a week before his death, referring to "Zinn, who has served us well and shown friendship and love and who in the future will continue to do so because he vowed to do so." There is little doubt that while jostling westward along the tracks, the two gentlemen discussed the bleak future of the Bismarck plant.[125]

Soon, the issue of the Bismarck brewery's efficiency became a moot point as North Dakota historian, Frank E. Vyzralek, described in a 1986 scholarly paper on that state's brewing history. By November 1887, alcohol production and sale in the Dakota Territory was becoming more tenuous, as the territory passed a law that allowed its counties to vote for local option, which allowed counties and towns to prohibit liquor vending. Of the 80 organized counties in the territory, 57 became dry, and by mid-1888 the future of the Milwaukee Brewing Company was determined. At that time, the Dakota Territory was on the verge of becoming North and South Dakota, and in July 1889 a convention in Bismarck assembled to write a constitution for the new state of North Dakota.[126]

On June 5, immediately prior to the convention, Ernest made another visit to the brewery to lobby the Bismarck citizenry against the dry clause. As usual, the brewers became involved "too little and too late." Vyzralek explained that the prohibitionists successfully inserted a clause into the constitution but resolved to have a separate public vote on this controversial matter. When the ballots were counted on October 1, 1889, the constitution was adopted by a large margin while the law prohibiting the sale and manufacture of alcohol passed with a majority of slightly over 1,100 votes out of 36,000 cast.[127]

This new law shocked and devastated the Millers and their Dakota employees, who had until July 1, 1890 to cease production. Rather than wait, they Millers shuttered their operation immediately and transported much of the brewing equipment by train to their Wauwatosa plant. Thereafter, the Dakota brewery's buildings were used mainly for storage. Since brewing was outlawed, the buildings' brewing-specific design decreased in value. On October 4, 1889, a column in the local newspaper lamenting the prohibitory clause noted that, irrespective of Frederick Miller's substantial investment, the family could not then sell the plant for more than $10,000. On October 20, 1900, the Millers sold the property for much less than that estimate. Temporarily, a seed business operated from the buildings. The buildings were gradually demolished, the last of them disappearing in about 1940. The site is now part of the grounds of Fraine Barracks, headquarters of the North Dakota National Guard.[128]

Unfortunately, there are only remnants of the reams of paperwork the Dakota-based Milwaukee Brewery produced, an insufficient amount to know its profitability in 1887 and 1888. The local newspaper's coverage was positive, but the extant business correspondences show otherwise. In all likelihood, despite the upbeat media reports, the Millers lost a substantial sum of money on this venture. Fred reported in a letter that he had invested $200,000 in it, which was considerably more than his original plan of $30,000.[129]

Certainly, Frederick Miller blundered by building the Milwaukee Brewery in Bismarck. The confident Fred pursued it because he had succeeded in most of his previous endeavors. He probably believed that the westward migration, which had populated the East Coast and then most of the states east of the Mississippi River, would continue by filling in the states of the Plains region. Unfortunately, he misread the demographics of the arid Northern Plains states, unaware that most travelers were passing through them on their way to the booming West Coast. Also, the prohibitory acts of the new state of North Dakota were an unexpected shock to the Millers and other

North Dakota brewery owners.

It is plausible that Fred pursued the Bismarck project to provide his sons with separate businesses at which to work, thus presenting them with opportunities to manage a business without interfering with each other. Fred erred in pursuing this project so late in life, when his sons were just five years away from naturally assuming the Wauwatosa brewery's leadership. At that time, they could have followed their own entrepreneurial ideas with a more reasoned and scientific approach. Unfortunately, this fiasco hurt the family's finances but, luckily, this period produced such large profits at the Wauwatosa brewery, that the Millers survived the Bismarck brewery's financial drain. Under slightly different circumstances, the cash drain from the Bismarck brewery could have forced Miller Brewery and its owning family into bankruptcy, significantly changing the brewery's history.[130]

Nevertheless, in 1889, Ernest continued to concentrate on the Miller Brewery. At that time, it advertised six kinds of beer; Export Pilsner, Extra Pale, Miller's Original Milwaukee Budweiser in bottles, (not to be confused with Anheuser Busch's similarly named product), Standard, Pilsner, and Muechener in kegs. This selection, compared to their two varieties eight years earlier, represented a growing sophistication in exploiting new market niches. Later that decade, other brands included Pale Bohemian, Porter (a dark beer), Culbacher, and Lager.[131]

In 1889, the Miller Brewing Company announced a twelve-building expansion, which would replace virtually all of the wooden structures. It is unknown whether Fred Miller had done some of the original planning for this expansion or whether the impetus came solely from Ernest and Fritz. The construction phase would occur over many years. Additionally that year, Miller Brewery continued expanding its sales network by building a large cold-storage facility in the Wisconsin town of Tomahawk. This building was constructed to supply beer to the northern Wisconsin towns of Tomahawk, Minocqua, Bradley, and Heafford Junction.[132]

Meanwhile, in Wauwatosa, a John Meihers filed a lawsuit

to enjoin Miller Brewery from operating a ditch between the brewery and the nearby Menomonee River because he stated that the ditch carried off refuse matter and bore an unbearable stench. This lawsuit demonstrated the incremental change from a woodland and farm-dominated region to one of industry and houses. The City of Milwaukee was growing westward and, eventually, in 1925, it annexed this portion of the Town of Wauwatosa.[133]

In 1889, Miller Brewery constructed a building to house an electricity-generating machine and a year later it was wired to Milwaukee's electrical grid. Prior to this time workers used candles or kerosene or oil lamps to light their way. It took years for all of the hand and steam-operated machines to be replaced or converted to electrical power. Also in 1889, sales topped 100,000 (116,082) barrels for the first time. At this point, the company was shipping beer to much of the Midwest and various foreign countries. The company also installed two De La Vergne refrigeration machines, one with a capacity of 150 tons, and the other with a capacity of fifty tons. Miller's sales rose rapidly between 1888 when the annual barrelage reached 80,212 and 1890 when it achieved 91,000. In 1891, it brewed 126,000 barrels, which kept it at fifth place among Milwaukee's brewers.[134]

In 1892, stockhouse A was completed at a cost of $60,000 and was the brewery's first building constructed completely with mechanical refrigeration. Unfortunately, in order to build stockhouse A, the workers razed the original Plank Road Brewery building. Currently, a replica of this building sits on a hill beside the Miller Inn on West State Street. The brewery lagered barrels of beer in racks in the stockhouse, above ground, more efficiently than they had done previously in its numerous caverns. Soon Miller Brewery's administration began construction of stockhouse B and completed it in 1894 for $41,000, leading to the abandonment of the 600-foot cave system. At present, the brewery uses the caves exclusively for the visitors' tour. In 1896, the Miller Brewing Company built an attractive brick stable to house the brewery's 53 horses at a cost of $32,000. The horses were kept on the second floor and the wheeled conveyances were stored on the first. Today the brewery uses it as a garage.[135]

In 1897, Ernest began construction of another brewhouse on the Wauwatosa property. This creation was a statement to the beer-drinking community that Miller Brewery was well-managed and that the Bismarck debacle was well behind them. In 1901, the brewery built a bottling house and the racking room was enlarged. (Breweries used racking rooms to fill kegs.) Simultaneously, the brewery produced 219,270 barrels of beer. Some of their labels at this time were Buffet, Bock, and Milwaukee Beer. In May 1904, Miller completed stockhouse C. Additionally, the old bottle shop was converted into a cooperage and new bottling shop. In 1906, stockhouse D was completed, which together with house C, cost $121,000.[136]

Parenthetically, in 1903, in a nearby garage unceremoniously painted with the words "Harley and Davidson," two men prepared to sell their first production motorcycle. Today, this enormous corporation's headquarters and Miller Brewing Company's headquarters are across the street from one another. Miller's current corporate headquarters, at 38th and Highland Boulevard, occupies the location of the original Harley Davidson garage.

In 1906, Miller Brewery occupied 44 acres, of which its buildings covered 25. The company had five hundred employees, which four years later grew to 1,000. It maintained a 500,000-bushel capacity malt house in Port Washington, approximately thirty miles north of Milwaukee, where it derived all of its malt. By 1910, the malt house's capacity had grown to 1 million bushels. By 1910 Miller Brewery had spent just over $500,000 to build a bottling house and a refrigeration or storage plant for lagering beer.[137]

In this period, the shipping brewers, of which Miller Brewery was one of the smaller ones, were constructing large, efficient, specialized buildings. It is worth taking a moment to examine the 1890 brewing process that since then has changed little. Miller's raw materials such as water, barley, adjuncts (corn or rice), hops and yeast were shipped to different buildings. The barley went to the malt house in Port Washington to be steeped in water, germinated, and then dry-roasted in a kiln. After it was dried and slightly browned, it was known as malt and then shipped to the Wauwatosa brewhouse. The adjunct, usually corn, was used to produce a beer of pale color that was less filling, with a snappier taste, and increased stability, especially of the bottled product. (Most breweries use corn as their adjunct but others, such as Anheuser-Busch also use rice.) Adjunct gave the brewers more soluble sugar to help make pale beers lighter than if they only had used barley. The ratio of malt to adjunct is roughly 10 to 1. Adjunct brewing, which constitutes most large-scale American brewing, is what separates most darker and heavier tasting European beers from their lighter American counterparts.[138]

Miller's water flowed from deep wells and was filtered and purified in the brewhouse. By this time, beer was not influenced by its water source, since breweries thoroughly filtered it to produce a clear stable liquid for brewing consistent tasting beer. The water, malt, adjunct, and hops were mixed and boiled in the brewhouse. In fact, the word brew means to prepare by boiling. Hops are the cone-shaped formations, representing clusters of blossoms of the female hop plant. In relation to malt and adjunct, hops are a lightweight airy crop with the taction of dried flowers. The brewhouse's final product is the hot wort, boiled with hops. Wort is the soluble matter that has been separated from the insoluble residue called spent grain. By nature of their operation, brewhouses were hot places with temperatures reaching ghastly heights in warm summers. Even today with modern refrigeration, Miller's brewhouse is closed to tours on many scorching summer days due to oppressive heat. Subsequent to the hot brewing stage, the wort was allowed to cool by atmospheric air, after which it was chilled by artificial refrigeration. Soon after yeast was added to the chilled wort, fermentation began to create beer.[139]

After beer was fashioned from the wort, and the yeast was extracted, the product traveled through pipes to the stockhouse for the lagering (aging) process. As the brewhouses were hot, the stockhouses were perennially cooled by large artificial refrigeration machines. Until well into the 20th Century the breweries used huge wooden tanks to lager the beer. Today, there are glass-lined metal behemoths to hold the beer at 30 to 34 degrees Fahrenheit until it is ready to be filtered and fill kegs or bottles in the bottling house. When Miller Brewery constructed its new brewhouse, stockhouses, and bottling facilities, it placed pipes between the buildings to simplify the transportation process. Previously, brewery workers moved the beer in wooden kegs.[140]

Following Fred Miller's death, Lisette lived in their substantial wooden house, staffed with servants, near the beer garden. Unfortunately, on February 14, 1889, her father, Gottfried Gross, died. With pluck and exertion, he had brought his family from Bavaria to Wisconsin and developed a farm and brewery. To exhibit their place in Milwaukee's Brahmin class, in 1901 the Millers built a palatial house some blocks away from the brewery, at 3200 West Highland Boulevard. One granddaughter later explained that Lisette wanted to live near other affluent German Americans so that her sons could find wealthy wives. Some of the other brewery owners were also displaying their wealth and status by constructing large brick and stone houses to complement their stunning business buildings. The seventeen-room Miller home, designed by the noted German-American architectural team of George Bowman Ferry and Alfred C. Clas, was at that time one of the finest residences in Milwaukee. The structure, apart from the furnishings, cost $45,000 to build with the total outlay at nearly $55,000.[141]

Highland Boulevard was also known as Sauerkraut Boulevard due to its many wealthy Germans residents. Lisette lived beside a Pabst, and near a Gettelman and a Blatz. Lisette's orange-brick house was typical of Milwaukee's renaissance chateaux being built at the time. Milwaukee architectural historian H. Russell Zimmermann noted that it was one of the most historically and architecturally interesting homes in Milwaukee. He wrote that, "Many of the older homes on

Highland looked like heavy stone fortresses, but not this one. The overall proportions were slender and the walls had a thinner look because the windows weren't recessed so deeply." He wrote that the home used a free interpretation of a number of styles and that the showplace of the home was the dining room with built-in materials alone costing $15,000 including one of ten fireplaces in the home. All of the dining-room woodwork, including the cabinets, ceiling beams, buffet, and mantel, were of mahogany imported from British Honduras. A central staircase divided at a landing into two smaller stairways. The design of the kitchen was especially interesting, according to Zimmerman, because the icebox was built into the wall so that the ice could be loaded from the outside. On the third floor was the ballroom or, as the family referred to it, the recreation room because it had a billiard table.

Each of the five Millers had a separate set of rooms. The family's living quarters were on the second floor and, as was customary in those homes, they socialized on the first floor. Ernest and Fritz kept their horses and conveyances in a spectacular coach house built in the same style as the residence and, daily, took a horse cart to work. At the brewery, the Millers stored their horse and cart at the company's stable. Servants were housed on the third floor and in the coach house to the rear of the building. Ever since her marriage to Fred Miller, Lisette had the luxury of servants. Three of them who in 1920 lived at the Miller mansion were Katherine "Katie" Dieringer, 49, Rose Schultz, 22, and Grace Border, 18. In 1942, Lisette's children gave the home to Marquette University, which converted it into a female dormitory called Lisette Lodge. In 1964, Lutheran Social Services bought the building and razed it in 1966.[142]

6.
FAMILY SQUABBLES

A simmering conflict surfaced in mid-1889 between Ernest Miller and his future brother-in-law Carl Miller. The actual events are lost to time but they involved Lisette, Ernest, Fritz, Carl, and Clara Miller. The problem's genesis was an intense rivalry between Ernest and Carl. Ernest was the business's president while Carl had no title but, with his commercial experience and likeable personality, had created a vital niche for himself at the brewery. In all likelihood, the crisis developed due to a combination of Carl's disregard of Ernest as the anointed and actual head of the brewery and Ernest's jealousy of Carl's business facility. Another reason for the conflict may have been Lisette Miller's fondness for the urbane immigrant that would have added to Ernest and Fritz's jealousy. One undocumented Miller family story notes that Ernest or Fritz "found" one of Carl's letters to his father in Germany, in his room, when he was gone, describing his new role at the brewery that might lead to his taking it over. The content of this letter would have seriously threatened the youthful Miller brothers. Other possibilities include accusations that Carl was misappropriating brewery funds or the resurfacing of a nefarious legal matter from his earlier life in Europe and Africa.[143]

In any event, Carl tried to acquit himself of the charges, but Ernest used the opportunity to extricate Carl from the business's headquarters by sending him to their Chicago agency to assume the bookkeeper's position until the brewery hired a replacement. This matter was complicated because, by this time, Clara and Carl were becoming a mutually exclusive couple. Lisette cried publicly as she saw Ernest and Fritz at odds with Clara and her future husband, Carl. This schism of Clara and Carl against Ernest, Fritz and, later, Emil and Elise continued, intermittently, for three generations. Due to the estrangement, Carl began to search for other employment. He wanted to become a partial or complete business owner to fully use his talents and prevent any chance of being fired or transferred again.[144]

On the morning of September 20, 1889, Ernest, who was suffering from a bad cold, and Carl Miller traveled by train to Chicago to the Miller Depot at 41 & 43 North Peoria Street where Adolph C. Lambrecht was the manager. Upon arriving, Carl took over the financial books and began to look for a replacement bookkeeper, which he judged would take no more than two or three weeks. As all employees, Carl worked six-day weeks of ten hours a day. After reviewing the office, the next day Ernest returned to Milwaukee leaving Carl in a small apartment or hotel room by himself. Carl was distraught to be apart from Clara and, daily, poured out his heart to her in extensive letters. Clara and Carl Miller thought that a secondary reason for Ernest exiling him to Chicago was to separate the two lovers and deprecated Ernest in their letters.[145]

Carl Miller's three-week assignment turned into months. Aside from the bookkeeping, he traveled about Chicago settling or improving saloon accounts, which included drinking liberal doses of beer as brewery agents were expected to buy rounds of drinks for all the present customers. One night, Carl complained of his headache from partaking in so many alcoholic drinks at the saloons. He feared that excessive drinking would harm his liver, which was already damaged from the severe case of malaria that he had contracted years ealier in Africa.

Every two weeks, Carl took a three-hour train trip to Milwaukee to spend the two-day weekend deepening his love affair with Clara and hunting for business prospects that would provide him, minimally, with his current $1,700 annual salary. Soon, Carl set his sights on the Beck and Schmidt Lumber Company, which had formed in 1888 at First Avenue at the foot of the Sixth Street Bridge. Milwaukee in 1889 was a great time and place to own a lumber company as the city was quickly growing with multitudes of immigrants arriving at its shores and train depots. These immigrants, as soon as possible, were buying or building new wooden homes.[146]

Carl enjoyed his meeting with the Beck and Schmidt principals, C.A. Beck and William Schmidt. He believed that they were trustworthy men with whom he could form a partnership. Carl envisioned himself buying into the company that sold lumber, lath, and shingles, to become a partner and officer. Carl asked his friends from Miller Brewery, William Marx and Albert Zinn, to review the Beck and Schmidt numbers and provide him with their assessments. It is unclear how much Ernest and Fritz Miller knew about Carl's plans but, presumably, they would have been pleased that he was planning on leaving the brewery. Against Lisette, Fritz, and Clara Miller's plus Marx's and Zinn's wishes, in mid-December 1889, Carl paid Beck and Schmidt to become a partner in the renamed Milwaukee Lumber Company. He used money from his savings and a bank note. One article reported that Carl's father had given him $5,000 when he came to America that he might have used to buy into the lumber company. Although Clara trusted Carl's judgment, she noted that he could take risks and live frugally as long as, after their marriage, he became financially successful. Carl immediately left the Miller Brewing Company to begin full-time employment at the lumber company. In approximately 1904, Carl returned to the brewery to assist with Chicago sales, which must have coincided with a downturn in his lumber business. On February 2, 1890, the lumber company incorporated with $50,000 in stock. From the start, as secretary and treasurer, Carl spent his energy guarding against risky lumber sales that previously had plagued the business.[147]

In 1889, Carl asked for, probably of Lissette, and received Clara's hand in marriage. Earlier, Lisette may have requested that Carl wait until Clara turned 20 and finished school. In the spring of 1890, Carl and Clara decided to marry in Carl's hometown of Friedrichshafen, Germany. Lisette, Fritz, Clara, Carl, Emil, and Elise Miller traveled by steamship to Germany for the nuptials. Afterwards, Lisette, Fritz, Emil, and Elise traveled to Vienna, Austria to pursue a medical treatment for the chronically sick Fritz, while Clara and Carl went to the Italian Alps for their honeymoon. They all returned to Milwaukee some four months later.

On December 22, 1891, ten months before their first child was born, Carl constructed a spectacular wooden home at 3036 Cedar (now 3037 West Kilbourn Avenue). This recently rehabilitated home stands relatively near the brewery. The gray painted wooden house had six bedrooms and was equipped with a backyard playhouse. It also was electrified and had running water. Behind the house there was a barn for a horse and two carriages. The kitchen had a wood-burning stove and an indoor-outdoor icebox into which, every other day, the iceman would put a hundred pound block. The third floor, to which one had access through a narrow rear stairway, was created for the two female live-in servants and featured a delightful circular reading room. The Millers' first house was more grandiose than many financially comfortable Milwaukee families could ever dream of owning.

Carl and Clara Miller wasted little time in beginning their clan and on October 20, 1892, Loretta Elizabeth arrived to twenty-eight-year-old Carl and twenty-two-year-old Clara. Fifteen months later on January 24, 1894, Anita Rose came into the Miller's home. On March 3, 1896, their third daughter, Claire, was born. On May 19, 1899 after their first three children were born, Carl Miller formalized the process that he had begun ten-and-half years earlier, and became an American citizen. Family lore maintains that Carl was without a middle name until soon after his marriage and, instead of a middle name, took the letter "A." Clara recommended that he take the letter "A", which was her middle initial, so they could both spell their names, C. A. Miller. Anyway, two years after baby Claire was born, on May 15, 1901, the Millers added their fourth child Marguerite. Dr. Jacob Lang assisted in Clara's first four home deliveries and interestingly, in 1888, also had treated her father, Fred Miller's, terminal cancer.

In 1902 with four daughters in tow, the Millers moved one block away to 3036 West Wells Street, an existing home in keeping with their growing financial status. Interestingly, the lots of their first two homes are contiguous. The Wells Street home was not appreciably bigger than their first home, if at all, but it gave the Millers a more prestigious address to match their growing success. It had a red-brick first floor and wooden second story that the Millers may have found more attractive than their prior all-wooden home. Also, Wells Street was one of Milwaukee's main east-west thoroughfares whose sidewalks were lined with grand mansions and which had a tracked electric streetcar running down its center. (Today there are few mansions yet standing on this area of Wells Street but, fortunately, the Miller home is among them.) This three-story house featured a large, front porch giving them ample opportunities, during the summer months, to entertain personal and business friends.

The Wells Street home, built in 1892 for Mr. Lin Boyd Benton (an inventor in the printing industry), has a *porte cochere* on its west side and a concrete driveway cutting to the back of the property. The attractive yard was ringed with lilac bushes. Before moving in, Carl built a three-horse and two-carriage coach house at the rear of the property. The house had an addition at its rear, which was connected directly to the kitchen, and where a piano, toys, and a twelve-person table were kept. Also, there was a large dining room with a fireplace, two sitting rooms; one for company and the other for family use in the evenings after supper. This home had several fireplaces but was heated by a coal furnace in the basement that provided hot air through grates in the house. Upstairs there were six bedrooms, one each for Carl and Clara, a sewing room, and a sitting room.

After Marguerite was born, there was nearly a five-year gap until February 26, 1906, when Frederick Charles was born to thirty-six year old Clara and forty-three year old Carl. After Fred, Charlotte was born on July 16, 1909, making six children in all. A year before Fred's birth, the Millers had traveled to Europe, stopping in Rome, to beseech Pope St. Pius X for a son. In 1906, a fearful Clara demanded that Carl circle the hospital until the last minute, at which time, she entered to give birth to Fred. The Millers believed that Fred, who one day would become a successful president of Miller Brewery, was their special gift from God.

Clara had lofty dreams for Fred, naming him "Frederick" after her father and not "Carl" after her husband. Carl Miller, who had interchanged Carl and Charles for his first name, provided his son's middle name. Interestingly, the Millers baptized Fred with the name "Carl" and, like his father, later changed it to "Charles." Fred received the Miller surname from his father who was biologically unrelated to Clara. Since the Millers' five other children were daughters and Clara's brothers died without children, Fred was the sole opportunity for the Miller name to continue.

Carl loved horses and rode them whenever possible. Before automobiles became commonplace and age took its toll on his joints, it was easier for him to indulge his equestrian interests. In the early days, Carl rode to the lumberyard in a two-wheeled carriage pulled by one horse. His daughter Claire remarked that when they lived on Wells Street, her Dad and her sister, Loretta, rode horses every Sunday in the summer.

The children of Clara and Carl Miller enjoyed the environs of their first two homes, which were substantially rural, as Milwaukee had not yet completely urbanized this area. Carl demanded that his children spend a lot of time outside to enjoy the nearby hills and woods. Also, the stern father expected his children to exercise a lot. It was common for the Miller children to travel to West Park (now Washington Park), some blocks north, and entertain themselves. Also, Carl was profoundly interested in nature and, on Sundays, took his children to the woods where he would patiently explain nature's secrets.

Clara and Carl Miller's household ran cleanly and efficiently; there were strict norms for the children to follow. Clara and Carl, for the most part, agreed upon their child-rearing principles and expectations. As necessary, the Millers meted out corporal punishment to their children and, at times, sent them to bed without dinner. The Millers raised their children to obey their parents, be respectful, attend school, practice Catholicism, marry suitable (Catholic and wealthy) mates, have children, remain loyal spouses, and visit Mama and Papa Miller regularly. During summers, the Millers rented a home on Pewaukee Lake in Waukesha County, twenty miles west of Milwaukee, where they, and their children's nurse Agatha, swam, boated, and fished. During this time, Carl stayed in Milwaukee to work.

Carl was a disciplinarian, who deplored idleness, but nevertheless, was well loved. He reared his children as he had been raised, which included schooling, work, cultural activities, and athletics. The Miller children took singing lessons and entertained family and friends. Claire McCahey said that her father endured military training under the Kaiser that gave him a life-long appreciation for punctuality and erect posture. Carl maintained a latent interest in military life encouraging his children to march, exercise, and have correct posture, even placing a stick under their arms to help them. His granddaughter Anita McCahey Gray said that he walked erect, despite a late-life arthritic hip, and expected others to do likewise. For emphasis, he would poke his finger into his grandchildren's backs and tell them to walk tall.

Beginning with their first home on Kilbourn Avenue, Clara and Carl Miller had resident servants. The Millers also had long-time non-resident help, such as drivers, nurses, and handymen. At a minimum, two people consistently lived with them. Chuck Bransfield says laughingly that his grandmother never cooked a meal in her life. In 1900, the Millers employed a new German immigrant Theresa Huenglia, 29, a single woman who spoke no English. Also empathetically, they hired Amelia Bartch, 29, a divorcee with eight children, born in Wisconsin to German parents. In 1920, they had two live-in servants, Stella Peterson, 24, who was born in Wisconsin, and Hilda Nelson, 20, who was from Minnesota. Finally in 1930, the Millers hired Ottilie Schulz, 34, a single woman born in Germany, as their cook, and Elizabeth Sauer, 28, also from Germany, as their maid.

The Millers socialized almost exclusively with first and second generation German Milwaukeeans. The majority of early Milwaukee residents, called Yankees, were from the East Coast, predominantly of English and Irish descent. In the 1870s and 1880s while Clara was growing up, there was animosity between the Yankees and the more-recent European immigrants. Many of the Yankees were threatened by the massive influx of non-English speaking immigrants. Chuck Bransfield noted that to Clara all Yankees were her life-long enemies. Clara, inheriting her father's attitude, spent her lifetime competing with Yankees and believed that they were trying to steal her money. To segregate from the Yankees, the Millers sent their children to school with other immigrants, socialized at German clubs, and worked with recent immigrants.

Even after Carl became an American citizen, his heart resided in Friedrichshafen, where he had many relatives. After his first return trip, during which he married, he and Clara regularly traveled there, to enjoy Southern Germany's hospitality, along with other European destinations. In the early 1930s, Carl's traveling became more extensive, after his son Fred took over his lumber business, when he began to travel overseas yearly staying for two summer months. He would take cases of Miller beer for his German relatives, with whom he maintained a lifelong relationship. Clara Miller McCahey remarked that the world wars crimped the Millers' overseas travels. So, each spring and fall during World War I, they voyaged to Excelsior Springs, Missouri where Carl maintained his regimen of bathing and drinking the mineral-rich water to treat his malaria. The Excelsior Hotel, near Kansas City, was the location where two of the Miller daughters met their husbands.

According to their grandson Chuck Bransfield, the Millers, wittily nicknamed lovebirds, argued constantly; often yelling at each other. Regardless, they worked and traveled together, with Clara holding various titular positions alongside Carl. Chuck notes that in the 1920s Clara discovered that Carl had a kept woman in one of the Millers' apartment buildings. Apparently, the employees who collected the rent broke the news to Clara. After this discovery, Clara evicted the woman and confronted her husband. Their relationship survived this episode but Chuck says that afterwards Clara was permanently chillier toward Carl.

After graduating from St. Rose Catholic Grade School, at 528 North 31st Street, the three oldest girls attended Milwaukee High School before transferring to the all-girls Woodlands Academy of the Sacred Heart in Lake Forest, Illinois, which is still operating. It was a highly regarded college preparatory school, run by an order of nuns called the Madames of the Sacred Heart, who operated similar schools throughout the United States. Their goal, as noted in their recently published history, was to teach young women of many religious, national, ethnic, socioeconomic, and racial backgrounds the value of serious study, social responsibility, and strong faith.

Like his sisters, Fred attended St. Rose School near his home. One priest remembered Fred as quiet, serious, sometimes moody and shy. Bishop William O'Connor of Madison said, "I remember with what shyness he approached me, took my hand, walked along without saying a word—and then said goodbye." In 1917, Carl and Clara built and moved into a home at 2909 East Newberry Boulevard near Lake Michigan. Due to this move, Fred did not follow his maternal uncles to Marquette University High School and, instead, entered the newly opened, private, nonsectarian Milwaukee Country Day School near his home. Before attending Country Day, Fred attended, for a short time, Milwaukee University School, then known as the German-English Academy, and St. Mary's Prep School in Kansas. Fred excelled at the exclusive, preparatory Country Day School finishing second in his class, with an average grade of 90, and starring on the baseball, basketball, and football teams. Fred was captain of the football team for three years while playing fullback and, as a senior, was captain of the baseball and basketball teams. In baseball, he was a home-run-hitting outfielder and in basketball he played guard. At graduation, he was awarded the James memorial prize that went to the boy whose influence had the greatest effect on the entire student body.[148]

Fred was a handsome boy with russet skin and straight dark hair. He had a slim build, even while playing high school and college football. He inherited big hands and feet. He had narrowly placed, deeply set, intense eyes and his mother's pronounced chin. As a young man, while being photographed, he would lower his large chin to diminish its prominence, therefore emphasizing his striking, penetrating eyes. Due to Fred's facial characteristics, some people assumed that he was an American Indian, a mistake that Fred enjoyed, as he had a life-long interest in Indians.

Carl's tough training of his male progeny, son and grandsons included, caused him difficulties with Frederick, who was more headstrong than Carl. From Fred's birth, the Millers raised him to become the family patriarch. Unfortunately, Carl and Clara had conflicting methods of raising him. Chuck Bransfield explains that Clara spoiled Fred, whereas Carl used a military approach.

Clara Miller's daughter, Claire Miller McCahey, kept a scrapbook that provides a delightful view into her and her family's life. For example, this 20-year old wealthy woman related a story of first meeting her future husband, James B. McCahey, Sr., in 1916:

"Mr. J.B. McCahey first came to our town [Milwaukee] when he visited Mr. Frank Dunn at the Sanitarium. He had been instructed to call Anita then one of our Convent friends, which he did. I was supposed to join the party but had a previous and more important date (with my dad) so did not meet Mr. McCahey in Milwaukee that day. Mother, Dad and Anita visited Excelsior [Missouri] in October 1916, and came back the first week in November. It was there they met Mr. McCahey for the first time tho [though] Anita had met him a while before in Milwaukee as stated above. Again I missed out in meeting him. But fate had decreed:

"I came into the Northwestern Depot, Chicago, Friday

November the tenth 1917, at four o'clock. Anita [Miller], Marion Boyle, Michael Bransfield, Lester Renipe and James McCahey met me there. That was the first meeting. After kissing all the girls I met the men and the man. We (the girls) went out to Marion's in Michael's "Loco" – got all settled and stayed there for dinner. We got all "dressed up" (donned the glad rags) and came downtown again and met the boys at the Sherman [Hotel]. We had no decided partners but in the rush for the theater, Mr. McCahey caught me. We sat apart from the rest of the party and by the time the show was over and we got together again I wore a "ring" for the evening. Then we went to the "Balle Fabarin" had a wine supper and danced until oh so late. That was the end of the first day.

"We had a steady fortnight of "high living" and then left for home. Saw all of the shows, went cabareting, to ball games (Chicago vs. Minneapolis), on auto trips etc. That was the life for us all! And all the time we saw lots of each other. Some sextette I'll say! Limousine service, touring cars, flowers, cards, all of the good things we enjoyed. That was my first visit to Chicago during my courtship.

"[I] Came to Chicago again February twelfth and went around with Jim and the crowd. Came down with Mother and Anita on a shopping trip, and we did some shopping! We went home for Fred's [Fred C. Miller] birthday, and the day after we got home, Marg [Marguerite Miller] took scarlet fever! That meant quarantine for four weeks for all of us. Then Jim and Michael [Bransfield] came up regularly to see us. Birthday parties, dances, etc. All weekend parties. Anita and I came to Chicago April twenty-first, five days after the boy's birthdays, [both Michael Bransfield and Jim McCahey's birthdays were on April 19] celebrated that night with Dad and Mother and we all. Then Dad went home and we stayed on. Then mother went home.

"May the second — Jim proposed at last! (This is a secret ssh!) Had my picture taken May third. And went home May fifth. Then Fred got the scarlet fever. Another rest for all of us. More weekend parties. Then we went on a weekend trip to Winneconne Wisc. Some trip. Mother, Loretta & Norm [Loretta and Norman Kopmeier], Anita and Michael, Jim and I had come back on Tuesday. Fishing, rowing, walking, lounging around, eating, walking thru the cemetery – all such exciting times we had there — but such fun!

"Our double engagement was announced Wednesday July the twelfth, in the morning paper. That evening Dad gave a dinner at the opening of the new Miller Hotel in the "Rose Room."

The Miller children were expected to marry according to their birth order; so, on October 20, 1913 Loretta had married Norman Kopmeier at St. Rose Parish. Four years later on November 12, 1917, at St. Rose, Anita Miller married Michael Bransfield and Claire married James McCahey in a joint wedding service. Anita and Claire married Chicago men and, after their Milwaukee marriage, settled there. Before the nuptials, Clara Miller researched her future son-in-laws' families and discovered that they could support her daughters, otherwise there would have been no marriages. The Millers gave each child $10,000 after their weddings to help them get established. In 1930, Carl Miller provided $65,000 mortgages to his daughters, Loretta, Marguerite, and Claire. In 1935, the Millers gave their five surviving children $15,000 each.[149]

Grandchildren soon followed the weddings. The first one was Charles "Chuck" Bransfield on September 10, 1918, followed by Rose Mary Kopmeier on March 18, 1919, and Claire McCahey on February 18, 1919. These three children, who are still living, were born before their grandmother Lisette Miller died in 1920 and, brought her joy in her last months.

Clara remained a devout Catholic throughout her life, attending Mass regularly, even on her many travels. She began her married life at the Miller family church, St. Rose of Lima, where the pastor, Monsignor Patrick H. Durnin, administered the family's sacraments. Clara's children attended the St. Rose Parish School, which, according to Claire McCahey, was quite strict. She remembered that Father Durnin and the resident

Dominican nuns would not hesitate to "switch" a child for poor behavior. At 11:45 a.m., the Miller children raced home for the large German-style dinner with Mama and Papa Miller, who served soup, meat, and potatoes. After eating, they returned for their afternoon classes.

Until 1917, the Millers lived on Wells Street, at which time; they moved into a spectacular home on Milwaukee's northeast side, that they had built at 2909 East Newberry Boulevard. This large home still stands on the southeast corner of Newberry Boulevard and Shepard Avenue. It was here that the Millers lived out the remainder of their years. It was near Lake Drive, providing easy access to Milwaukee's downtown and the northern part of Lake Michigan's developing shore. Additionally, it was one block from the elegant Lake Park, which provided myriad recreational opportunities for Milwaukee's residents.

Milwaukee's well-known home restorer and historian H. Russell Zimmermann noted that this Italianate style residence was designed by architect Charles W. Valentine. It was spectacular in its size and dominance of the property. It was built simply, with featureless Indiana limestone block, inset windows, and a green tile roof. Its front door was adorned with columns in relief, and an unobtrusive balcony circles the moderately sized porch. Its façade had two wrought-iron balconies and its most spectacular exterior feature was a large two-story coach house attached by a two-story passageway.

The interior, dramatically different from the exterior, was where the Millers lavished their money. The two large, high-ceilinged parlor rooms, each sporting a large glazed-tile fireplace, had many tall windows. A dramatic sweeping stairway led to the second floor and featured an exquisite, four feet by six feet, stained-glass window that portrayed the biblical story of Pharaoh's daughter discovering baby Moses at the Nile River. This stained glass may have been created by the Tiffany workshop and rivaled any in area churches. This depiction possibly was influenced by Carl's visit to the Victoria Falls on the Zambezi River.

Carl flourished on Milwaukee's East Side. By 1920, he

was financially secure and his oldest children were beginning to marry and leave the house. In the 1920s and 1930s, his children and grandchildren frequented his home. Carl Miller's granddaughters, Gail Miller Wray and Elizabeth Blommer remember he regularly puffed on short Cuban cigars in a white ivory holder. Chuck Bransfield, and other grandchildren recall Carl preparing for bed with his long underwear and red fez that kept his hair straight. He visited his children's winter and summer lake homes where he took a special interest in his grandchildren. In Milwaukee he was popular and on friendly terms with Catholics, Protestants, and Jews. Even though he died in 1949, an occasional resident still remembers the avuncular and erudite Carl Miller chatting with neighbors as he strolled the sidewalks.

On January 27, 1920, Anita, 25, Carl and Clara's second child, died suddenly of the pandemic Spanish influenza in Chicago. She, and her unborn child, became sick and perished within three days, leaving her sixteen-month old son, Chuck, and her husband, Michael, to fend for themselves. According to Chuck Bransfield, previously his mother had been in good health and, during the 1919 Christmas, had visited Mama and Papa in Milwaukee. Anita's death, three days after her birthday, left the Millers in shock. To come to grips with their sorrow, the Millers commissioned a Marian statue at St. Rose's Parish, where Anita had attended grade school and received her sacraments. This statue, yet standing, faces south on the outside of the school. Anita was buried in the Bransfield family plot in Chicago's south side Mt. Olivet Cemetery.

After Anita's death Chuck became somewhat of a lost soul. For five years Chuck's spinster aunt, Mary Bransfield, lived in their home and cared for him, but for long periods of time, beginning in 1924, his Miller grandparents took him into their Newberry Boulevard home. Clara was 54 years old and Carl was 61 years old when they began to care for 6-year-old Chuck, providing him close attention and strict training. Until his adult years, Chuck lived with them intermittently, and later, chronicled his humorous memories in his self-published book, *Mama*. Three-and-a-half years after Anita's death, Michael Bransfield married her younger sister Marguerite. The couple had four children: Marguerite in 1924, Michael in1929, Frederick in 1930, and Joan in 1934. Marguerite never legally adopted Chuck even though she put considerable effort into raising him. Currently, Chuck regards himself as a full brother to his younger siblings and they remain close.

7.
FIRE DESTROYS
THE BEER GARDEN

On Independence Day 1891, two boys set the large Miller Garden dance hall afire, with their rocket firecrackers and Roman candles. On this Saturday night, they had stayed behind after most of the revelers had departed, including a Lutheran Church society. The near-midnight event created a spectacular scene, as the beer garden was high upon a bluff giving it great visibility from Milwaukee. After the brewery's firefighters were overwhelmed, the business's loud siren summoned fire departments from Wauwatosa and Milwaukee. The fire also demolished a storage facility valued at $1,150. Two days later, the brewery recognized the Milwaukee Fire Department's efforts by presenting a $50 check to Fire Chief James J. Foley. This fire signified the slow diminution of the beer garden's importance to the Miller Brewery. It had been many years since the Millers had managed the property and, due to the brewery's fantastic growth in beer sales, the garden became a minimally profitable sideshow. No doubt, the Millers put less money and time into maintaining the garden, which led to its demise in 1909, when its last traces were razed.[150]

At the brewery's stockholders and directors annual meeting on September 7, 1891, Ernest stepped aside as brewery president and Lisette took his place. Ernest's health, never great, was the reason for the change. It had declined and in the summers of 1891 and 1892 he went to Western Europe to seek a cure for his physical and emotional problems. Since his father died, Ernest had poured his energies into the business, understanding that it was the sole means of support for his mother and most of his siblings. Ernest took his job seriously. A man well acquainted with Ernest explained that he was, "too wrapped up too much in business; he is too conscientious. Everything must be just so; the barley, malt and hops must be the best that money can secure."[151]

Miller's directors returned Ernest to the presidency at the September 5, 1892, corporate meeting. Because the brewery's sales generally grew and the company's profits flowed into the Millers' pockets, there was little reason to change the management team of Ernest, Fritz, and Emil. Ernest continued as president until January 30, 1904 when his brother Emil assumed the position. Ernest, Fritz, Emil, and Elise worked full time at the brewery. Clara had various corporate titles but never worked full time at the brewery.[152]

Though the Miller family controlled the directorships and officer positions, non-family managers helped to manage the business behind the scenes. These men, who were highly regarded and compensated, loyally performed the mundane tasks that gave the Millers opportunities to travel or rest while comforted that the brewery was operating efficiently. This system was created by Frederick J. Miller and continued by his children. The system was successful because by 1892 the Miller Brewing Company's assets had grown to over $1 million and the plant occupied thirty-one acres.[153]

Miller Brewery's internal operations manager in 1892, Eugene Salbey, was born in Germany in 1857 and, in 1880, came to America where he studied English and business methods at the Milwaukee Mayers College. He began working for Miller Brewery in 1884, where his previous experience in the mercantile trade benefited him. At the brewery, he quickly gained the Millers' confidence by helping them to manage the internal operations. He eventually became Lisette's confidant and lived with his wife, Clara, on Highland Boulevard next to his employers. His job, for which he was paid $5,000 annually, included personal work for the Miller family, especially regarding their financial matters. In closely held corporations, various company employees commonly spend some of their time assisting the stockholders with their personal matters. Customarily, the company's accountants track this time and charge it to the stockholder. Of course, often these expenses are undercounted or overlooked.[154]

Henry Eimer, who managed Miller Brewery's outside sales, was born in Milwaukee in 1850, and his previous jobs included a bookbinder apprenticeship, a physical education teacher, and owner of a clothing store for gentlemen in downtown Milwaukee. In 1882 he opened a country store in Neosho, Wisconsin. Eimer began his employment with the brewery in 1888, and soon assumed supervision of the brewery's numerous sales agents. John U. Kraft, who married and had four children, was Miller Brewery's noted brewmaster. In 1857, Kraft was born in Wannbach, Bavaria where he studied brewing before coming to the U.S. in 1873. His first job was an eight-year stint with the Cincinnati-based Windisch-Muhlhauser Brewing Company, where he served as foreman after 1881. Afterwards, he was a brewmaster in Youngstown, Ohio for five years. He then enrolled in a four-month brewmaster course in the Schwartzen Academy in New York City. Subsequently, he worked for two years at the Phoenix Brewery in Cleveland. In 1891, he was hired by Miller Brewery as brewmaster. A spokesman for the Miller Brewery crowed, "There is no better brewer in the United States, in our estimation, than Mr. John U. Kraft."[155]

8.
HIGH LIFE AND THE GIRL IN THE MOON

In 1901, Miller Brewery began to search for a new beer to augment its line. Brewing had changed dramatically since Fred J. Miller created his carbonated products. At that time, most of the beer consumed was a heavy and dark beverage that German-American males liked. Over time, the American taste changed and lighter beers came into vogue. Many Americans could imbibe more of the lighter beer without feeling bloated. It was these lighter pilsner beers, originally from Pilsen in Bohemia (now Czech Republic), which were clearer and had a stronger hop flavor, that the large brewers created in great volume. Miller Brewery wanted to develop a high-quality lighter beer to boost its position in the marketplace. In all likelihood, they already brewed this product under another label and wanted to find a pleasing name and popular marketing strategy to boost it. Ernest and Fritz began to travel about searching for a name. Unsubstantiated family lore maintains that Ernest traveled to Kansas City, Omaha, and, finally, New Orleans where he walked down to the docks and saw High Life Cigars, a large, defunct factory. After a series of phone calls to Miller Brewery's headquarters, the family decided to offer the owners $15,000 for the rights to the name "High Life." Negotiations followed during which the factory owners wanted more than the primary offer. Finally, Ernest said that he would pay the owners $25,000 for the rights, to which they agreed.

Another version of procuring the name "High Life" maintains that the brewery held a contest to select a name for their new product. Previously, the name "High Life" had been used for various products. Clara's oldest daughter Loretta Kopmeier reported late in her life that Ernest and Fritz went to Florida soon after the turn of the century and liked the tranquil pace of life there. They began to refer to it as the High Life and then used that moniker for their new beer. Nevertheless, Miller Brewery obtained a trademark to use it in association with beer but other companies could continue to exercise it in connection with their products. From that point forward, Miller aggressively had to pursue other American brewers to prevent them from using the name "High Life." Regardless of the veracity of any of these stories, the Millers developed and marketed a premium beer that blossomed and remains one of its core brands.[156]

Miller Brewery's High Life hit the market on December 30, 1903. It came in a clear bottle and was an immediate success. High Life was not Miller's first beer sold in a clear bottle but it was their first exceedingly popular one. Most beer was sold in brown glass bottles to filter out the product-damaging ultraviolet rays. The brewery explained, "We use light (clear) bottles exclusively for this high grade beer—common beer comes in dark bottles."[157] They also noted that High Life was a stable beer, due to the liberal use of the best materials, extreme care, and skill in brewing. The Millers used clear bottles to demonstrate the beer's purity but made concessions to light's deleterious effects. They encouraged their vendors to keep it away from windows and not stock more upon the shelves than was quickly sold. It was not a problem, as High Life flew off the shelves necessitating Miller's construction of another brewhouse by May 1904.[158]

To complement its new beer, Miller Brewery sought a likeable image to promote High Life. In 1902 or 1903, Miller developed the famous "girl in the moon" for this purpose. At the time, a Miller employee bought a burnt-wood plaque in an oval frame from a traveling salesman, which had an image of a Spanish senorita standing on a box with a wide-brimmed hat, a rose in her hair, and a whip in her hand. Miller Brewery's historian, Tice Nichols, describes her as a French-style circus performer, such as a lion tamer or an equestrienne, a woman who rides horses or performs on horseback. Soon after, the brewery's advertising department put the whip under her arm, a tray of full beer glasses in a her hand, and the words "High Life – Milwaukee's leading bottled beer" on the box that she was standing on. Afterwards, Miller's advertising manager, Albert C. Paul, took it upon himself to find a unique place for this young lady. Lore has it that one day while hunting in the northern Wisconsin woods Paul lost his way. After a time he lay down to rest his head and soon found himself asleep. In time, he dreamed of a young woman sitting on a quarter moon beckoning to him. He followed her until he found a road, then he woke up. Inspired, Paul used this image in Miller Brewery's new advertising campaign. The brewery began using the image in December 1903, and four years later Miller Brewery received federal trademark protection for their image of the *senorita*, holding a whip, sitting in a crescent moon.[159]

Over the years, there has been uncertainty regarding the identity of the model for the original paintings of the "girl in the moon." Different Miller family branches boast that their grandmother or great-grandmother was the model. For instance, Rose Mary Bradford Hewlett, Clara and Carl Miller's granddaughter, told of her grandfather Carl Miller's story regarding the origin of the "girl in the moon." In 1903, Carl was touring the brewery with his 11-year-old daughter Loretta, Rose Mary's mother, when he sat her upon a bar in the dining room. Loretta impulsively posed with her hand in the air, which became the inspiration for the girl in the moon. Supposedly, Fritz Miller, who was an amateur artist, sketched Loretta. Soon after, the advertising department went to Clara Miller's house to get a photo of Loretta. In all probability there were several models and the advertising department could have painted different versions of the available young Miller family females, then created an amalgam of all of them. The possible candidates were Fred and Lisette's youngest child, Elise, 23, or Clara and Carl's daughters, Loretta, 18, and Anita, 16. At any rate, one can see this young woman on bottles, billboards, and buses the world over gaily sitting on a crescent moon.[160]

In the early years of the "girl in the moon's" popularity there were large shipments of the bottles to disparate locations. At one moment, the Millers had shipped 40,000 bottles of the gaily-designed bottles to Kingston, Jamaica, where they were being stored in a warehouse of an English brewery agent. "An earthquake shook the structure, pitching the smiling girls upon the amber bottles into the ocean." The Millers offered to pay for half of the lost product. Years later, Fritz Miller recalled, "But would you believe it, he wouldn't take a cent. Well, he was the most honest Englishman we ever had anything to do with." At this same time, Fritz remembered that during the army-like invasion of the Gogebic Mountain Range in Michigan's Upper Peninsula to extract iron ore, the demand for High Life was so intense that the Millers were unable to meet it. Fritz noted that the Girl in the Moon's services were "pathological as well as social" because typhoid fever was ravaging the area and, to keep from spreading the disease, the miners drank High Life instead of water, In fact, they even washed themselves in it. Fritz intoned, "It is certain that the Miller maid's presence saved many lives."[161]

To complement High Life, Miller Brewery, in 1903, installed mechanized filling, labeling, and capping equipment in the bottling departments. In 1905, the first motorized truck was used to deliver product to the south side depot, at 538 South 12th Street, where later Herman C. Mueller was the manager. By this time the sales in barrels reached 308,498. In 1906, the brewery began using the slogan, "The Champagne of Bottle Beer" to promote High Life in its elegant long-necked clear bottles. The light-colored product sparkled like Champagne when held up to a light. This bottle, still in use today, became known as the "Miller High Life Streamlined Bottle."[162]

9.
THE BOTTLING
PLANT

The bottling facility, with a 1,000-bottle daily capacity, was used exclusively for the booming High Life brand. These bottles were placed in substantial wooden twenty-four-container cases branded with Miller Brewery's name and logo. The brewery used electricity throughout the plant to operate the automatic rotary filling and crowning machines.[163] Beer bottling had progressed significantly since its earlier days in the mid-19th Century. Beer and ale, with effervescence that could not be captured, had been bottled for centuries but only for immediate consumption. Railroads provided a quick distribution system to distant places, encouraging breweries to develop improved bottling techniques.

Previous to the extensive use of bottles well into the 20th Century, people purchased beer poured from a keg at their local saloon for immediate consumption or to take home. At times, neighborhoods would buy a barrel of beer and have each household draw off its respective share or families would brew their own beer on their stove. Often they would bring a small tin pail or growler to the saloon, fill it, and then carry it home for their evening pleasure. It was for this local use that saloons were ubiquitous in pre-Prohibition America. Because refrigeration came slowly to non-industrial uses, the beer in saloons was room temperature rather than the frigid liquid of today. It was not until artificial cooling methods arrived in saloons and homes that Americans were able to drink cold beer.[164]

Slowly bottling became important to the brewing industry, with 20% packaged by 1900. By 1940, over half of the beer was bottled and, by 1976, 90% was sold in cans or bottles. Early brewers used fired-clay bottles, which were made at local pottery works, to hold their beer. These thick, often unevenly created, bottles usually had their brewery's name stamped into them. On September 1, 1880, the Chase Valley Glass Company made the first locally manufactured glass bottles on Milwaukee's South Side. Bottles usually had the name of the breweries embossed on them. After glass bottles became accessible, brewers soon stopped using pottery containers. The breweries experienced difficulty maintaining the effervescence in bottled beer while excluding impurities until the customer opened it. Previous to the 1870s when pasteurization began to be widely used, bottled beer was likely to spoil if not immediately consumed. The breweries pasteurized their beer in kegs and bottles, which killed any living organism within it, giving it a much longer shelf life. The brewers pasteurized the beer by placing the kegs and bottles into tubs of water that steam slowly heated to 160 to 170 degrees Fahrenheit. Some purists claimed that the high temperature damaged the beer's flavor, and brewers began a long process to develop a method to filter the product without heating it. Today, the Miller Brewing Company brews Genuine Draft that is filtered without heat. Brewers, as did vintners and distillers, used corks with wires to contain the beverage and keep the internal pressure from popping the top. In 1892 William Painter, of Baltimore, invented the crown bottle cap, which is still in use today. The crown cap, so named because when inverted it resembles a queen's crown, necessitated a change in bottle manufacturing. The transition from the cork bottles to the crown tops was completed in the bottle industry by 1910.[165]

At about the turn of the century, paper labels began to replace embossing as a cheaper alternative for designating the bottles' brewer and contents. Labels allowed the breweries easily to denote their many varieties of beer compared to the more expensive plate moulds bottlers used for embossing. The advent of labeling brought an exciting change to beer distribution because paper allowed designers an almost limitless palate for colors and patterns. Today, breweries use labels to position a beer brand in the marketplace, competing to create the most exquisite and eye-catching designs. Early bottling was a manual affair, with each bottle individually washed, filled, and corked. Early machines helped wash and fill the bottles. Eventually, technology allowed for automatic soakers, washers, fillers, crowners, pasteurizers, and labelers.[166]

In 1906, much of Miller Brewery's trade extended throughout the Mississippi Valley, from the Gulf of Mexico to the Dominion of Canada, which was, "exceptionally large and remunerative." At this time, the brewery had an annual brewing capacity of 1 million barrels though only during its peak months did it approach it. The brewery bragged that its brews were not placed for sale until they were lagered for at least two months, making them superior to competitive brews that were sold after only two or three weeks of storage.

At this time, the brewery noted that it had one of the most up-to-date facilities in the nation, featuring the newest machinery and appliances. It bought barley from Wisconsin, Minnesota, Montana, California, and Canada and hops from New York, the Pacific Coast, and Bohemia. Even though the prohibition movement had hurt its sales, the brewery boasted of a 5% increase in 1905's annual sales. The management expected a slight increase in 1906's sales despite prohibition's tightening noose. In 1906, the company employed 500 workers, which four years later had grown to 1,000. The brewery had forty-four agencies (branch houses), of which the principal ones were in Chicago, Minneapolis, Memphis, Cleveland, St. Louis, and Kansas City. Some years later, the branches of Jacksonville, New Orleans, San Antonio, New York City, Boston, Montreal, and San Francisco were developed. In addition, there were over 200 carload customers who bought in bulk directly from the factory. The brewery, under the direction of the new advertising manager, R.R. Johnstone, was beginning to blanket the principal cities of the Midwest with a substantial advertising campaign promoting "The Best" Milwaukee beer. Johnstone designed a campaign to plaster the area with striking posters and other advertising matter promoting their two primary products, "High Life Beer" and "Miller's Malt Nutrine," a low-alcohol product that people who lived in dry counties could buy and then add alcohol to make beer.[167]

10.
TWO WEDDINGS
AT ST. ROSE CHURCH

In a time and place lost in history, Elise Miller met Harry George John, a gadabout and former Lutheran, six years her elder. Over time, they dated and then made plans to marry. Harry G. "Buddy" John, Jr., their son, noted, "Elise married Harry for his looks, and Harry married Elise for her money." Harry was comely and without peer in living an entertaining life. His ebullient personality was an elixir for the reticent socialite. His drop-dead good looks helped him maintain a life-long healthy self-image. Bill Miller, a friend, called him a man's man. His daughter-in-law Erica Novotny John remembered that he was charming to women and capable, until his final years, of winning a woman's heart.

After attending Milwaukee Public Schools, Harry John entered Concordia College then located at the family's Trinity Evangelical Lutheran Church. While there he excelled at baseball, and he got a tryout invitation from Connie Mack, the legendary owner and manager of the Philadelphia Athletics. Between 1897 and 1900, Mack was the manager of the Milwaukee Brewers, a minor league team, and it was likely that Harry tried out for this club. In 1893 after completing his education, he worked as a clerk and then a salesman and undoubtedly, due to his winning ways, performed well. Throughout this period he lived with his mother and younger brothers. Eventually he worked as a commercial traveler, and by 1908 his older brother Charles employed him at the Wollaeger Company, an office furniture designing and manufacturing business that Charles had come into by marriage.

Since their youth Harry and Elise had numerous opportunities to become acquainted as both sprang from large, prominent, West-Side Milwaukee families that socialized in the same circles. Miller family member Gail Miller Wray explained that their marriage was an arranged affair, which referred to a system of finding an acceptable mate rather than to the ancient Asian practice of pairing two children who would later marry. Generally, upper-class parents strove to find compatible singles, from their own economic class, to whom they introduced their unmarried adult children. They threw lavish parties to which they invited their socially acceptable friends and their children. They also belonged to clubs, which hosted similar parties. The Millers and Johns surely brought their adult children to these events in hopes of their meeting a future acceptable spouse.

On June 18, 1912, Elise and Harry wed at St. Rose Parish. Harry's father had been a prominent Milwaukee homeopathic doctor, who had died well before the wedding, so the couple was given away by their mothers. The combination of such prominent families normally would have generated newspaper coverage, but there was none. Possibly Lisette was embarrassed that Elise was marrying a non-Catholic.

After the wedding, the Johns rented a floor at a substantial two-family wooden Victorian house at 955 North 29th Street. In all likelihood their first child, Lorraine, was conceived in this dwelling. Some time later, yet before Lorraine was born on September 7, 1913, the Johns inhabited a two-story brick house at 3221 Highland Boulevard replete with two large stone lions "guarding" their front walkway. This magnificent though not ostentatious home on the prominent Highland Boulevard that also included the Davidsons of the Harley Davidson Motorcycle family, Pabsts and Blatzes, demonstrated the couple's high social standing. Lorraine, as well as Harry G. John, Jr. (Buddy) who was born on December 19, 1919, came into the world at St. Joseph Hospital at Fourth and Reservoir Streets. In between Lorraine and Buddy, Elise miscarried a late-stage son who is buried at the Miller Family plot in Calvary Cemetery. According to a later account by Lorraine, Elise was playing the piano when a chandelier fell, startling her. Then, feeling cold, she went to the cellar to shovel coal into the furnace, after which, she began to hemorrhage and then lost her baby boy. Elise had two children, who survived childhood, and wanted more offspring but failed due to her advancing age and miscarriages.

Throughout his life Harry John, Sr., liked speed, which as a young man was expressed through horses and, later, automobiles. He loved to race and was a regular at local racecourses from the end of the 19th and into the 20th Century. He was an officer of the Gentleman's Driving Club, which hosted horse races at area courses especially the west side Cold Spring Park, located on the current McKinley Boulevard between 27th and 35th Street, which was near the Miller Brewing Company. At these races Harry rode sulkies pulled by his horses, Kalmia and Irish Elder. The large dirt ovals provided Saturday summer entertainment and betting for many Milwaukeeans. Undoubtedly, Harry partook in the betting, drinking, and socializing that racetracks offered. In the winter, on Sunday afternoons, snow conditions permitting, Harry raced cutters up and down Grand Avenue, now Wisconsin Avenue, with a large buffalo robe on his lap to keep him warm. John Gurda wrote in his 1980 book, *The West End,* that these light sleighs sped up and down the avenue from the main Milwaukee Public Library to 35th Street. The fun was heightened because there were no police or stoplights, and people knew enough to stay off of the streets. In later years Harry kept an iceboat at his Oconomowoc Lake home, which his son, Buddy, and his friends enjoyed.

Elise's Catholic faith saw her following a westward migration common to many Milwaukeeans in this growing metropolis. In 1880, she was born into St. Joseph Parish, at 11th and Cherry Streets, to which she belonged until 1895 when, Father Joseph Holzhauer, its founding pastor, died. At that time, the Millers, (Lisette, Ernest, Fritz, Clara, Emil, and Elise), joined St. Rose of Lima Parish at 528 North 31st Street, a newer congregation closer to their Highland Boulevard and Kilbourn Avenue homes. (At this time Clara and her husband Carl lived near Lisette and had not yet moved to Milwaukee's East Side.)

Elise was vitally involved with this parish and was a daily communicant. Father Patrick H. Durnin, the first archdiocesan priest born in Milwaukee to English-speaking parents, was the pastor and ministered to the Millers. Lorraine and Buddy matriculated at St. Rose Parish School. In September 1939, Elise changed to St. Sebastian Parish at 5400 West Washington Boulevard, which was closer to her new home in the Wauwatosa Washington Highlands. Elise provided considerable financial support to St. Rose and St. Sebastian Parishes.

The Highland Avenue home represented the highlight of Elise's married life as the place she raised her children and enjoyed her mother and brothers living across the street. Their immediate neighbors were the Lemkes and Wittigs, both close friends. Peter Sanfilipo, Buddy's childhood chum, noted that, on winter nights, Walter Davidson, one of the founders of Harley Davidson and a neighbor, brought out floodlights to illuminate a homemade ice rink on the Concordia College campus to where neighborhood children gathered. After an evening of skating and falling, the Johns would invite some of the children to their basement where Elise served hot chocolate, apple juice, and their cook Rose Eisenmann's delectable cookies.

On October 29, 1912, the 45-year-old Fritz married the 32-year-old May Frances Gibson at St. Rose Parish. The pastor, Right Reverend Patrick Durnin, officiated and Fritz's brother, Ernest, and his niece, Loretta Miller Kopmeier, were the witnesses. Before marrying Fred, May nursed Fritz during one of his prolonged illnesses, though she was not a trained nurse; rather a stenographer and bookkeeper at a haberdashery. Apparently, Fritz married May for companionship as they both were beyond their optimum parenting years and remained childless.

May was a pleasant yet plain-looking woman with a round face and hair that she tied in a bun. Her Scottish father, William C. Gibson spoke predominately Gaelic and managed the farm at the National Soldiers Home on Milwaukee's southwest side where he and his family lived. May's mother was Amelia

Hammer Gibson, her older sister was Christine, and her two younger brothers were William L. and Ralph. No doubt they were amazed to see one of their working-class family marry a wealthy scion of Milwaukee's elite.

The federal government had created the Soldiers' Home in 1867 to house and care for injured Civil-War veterans. The Home became so successful that it turned into a kind of nursing home for elderly veterans. The grounds are outstanding with rolling lawns, knolls, ponds, and marvelous wooden and stone structures placed about. Surely, the Gibsons loved living on its marvelous 400-plus acres. Marquette University professor James Marten, in the Spring 1999 *Milwaukee History* magazine, noted that the Home's grounds became a popular excursion destination for thousands of Milwaukeeans who were looking for a clean restful place to picnic. Independence Day brought the largest crowds for sumptuous dinners, military bands, and an impressive fireworks display.

In 1905, to complement their Highland Boulevard home, Fritz Miller built a substantial, beautiful home on the east shore of Lake Nagawicka in Waukesha County that is still standing. Early on, Lisette, Ernest, and Fritz enjoyed their summers in fine fashion by riding the train to this lake home. At this summer home, Fritz, an amateur botanist, planted numerous trees and shrubs of myriad varieties; many of which are yet living.

Miller Brewery's sales reached 435,098 barrels in 1910 and the following year achieved the highest pre-Prohibition total of 473,049. The brewery sold most of its beer in the central states, particularly Wisconsin. The sales produced a $616,885 net profit for the business in 1911. By 1918, barrelage sales had dropped to 276,847 due mostly to more states becoming "dry." Ernest continued managing the business's operations with the help of the First National Bank. In 1918, he invested at least $68,000 with Byron Kanaley of the Chicago venture firm Cooper Kanaley and Company. Byron's daughter, Adele, would marry Clara and Carl Miller's son, Frederick, in 1931.

The Millers had lost their Bismarck brewery due to the Prohibition forces and that gave them as much direct experience with this movement as any other brewer. These lessons were not lost on Ernest and Fritz. Well before national Prohibition was enacted, they began to prepare their business and themselves for its eventuality. On September 11, 1918, they incorporated the Miller Ice and Cold Storage Company with $100,000 of capital stock. Emil Miller was named president; Fritz Miller — vice-president; and Arthur L. Kleinboehl — secretary. They created this business to replace income from the loss of beer sales. The purpose of the corporation, "was to manufacture, buy, sell and deal in ice, to own and operate warehouses and cold storage plants for the storing and custody of food and daily products and other articles of all kinds."[168] The new company allowed the Millers to earn money from their delivery trucks and refrigerated stockhouses that were not used to capacity. This business also was an appropriate way for Ernest and Fritz to keep their brother Emil busy while protecting the financially important brewery.[169]

From 1908 to 1914, the brewery's yearly profits fluctuated between $642,500 and $768,500 while its total assets increased from $6,157,000 to $9,048,000. The 1916 profits were a healthy $867,000 before dropping precipitously to $472,000 the following year. Ironically, 1919 was a strong year with $744,000 in profits, but they declined thereafter due to Prohibition's reach. In 1919, the brewery owned some 300 saloon properties locally, including in Milwaukee the Miller Hotel, Miller Block, and the Strand Theater.[170]

Miller Brewery in 1914 announced plans to build a two-story building at Grand Avenue (now Wisconsin Avenue) and Fifth Street that included a glazed terra cotta front. It would have 143 feet of frontage on Grand Avenue and 80 feet on Fifth Street. The multi-use building was to feature a theater, eleven stores, and twenty upscale apartments. The theater proper, expected to open on September 1 of that year, would be detached and located behind the stores with a seating capacity of 2,000 and designed to accommodate moving pictures or a vaudeville theater. A unique heating and ventilating system was built, to provide for the patrons' comfort. The architects remarked that the building was designed to last for 10 or 15 years, at which time it would be razed and replaced with a skyscraper. This building served as a theater in Milwaukee's downtown for many years until it was razed.[171]

This building represented the considerable amount of money that the brewery was earning from the enormous number of barrel sales. The Millers continually looked for novel ways to invest their dividends. Additionally, with prohibition forces close to realizing their dream, the Millers sought ways to hedge their assets in case beer production ceased or was dramatically reduced. Eventually, real estate ownership and management became an important part of the Millers' portfolio.

Miller Brewery's management leased a train in August 1916 to carry 150 of its white collar employees to a Grafton, Wisconsin, park, about 15 miles north of the brewery for a day of games and levity. In a baseball game, the young men defeated their senior co-workers, 14 to 6. The partiers also caught over forty pounds of fish.[172]

Clara and Carl Miller continued to concentrate their efforts on their own business. Their lumber company was financially successful, allowing them to buy a series of beautiful homes replete with servants and horses, provide private school education for their children, and enjoy annual vacations to Europe. By 1896, Carl had bought out his partners, becoming the sole owner of the Milwaukee Lumber Company. Concurrently, Carl opened another lumberyard at 30th and Lisbon Avenue on Milwaukee's west side. Also that same year, Clara became vice-president remaining involved for many years. Her grandson, Charles "Chuck" Bransfield noted that she was always pushing Carl to do a good job. He said that, in the early 1900s, Clara encouraged Carl to salvage lumber from the October 1871 northern Wisconsin Peshtigo fire, which killed 1,200 people and took place at the same time and year as the famous Chicago fire. The Peshtigo conflagration scorched 1.5 million acres of timber leaving a grand salvage opportunity. In 1906 they opened another branch on Milwaukee's south side at the corner of Becher and Clinton Streets. By 1912, the Millers had renamed their business, the Carl Miller Lumber Company.[173]

On her twenty-first birthday on October 20, 1913, Clara and Carl Millers' oldest daughter, Loretta, married Norman Kopmeier, 34, of the Wisconsin Ice and Coal Company, (since renamed Hometown, Inc.). On March 18, 1919, the Kopmeiers had a daughter, Rose Mary, and on May 16, 1925 they had a son, Norman, Jr. Many years earlier, John T. Kopmeier, Norman's grandfather emigrated from Germany and started a farm at a site which is now on Milwaukee's South Side. He dug a large hole on his property and lined it with straw to store ice. In summers, when he drove a wagon into Milwaukee to sell his milk, he preserved it with ice. Housewives wanted some ice along with his milk, so in 1849 he began the ice business. His ice delivery business grew and he began to cut frozen blocks from the Milwaukee River and nearby lakes. The company stored it in a dozen or more large icehouses for distribution during the summer months. In 1892, it was known as the Wisconsin Lakes Ice Company and the Miller Brewing Company purchased 1,732 tons of ice from them at 75 cents a ton for a total of $1,299.[174] In early 1893, six firms, Kopmeier Brothers, Helms Brothers & Co., Sanborn, Haisler, Meyer Brothers, and F. A. Reinecke, incorporated as Wisconsin Lakes and Cartage Company with headquarters at 432 3rd Street. The company owned icehouses at the lakes of Spring, Pewaukee, Shawano, and Silver Spring and the Milwaukee River and also obtained ice from North, Pewaukee, Spring, Dousman, Pike, and Barton lakes. Storage capacity was approximately 225,000 tons and it used between 1,200 and 1,500 men during the winter harvest time. In the warm months, 300 horses and a small army of workers delivered ice throughout the Milwaukee metropolitan area. In 1917, the firm entered the coal delivery field and changed its name to the Wisconsin Ice and Coal Company. It stopped harvesting natural ice in 1924 and built refrigerated ice plants. In 1930, it added the sale of fuel oil to homes and businesses to its line of services.[175]

Over the years, Lisette Miller continued with her estate planning. On January 30, 1899, she signed a document giving power of attorney to her sons, Ernest and Fritz. Her daughter, Elise, and William Marx, a Miller Brewery manager and neighbor, were the witnesses. Power of attorney allowed Ernest to vote Lisette's brewery stock and expedite decision-making on the construction of their new Highland Boulevard mansion, in case Lisette was away or became incapacitated. The document gave Lisette the freedom to travel and skip brewery board meetings without concern for her finances. On January 5, 1914, she signed a note explaining that all of the gifts, which she received from any one of her children, be returned to that child after her death.[176]

Clara's third child, Claire, and her husband, James McCahey, had five children: Claire in 1919, James, Jr., in 1921, Anita, 1923, Frederick in 1925, and Carol in 1927. As each of Clara and Carl's six children married, they set $10,000 aside for them and, regularly, sent them the interest. When the children sometimes requested more than the interest due to hard times, they endured their father's stern lectures on thrift and preserving capital. Their oldest daughter, Loretta, bought a house near her parents' home with her $10,000 and the Millers tried unsuccessfully to get their two Chicago-based daughters to move to Milwaukee. In 1920, Carl Miller unsuccessfully implored his son-in-law, James McCahey, one of the Chicago men, to buy into his lumber company and then work there, as the 57-year-old Carl was looking to semi-retire. It would be 10 more years before his second-youngest child, Frederick, graduated from college and assumed management of the business.

11.
PROHIBITION STALKS
THE BREWERY

The anti-alcohol movement increasingly affected the Miller Brewery. From Fred and Josephine Miller's first days of beer brewing, they coexisted with the ebb and flow of temperance and prohibition movements. Because the Millers were steeped in the German culture and language, they did not fully understand the depth of this sentiment among many Yankee Protestant Americans. As long as the Millers could sell their beer in the burgeoning American cities, overflowing with immigrant Catholics, they generally were unconcerned with the anti-alcohol movements that intermittently simmered and boiled in America's rural areas and small towns. Ernest, however, would have his tenure at Miller Brewery seriously marred by the prohibition movement.

Since the Pilgrims arrived on America's shores, there had been a see-saw action among people who desired, unencumbered, to drink a pleasing alcoholic beverage and others who would quash this activity.[177] For reasons of religious motivation or personal experience, temperance advocates beseeched others to avoid alcoholic beverages. Unlike prohibitionists, they relied on one's self-control instead of governmental proscription. There have been secular organizations and Christian denominations that have demanded temperance as integral to their members' belonging. Also, many families had excluded alcoholic beverages from their homes for personal reasons. Prohibitionists, however, strove through government dictate to eliminate alcohol consumption by stopping its manufacture, transportation, and sale. The 1850s and 1890s saw successful surges in the prohibition movement. After these surges, which resulted in many dry counties and states, the anti-prohibition forces prevailed and rolled back most of these laws.[178]

A wave of state prohibition legislation followed the creation of an anti-alcohol law in Maine that lasted from 1846 to 1851, the first of its kind in America. Thus, the emphasis shifted from temperance advocacy to outright demand for government prohibition. The 1850s saw a burst of fervor in the anti-alcohol movement in which thirteen states adopted some version of prohibitionary legislation. It lost steam during the Civil War when most of these laws were revoked. From 1860 to 1880, only three states were continuously dry. Nevertheless, the movement was still alive, and from 1869 on, the newly formed national Prohibition Party ran candidates in presidential and many state elections.[179]

The Wisconsin Graham Law of 1872 required a $2,000 bond from licensed liquor sellers on which they could be sued for any of a long list of possible civil offenses. The Graham Law motivated Wisconsin brewers to organize and, on August 6, 1873, they, including Frederick J. Miller, met in Milwaukee. The brewers decided to back Democrat A. N. Taylor for governor. He won the seat and effectively killed the Graham Law. The brewers emphasized that they stood for temperance, trying to disassociate themselves from the hard-liquor industry. The beer and ale brewers, for self-preservation, had joined the temperance movement and promoted their products as pro-temperance drinks. They argued that beer and ale were superior to hard liquor because the imbiber would consume less alcohol by volume with their brews. A beer quaffer usually would become sated long before he became seriously drunk, unlike stronger alcoholic-content drinks like whiskey and brandy. The brewers argued that beer and ale promoted family togetherness because parents would drink it while picnicking or socializing with their children, whereas, men usually drank stronger liquors in saloons away from their families. The brewers did not realize that the prohibition movement eventually would overtake the temperance movement to harm all legal alcohol producers.[180]

In 1874, the Women's Christian Temperance Union was founded in Ohio to advocate for prohibitory legislation. It began to organize millions of Protestant churchwomen for a crusade against all liquor. In 1881, the state of Kansas wrote an absolute prohibition clause into its state constitution and South Carolina adopted a liquor-control system. At this time, Illinois established local option, which allowed each of its counties or townships to decide the liquor sales question for itself. A portentous event occurred in 1887, when Senator Blair of New Hampshire introduced a failed prohibition amendment to the federal constitution. Although, by the early 1890s, public apathy and failure of the existing laws saw prohibition efforts reach low ebb.[181]

In July of 1892, Ernest remarked in a newspaper interview:

"Any law which would be detrimental to the general use of lager beer I have always opposed. Lager beer has always appeared to me as a temperance medium ever since I could speak. The Maine law has never been advocated by any man worthy of the name of statesman, and I challenge any living man to mention such an individual. It is not in the sphere of legislation to attempt to suppress the liquor traffic, and all theologians and jurists of ability are united in this opinion. Against such legislation a firm stand should be taken by every true statesman."[182]

At the same time Fritz Miller said: "I do not believe that there can be found an individual who dare assert that lager beer has been injurious to true temperance in this country. Penal measures and private efforts can hardly lessen the evil, and I am satisfied cannot eradicate it. There should be an abolition of taxes upon wholesome beverages, and I am anxious for such legislation, and the hopes of the United States and of the world lie in this great national beverage."[183]

The Anti-Saloon League of America, begun in 1893 by Reverend H.H. Russell, finally was able to unify the disparate prohibitionists and temperance advocates into one national campaign. Russell harnessed the power of the affiliated church groups, mainly the Methodist, Baptist, Presbyterian, and Congregational, against the institution of the saloon. These establishments were the sales outlets for the alcohol-producing industry, as bottles, which allowed for home consumption had not yet achieved widespread use. Some of these ubiquitous, male-dominated institutions hurt their cause by featuring gambling and prostitution to boost profits. Though most saloons were respectable institutions seeking law-abiding clients, many Americans viewed saloons as America's most despicable feature, blaming them for much of the population sleeping in poorhouses, jails, and insane asylums. Many southern ministers effectively aligned alcoholic beverages, even beer, with the devil in the minds of their flocks. The Anti-Saloon League from 1905 to 1913 put its major emphasis on the winning of local option in the rural districts. It also advocated eliminating saloons, its avowed enemy, and supported dry political parties. By 1906, thirty states had local option laws, and three had special systems of liquor control. Even in Wisconsin, more than 600 small villages and townships abolished saloons. The movement did not stop the consumption of beer, as no states, even the dry ones, prohibited anyone from drinking. Rather, the movement made it increasingly difficult for an upstanding citizen to get a legal alcoholic drink. There was a clear shift in tactics in 1913 when the Anti-Saloon League supported the enactment of a federal constitutional amendment to ban alcoholic drinks.[184]

Prohibition, along with the advent of World War I in 1914, brought an end to Milwaukee's German high-cultural period and made the League's victory more certain. The prohibitionists used the brewers' German ancestry against them, branding them pro-German and, thus, anti-American. No longer did the German-Americans proudly flaunt their ethnicity at political and cultural gatherings. The anti-German sentiment that swept over the country left many Milwaukeeans of Teutonic heritage silent and ashamed. This era put the final nail in the coffin of the city's beer gardens. Fortunately, many of the private parks and beer gardens became the foundation of today's Milwaukee County Park System since they occupied open spaces in developed residential areas. Regardless, today there are vestiges of Milwaukee's beer gardens, for instance the Bavarian Club's Heidelberg Park sits in the northern Milwaukee suburb of Glendale and gloriously offers German dishes along with Polka bands various weekends of the summer and fall. Before Prohibition, Miller Brewery, as the other breweries, supported myriad Milwaukee social events, which, due to their tremendous wealth, gave this city a grand supply of concerts, plays, and dances. The Saengerfest (German-language singing festival) was a fine example of this generosity.[185]

Saengerfest was the major yearly event of the Sangerbund (singing confederation) of the Northwest. The four-day festival, one of which took place in 1904, from Thursday July 28 until Sunday July 31, attracted thousands of out-of-town visitors in addition to many Milwaukeeans. Mayor David S. Rose implored Milwaukeeans to decorate their homes, factories, and stores. "Blue and white streamers intertwined with the American colors, and here and there, with those of the fatherland, gaily pick up every breeze that passes through Milwaukee's thoroughfares, giving to the city a festive appearance such as it has not had in many months." The event centered at the grand Industrial Exposition Building, which hosted five concerts. Milwaukee historian John Gurda explained that this brick and glass palace was completed in 1881, but burned down in 1905. It covered the entire block bordered by State Street and Kilbourn Avenue between 5th and 6th streets. The Saengerfest featured soloists, orchestras, choruses, and parades. The giant concerts featured a male chorus of 2,500 voices, a mixed chorus with 1,500 voices, and a children's chorus of 3,000. Miller Brewery, as did other local German-American breweries, sponsored parts of the event and advertised liberally to the visitors to taste some of their beer while in town. Miller Brewery managers expected that the visitors would taste their beer, like it, and then request it at their local saloons in other Midwestern states. World War I brought an end to the Saengerfest and other similar ventures, extinguishing Milwaukee's reputation as the "German Athens of America."[186]

During World War I, the Milwaukee brewing families felt the cold accusing hand of many Yankees who believed that the German-Americans were helping the German kaiser politically and financially. At this time, Carl and Clara Miller had vegetables thrown at their home, about which the irrepressible Clara blustered that it was unfortunate that they were not fresh because then their cook would have prepared them. This hysteria brought great victories to the prohibitionist forces between 1917 and 1919, especially regarding legislative elections. For example, in 1918, John Strange, a papermaker and Wisconsin's lieutenant governor from 1909 to1910, said, "We have German enemies across the water. We have German enemies in this country too. And the worst of all our German enemies, the most treacherous, the most menacing, are Pabst, Schlitz, Blatz and Miller."[187] In December 1917, the Eighteenth Amendment banning the manufacture, transportation, and sale of intoxicating beverages was introduced in the Senate where it passed easily there and, then, in the House of Representatives. Twenty states were already dry when the amendment went to the state legislatures.[188]

On June 7, 1916 Miller ran a large newspaper advertisement, which promoted the health benefits of its flagship brand, High Life. After noting the importance of natural moderation, it explained how beer's "digestive qualities. . . assist in building bodily endurance." For proof they noted that, "France and Germany today are exhibiting most wonderful — almost superhuman strength and endurance. They partake moderately of mild stimulating beverages [wine & beer]. They have proven their worth."[189]

In mid-December 1916, Emil Miller struck back against the apparently unstoppable prohibition movement. He sent an open letter to Milwaukee's merchants requesting that they bar their employees from attending religious services at the Forsythe Tabernacle on Vliet Street. He explained that these meetings were simply a forerunner of the well-known evangelist, Billy Sunday, coming to Milwaukee to begin, "an organized effort to swing Wisconsin and the City of Milwaukee into the prohibition column. If you want to prevent such a calamity [, I] think it advisable to tell your employees not to patronize these meetings." This letter angered prohibition advocates who then aligned Miller Brewery to an antebellum plantation owner who restricted his slaves. They queried, "Does slavery exist in Milwaukee?" then added that Miller's request of the mercantile houses was, "as tyrannical and diabolical in spirit as ever was uttered by a southern planter to a Negro slave."[190]

12.
WORLD WAR I AND THE WASHINGTON TIMES AFFAIR

In May 1917, near the end of World War I yet only one month after America's formal entry into the conflict, Arthur Brisbane, a prominent national newspaperman, purchased the *Washington* (D.C.) *Times*. (This newspaper is not connected to the present-day *Washington Times*.) The Miller family was involved with the newspaper's purchase, which later garnered it some unwanted publicity.

Arthur Brisbane was born on December 12, 1864, in Buffalo, New York, and later became well acquainted with the famous Milwaukee socialist Victor Berger. Though not a socialist himself, Brisbane shared some of the party's view of opposing large business trusts. Brisbane was also a close associate of the American publishing mogul William Randolph Hearst. While best known as a newspaper columnist, Brisbane became a newspaper publisher, too. In 1918, he purchased the *Evening Wisconsin* and Milwaukee's *The Press* and merged them into the *Wisconsin News*.[191]

At the time Brisbane purchased the *Washington Times*, he sought and received financial support from America's brewing families who were looking for a national forum to promote their anti-prohibition views. The Millers provided $15,000 while Gustav Pabst of the Pabst Brewing Company gave $50,000 and Joseph E. Uihlein of Milwaukee's Schlitz Brewing Company offered $50,000. The list included many other Milwaukee and national brewery owners. It was this connection with German-

American brewing families during World War I that caused a furor in Washington, D.C. Soon after the Armistice ended the war, the U.S. Senate Judiciary Committee investigated this source of funds. The contributing brewery owners, including all five of Fred J. Miller's children, were of German ancestry, which put them under suspicion during this period of national anti-German feeling.[192]

Whether their real belief or an attempt to attack a controversial journalist, various government witnesses testified that the *Washington Times* was part of a German propaganda effort to influence American public opinion. Brisbane testified that the brewers gave him the loans on extremely favorable terms because they desperately needed a national mouthpiece to oppose the gathering momentum for Prohibition.[193]

In September 1918, Fred and Lisette Millers' children, who each had given $3,000 to Brisbane for his purchase of the *Washington Times,* were suddenly thrust into the front pages of the Milwaukee newspapers. A reporter tried to contact Ernest Miller, Miller Brewery's president, and Emil Miller, its secretary-treasurer, but was told that they were "not here." Instead, Carl Miller spoke on behalf of the family. He noted that the Millers' $15,000 distribution represented a business investment in a publication that would advocate the use of beer and light wines. According to Carl, the Millers did not pay much attention to the investment. They were "sold" on it in much the same way that they were solicited for railroad or Liberty bonds. To that date, they had received no return on their loan but still expected one. He denied any disloyal intention or attempt to keep the transaction secret from the public or to conceal the purpose of the *Washington Times* to fight Prohibition. He continued, "No one can deny us the right to make a fight to save our business, and that was what we were doing." Carl noted that the investment, which took place three years earlier, was not in any way intended for propaganda about United States' involvement in World War I. He intoned that the charge was unfair and was taking undue advantage of the brewing industry. Obviously upset, he said, "We are getting it in the neck without deserving it. This [the investment] was done upper handed."[194] Carl remarked that, "There was absolutely no politics in it and no connection with pro-German propaganda." He concluded that, "everybody in Milwaukee knows where we stand on loyalty. Our action was absolutely loyal and legitimate. It is simply that where you have enemies, they will take advantage of all chances to hurt you."[195]

The Miller Brewery was still successful during these difficult times. In 1917, it sold the second most beer in Milwaukee of any brewery and the, "largest sale of any brand of bottled beer in Chicago's Loop." At this same period, Hannan and Hogg, owners of one of the largest Chicago saloons, deserted a celebrated St. Louis beer in favor of the charms of the High Life maid. At its highest quantity in the years immediately preceding Prohibition, the brewery brewed 473,049 barrels. Of that number, it sold 250,000 barrels to Milwaukee patrons. In fact, at this time, beer sales reached the brewery's production capacity and, thereafter, the sales department ceased taking, "orders outside of a 300 mile radius from Milwaukee."[196]

The forces of prohibition were formidable and the necessary ratifications of the amendement by three-fourths of the states quickly were secured with even Wisconsin doing so on January 15-16, 1919. The last state ratified the 18th Amendment on January 29 of that year. The Volstead Act of October 1919 defined intoxicating beverages as those containing over 0.5% alcohol. On January 29, 1920, exactly one year after the final state had ratified the amendment, the 18th Amendment went into effect. Alcoholic products used for manufacturing and medicine were exempted.[197]

The actual onset of Prohibition began even earlier. The Wartime Prohibition Act, passed by Congress in November 1918, banned the sale of intoxicating beverages after June 30, 1919. National Prohibition thus began even before the Eighteenth Amendment went into effect.

Due to Ernest and Fritz's painful experience concerning their Bismarck-based Milwaukee Brewing Company, they were able to prepare themselves and their business for Prohibition.

Nevertheless, its enactment was a devastating blow to the family and to the business' employees. Miller Brewery survived Prohibition due to its significant cash reserves, a belief in Prohibition's eventual termination, and adept management.

13.
DRY TIMES

Prohibition eviscerated the Miller Brewing Company and should have diminished the potential earnings of its controlling family. But the Millers thrived both personally and financially in this unique period. Baby Millers were born to the world while their parents increased their wherewithal, despite Prohibition's strictures. With determination and intelligence, the brewery's management implemented various means to survive the interregnum. No doubt, the dry period decreased the family's earnings, but when it ended they were substantially richer with most of their income coming from brewery dividends.

In 1919, the 18th Amendment to the U.S. Constitution became law, forbidding the production, shipment, and sale of alcoholic beverages. In October, the Congress enacted the Volstead Act, which specified an intoxicating beverage as one containing over one-half percent alcohol and, therefore, illegal. The "noble experiment" took effect on in January 1920, leading to the permanent shuttering of numerous American breweries. Milwaukee historian John Gurda wrote that, "Milwaukee without beer was as unthinkable as Detroit without cars or Hartford without insurance." Besides quashing much of Milwaukee's vibrant, delightful, Germanic culture, Prohibition also diminished the city's financial health, as brewing added considerably to the city's coffers. In 1918, Milwaukee had nine breweries with 6,540 employees, which produced $35 million worth of beer annually. Along with the foundering breweries, ancillary businesses such as coopers, box makers, and makers of glassware and bar fixtures were in financial trouble. Milwaukee's Common Council was exasperated with their loss of taxes and in 1921, by a vote of

29-1, implored Congress to end Prohibition.[198]

During Prohibition, much of the income that the federal government denied the breweries, distilleries, and vintners was transferred to criminals. Illegal producers, transporters, and sellers of alcoholic beverages had a massive increase in "business" as many Americans continued to drink, regardless of who was producing and distributing the "hooch." Gurda noted that: "If someone wanted to find a drink, a drink could always be found."

Many Americans turned toward legal personal production of alcoholic beverages for familial and friendly consumption, often with uneven results. Many Milwaukee families manu-factured wine made from local berries or dandelion flowers in basements or garages. Vintners produced a type of grape jelly called Vine-Go, which, in two months, became a strong wine after water was added. Also before Prohibition's enactment, scores of people stockpiled their favorite liquor.[199]

Gurda revealed that: "Prohibition was selectively enforced by the police and widely ignored by the public."

In many cities, particular neighborhoods featured several illegal drinking establishments on each block. In Milwaukee, the Italian-dominated Third Ward, which is immediately south of the downtown area, served this purpose. Also the areas of Blue Mound Road and National Avenue, tangent to the U.S. Soldiers' Home, provided alcoholic drinks to convalescing vet-erans. Speakeasies served alcoholic beverages brewed illegally in America, smuggled from Canada and other foreign countries, or stockpiled before 1920. As saloons had done, some of the speakeasies earned money from gambling and prostitution. Many were not actually speakeasies, protected with code words and subterfuge; rather, they functioned openly in the same space where, previously, a saloon had operated. The word speakeasy originated before Prohibition from people who wanted to en-ter a secret bar having to "speak easy" and credit whoever sent them. By the interregnum's end, speakeasies had, "defeated the Volstead Act, opened bars to women, and romanticized the mob."[200] Since major American cities were full of immigrants who despised the noble experiment, their politicians ignored the flourishing speakeasies. Frequently, politicians and municipal policemen drank at these secret bars overlooking the rowdy roadhouses outside municipal boundaries. Municipal governments viewed Prohibition as a national matter and often dismissed or hindered the enforcement activities of federal authorities. When marshals from the Federal Prohibition Bureau made an occasional public splash raiding a prominent speakeasy, it was common for it to reopen at that same site. Sometimes, the local constabulary, who may have been on the take, would notify the owner before the federal officers arrived for the bust. Then the feds would break in to find it devoid of intoxicating beverages, yet filled with people placidly playing cards and smoking cigars.

Prohibition precluded the Miller family from brewing beer but it could not deny them a drink. In anticipation of the dry period, the Miller boys, Ernest, Frederick A. "Fritz," and Emil, who lived on Highland Avenue, stockpiled at least 45 quarts of whiskey, 160 bottles of Ohio wine, and 10 gallons of Port wine. Possessing alcoholic beverages was legal, only their production, sale, and transportation were illegal. Also, Clara and Carl Miller used the services of Milwaukeean Jacob Best, who set up a legal winemaking operation in their basement on Newberry Boulevard. Additionally, Clara and Carl's son, Frederick Carl, occasionally visited Peter Guardalabene's famous joint, Monte Carlo, at Detroit (now St. Paul Avenue) and Jackson Streets in Milwaukee's Italian Third Ward to wet his whistle. Not to be outdone, Harry G. John, Sr., Elise's husband, traveled with his brother-in-law, Emil Miller, to Chicago's clubs for drinking, gambling, and womanizing. Also, Emil frequented Waukesha County's Blue Mound Road House and Club Madrid, examples of rural establishments that catered to those desiring gambling, imbibing, and visiting prostitutes. These activities were difficult to offer consistently in large municipalities under the ubiquitous, yet uneven, eye of law enforcement. Often it was easier to bribe officials in scarcely populated rural areas than in crowded cities.[201]

Lisette Miller, due to her children's perspicacity, reached the Prohibition era with a solid financial portfolio. They assured that their mother had the financial wherewithal to live comfortably in her later years. Since 1901, Lisette had been living in the impressive mansion at 3200 West Highland Boulevard with some of her children. This *grand dame* lived her last years surrounded by her children, grandchildren, and eventually her great-grandchildren. Lisette was a good mother but an esteemed grandmother. In recompense for her loving parenting, Lisette's children and grandchildren offered her joyful garden parties and afternoon teas. Her daughter, Clara, gave her the first six grandchildren: Loretta in 1892, Anita in 1894, Clara in 1896, Marguerite in 1901, Frederick in 1906, and Charlotte in 1909. Her daughter Elise provided the next and last grandchildren: Lorraine in 1913 and Harry in 1919. At the time of her death in 1920, Lisette left 3 sixteen-month old great-grandchildren, Charles "Chuck" Bransfield, (Anita and Michael Bransfield's son), Rose Mary Kopmeier (Loretta and Norman Kopmeier's daughter), and Claire McCahey (Claire and James McCahey's daughter). These three individuals are alive today.

Lisette's granddaughter, Claire Miller McCahey, contended that Lisette, "was in a true sense a very German housemother." She was always smiling and sweet while being proud and dignified. Lisette's granddaughter, Loretta Miller Kopmeier, noted that, in her latter years, she was a beautiful and elegant woman at peace with herself. Lisette's last photos portray a woman, while somber, proudly holding her head high. McCahey reminisced that her grandmother always wore a little black bow on her head and a beautiful handmade apron over her silk skirts that the children heard swishing through the house. She kept her hair up and decorated it with a flower and handkerchief. She was strict about her grandchildren's homework and getting them to school or bed on time. Until the end, her relatively good health allowed her to keep busy in her house. She loved music and gave chamber parties for her friends and family. Like clockwork every afternoon at four o'clock, Lisette had tea with her adult guests and milk for the children, plying them with tasty sweet rolls. Over the years, Lisette pursued her passion in flowers; at her last two homes, she had beautiful flower gardens with trellises.

Due to Lisette's substantial assets, she received large incomes. For instance in 1913 she earned $16,500, equivalent to $300,000 today. In both 1914 and 1915 she earned about $20,000. In 1917, her income rose to approximately $22,000 of which $20,000 was from mortgage interest and $1,000 was from bonds. That year she made a $3,000 donation to Marquette University where her sons had attended. In 1918, she garnered $16,000 and made tax-deductible donations to her parish, St. Rose of Lima — $47, St. Michael Parish — $79, St. Benedict the Moor Negro Mission — $100, Columbia Hospital — $200, and Marquette University — $1,000. In 1919, she earned $22,000 and made donations to Fr. Gerend, who was assisting at the Catholic School of Deaf Mutes — $20, St. Michael Parish — $36, St. Rose — $47, and Columbia Hospital —$300. In 1919, Lisette used $10,000 for household expenses, while letting one of her sons talk her into buying a new $5,100 Cadillac car and selling a used one for $700. She had $394,000 in assets, primarily mortgages. In 1920, her income dropped to $14,000 while she made donations to an unknown West Allis Catholic parish — $12.50, the German-Austria Relief Fund — $50, the American Welfare Association of German Children — $200, and the Milwaukee Children's Hospital Building Fund — $500.[202]

In the summer of 1920, the 79-year-old *grand dame* was suffering from cancer in Milwaukee's St. Mary's Hospital. The Miller children left no stone unturned in assisting her. Doctors E. Wyllys Andrews and Bertram W. Sippy traveled from Chicago to consult on Lisette's case and, on August 2, Dr. W. C. F. Witte operated on her with Dr. L.F. Jermain assisting. Milwaukee based Dr. George J. Jures also helped on the case. Four days later, seven months after the enactment of the "noble experiment," Lisette succumbed to her disease. The final member of Miller Brewery's founding generation was gone, as

Josephine Miller, Frederick's first wife, had died in 1860 and Frederick in 1888. The S. F. Peacock & Son Funeral Home, of 1028 North Van Buren Street, prepared the body for interment and laid it in state in a silver coffin at her Highland Avenue residence that Claire Miller McCahey noted was a family-only event. The grand funeral service was held at St. Rose Parish and officiated by family friend and pastor, Rev. Msgr. Patrick Durnin, and Father O'Connor, an assistant pastor. Mary Baez and the St. Rose Parish quartet sang. The funeral procession was replete with four coal-colored horses drawing the hearse. Each steed was festooned with large black feathers upon its head and had shiny burnished hooves. The family rode behind the hearse in a horse-drawn carriage followed by many mourners in motorcars. Lisette was buried in the Miller family plot at Calvary Cemetery beside her husband, with a simple gray granite headstone mined in Barre, Vermont, inscribed with her name, life span, and the word, "mother."[203]

Lisette Miller's will that was written by the law firm of Quarles, Spence and Quarles, (now Quarles and Brady), provided each child with a $10,000 advance on their share, within a year if they wished, because traditionally large estates took years to meander through probate court. Lisette's sons, Ernest and Fritz, were the executors with her youngest son, Emil, the alternate. The document divided her estate evenly among her five surviving children: Ernest, 55; Fritz, 53; Clara, 50; Emil, 43; and Elise, 40. Lisette left assets valued at $450,000, ($400,000 in personal property and $50,000 in real estate.) Lisette had a relatively small estate because she did not own any Miller Brewery stock as, earlier; Fred Miller had willed much of it to his children.[204] If the children were so inclined, they could inhabit the family's mansion at 3200 West Highland Boulevard rent-free until their deaths; otherwise, they could sell it and evenly divide the proceeds. At that time, Ernest, Fritz with his wife, May, and Emil were living in this house. Lisette provided two $200 bequests, one each to the Little Sisters of the Poor, (an order of Catholic nuns who served the poorest of the poor), and the House of the Good Shepherd, (a Catholic girls' home at 5010 West Blue Mound Road). Previously, she had added a codicil, which gave $1,000 each to her husband's niece, Sophia Meyer, who had died by the time the estate's proceeds were distributed on August 1, 1921; her long-time cook, Katherine "Katie" Dieringer; and cousin, Phyllis Engelhardt. She had signed another codicil, on December 29, 1919, which directed $500 to the Discalced Carmelite priests, at the Hubertus, Wisconsin, Holy Hill Shrine, to celebrate Masses, including Gregorian, for her soul. Gregorian Masses are interspersed with haunting medieval chants that many of the faithful find soothing and meditational. The codicil also provided $500 to the Commissariat of the Holy Land, at Mount St. Sepulchre in Washington, D. C., for Masses, including Gregorian.[205]

Lisette's death did not have a significant effect on the Miller Brewing Company, as, for quite some time, her role had been honorary. In fact, in 1899, she had given Ernest and Fritz the power of attorney to act on her behalf in financial and brewery matters. Lisette had provided her husband Frederick with heirs to perpetuate his legacy. She was a remarkable wife and mother. Her long life allowed her to attend to all of her eight grandchildren. Mrs. Miller's legacy was her steadiness and grace. She was a staunch ally of Fred and later of her sons. From her early days as a cook for the employees, to her time as a conscientious stockholder and board member, this family matron helped to create a strong regional brewery. Lisette began her association with Frederick Miller as a thin, shy, young woman and, due to her tenacity, completed her life as a resolute family matriarch.

Previously, Fred Miller Heirs was a partnership run by Eugene Salbey, who was Miller Brewery's general manager until March 1, 1918. On December 31, 1919, as a way to manage their finances, Ernest, Fritz, Emil, and Elise Miller created Fred Miller Heirs, Inc. with each investing $1 million, therefore establishing $4 million in authorized capital stock. The three brothers each had 15,000 shares and Elise had 12,600. Before the end of 1922 their additional investments totaled $536,000 for Ernest, $559,000 for Fritz, $506,000 for Emil, and $262,000 for Elise. At first Fritz served as the president of Fred Miller Heirs, but in 1921, deferred to Elise. The Millers created this corporation for two purposes; primarily, to share the administrative costs of their growing portfolios, such as hiring a bookkeeper to manage them and, secondly, to keep their capital at arm's length and live off a reasonable allowance. Clara did not participate in this undertaking, because she and Carl had their own financial advisors. Carl and Clara, (known as the East Side Millers, because of their Milwaukee East Side Newberry Boulevard home), when possible, kept their finances apart from Ernest, Fritz, Emil, and Elise, who were known as the West Side Millers. The only exceptions were brewery and estate matters that required their cooperation.[206]

Oscar F. Treichler, a bookkeeper by training, managed Fred Miller Heirs, Inc., located in downtown Milwaukee in the Pabst Building at 1302-04 Wisconsin Avenue. Treichler was the first of many people that the Miller family employed, apart from the brewery, to manage their finances. Treichler began work at Miller Brewery's office on August 15, 1904, as a stenographer earning $50 a month. In 1919, Treichler stopped working at the brewery to serve the Miller family full time as supervisor of Fred Miller Heirs, Inc..[207]

Until March 1918, the Millers had used brewery personnel, such as Eugene Salbey, to supervise their personal finances. They found it prudent to keep their own money geographically separate from the brewery's and hired men distinct from the brewery to manage it. This division made self-serving business deals less possible. On January 1, 1920, Treichler also began administering Lisette's estate and shortly thereafter managed Ernest's assets as well. Eventually, he became Ernest's personal secretary before branching out to assist the other Millers. He remained with them, until the late 1940s, while receiving a $3,000 to $4,000 annual salary.[208]

Oscar Treichler and B. H. (Bertram Henry) Protzmann, his long-time assistant, kept meticulous monthly statements for the Millers, completing their tax returns and other government reports. Occasionally as needed, Treichler provided the newspapers with information regarding the Millers' finances, as Ernest and Fritz were loath to speak publicly. Treichler traveled to Florida, Chicago, Detroit, and Canada to review the family's income properties. For the most part, Treichler worked for Ernest, who supervised the family's business and personal finances, except for Clara, of course, who did not participate in this system. In many ways, these personal employees became *de facto* members of the Miller family because they acted as intermediaries among the siblings. Due to their duties, they also learned many of the family's most guarded secrets.

Fred Miller Heirs operations were confined principally to the investment of its cash in municipal bonds and mortgages and, between 1922 and 1926, paid $400,000 in cash dividends to its stockholders. Ernest, Fritz, and Clara enjoyed visiting Florida and all eventually bought land there. On January 17, 1921, Ernest bought a $275,000 piece of land for Fred Miller Heirs in Key Biscayne. According to Dr. Frederick Olson, the eminent Milwaukee historian, personal mortgages were common investments at that time as relatively few people held common stocks. Often, wealthy people held numerous home mortgages, whereas, today it is rare for individuals to own mortgages of unrelated people. Bankers would take the safest mortgages for their own institution and give their wealthy friends leads on riskier mortgages, which provided higher yields. Investors also procured mortgages by lending money to poorer friends and acquaintances and by assuming distressed mortgages. Due to Ernest's death in 1925, Fritz, Emil, and Elise dissolved Fred Miller Heirs on November 30, 1926, providing $1.6 million each to Ernest's estate, and to Fritz, Emil, and Elise.[209]

On February 14, 1913, the Millers created the Oriental Investment Company to manage, buy, and sell their investment properties. It existed only on paper until May 31, 1917, when the Millers transferred $3.5 million of property to it. The Millers also created the Occidental Realty Company at this same time but dissolved it in December 1920.[210] The Millers created the Oriental and Occidental realty companies to diversify their assets that they believed were in danger of being dissipated if

Prohibition became law, a threat that, monthly, was growing more feasible. If the brewery were to become bankrupt due to Prohibition, the Millers could retain their numerous properties. At the time of its inception, the Oriental Investment Company, a wholly owned subsidiary of Miller Brewery, began to receive transfers of buildings from the brewery. The Oriental Investment Company existed until August 26, 1927, when it was dissolved. Subsequently, on December 31, 1936, the Oriental Realty Company was created with 10,000 outstanding shares, wholly owned by the Miller family. At this time the Oriental Realty Company wholly owned the Miller Brewing Company's stock. Eventually, the Oriental Realty Company became an important source of revenue for the second and third generation of the Miller family.[211]

Miller Brewery, much like other breweries, had purchased numerous pieces of real estate since the 1890s. In fact, on June 28, 1897, the stockholders of the Miller Brewing Company, then known as the Fred Miller Brewing Company, held a special meeting to amend the corporate bylaws allowing the officers to buy real estate and make contracts without prior authorization of the stockholders. This change allowed the brewery's officers to buy and sell properties without the pre-approval of the stockholders.[212] Acknowledging the paucity of information regarding Miller's properties, excluding its production facilities at 40th and State Street, it is reasonable to infer from Pabst Brewery's existing voluminous records that Miller Brewery began purchasing saloon locations in the 1890s. Much of Miller Brewery's corporate life followed that of Pabst, which for most of its existence, was much larger than Miller Brewery and an industry leader. The Pabst Brewery began to purchase its saloons and investment properties between 1887 and 1900. As an example, by 1893, Pabst had 20% of its net worth invested in such properties.[213]

Breweries' saloon properties were known as "tied houses" because they were tied to one brewery. Miller's properties were clustered in the Midwest where their sales were the highest. Breweries procured the best locations, usually prominent corners, to sell their beer. It was not unusual for a brewery to buy a street corner simply to keep it out of the hands of its competitors. The large breweries also built attractive two-story brick buildings, with the brewery's insignia inlaid in the brick, where the custodian and his family could live above the saloon. Several of Miller Brewery's Milwaukee tied houses still stand with other uses. Pabst also bought land and then built investment properties such as hotels and restaurants. "At the peak of its property holding, Pabst owned nine large hotels and restaurants in New York, Chicago, Milwaukee, Minneapolis, and San Francisco."[214] Miller Brewery had built the Miller Hotel and Theater in Milwaukee in 1917, but for the most part, its real estate holdings involved tied houses, distribution sites, and icehouses.

After Prohibition was enacted in 1920, the breweries, Miller included, began to divest themselves of these vacant properties. They sold these properties, numbering in the thousands slowly, because an indiscriminate sale might have depressed prices. Miller disposed of these tied houses in a reasonable manner over thirty years. Fortunately, land prices remained high during Prohibition as it coincided with the robust economy of the 1920s, therefore providing the brewing family's substantial income. Simply said, while beer was outlawed, the Millers gained a considerable income from their properties' rents and sales. On December 14, 1926, the Miller Brewing Company transferred ownership of their prize possession, the $625,000 Miller Block building at Wisconsin and Water Streets, to the Oriental Investment (Realty) Company to manage. Over the years, Oriental Realty came to own and manage residential properties also.[215]

Because the Millers did not sell any stock until 1961, they could not profit from their brewery shares except through dividends. They declared the first dividend the day after Christmas in 1898 at a special stockholders' meeting. Dividends gave the Millers who were not employed by the brewery, such as Lisette, Clara, and Elise, a chance to profit from it. All stockholders profited equally according to the number of shares that they owned. In all likelihood, Clara and Emil demanded dividends because Lisette had a substantial estate for her support. Ernest and Fritz were employed full-time by the brewery and, as directors and officers, could set their own salaries, while Elise was an 18 year-old student comfortably enjoying her mother's home and largesse. Clara was employed by the Carl Miller Lumber Company, not the brewery, and was interested in being compensated as a brewery stockholder. The impetuous Emil may have wanted a dividend declared to receive more money than he was being paid as a company bookkeeper. No doubt, Ernest and Fritz wanted Emil patiently to scale the corporate ladder, but Emil wanted his due sooner than later. In all likelihood, Ernest and Fritz fought the declaration of dividends in order to give the business more money to accomplish its goals. Once money flowed from the corporation to its stockholders, it was lost for expansion or surviving difficult times. At the same meeting, they empowered Ernest and Fritz to set a price on the company's stock and offer it for sale. (As we know, they did not sell their stock to an outside concern.) The stockholders declared stock dividends of unknown quantity on April 4, 1905 and May 5, 1909.[216]

Between 1914 and 1917, Miller Brewery's stockholders declared $8.3 million in dividends. The substantial transfer of value from their business to their personal accounts, as Prohibition neared, demonstrated their fear that their company might close. In 1920, 1921, and 1922 the brewery declared stock dividends correspondingly of $3.8 million, $380,000, and $225,000. Stock dividends were dividends of additional stock to existing stockholders. Stock dividends gave stockholders a better opportunity to pass their holdings to their heirs or in theory to sell them publicly. Additional outstanding stock generally lowered the price per share making each one more affordable. In 1924 they declared a cash dividend of $100,000 and in 1926 of $230,250.[217]

The forced closure of the Millers' Bismarck-based Milwaukee Brewing Company in 1890 gave Ernest and Fritz Miller indispensable experience in dealing with the chaos caused by prohibitionary forces. By the early 1890s, Ernest and Fritz Miller believed in the probability of a national proscription law, giving them a head-start to plan for a possible business interruption. They had seen Prohibition's steady march and were not surprised at its eventual arrival. Fortunately, they had sufficient personal and business capital to survive it.

In the decade before Prohibition, many breweries began to brew alcohol-free or low-alcohol malt drinks, also known as "near beer" that became popular due to the increasing number of cities, counties, and states that outlawed regular beer. In March 1917, Miller Brewery began production of their near-beer products, Milo and Vivo. Ries Behling, a Miller Brewery contract historian in the mid-1950s wrote that, "Milo was a wheat cereal beverage and Vivo was a barley cereal beverage, both containing less than one-half percent alcohol." In March 1917, the Millers introduced the Milo Beverage Company that was wholly owned by the family, to brew and sell Milo. They gave the Milo guarantee, assuring the public that, "this soft drink in every sense," was created differently than beer and was absolutely non-intoxicating. Their product was, "an absolutely pure, wholesome and refreshing drink, thoroughly pasteurized, with a delightful hop flavor peculiar to itself, and is placed on the market to satisfy the public which demands a non-alcoholic beverage." It was sold in ten-ounce bottles, sealed with a crown stopper.[218]

"'Near Beer,' introduced in January 1919, under the High Life label, was the only cereal beverage the Miller Brewing Company marketed after September of that year," as it had discontinued Milo and Vivo and, likely, eliminated the Milo Beverage Company. The non-alcoholic High Life product was dramatically different from the wildly popular alcoholic version of pre-Prohibition days and was advertised as a pure tonic beverage.[219] The brewery's management discovered that the High Life name was easier to market, due to its residual value, than creating new images for Milo and Vivo. Also, they surmised that promoting the High Life name would give the regular High Life beer a boost after Prohibition's repeal. They guessed correctly as High Life's sales grew enormously after Prohibition's repeal.

Miller's first low-alcohol products did not require significant changes in the brewing process. The master brewer slowly fermented slightly heavier wort at unusually low temperatures until the alcohol reached one percent. Next, they diluted the mixture until it reached the legal limit. Many beer drinkers bought these legal malt beverages and added alcohol to them or simply drank them unadulterated.[220]

The Millers were determined to defeat the forces of Prohibition that sought to destroy all producers of alcoholic beverages. They resolved to keep their father's company afloat. They held long meetings during which they chose to make the changes necessary to remain a viable operation. It took considerable willpower and *chutzpa* to create new corporations and products in order to survive for the duration. This dilemma was on a scale of any predicament their father, Fred Miller, had encountered during his thirty-three year tenure.

The Millers countered the effects of Prohibition on many fronts, creating various enterprises with the hope that one or two of them would save the brewery. With Prohibition's storm clouds on the horizon on October 9, 1918, the Millers incorporated the Miller Ice and Cold Storage Company with $100,000 in capital stock. Each of the five Miller children owned 40 shares. The directors elected Emil Miller — president, Fritz — vice-president, and Arthur L. Kleinboehl — secretary. Its headquarters were at the brewery's main office. The Millers developed this company for two reasons; the first was to give Emil a task into which he could put his energies and the second was to more fully utilize the brewery's delivery trucks and huge cold storage facilities, as Prohibition encroached, decreasing beer sales. Emil, the youngest brother, was energetic and strove for a chance to demonstrate to his family his business talents. In all likelihood, the Millers did not provide much advertising or capital improvements for their ice and cold storage company; instead, they continued to focus on their core business, the beverage operations. Another strike against Miller's ice company was Ernest's nephew, Norman Kopmeier's, formal association with his family's ice company, Wisconsin Ice and Coal. Over the years, the brewery had purchased ice from this local concern.[221]

From 1920 forward, Miller Brewery attempted to retain its best employees out of loyalty to them and in the event of Prohibition's repeal. It was important to keep a skeletal operation in order to retain their valuable, skilled employees, otherwise, they would have found other work, albeit less remunerative and fulfilling. To keep operating, Ernest and Fritz Miller scaled back their variable costs, such as temporary labor and brewing ingredients, except for the diminished quantities they needed for non-alcoholic malt beverages. The Millers reduced their fixed costs by shuttering or renting their unused buildings and covering the remaining costs with new products. Despite the myriad products breweries created during the "noble experiment," rental income was their best source of income. During the dry years, Miller Brewery sold alcohol free or low alcoholic malt products, alcohol for medicinal purposes, and carbonated sweet drinks. Milwaukee's other breweries also made divergent products; Blatz — soft drinks, Schlitz — "Eline" candy bars (a play on the owners' name Uihlein), Pabst — "Pabst-ett" processed cheese, and Gettelman — snow plows. This valiant effort to remain viable had uneven success as, for years, breweries idled millions of dollars of brewing equipment.[222]

Non-alcoholic malt syrup was the most profitable product that Miller sold during the dry years. Miller Brewery sold it in 2.5- to 3-pound cans and barrels under the Miller name, while also allowing dealers to market it under their own moniker. The brewmaster formulated this syrup by producing regular beer and then evaporating it into a thick concentrate with approximately eighty percent solids. It was used by bakers and pharmaceutical companies, besides being perfectly suited for home-based beer makers. The brewery advertised it as a flavorful enhancement to many baked and cooked foods. Nevertheless, home brewing constituted its largest market. Home brewers would add yeast, available by mail, to the syrup and, together with boiling, cooling, and storing, brew their own beer.[223]

The sales of the near beers was significantly lower than the alcoholic beverages. In July 1920, Miller Brewery supplemented its product line with root beer. Slowly they added more flavors, such as grape, ginger ale, cherry, lemon, orange, and white soda. They marketed them in bottles except for root beer, which was also sold in barrels. Ironically, Miller Brewery created and marketed sugary children's drinks after spending their history brewing bitter-tasting adult alcoholic beverages. In fact, the acquisition of a taste for beer often is seen as part of one's passage to adulthood. Certainly, Miller long-time German-American brewmaster John U. Kraft disdained these new products, yearning for beer's return.[224]

On April 23, 1920, in order to represent its current value more accurately, Miller Brewery's stockholders increased its capital stock to $4 million. In late 1920, the brewery purchased equipment, with some of the $344,500 in profits it made that year, to produce malt syrup and alcohol more efficiently. In order to produce and sell medicinal alcohol, the federal government demanded that all distillers, including Miller Brewery, buy a bond to insure the alcohol's proper distribution.[225]

On December 23, 1920, Miller Ice and Cold Storage Company's stockholders changed the corporation's name to the Miller Products Company as they discovered that the ice distribution and cold storage businesses were less profitable than low and non-alcohol products. It was reasonable to name the new company Miller Products because it sold many items that were unlike alcoholic beer. On December 29, 1920, Miller Brewery converted stockhouse A into an industrial distillery and transferred its title to the Miller Products Company. At this time, they converted stockhouse B into a malt syrup factory. After Miller Brewery purchased a de-alcoholizing apparatus, they amended their method of producing near beer. Thereafter, they brewed and fermented 4% beer and then boiled off the alcohol, losing about one-third of the product in the process. After reclaiming and distilling the alcohol, the brewery sold it for medicinal purposes.[226]

In 1922, the Miller Brewing Company, then known as the Fred Miller Brewing Company, made $133,000 in profits. At this time, to create a more flexible operation, the Millers transferred many of Miller Brewing Company's assets to its wholly owned subsidiaries, the Miller Products Company and the Oriental Realty Company. Also, by creating two divisions, they could manage the real estate portion of their business profitably without being affected by the depressed brewing business. Regardless, the brewery continued, in 1923 — their profits were $224,300, in 1924 — $176,000, in 1925 — $195,000, and in 1926 — $166,000.[227]

Since his marriage to Clara Miller in 1890, Carl Miller had an important yet low-key role at the Miller Brewing Company. The lumber company executive never owned any stock nor held a director's or officer's position, as his wife had. Yet, Carl was the family's breadwinner and Clara followed his advice regarding her brewery stock. In order to receive Clara's cooperation, the West Side Millers dealt with Carl. Over the years since their estrangement in 1890, Ernest and Carl communicated coolly regarding their personal and business affairs. Yet by 1925, Ernest and Carl had developed a civility that allowed them to cooperate on various matters. For instance in September of that year, only days before he died, Ernest agreed with Carl's promotion of German bonds. Carl was an active investor in German bonds and, as he had been born in Germany, traveled there annually, and had many family members still there, he was able to attend to their research, purchase, and sale.[228]

In this period, Ernest, Fritz, and Emil spent long periods away from the company, each for their own reasons, while Arthur Kleinboehl ran the brewery. Over time, the Millers grew dissatisfied with Kleinboehl's abilities. In all likelihood, he paid little regard to the Millers' wishes. Ernest believed that Miller Brewery should be selling substantially more malt syrup and that Kleinboehl was rapidly missing an opportunity to do so. In 1925, Ernest complained to Carl that, "Emil and K [Kleinboehl] are the two extremes." He noted to Carl that

Kleinboehl employed only one traveling salesman from January to June of 1925, which was well below Ernest's expectations. On the other hand, Emil, who was taking a larger role at the brewery, wanted dramatically to increase their promotional efforts. Ernest noted that the brewery, with only one traveling salesman, had sold merely 15,000 barrels of malt syrup in 1924 and 30,000 by September of 1925. He figured that if the brewery could at least sell, "50,000 barrels this year [1925] of beer and syrup we can make some money." [229]

As a way to reduce Kleinboehl's authority, Ernest Miller offered him the opportunity, "to run all except sales and he refused." In a final exasperated remark, Ernest damned Kleinboehl's inability to make brewery repairs; the, "roofs leak and the paint is nearly off." Noting Emil's propensity for overindulging in alcohol, Ernest was apprehensive about giving his brother the sales and marketing position because he would again, "become a drunkard." Ernest was grateful that since, "July 1st he is as good as you [Carl] or me."[230]

Ernest was never a physically hardy person, and the pressure at the brewery, along with his mother's death, took a toll on him. In all likelihood, he had numerous maladies, especially hypertension (high blood pressure). Due to his deteriorating health, Ernest took stretches of time away from the brewery. Finally, on December 18, 1920 he resigned as Miller Brewery's president, remarking that he had made Miami his permanent home. Actually, Ernest spent winters at the Casa Marino Hotel in Key West, Florida, and summers in Milwaukee. During his three to four month absences, Oscar Treichler controlled the family's finances and investments. As his time and energy permitted, Ernest donated his expertise and critical thinking to brewery matters. He trusted that Fritz, Emil, and the non-family managers, such as Arthur L. Kleinboehl would succeed in his absence. He collected his last $5,000 pay in 1921 and, thereafter, received no further salary from the brewery.

Ernest was a loving uncle to his nephews and nieces. Loretta Miller Kopmeier was especially fond of her Uncle Ernest. Due to their nervous natures, both Ernest and Fritz disliked going to Clara and Carl Millers' house with the accompanying noise from their children. On the other hand, the brothers enjoyed having their oldest nieces, Loretta, Anita, and Claire play pool in the basement of their stately home on Highland Boulevard. Claire remembered that, to relieve stress, Ernest, who had arthritic hands, nervously would crack his knuckles.

Like his parents, Ernest practiced his Catholic faith and, as he aged, spent an increasing amount of time and energy promoting it. As with many Catholics, Ernest kept saints' relics as reminders to live a holy life. He grew up at St. Joseph Parish and then, around 1900, transferred to the new nearby St. Rose of Lima Parish where he was, in all likelihood, a daily communicant. Ernest had donated a large sum to this parish to build their school, which became one of the finest parochial school buildings in the state.[231]

It is unknown whether Ernest, the life-long bachelor, ever dated women. He may have been homosexual. His niece, Claire Miller McCahey, who was born in 1896 and knew her maternal uncles well, noted that Ernest was timid with women as well as, generally, being quiet and shy. McCahey even said that he was afraid of women. When her grandmother, Lisette, arranged a dinner at the home of one her neighbors, who had an eligible daughter, Ernest ran home before the meal began. McCahey also noted that Lisette arranged events so that young ladies could meet her boys—expectantly, they would duck the party and ensconce themselves in the basement to play pool. Ernest also took solo trips to Miami, San Francisco, and Europe where he would have been free to indulge in male trysts. One can imagine, if Ernest was homosexual, the intense angst he experienced while maintaining his Catholic religion, living with a conservative German-American family, and finally, operating a large regional brewery.

By 1925, Ernest had a net worth of $4 million due to his brewery stock, real estate, and bonds. In 1913, he earned $20,000, of which $15,000 was from mortgage interest. From 1913 through 1921 Ernest earned a $5,000 yearly salary, the most he ever earned from the brewery. Due to his stock owner-ship in the Miller Brewing Company and subsequent sizeable dividends, Ernest did not need to increase his salary. In fact, his modest salary allowed him to maintain his siblings' and managers' moderate incomes by noting that his was likewise. This practice benefited the brewery as long as the employees did not seek higher pay elsewhere. In 1914, Ernest's taxable income rose considerably to $49,000 and in 1915 to $53,000. In 1916, due to $800,000 in Miller Brewery dividends, his income was an astronomical $827,000. In 1917, he received another dividend that increased his income to $879,000. As Prohibition approached the Millers withdrew funds from the brewery to protect themselves from a potential bankruptcy. By 1919, his dividends had been invested in mortgages and bonds, providing him with a respectable $85,000 income. In 1920, he gave tax-deductible donations to the German War Relief Fund — $10, the Missionary Association of Catholic Women that was located in Milwaukee — $1,375, and the Marquette University Building Fund — $2,500. In 1921, Ernest earned $38,000 in income and gave a respectable donation of $11,000 to the Women's Missionary Association. In 1922, he brought in $44,000 and in 1923 — $33,000. In 1924, his income rose to $71,000.[232]

Due to his declining health, Ernest increasingly turned his attention to philanthropy. In the early 1920s, he became a major contributor to Catholic missions, both domestic and foreign. Ernest Miller often sought out persons in dire straits to aid them. To his credit, driven by his subdued German-like personality, his greatest financial philanthropic efforts were anonymous. His principle was, "Let not your right hand see what your left hand does."[233] Ernest Miller, who had spent his lifetime working for others, in his last years, maintained his frugality even though his nearly $4 million fortune would have afforded him considerable luxuries. Instead, Ernest started a family tradition of philanthropy that saw its impressive fruition in his nephew, Harry G. "Buddy" John, Jr., who donated his Miller Brewery stock, valued in 1970 at nearly $100 million to

Catholic causes worldwide.

The Catholic St. Benedict the Moor Parish Mission on 9th and State streets had a special place in Ernest's heart. In 1908, the Archdiocese of Milwaukee founded this mission to serve the growing black community, as it later created Our Lady of Guadalupe Mission (now Holy Trinity – Our Lady of Guadalupe Parish on South 4th Street) on Milwaukee's South Side to serve the Hispanic community and the Parish of the Great Spirit for American Indians. The mission's namesake, St. Benedict the Moor, was a Catholic saint born in Ethiopia, who lived in the mid-1500s in Sicily and dedicated his life to aiding society's poorest members.

In 1913 St. Benedict Parish's pastor, Father Stephen Eckert, O.M. Cap., created a school for black students and soon realized that he needed to board many of the students. The November 1925 *Seraphic Chronicle*, the monthly bulletin for members of the Third Order of St. Francis, noted that St. Benedict's Boarding School, the only institute of its kind in the Midwest, was favorably known throughout the Union. Over the years, such luminaries as Chicago Mayor Harold Washington, musician Lionel Hampton, and comedian Redd Foxx studied there. Fr. Stephen had the heart of a martyr and sacrificed himself wholly for the cause of the mission. On February 16, 1923, Father Stephen died and, despite his great work, St. Benedict Parish lacked the funds to fulfill his dreams.

Shortly thereafter, Father Philip Steffes, O.M. Cap. became pastor and primary fundraiser. At this time, Ernest G. Miller became involved financially at St. Benedict's Mission in a story best told in the mission's *1975 Reunion* booklet. On July 3, 1923, months after Father Stephen died, Father Steffes was in his office poring over the construction paperwork when he answered a knock at the door. The tall stranger, declining a chair, drew his business card from his vest pocket, and placed it on the priest's desk. It said, Ernest G. Miller, President, Miller Brewing Company. The brewer, previously unknown to the parish, asked the pastor why they were excavating a large hole on their property. The pastor explained that they were building a church. Then Ernest queried, "Who is going to pay for it?" to which the priest rejoined, " I don't know yet." Ernest, holding his gray fedora, serenely continued, "Would you mind if I paid for it?" Father Steffes stood dumbfounded, then swallowed hard. Ernest posed, "How much will it cost?" and the priest replied, " I think about $35,000." Ernest Miller paused and then invited the pastor please to send him the bill. He also asked the rector, presently, to keep his gift anonymous and then, in time, insert his name as a donor. After a few polite comments, Ernest departed while Father Steffes uttered a prayer of thanks.

Three months later, Ernest Miller heard that the Jesuits of Marquette College were planning to sell their old four-story school, with its block-long campus, directly across the street from St. Benedict's mission. Previously, the college had moved to its present location on Wisconsin Avenue. Ernest sent a check to Father Steffes to purchase that building for a larger school for the black students. Remarkably, Ernest provided funds to purchase the building where, over forty years earlier, he had attended high school. Altogether, he provided the mission with $122,000 to help them build their church and buy his vacated alma mater.

In the spring of 1925, Ernest took an extensive ocean voyage to Rome, Cairo, and Jerusalem where he fulfilled his ambition to see the geographical cornerstones of his Catholic faith. It was a physically difficult trip for the ailing man, but he delighted in praying at the famed religious sites. On April 10, he wrote his sister Elise that Jerusalem was very interesting but cold and with no bath to be had. He also noted that he had been in the house where Jesus of Nazareth's father, Joseph, had worked as a carpenter. Ernest relished visiting Rome during a Holy Year, providing him with the rare opportunity to experience Catholicism's splendor.

Soon after returning from his pilgrimage, on Labor Day, September 7, 1925 the Mission of St. Benedict the Moor celebrated the dedication of its new school building. Msgr. Joseph Rainer, rector emeritus of St. Francis Seminary, officiated at the 10:30 a.m. field Mass and ceremony. Immediately afterwards, Msgr. Rainer presented Ernest both with a St. Benedict diploma and, most importantly, the decoration *Pro Ecclesia et Pontifice* (for the church and the pope), in recognition of his substantial Catholic philanthropies. The Church bestowed this honor to individuals for their extraordinary zeal in the exercise of the lay apostolate. It was a valuable distinction awarded by Pope Pius XI himself. Ernest had earned this decoration with liberal donations to the papacy, St. Rose of Lima Parish, Chinese Catholic missionaries, and St. Benedict the Moor Mission.[234]

At the ceremony he said: "I wish to thank the speakers for the nice things they said about me. I wish to thank the Holy Father for having decorated me. Furthermore, I thank God for having inspired me into the Negro and Chinese Missions. When you think of this institution, please do not think of me, but think what this institution stands for and what it is trying to accomplish; and above all, I ask that you give all you can to aid this institution. Give every way to the fathers here that are doing hard work, dedicating their lives for this cause, and to the Sisters. I guess this is all I care to say."[235]

The *Seraphic Chronicle* noted that Father Weyer, the orator of the day, explained that, "an everlasting glory awaits all of our Catholic laymen for their help in building up of this mission." He continued, "In the vestibule of this building, you will see two wood carvings, the two elements — the spiritual and the material; one represents Father Stephen and the other Mr. Ernest G. Miller." These beautifully painted wood-carvings were prepared in Italy by the International Statuary Company. Currently, this carving rests with the author.

On September 13, 1925, seven days after the dedication, the 60-year-old Ernest had a cerebral thrombosis (stroke) that incapacitated him. As he lay deathly ill, the members of St. Benedict the Moor Mission looked for ways to help. The *Seraphic Chronicle* reported that the priests, nuns, lay persons, and black children prayed fervently for their hero. They kept ten candles burning in the chapel before the altar of St. Joseph and the priests said daily morning Mass for him. It was stated that shortly before his death on September 21–he was unconscious for two days–a smile lit up his face and remained there even after his soul departed to receive the laurels of celestial bliss. At the end, Fritz and brother-in-law Carl Miller stood at his side comforting him.

Msgr. Patrick. H. Durnin, St. Rose Parish pastor, officiated and Father Steffes assisted during Ernest's funeral, held at St. Rose Parish on September 24. The St. Rose quartet sang under the direction of Raphael Baez, organist. Ernest was buried in the Miller plot at the Calvary Cemetery.

Ernest had dedicated his life to his family's business and left a meaningful legacy for his siblings and nephews and nieces. His friends knew him as a quiet, studious man, hating show and ostentation.[236] With his personality, under different circumstances, Ernest could have been a successful police detective or English teacher. Fritz, Clara, Emil, Elise and their descendants owed a lot to Ernest, who dedicated much of his life to their well-being. Generally, they were appreciative of his sacrifices on their behalf. He assumed control of the Miller Brewery a year before his father's death in 1888 and continued to manage it, (except for a one-year hiatus in 1891), until his health deteriorated in the early 1920s. His presidency saw the brewery expand immensely and provide a good living for many brewery employees and the Miller family. Ernest gave his life and soul to the brewery and helped it navigate Prohibition's strictures. In all likelihood, the Miller Brewery would not have remained viable nor controlled by the Miller family had he not served as its president.

Ernest had created his last will and testament on September 8, 1924, with the help of his attorney, J. V. Quarles, and named his brother, Fritz, and sister, Elise, as executors. The will noted many bequests such as $8,000 for St. Joseph Hospital, $1,000 each to twelve local predominantly Catholic organizations, and $500 to the Catholic shrine at Holy Hill in Wisconsin. He left $1 million to the Missionary Association of Catholic Women. He also provided $500,000 to Milwaukee's St. Francis Seminary that used some of the munificence to construct the Ernest G. Miller Memorial Gymnasium, which Archbishop Sebastian B. Messmer dedicated on in 1927 and is still used today. Ernest dictated that $200,000 of his bequest to the seminary be used to create a trust fund to aid its poor students. Furthermore, he gave $200,000 to the St. Benedict the Moor Negro Mission,

$50,000 to the Pope Pius XI, and $30,000 to the Catholic Vicariate of Foochow, China.[237]

Ernest directed the remainder of his estate that included his stock in the Miller Brewing Company, be divided among his four siblings. Fritz and Elise each received an undivided two sixths, Emil and Clara each received an undivided one sixth. Ernest left no written explanation regarding the uneven allocation. He provided a lesser share to Emil, because he was an uncontrollable alcoholic who could not manage his own money. The reason for Clara's reduced share is murkier. Family oral history notes that Ernest was more empathetic toward Elise because her husband, Harry, was less financially successful than Clara's husband, Carl, who owned a thriving lumber business. Another reason may have been the enduring rift between Clara and Carl Miller and the West Side Millers. Early in their relationship, Ernest and Carl had severe disagreements that may have never completely been resolved.[238]

Fritz and Elise, the will's executors, used the law firm of Miller, Mack and Fairchild (now Foley and Lardner) at the First Wisconsin Bank building, whose fees reached $35,000, to process Ernest's estate. On September 2, 1927, they filed legal papers in Circuit Judge John Karl's courtroom, establishing the estate's value at $3.97 million, from which the State of Wisconsin deducted $374,000 in taxes. At his death, Ernest owned forty shares of the Miller Products Company, 15,361 shares of common stock in the Fred Miller Heirs Company, 9,210 shares of common stock in the Fred Miller Brewing Company valued at a little over $1 million, and 8,880 shares of common stock in the Oriental Realty Company valued at $1,145,520. The Oriental Realty Company owned the Milwaukee properties of the Strand Theater, the Miller Hotel building, and the Mack building. Fritz and Elise were to receive assets worth $506,000 and Clara and Emil were to receive assets worth $253,000. Due to the difficult and painstaking manner of processing the large estate, the heirs did not receive the majority of the funds until 1929.[239]

14.
ESTATE BATTLES

Not since Frederick J. Miller's death in 1888, had a passing so impacted the family and its business. Even though Ernest had withdrawn from many of his considerable daily duties, he was the person most responsible for directing the family's corporations. He was the glue, especially among the West Side Millers. While in authority, Ernest, Fritz, and Elise controlled the majority of the stock. For the West Side Millers, there was no reason to change this formula while Ernest was alive since generally they prospered. Upon his death, there remained four Millers: Fritz, who was uncomfortable with leadership; Clara, who was uninterested in cooperating fully with her siblings; Emil, whose personal problems made him increasingly undependable; and Elise, who was unwilling to confront the obstinate Clara without Ernest and Fritz at her side.

After Ernest's death, Fritz counted on Elise's continual and Emil's sporadic support. Fortunately, if Emil was ensconced in gambling and drinking, Oscar Treichler later would procure his signature on the appropriate corporate documents. Since Fritz and Elise were the executors of Ernest's estate until it was disseminated in 1929, they voted his stock in support of the existing order, therefore maintaining control over the corporation. On November 28, 1925, two months after Ernest's death, the four surviving Millers gathered for a special shareholders meeting at the family's homestead at 3200 West Highland Boulevard. Doubtless, they had begun holding shareholder and directors meeting there when Lisette was ill with cancer. The Highland mansion was more luxurious and private than the cramped Miller Brewing Company headquarters on State Street, where corporate meetings might have distracted the office workers.[240]

The stockholders' first order of business was to elect Emil in place of Ernest, joining Fritz and Clara as directors. Emil then attempted to establish himself as the next brewery leader, figuring that Fritz and Clara were uninterested in the position. Emil reported that since the Prohibition Amendment had been adopted and enforced, there had been insufficient expenditures for renewals, repairs, and upkeep of the brewery, bottle house, and machinery, creating an, "unsatisfactory dilapidated and run-down condition." This report was an implicit condemnation of Arthur Kleinboehl, the brewery's manager. He continued that, "many thousands of dollars worth of cooperage, bottles and cases, and other equipment have become practically worthless as a result." He said that the steam plant, brew house, and cooker kettles were worn out and in need of replacement.[241]

Emil testified that the, "condition of the refrigeration buildings is causing much trouble and annoyance." Due to neglect and disuse they have been damaged by decay, mold, and corrosion. He explained that these problems have led to a, "cellar and sewer odor," that was tainting the beverages. Even a consultation with the outside expert, Mr. E. A. Siebel of Chicago, offered no resolution. Emil's report was an exaggeration of the existing conditions because the brewery's management had modified the buildings in order to create new products, albeit without the financial success of earlier periods.[242]

After Emil finished his report, the Millers had an extensive and heated discussion regarding retaining the business and repairing it or simply selling it. The siblings each had sufficient personal funds to invest in the brewery to ameliorate its shortcomings, but they were reluctant to risk them. Finally, they decided to sell the brewery. Certainly if Ernest were alive, they would have invested in the business instead of trying to sell it.[243]

In an apology to future generations regarding their decision, Fritz added to the unanimously accepted resolution that, "there was much grief and worry incident to and connected with the brewing and beverage business and, in our best judgment, the corporation's best interest and the interest of its stockholders will be conserved by affecting the sale of the brewery, bottling house and other property and assets of this corporation pertaining to the brewing and beverage business." They resolved to sell all of the land, buildings, machinery, auto trucks, supplies, leases, trade name, good will, merchandise and material, and properties listed in the city or county originally purchased in connection with the brewing business. The transaction also included brewery properties throughout the Midwest that had been used for storing beer and ice. They excluded the profitable Mack Block building in downtown Milwaukee (that had since been renamed the Miller Block), and bonds, real estate mortgages, and cash and bank accounts. The exclusions were financially significant and contained much of the family's worth.[244]

Subsequent to the resolution, Emil unexpectedly made a $75,000 offer to purchase the 800 shares of the capital stock of the Miller Products Company, then held by the Miller Brewing Company. In other words, he tried to buy a portion of the brewing component of the business. At that time, the Miller Products Company had various products and brewing facilities within the Miller Brewing Company, but not all of the brewing equipment and properties on State Street. The Millers rejected his first offer but accepted a second one of $78,000, for which he was to provide a 5% note payable on or before June 10, 1927. Thereafter, the directors met, namely Fritz, Clara, and Emil, to review the actions of the stockholders and then resolve to contact real estate brokers and other such people to find buyers for the remaining assets of the Miller Brewing Company.[245]

The next stockholder meeting was held on January 28, 1926, at which time, it was reported that A.L. Kleinboehl had resigned as general manager and secretary of the corporation. The Millers hired Frank A. Miller, who was no relation to the Miller family, to replace him. Also since the last meeting, the stockholders had entertained one $200,000 offer to purchase the Miller Brewing Company's stock that they had rejected. In his inimitable way, Emil offered $250,000 for the stock, which his siblings also refused. No doubt, Fritz, Clara, and Elise did not want the problematic Emil to increase his offer and buy the company because, currently, he was contracted to purchase the 800 shares of the Miller Products Company. They were doubtful that Emil would fulfill his end of a sales contract. Certainly, there was a period of heated discussion, after which, the Millers completed the conference with a fervent request for everyone present to make "further aggressive steps" to sell the brewery for $300,000 or not less than $275,000.[246]

The Miller stockholders had their regular meeting on May 26, 1926. Fritz reported that the best offer for the brewery's assets was $275,000. Immediately thereafter, Emil made a $503,000 offer for the brewery stock. The amount of Emil's offer came from the brewery's total gross book value ($2,367,221), minus the deduction for reserves on the books for depreciation and obsolescence ($1,864,221) that equaled the net book value ($503,000). After a discussion, consideration, and change of mind, the directors were instructed to accept Emil's offer to purchase. The shareholders then directed the officers to execute the necessary contract to consummate the sale on about July 1, 1926. Following the shareholders' meeting, the directors met, during which Clara was elected president; Fritz, vice president; Elise, treasurer; and Frank Miller, secretary and manager. After the elections, Emil addressed the group concerning his $503,000 offer to purchase the brewery, stating that, "although he considered his offer liberal," nevertheless, he was willing to give the board of directors until June 20 to secure a higher bid for the property and assets.[247]

Since no improved bid was received by June 20, the corporation's attorneys drew up a contract two days later. It called for Emil to pay the stockholders in cash, stocks and bonds, and secured notes by September 1, 1926. Upon payment, the stockholders would transfer the assets to him. Emil financed his purchase with a $353,000 promissory note dated June 30, 1926, that he collateralized with $150,000 in U.S. Liberty bonds, $150,000 in his shares in the Oriental Investment Company, and 4,800 shares of the Miller Products Company. At a special Miller Brewery stockholders' meeting on September

2, 1926, Frank A. Miller explained to Fritz, Clara, and Elise that the corporation showed a surplus of $489,988. Ethical business practice dictated that Emil excuse himself from these discussions while the sale was pending. Soon thereafter, the stockholders declared a $5.00 per share dividend, totaling $230,250.[248]

Not surprisingly, Emil failed to meet his payment deadlines and, therefore, on December 15, 1926, the Miller Brewing Company's stockholders regained control of the brewing, bottling, and beverage business. In all likelihood, Emil never intended to buy the brewery and operate it, as it was not in his character to do so. Rather, he demonstrated to his reluctant siblings that the brewery was worth keeping and promoting. In a manner of speaking, Emil saved the brewery for the Millers, who reaped substantial financial gains after Prohibition's repeal. Regrettably, Emil did not live to enjoy these rewards. By early 1927, the atmosphere at the brewery improved sufficiently to give the Millers hope and confidence that it would survive Prohibition. The chief reason that the Millers became more optimistic was that Frank Miller had taken over the brewery's management from Kleinboehl. The transition from a lackluster manager to one who communicated well with the Millers, while promoting their vision, reinvigorated them and gave them hope for its future.

During a stockholders' meeting on January 8, 1927 at the family residence at 3200 Highland Boulevard, the family unanimously agreed to liquidate the Miller Brewing Company, then named the Fred Miller Brewing Company. Upon dissolution, the brewery had outstanding stock worth $4.6 million. The liquid assets were distributed to the stockholders and the plant and non-liquid items were sold to the Miller Products Company. The result of failing to sell the brewery except to an existing stockholder, who eventually reneged on his contract, led the stockholders to reorganize the business. They permanently separated the brewery operation from the Oriental Investment Company. Miller Products Company would become their primary brewing corporation since it owned most of the brewing assets. On February 17, 1927, the stockholders changed the Miller Products Company's name to the Miller High Life Company. It was natural for them to use the words High Life in the appellation because it was the only brand name that they were currently selling.[249]

Ernest's death gave Fritz the opportunity to assume a larger role with the family and the brewery. He was well prepared for his role at the brewery, having been its second-in-command since 1888; nevertheless, he was not a natural leader. He preferred to assist the president rather than stand in the limelight. Throughout his adulthood, Fritz assumed whatever business position was appropriate depending on the situation, including the presidency, but he was most content as the second fiddle. After Ernest died, Fritz supported his younger siblings while they took turns serving as brewery president. Fritz was a fastidious worker with the same dedication to the brewery as his older brother. Fritz was not always appreciated for his efforts. On June 24, 1930, he noted to his sister, Clara, "I can hereby see how much you appreciate my services and in gratification thereof I will in the future ask for pay as my services are so little considered. I gave my services in the past without compensation for the benefit of the family [regarding his father and mother's estates], and have neglected my personal affairs to attend to brewery work."[250]

As an adult, Fritz focused on the brewery, his wife, and his Catholic faith. "Of a quiet, reserved nature, Mr. Miller engaged in little activity outside the brewing business."[251] Ironically, the physically frail Fritz survived his teenage illnesses to live a longer life than his healthier brothers. He had a glass eye and was so embarrassed by it and his skeletal appearance that he avoided photographic opportunities. Nevertheless, to his associates and subordinates, "he was a person extremely kind and considerate." He was a gentle man who was happiest watching others enjoy themselves. Fritz was very thin, with loose joints, and while sitting with his legs crossed both of his shoes were flat on the ground. At times, his colitis (an inflammation of the intestine) caused him problems and may have led to his perennial gaunt-ness. His great niece, Anita McCahey Gray said that he was a kind-hearted man who was fond of engaging his nephews and nieces and their children.

Fritz and May's investments in 1918 equaled $2 million, with most of it held in family-owned businesses and munici-pal bonds. Fritz and May were awash with cash after recently receiving an $804,000 cash dividend from the Miller Brewing Company. At this time, Fritz took a hiatus from work to build a substantial home on farmland that he purchased in 1916, on the eastern-most shore on Lake Nagawicka, about 25 miles west of Milwaukee. Previously, he and his wife, May, had sum-mered at the Hoffman Cottages at Pewaukee Lake. Fritz put a lot of his time and energies into making this sizeable property an attractive place. This amateur botanist was a gracious host, entertaining his mother, siblings, and nephews and nieces on the sizeable spread on Lake Nagawicka that by 1918 was valued at $20,000. On his lake estate he could be found most summer afternoons, "planting, pruning, and casting fond looks upon his spruces." If there was anywhere a spruce of a shade in color, shape of branches or texture of bark that was not on his property, he wanted to hear of it.[252] His 1918 federal tax return noted no profession; rather, he was content to live at his new home with his wife May, while passively collecting $62,500 from interest, mortgages, and bonds. He had expenses for grading the road, outfitting the house, wiring the garage, installing a culvert, and home insurance.[253]

In 1919, the retiring Fritz enjoyed a net worth of $2.1 mil-lion while, monthly, giving May $200 to $400 for spending. Not all of Fritz's investments were successful as he claimed an $11,000 loss after selling Racine Manufacturing Company stock. In December of 1926, Fritz and May were living and receiving mail at their Nagawicka Lake house. In March of 1927, Fritz and May took a long vacation at the Arlington Hotel in Hot Springs, Arkansas. That same year, they also bought a $318 radio to pass the evenings. Fritz Miller was deeply religious and made various donations to Catholic causes.

For instance, he gave $350 for the St. Rose Parish Building Fund. He also gave $500 to a Chicago Benedictine Convent for Perpetual Adoration. It was not uncommon for Catholics to make these gifts to cloistered orders that would pray for the donor's special requests.[254]

In 1930, Fritz and May built a spectacular three-story home at 6300 Washington Circle in Wauwatosa's Washington Highlands, for $62,000. No doubt, Fritz wanted another residence apart from his troublesome brother, Emil, who also lived at 3200 Highland Boulevard. On June 24, 1930, Fritz reported to his sister, Clara, that for the past three years that he had lived in the Highland Avenue house, he had his, "nerves wrecked, and for the privilege, paid at the rate of $4500.00 per year for three months occupancy each year."[255] It is curious why this quiet, middle-aged, childless couple constructed such a large mansion. They spent only a few months a year there as they also lived in Florida and on Lake Nagawicka. The Washington Highland's seven-bedroom home currently sits on two lots and was fitted with a gothic-style "M" for Miller carved into the keystone of the porch. It was constructed of white, locally quarried limestone and crowned with a red tile roof. A molded tile, portraying St. George slaying the dragon, graced the back of the fireplace in the first floor parlor.

By 1920, Carl and Clara lived a comfortable existence while earning money from their brewery stock and lumber company. They had a mortgage-free mansion, sent their children to private schools, took yearly European vacations, enjoyed summers in lake homes, and belonged to local social clubs. For most of their adult lives, Carl was the lumber company's president and Clara its vice-president. By the mid-1890s, their lumber company that began in 1888 at 1st Avenue and East Street, had opened a West Side branch at 3002 West Lisbon Avenue that became their new headquarters. By 1906, they had closed the East Street location and opened two South Side branches, one at Becher and Clinton Streets that they called the Farmers' Lumber Yard, and another one at 725 Clinton Street. At this time, they advertised lath (thin boards), shingles, and posts, etc. By 1912, the Millers had renamed their business, from the Milwaukee Lumber Company to the Carl Miller Lumber Company, and employed Herman R. Boese as their corporate secretary. Boese also served as secretary for the Miller Brewery's enterprises.[256]

The February 28, 1949, *Milwaukee Journal* reported that in 1925 Carl organized a finance and investment company, the Carl Miller Company, for the development of residential property in Milwaukee and vicinity. Carl built many attractive apartment buildings on Milwaukee's northeast side. Not later than 1927, Carl and Clara Miller had opened their lumberyard's final location at 2nd Street and Hampton Avenue on Milwaukee's northeast side. By 1930, they had moved their headquarters there and closed their other yards. This same year, the Millers lived with their son Frederick, 23, and their daughter Charlotte, 19, in their $100,000 home on Newberry Boulevard. The Millers had a cook, Ottilie Schulz, 34, and a maid, Elizabeth Sauer, 28, living upstairs.[257]

Carl's grandsons, brothers Chuck and Frederick Miller Bransfield, who worked at the family lumberyard, explained that their grandfather was a taskmaster. They were expected to remain busy, even performing make-work tasks such as picking weeds, in the lumberyard lot on hot summer days. Their lessons were buttressed with barked commands smothered in a German accent. His granddaughter Joan Bransfield, who remembered Carl's gentler side, listened to stories on his lap while watching him open his pocket watch for her to hear its enchanting chime.

Clara, called Mama by her children and grandchildren, was wealthy but, according to her granddaughter Gail Miller Wray, was not an aristocratic socialite. Milwaukee's wealthy socialites never warmed to Clara who would not cater to their high-class mores. Rather, her priorities were her children, grandchildren, and then great-grandchildren. Clara regularly ate dinner at the Deutscher Club (now the Wisconsin Club) and was a member of the women's Rosebud Card Club, which met weekly at one another's houses. Clara loved to flirt with men and, at parties, would find the comeliest man, make a beeline for him, and then dominate their conversation with an ebullient manner. Chuck Bransfield noted that Clara could hold her bourbon better than anyone, and if dancing was part of the program she cavorted until the last note faded from the violins.

Emil Miller was the youngest of Fred and Lisette's three sons and, arguably, the most intelligent of the children. He received superior grades at St. Joseph Parish School and Marquette Academy. Of the Miller boys, he had the liveliest personality and relished pursuing new interests, especially music. Emil was 11 years old and finishing sixth grade in 1888 when his father died.

Emil probably suffered from bipolar disorder; a mental illness that, slowly over time, caused him to fluctuate between manic highs and paralyzing lows. There is no official diagnosis extant regarding Emil's bipolar disorder. Any mental disease besides alcoholism is suggested by the author. Individuals afflicted with bipolar disorder have a difficult time maintaining a stable lifestyle. They can swing between a messianic complex, able to fix all the world's ills, to being emotionally paralyzed in their room wishing for death. Of course, there are varying levels of this illness. Emil discovered that massive amounts of alcohol could help him escape temporarily from this painful cycle. Today, psychotropic medicines can mitigate its symptoms. Unfortunately, the consumption of copious amounts of alcohol caused him other problems. It is unclear when he first manifested bipolar disorder and whether he ever was treated for a mental illness. Nevertheless, he received numerous treatments for alcoholism. Aside from Emil's restless spirit, he was a kind-hearted man who was loved for his sweet demeanor. Before his diseases ravaged him, he was a gregarious man who made friends easily; his self-destructive path, therefore, was all the more painful for his family and friends.

The clean-shaven Emil found pleasure in mundane activities and brought good cheer to others. He had a penchant for writing poetry in German and some samples remain. Early in his adult life, he was an energetic fellow who saw opportunity where others saw despair; exuded energy where his brothers, often, were more lethargic. Emil's grandnephew, Charles Bransfield, noted that his mother, Anita Miller Bransfield, regarded her uncle Emil as great fun and enjoyed socializing with him. In several photographs, Emil and Anita, adult uncle and 8-year-old niece, are represented politely posing together. Chuck also noted Emil's impulsivity that showed itself soon after February 26, 1906, when Emil's nephew Frederick C. Miller was born. Previously, Frederick's parents, Clara and Carl Miller, had traveled to Rome to beseech the pope for a son, since the couple already had four girls. The Millers were granted their request when Frederick was born. When Emil came to the house to congratulate his sister and saw the baby boy he remarked that, indeed, their prayers were answered; they had been blessed with a baby as ugly as the pope.

Emil used his imaginative skills to accomplish his goals. Family raconteur Chuck Bransfield related that in the late 1940s, while working for Miller Brewery as a Wisconsin beer salesman, he had entered a bar in Green Bay, Wisconsin, and queried the owner on his business prospects. As the owner spoke, Chuck noticed that the establishment was dominated with Miller products and advertising pieces. After asking the owner how this came to be, the proprietor noted that thirty years earlier, his bar was beholden to another brewery until a Miller salesman appeared in a horse carriage, well-heeled, and escorting two comely lasses. This man asked the owner why the bar did not have Miller beer, to which the keeper gave the traveler an unacceptable answer.

Promptly, and without warning, the Miller representative began smashing the bar's paraphernalia with his metal-tipped cane. The startled owner watched, with mouth agape, at the demolition. After some minutes of destruction, the salesman stopped and caught his breath. Then, he reached into his vest pocket and withdrew a Miller Brewery checkbook, subsequently writing out a check for $5,000, which greatly exceeded the costs of the damage. The salesman, who was Emil Miller, noted tersely that, from that day forward, the saloon would serve Miller Beer and none other. The chuckling bar owner told Charles Bransfield that due to Emil's imaginative sales approach, ever since, the establishment had served Miller Brewery's products.

The 1919 onset of Prohibition provided Emil with a new world to explore. He came, money in billfold, lit cigar in mouth, bowler hat on head, and cane in hand to hotels, speakeasies and roadhouses; gambling, buying liquor, and indulging in prostitutes. Occasionally, Emil would gamble ceaselessly, and lose, daily for a month and a half straight. Emil's gambling losses were an expensive means for him to maintain human contact after he had alienated his family and previous friends. He spent many nights in Milwaukee's finest downtown hotels such as the Plankinton, St. Charles, Pfister, Jefferson, and Schroeder gambling with countless Milwaukeeans.

Chuck Bransfield related an episode that took place in Chicago in the early 1920s. Mont Tennes, the Windy City's gambling titan, had kidnapped Emil for not paying $25,000 in gambling debts. Emil pleaded with his family to rescue him by fulfilling his obligation. Chuck noted that the Milwaukee Millers were so exasperated with Emil and his behavior that a week passed before they decided to pay the balance.

At the same time as Emil's late 1920s infamous news coverage, his sister Clara's son Frederick C. Miller was garnering positive publicity for his exploits on the gridiron at the University of Notre Dame. In 1928, one could read about Emil's exploits on page one of a newspaper and then in the same issue peruse an item on Fred's selection to a football all-star team. Stories of Emil's exploits shocked the generally staid Millers and, even today, reverberate among them.

In 1894, Emil, 18, began to work at the brewery as a manager. By 1895, he was in charge of the bottling department and later moved into the bookkeeping department. In 1900, he listed himself as the brewery's manger and six years later he had become the brewery's secretary/treasurer.[258] In 1919, Emil received a $5,000 salary from the Miller Brewing Company and had $2.4 million in assets. As Ernest and Fritz aged, they looked to the energetic Emil for relief. He was the president of Miller Brewery as early as 1919. In this period, all of the Millers took turns fulfilling the president's seat of all of their corporations while hired managers ran the companies. For a long period before alcoholism consumed his life, Emil was an active participant in the family's finances and businesses. For instance, in 1912 he attended board meetings at the Racine Manufacturing Company, in which the Millers owned stock. After the meeting he wrote lucid reports of the affair. Sometime in the middle 1920s Emil lost control of his drinking, ruining his relationship with his siblings. He endured countless lectures and threats from his family and friends. In the 1920s in order to get away from his "overseers," he lived infrequently at the Highland Avenue house, and, instead, resided most of his time in hotels throughout the Midwest. For instance, on September 29, 1921, he was receiving mail at the Webster Hotel in Chicago.[259]

Anybody who could keep Emil away from his own money did so. On September 29, 1921, Ernest Miller, as Lisette's estate executor, began sending checks of $74,264 to each of his siblings, except for Emil. Instead of giving funds directly to the 45-year-old carouser, Ernest transferred the money into another account over which he and Oscar F. Treichler had some control.[260]

After Ernest's 1925 death, the remaining Miller children pressed Treichler to help extricate Emil from his periodic disasters. Ernest's death brought Emil a financial windfall when his estate was distributed among his survivors. Beginning in September 1927, Emil Miller began receiving his portion of his brother's estate. At this time, they excluded him from any elected or chosen position at the brewery. Oscar Treichler managed Emil's $3 to $4 million portfolio and, yearly, meted out $100,000 to him, exclusive of his profligate spending sprees. Apparently when sober, Emil was rather cooperative with his Milwaukee handlers and appreciated their assistance. Ernest

Rahtjen, Emil's personal secretary and assistant secretary of the Milo Beverage Company, termed his boss, "a spendthrift when he was drinking but a frugal man sober, who lived modestly between his sprees." When drinking, either Treichler or Rahtjen would follow the poor soul, figuratively and literally, to protect him and, subsequently, repair his financial messes. Rahtjen testified that when Emil would return from a trip he would ask Rahtjen how much money he had spent. "Then he would instruct me to pay out the money." Rahtjen said that, "When he [Emil] was sober, he was eccentric and of a suspicious mind. He didn't stay sober long enough to be competent to handle his affairs." Though, "At times, his mind was clear."[261]

Two of Emil Miller's unofficial handlers were Charles Serio, a.k.a. Charles Nelson, a nightclub operator and Joseph J. Bove. They provided Emil with food and drink upon his request. Rahtjen admitted that, "Miller preferred Serio and Bove to others." They remained at Emil Miller's "beck and call," living with him for long periods at local and out-of-town hotels. Supposedly, Emil paid them $100,877 for clothing and shelter valued at no more than $10,000. Reportedly, Serio was the general manager of Emil's pleasure excursions and Serio paid the bills. Additionally, they drank and played cards with him at his request. They also performed numerous personal services relating to his physical comfort, such as nursing him and giving him alcohol rubs.[262]

At this time, Emil was living with three female servants and lavish furnishings, rent-free in his deceased mother's house. After Emil squandered his monthly remuneration, he looked for ways to get more money for his activities. Beyond his yearly $100,000 stipend, money for these other activities were $109,000 in 1929, $64,000 in 1930, $69,000 in 1931, $87,000 in 1932, $79,000 in 1933, and $85,000 in 1934.[263]

To fund his sprees, Emil used blank checks and I.O.U.s [promissory notes]. He realized that his name was worth several million dollars and that his trustee, Oscar Treichler, and financial institutions, like the First Wisconsin National Bank, the City Bank, the Marshall and Ilsley Bank, and the 16th Ward

State Bank were legally obligated to redeem his checks and I.O.U.s. Many of the checks that Emil wrote did not have his bank's name or identifying numbers until he created them and his I.O.U. was scrawled on any ready scrap of paper. Sometimes when severely inebriated, he would fill out promissory notes with a shaky hand that produced words like a 7-year-old's scribbling. When he was sloppily drunk, others would fill out his checks and I.O.U.s and he would sign them with Emil P. Miller, E. P. Miller, or simply E.P. M. His banks eventually tried to slow his spending by requiring his countersignature, along with the payee, on the back of every check. After returning from another trip of profligate spending and then sobering up, Emil would meet with Rahtjen to decide which of his I.O.U.s should be honored.[264]

In December 1928, Emil, with the help of his attorney, wrote a form letter with blank areas to fill in any name to help defend himself against his numerous I.O.U.s:

TO WHOM IT MAY CONCERN:-
This is to certify that on or about December 5th, 1928, some person, whose name I do not at present remember exerted undue influence over me and to the best of my knowledge, information and belief, for some fraudulent purpose, persuaded me to sign my name on a blank piece of paper.

Also, Emil frequented the Waukesha County Blue Mound Road House, the Golden Pheasant, and Sam Pick's Club Madrid, examples of rural establishments that catered to people desiring gambling, imbibing, and visiting prostitutes. These activities were difficult to offer consistently in large municipalities under the omnipresent, yet, uneven eye of urban law enforcement.

By December 1928, Emil was estranged from his friends and family and enjoying Milwaukee's illegal nightlife, while encountering opportunistic toughs and scammers in those places. Emil and two week-old Milwaukee acquaintances, Charlie Metrie, a former pugilist and gymnasium manager, and Frank Scaler, a restaurateur who had been convicted of a liquor violation, decided to travel to a health spa in French Lick, Indiana, for seven days. This escape was not uncommon for Emil and the other Millers, who liked to soak in the warm springs to assuage their ills. At this time, it was probable that Emil left Milwaukee to escape dangerous underworld characters, who were threatening to hurt him if he did not continue to pay off his gambling losses. In fact by mid-1927, Emil and his siblings were sufficiently concerned for his safety that they hired Thomas McAneny and Colonel Hunter to accompany him on his sprees. Although at times, such as this proposed trip to Indiana, Emil eluded them.[265]

Their adventure was sidetracked in Chicago at the Morrison Hotel where they engaged an expensive suite and started a party. At this time, Chicago was awash with speakeasies, gambling establishments, and prostitutes. Predictably, Metrie and Scaler engaged him in an interminable dice game. Soon, the pitiful, besotted Emil was helpless and, daily, $1,600 left his billfold. Quickly, he was broke and resorted to writing three $1,300 checks to keep the party going. Metrie and Scaler were greedy for more cash, so Metrie drove to Milwaukee and, expecting immediate payment, presented the checks to Emil's personal secretary, Ernest Rahtjen, who refused to comply.[266]

Rahtjen called the Milwaukee Police Department for help. Detective Arthur Burns tailed Metrie to the Chicago hotel and its revelers. Upon discovering evidence of alcohol consumption, gambling, and whoring, Officer Burns enlisted Chicago's finest to break up the gathering. One hopes that Emil was not surprised when a police officer discovered two pair of loaded dice in the pockets of one of Emil's "jolly good fellows." The delusional Emil told Milwaukee Detective Burns, "Give me a Schnapps and take me home." And, "I'll stay home and behave thereafter." The whole gaggle was escorted to the police station where Rahtjen convinced the officers of Emil's innocence due to his alcoholism and asked him to be released to his care. Also, the public defenders may have been moved by Rahtjen's story that, eight months previous in Chicago, Emil had been fleeced of $92,000 by "Big Tim" Murphy who also used a pair of loaded dice. Immediately thereafter, Rahtjen placed Emil on a train bound for Dwight, Illinois, the home of the Keeley cure. William L. White in his book, *Slaying the Dragon: The History of Addiction Treatment and Recovery in America*, noted that the Keeley Institutes were a hugely successful chain of privately owned miracle cure centers purveying injections of a secret formula allegedly based on chlorides of gold that supposedly removed the desire to drink alcohol or use drugs. The formula was later shown to be placebo. Nevertheless, the Keeley Institutes helped many thousands of alcoholics achieve long-term abstinence. Meanwhile, Emil's two accomplices, while complaining vigorously, were held in Chicago cells without charges to allow the fleeced one a head start to get away from them.[267]

The Keeley cure was unsuccessful and, two months later on February 11, 1929, Emil returned to Chicago. There were two reasons that Emil enjoyed reveling in Chicago. First, it was a center of unfettered illegal fun, far out-shadowing Milwaukee's ability to entertain. Enough politicians looked aside that saloons and gambling establishments operated openly, serving the anonymous and famous alike. Secondly, Emil may have wanted to spare his family the embarrassment of his behavior and had the mistaken belief that if he cavorted in a city ninety miles from his home he could do so in relative obscurity.

After a short stay in Milwaukee, Emil took another area-wide romp visiting inns and speakeasies in Wisconsin municipalities such as Madison, Marinette, Fond du Lac, and Pewaukee. He also returned to Chicago and French Lick, Indiana. For instance, on February 17, 1929, Emil Miller was at Chicago's Congress Hotel where he had gone, primarily to gamble and secondarily to drink and frolic with prostitutes. Emil, with his rapidly disappearing cash and a supply of blank checks, was determined to paint Chicago red. Soon after the brewery executive made clear his interest in distributing his money, new "friends" coalesced around him. Men explained to Emil that they could show him the best gaming establishments in town while, simultaneously, protecting him from thugs. Women appeared, some who lived in these hotels, to pleasure Emil and his friends for money and gifts. The hotel management gladly, though illegally, procured alcoholic drinks that often they disguised on their invoices as grape juice or ginger ale.

The Milwaukee Millers and their dutiful assistant Oscar Treichler were exasperated with their inability to keep Emil from leaving on yet another dangerous binge. They hired Chicago Attorney John J. Sonsteby at 19 LaSalle Street, who in turn engaged the Edward J. Hargrave Secret Service Company with offices in Chicago and St. Louis. In 1929, the Hargrave Company billed itself as having forty-two years of experience in detective work. Attorney Sonsteby asked them if, for their daily $15 fee, they could shield Emil from being physically harmed or arrested; two probable occurrences.[268]

Immediately, the Hargrave Agency put agent Anton Maunitsen on Emil's case to monitor the brewery executive unobtrusively. When the conditions became overly dangerous or expensive, the "private dick" would spring into action. Mautinson could not be overly intrusive because Emil would have slipped away and the agency would have lost a good client but, conversely, he needed to be sufficiently involved to satisfy Treichler, who was paying the invoices and to whom the agency reported. Anton Mautinson stayed with Emil for 45 days through a panoply of fantastic adventures. Imagine his job description: trail and stay engaged with a pleasant, wealthy man who is intent on spending his way into the poorhouse while drinking, gambling, and carousing.[269]

An example of Emil and his guest's expenses for a single day was: $1.25 for barber service (at that time, it was common for men to have a daily barber shave), $14 for whiskey, $9.90 for breakfast and dinner for Emil and two of his girlfriends, $6.50 for cigars and tips for the cigar girls, $15 for the singer, piano player, and officer at the Beau Monde Lounge, and lastly $40 for two women for entertainment.[270]

By mid-March 1929, while still in the Windy City, the overweight and overwrought Emil was spending one to four thousand dollars daily for gambling, living, and prostitutes whom he was changing as one changes pants; paying $100 to $1,000 for their services. On March 12, George Hargrave, of the Chicago-based, Hargrave Secret Service, reported to Oscar Treichler that, "Dr. Jetty, of Commissioner Kegel's office, said that if Emil did not come out of this drunk before very long, he would go blind and have delirium tremens."[271] This 1929 *fiesta* progressed from mid-February into early June with one of Emil's "friends," daily sending his party two new prostitutes. Catherine, Corene, Ella, Elsie, Frances, Harriet, Helen, Jean, Margaret, Marion, Viola, and Virginia to name some, took their place at Emil's side and collected a considerable I.O.U. for their service.[272]

On June 3, Emil went to South Bend, Indiana, to support his nephew, Frederick C. Miller, who had just graduated cum laude from the University of Notre Dame. This side trip interrupted Emil's extended fling and had a profound effect on the emotionally and physically exhausted reveler because, on June 5, 1929, the binge ended and he returned to Milwaukee. Thereafter, the guards, bookkeepers, and lawyers did their best to repair the damage and keep the characters, with their I.O.U.s, from coming to Milwaukee and pleading their cases to the brewery or to Emil's siblings. The Hargrave Agency collected the checks and I.O.U.s from Emil's "friends" and negotiated lower payments while, simultaneously, procuring legal releases from them. Chicago citizens, rich and poor alike, had their pocketbooks enlarged by this spendthrift brewery executive who left stories to last generations.

Elise, then 32, married 37-year-old Harry G. John, Sr. on June 18, 1912, which was the first and only marriage for both of them. Even though Harry's father, Frederick John, was a prominent Milwaukee medical doctor, his untimely death in 1892 left his wife and eight children with moderate means by the time Harry married. As an employee, stockholder, and loan guarantor of the failing Milwaukee Motor Company, Harry brought only debts into the marriage. The Milwaukee

Motor Company manufactured car engines. Harry's brother, Charles, started the company, which also built the Stutz engine that experienced success at early Indianapolis auto races.[273] Despite his debt in the company, Harry convinced his new brother-in-law, Ernest, to invest in this endeavor. In October of 1912, four months after Harry and Elise's wedding, Ernest guaranteed a $10,700 note in the Motor Company that Harry and his brother, August, owned. In the spring of 1913, it went bankrupt, at which time, Ernest helped out his sister by hiring Harry at the Miller Brewing Company at a $2,500 salary. Eventually, Harry became Miller's city sales manager. Ernest spent years trying to regain his money or, at least, deducting it from his taxes. No doubt, Elise was embarrassed by her husband's actions, which brought difficulty to her brother Ernest. This business transaction surely caused some moments of angry discourse among the Millers or, at a minimum, stretches of unpleasant silence.[274]

After their nuptials, Elise managed the household and did not work outside of the home until much later when she became an active officer of her family's brewery. On September 7, 1913, while the Johns lived at 277 29th Street (in the city's former numbering system), their daughter Lorraine was born. That same year, Elise had an income of $4,108 that came exclusively from interest. The bookkeepers noted both mortgage income and cash account revenue as interest. In 1914, the Johns paid taxes on the combined income of interest and salary of $15,800 and Miller Brewery dividends of $25,000. On April 21, 1915, the Johns bought a house at 3215 West Highland Boulevard, across the street from Elise's mother Lisette, for $19,143. In 1916, they collected a substantial $800,000 in Miller Brewery dividends and received $11,860 in interest. At this time, they owned residential income properties in New York, Chicago, and Milwaukee, which Ernest and their bookkeeper, Oscar Treichler, had purchased for them. In 1918, Harry received a $3,600 salary as Miller's manager of city sales, while the couple had an additional $46,433 in interest income.[275]

On December 12, 1919, the Johns welcomed their second

and last child, Harry "Buddy" George John, Jr. They had $1.8 million in assets, mostly in bonds and mortgages. In 1920, the year that Prohibition was enacted, Harry maximized his income at $4,200, while their investments brought in only $16,548, primarily from interest. It is clear that Elise and Harry's income fluctuated wildly, year to year, but thanks to Oscar Treichler, who contained their spending, they lived comfortably on a stable allowance. February 28, 1921 saw Harry's last day as a Miller employee or as an employee—period. It is unknown why he was terminated. At age 46, he was either released due to the effects of Prohibition, or behaved in a way that forced his brothers-in-law to fire him. Harry never again worked for a salary. His philandering ways possibly crossed Ernest and Fritz, who would have supported their baby sister. Whatever the reason, Elise's substantial assets precluded any financial reason for Harry ever to reenter the work force.[276]

In 1922, the Johns' investments brought in $28,000 of which $25,500 was interest income. Also, Elise deducted $149 in donations to Catholic causes, namely St. Rose Parish, the Archdiocese of Milwaukee, and St. Charles Boys' Home. As her donations became known, she was besieged with numerous bequests and by 1925 gave $382 to nineteen primarily Catholic causes. By 1931, she gave $4,120 to thirty-one organizations. Concurrently, Harry made a few donations to Missouri Synod Lutheran organizations, the faith of his childhood. The Johns' home or the Sacred Heart Sanitarium, where Elise occasionally lived, had a constant queue of priests, nuns, and family friends socializing with her. While Elise made many donations, she never came close to tithing.[277]

In 1924, the Johns earned $63,018 of which $61,808 was derived from dividends from the Miller Brewing Company, Fred Miller Heirs, and the Oriental Investment Company (a Miller owned company). On September 21, 1925, Elise's oldest brother Ernest died, leaving a considerable estate. In 1926, the Johns' portfolio became more complicated as Fred Miller Heirs was dissolved, providing them with a lump sum of $1.5 million. The basis of this stock dissolution was $1.2 million leaving them with a taxable income of $300,000. Other income equaled $144,000. These increases gave them a net worth of $2,353,050. In 1926, Elise and Harry were living on $2,000 to $4,000 a month, which is $20,000 to $40,000 at today's prices, for out-of-pocket expenses because their bookkeepers paid most of their bills with checks.[278] Even though Elise brought all of the money into the marriage, the Johns co-signed these cash checks, so they both knew how much of an allowance they were receiving. Presumably, the Johns used this allowance for expenses that they did not want tracked by their bookkeepers such as, entertainment, gifts to friends, and hunting supplies. In 1927 the Johns, with a net worth of $3,573,453, continued to summer on Waukesha County's Beaver Lake where, that year, they built a shed for 7-year-old Buddy's pony and cart. They motored there in either their Cadillac or Lincoln automobiles.[279]

In 1928, they realized $176,000 in interest income and real estate sales, which gave them a growing net worth of $4,061,892 or $44 million at today's prices.[280] Also, they had Irene Doberstein living with them as their housekeeper. That same year, they received from Ernest Miller's estate, 13.33 shares in the Miller Products Company valued at $1,667 and 2,960 shares of Oriental Realty stock valued at $429,844. At this time, the Johns were still living at 3215 West Highland Boulevard. Highland had been a splendid street for Milwaukee's German-American elite, but the automobile had made suburban living more feasible and Milwaukeeans were beginning to leave these exclusive urban neighborhoods. Harry was enamored with Milwaukee's East Side and on June 5, over Elise's objections, purchased vacant land for $84,000 on Milwaukee's exclusive Lake Drive in order to build a mansion. On March 19, 1930, Harry bought an adjoining lot for approximately the same amount. In 1930, they paid the Milwaukee architect Richard Philip $7,431 to create a set of drawings for Santhe proposed residence. After various false starts, the Johns decided against building this home. In 1929, the Johns, with a net worth of $4,434,983, bought farmland for $10,042 in Arizona, presumably for builing a winter home. The Johns fell in love with Arizona after their extended trips there, beginning in 1926, which they took with their son, Buddy, because of his scarlet fever and subsequent case of asthma. They never built anything on these two properties. On July 2 of that year, the Johns bought a house and land, for $25,000, on Oconomowoc Lake in Waukesha County, and immediately, made use of it. Additionally, Elise splurged on a $15,067 diamond and pearl necklace.[281]

In 1930, Elise's brother, Emil, continued his extraordinary rate of carousing in Milwaukee and Chicago hotels. At this time, he was losing a considerable sum in card games with con artists. Concurrently for a year or two, Elise's monthly cash allowance grew from $2,000 to almost $8,000. No doubt, she was giving Emil money to fulfill his gambling debts that often he owed to dangerous men. Emil had sufficient assets to afford his lifestyle, but Oscar Treichler made it difficult for him to get cash, and also tried to discredit many of Emil's scrawled I.O.U.s that he used as currency. In at least one long-distance call from Chicago, Emil begged his younger sister to give him cash to extricate him from his difficult plight.[282]

The year 1931 found the Johns enjoying three cars: a 1929 Ford sedan, a 1930 Cadillac sedan, and a 1930 Cadillac coupe. In November the Johns, with a $4.9 million net worth, gave their nephew, Frederick C. Miller, and his wife, Adele, a $200 wedding gift. The Johns owned two homes that needed considerable upkeep, for which they occasionally used maintenance workers from Miller Brewery while Oscar Treichler dutifully charged them for these services. The couple had four domestic employees: their cook, Rosa Eisenman, who earned $1,000 per year plus room and board; their housekeeper, Agnes Sternig, who earned $524 plus room and board; their chauffer, Clarence Schermeister, who earned $110 per week; and their gardener, Clarence Shannon, who received $120 a month plus free room and board for his wife and himself at the Oconomowoc Lake property's caretaker house. In 1933, the Great Depression dramatically depressed consumer prices and moved the Johns to decrease their servants' incomes by approximately 10%. This action was petty considering that the Johns earned $156,000 that year or $2.2 million at today's prices.[283] At that time, the Johns started giving their twenty-year-old daughter, Lorraine, a $150 monthly allowance where previously she received money as needed. They also bought a new Cadillac V16 Roadster Sedan for $4,885. During this period, the Johns' portfolio grew dramatically and they began to enjoy the fruits of the additional money. It seems ironic that their net worth doubled during Prohibition, but it reflects the Miller family system of careful money management and wise diversification of assets.[284]

On June 2, 1929, Frederick C. Miller graduated from the University of Notre Dame and immediately began working at his family's lumberyard, from which his 66-year-old father had been trying to retire for 20 years. Fred Miller quickly assumed the company's leadership from his father who finally could withdraw knowing that the family business was in good hands.

At Country Day High School, Fred had become acquainted with Clarence H. "Razz" Rasmussen, a physical education teacher and the first coach for the football program that had begun in 1920. Razz became a major influence in Fred's life and the two grew close culminating in this handsome, youthful coach being the best man at Fred's 1931 wedding. Obviously, Razz saw talent and drive in the raw-boned young man who, literally and figuratively, stood head and shoulders above his teammates. A photo of Fred's baseball team in his junior or senior year shows him, in the top row, looming over his mates.

Razz was a physical fitness guru and, along with Fred's father, passed this habit to Fred. During summers, Razz operated the all-male Red Arrow Camp of sports at Woodruff in northern Wisconsin. Chuck Bransfield, Fred's nephew, reported that, at this camp, his uncle grew strong and confident in his athletic ability. The rustic surroundings where the boys swam, boated, and hiked melded with weightlifting and running to make tanned, ambitious athletes. In later years, Fred returned as a counselor.

Fred enjoyed curious challenges. In the summer of 1928,

Fred, Razz, and Bob Pieper, a Country Day alumnus, were camping on Basswood Lake in Canada. One day, Fred and Bob were fishing from a boat while Razz stayed on the shore. Suddenly, one of the boaters hooked a feisty 40-pound lake trout, a rarity at that size. The pole was strung with light line that was in danger of breaking when Fred disrobed, grabbed a knife, and jumped into the cold water. Fred killed the fish and then, instead of returning to the boat, put it under his arm and swam to shore. On another occasion "up north," Doc Feiseler of the University of Iowa removed an imbedded fishhook from Fred's back while he placidly munched on an apple. Razz was amazed stating, "I have never seen such a fellow so unconcerned about physical pain. He just takes it."[285]

Frederick's scholastic and football prowess brought him to the attention of major college football schools such as the University of Wisconsin and the University of Notre Dame. In August 1925, Fred traveled to Notre Dame to begin a four-year term. Knute Rockne, Notre Dame's football coach, became Fred's third significant male mentor, following his father and Razz. Rockne had been a Notre Dame football player and 1914 *cum laude* graduate who successfully participated in the student newspaper and yearbook, played flute in the school orchestra, and had a major role in every student play. Obviously, Rockne saw something of himself in young Fred, an intelligent, self-motivated player who eagerly followed his directions. Rockne admired Fred's aplomb regarding his family's wealth. One evening during Fred's junior year, the coach gave a speech at a banquet in Whiting, Indiana, during which he bragged that money did not affect a player's status at any large Midwestern university. He added that, there was a boy on his own football team worth $5 million playing next to a lad paying for his own education. Rockne's statement, regarding the Miller's wealth, found its way into the newspapers and had the unintended effect of embarrassing Fred, who worked hard at being judged on his own merits, not his family's affluence.

Jack Elder, Fred's teammate, noted in an article written by Joe Doyle titled *Fred Miller—Hall of Famer*, in Notre Dame's

November 2, 1985 *Touchdown Illustrated Magazine*, that he could never remember Rock "getting" on Fred or being sarcastic about him. Elder remembered Fred as a perfectionist who also was physically tough. He noted that when Fred blocked and tackled, "he did it right." In Fred's first year, he was a regular on the freshman team. Doyle wrote that in Fred's sophomore year, the 6 foot 1 inch, 195-pound scholar-athlete became a starter at left tackle, a rarity under Rockne, as the coach rarely started second-year players. Before an early October game in Minneapolis against Minnesota's Golden Gophers, the 220-pound Joe Boland broke his leg and Fred, number 44, substituted for him. Thereafter, he became a regular starter, playing both offense and defense, as did many players at that time. In February 1928 before his senior year, Fred was chosen team captain. Fred finished his fourth season by being named first-team All Western by Walter Eckersall and, then, first-team All American by Davis J. Walsh. He gained a posthumous honor in 1985, when he was inducted into the College Football Hall of Fame as a tackle.

The summer before his senior year, Fred, as he had every year, took a month out of his summer vacation and, with two teammates, participated in Razz's camp and then went to Canada for two weeks camping and fishing while toting their pigskin for impromptu practices.[286] His camp stay was a sabbatical from the multitude of distractions that he faced in Milwaukee, but also a respite from his demanding father who wanted his son, over the summer, to toil at the lumberyard. Furthermore, Fred's nieces and nephews each wanted to spend time with him, further distracting the footballer.

While at Notre Dame, often Fred and his roommate (and fellow footballer) John Law quietly did their school work while their dorm mates chatted and smoked in their rooms. His diligence was rewarded on June 2, 1929, when he graduated *cum laude*. His daughter Kate Kanaley Miller noted that her father, for many years, carried the highest grade-point average of anyone in the Notre Dame Monogram Club, an organization for athletes who lettered. Fred also had a light side, for instance he donned a foppish medieval costume, tights, and oversized hat included, for a December 1929 Milwaukee ball.

Eventually Knute Rockne became one of America's most esteemed coaches. As Rockne admired Fred, Fred admired Rockne, in later years, naming him as one of his heroes. In his thirteen-year Notre Dame head coaching tenure (1917 to 1930), the Fighting Irish won six national championships, the 1925 Rose Bowl, and played five unbeaten and untied seasons. Also, Rockne won the last nineteen games that he coached. Simultaneously while coaching, he served as Notre Dame's athletic director, business manager, ticket distributor, track coach, and equipment manager. On March 31, 1931, Rockne boarded Flight 599 from Kansas City to Los Angeles, to help make a football demonstration movie, when the plane flew into a storm, became covered with ice, and crashed into a wheat field near Bazaar, Kansas. There were no survivors.

After graduation, Fred may have toyed with the idea of playing professional football but his family's wealth and his father's advancing age precluded it. Although soon after graduating, he played in some Notre Dame "Irish" gridder all-star charity matches. The time had come for Fred to return to Milwaukee, to accept the role of bourgeoning city icon. Besides, the pay of professional football's in those days was a pittance compared to his family's wealth. Fred headed for his predetermined job, working at his father's lumberyard. The young man stated that Dad is, "beginning to look for someone to fill his shoes, and I'm after the job." According to Chuck Bransfield, Carl Miller had little regard for formal education and believed that the best learning came on the job, as he had received. Strangely, after laboring at a prestigious school, Fred shared this view, opining that books are one thing, real business another. He continued, "After you get out, you find out that while what you did was good, a lot of it was hokum."[287]

Beginning with his senior year at Country Day High School, Fred became a magnet for newspaper publicity that continued until his death. The *Milwaukee Journal* had anointed Fred, with his mother's urging, as a man to be tracked. There was a bright future for this man who was intelligent, athletic, handsome, well connected, and driven. The scads of articles, which grew in frequency until his death, seemed, at times, a daily chronicle of his life. Then for many years after his death, his widow, Adele Kanaley Miller, continued this public role. Fred's mother, Clara Miller, certainly encouraged this coverage. She underplayed herself, her husband, and her daughters, but her son best represented her father to her, thus making him worthy of considerable exposure. Besides, she believed that this coverage would give Fred an advantage when he began to work at Miller Brewery.

Fred, at 24 became romantically interested in 18-year-old Adele Kanaley of Winnetka, Illinois. She was the tall, elegant daughter of Kate Buddeke Kanaley and Byron Vincent Kanaley—a Notre Dame and Harvard Law School graduate and a founder of the Chicago bond and mortgage house Cooper, Kanaley & Company. Adele was bright, beautiful, and graceful—a genuine star. She had delightful round eyes, blond hair, a straight nose, and small mouth. She had a playful personality belying her sharp, inquisitive intellect. Their families had known each other for many years, as Fred's sisters had attended high school with Adele at the Convent of the Sacred Heart in Lake Forest, Illinois. Previous to the Sacred Heart Academy, Adele had attended Roycemore in Evanston, Illinois, and, subsequently, traveled to Philadelphia to matriculate at the Ogontz school. At times, Fred, looking for private time to court his sweetheart, asked his niece Anita McCahey to row them around Oconomowoc Lake away from his sisters' prying eyes. On May 31, 1931, Fred and Adele announced their engagement and August 22, 1931, wedding.

This engagement announcement began a long series of parties, held at private organizations like the Milwaukee Club and the Wisconsin Club, in which the Millers introduced the couple to Milwaukee's high society. The Kanaleys did the same in Winnetka. The Millers beamed with pride at their son's decision to marry a society girl, although, it took Clara years to accept Adele into her heart. In late July, Fred and Adele announced their attendants: Audrey Kanaley (Adele's sister) as the maid of honor, and Blanche Cooper; Charlotte Miller (Fred's sister); Mildred Lawrenze, Jean Jordan, Virginia Wiley, Helen Badham, Jessica Rankin, and Catherine Cyne as the bridesmaids. Clarence "Razz" Rasmussen was the best man while the ushers were: Herbert Hirschboeck (a Milwaukee attorney); Norman Ott, Layton Busby, Edward Keogh, Clayson Swallow, Bernard Blommer (Charlotte Miller's future husband), Allan J. Moore, and John "Jack" Chevigny (a teammate who later died on Iwo Jima).

On August 22, 1931, Adele, 20, and Fred, 25, married at Sacred Heart Parish in Winnetka, Illinois. This French gothic church that is tightly surrounded by spectacular homes in this wealthy northern Chicago suburb, dominates the block with its limestone façade and conspicuous corner bell tower. Years later Fred's daughter, Gail, in order to honor him, also married there. After the wedding, the Millers left from Los Angeles on a ship for a Honolulu honeymoon.

Fred and Adele Miller returned from their honeymoon to live at 4614 North Murray Avenue in Whitefish Bay, a suburb on Milwaukee's North Shore. Afterward, they lived in a succession of Milwaukee-area residences all built by his father. Eventually they moved into a year-round home at 50 Beach Road on Oconomowoc Lake. They had eight children: Claire in 1932, Frederick Carl "Freddy," Jr., in 1934, Loret in 1936, Kate in 1937, Marguerite "Gail" in 1939, Carlotta in 1940, Adele in 1942, and Carl Anthony in 1944.

Clara's doting on and pampering of Fred made her husband Carl jealous of their son and, throughout their life, Fred and his father vied for Clara's attention. Chuck and Frederick Miller Bransfield, (who were brothers and Fred's nephews), said that their uncle was headstrong and often disagreed with his father's suggestions. Once when Carl was on one of many trips to Germany, Fred bought a new Packard automobile, without his father's foreknowledge, and upon his return gave his Dad the invoice. Carl became enraged, yelling at Fred, but in the end he acquiesced and paid it.

Buddy John was born to Elise and Harry John on December 12, 1919. Just like his older cousins, Bud was raised in the Catholic Church, though not without difficulty. Before Buddy's second-grade First Holy Communion Mass, he inadvertently drank a glass of milk, which, due to the church's rules, prevented him from receiving Holy Communion. Frantically, Elise called the pastor who determined that Buddy would not walk down the aisle with his class to receive the host. Buddy was embarrassed by missing this event but happy for avoiding a mouth-full of soap from his devout mother.

On September 29, 1928, the 9-year-old Buddy was among New York Governor Al Smith's supporters as he campaigned for the presidency as a Democrat when suddenly he found himself in the campaigner's path. The Johns, especially Elise, had supported the first Catholic to run for president on a major ticket. Al Smith, during his and his wife's forty-two hour Milwaukee visit, pushed or rather urged Buddy aside as he worked the crowd. This incident was Buddy's sole boyhood brush with fame. On May 11, 1931 while in sixth grade, Buddy successfully was confirmed in the Catholic faith with his maternal uncle Frederick Andrew Miller as his sponsor. He took the name Frederick to honor him.

As a child, Buddy contracted various illnesses including, at age 9, a nearly lethal case of scarlet fever. Due to the Johns' substantial finances, they obtained the best Milwaukee-area doctors who nursed the boy back to health while, due to the prevailing medical wisdom, quarantining him from all but a few masked people and his pet dog. He was isolated on the second floor so that his family, while avoiding this dangerous disease, could live safely on the first floor.

Buddy had a life-long case of allergic reactions to airborne particulates, especially ragweed pollen, which later developed into asthma. As a young boy, he also suffered from a severe case of whooping cough. As an older adult he remarked that, due to his breathing difficulties, he could never remember having a restful night's sleep. Often he would sleep while sitting in a chair. Years earlier, the Johns were concerned about their son's respiratory ailments and tried various methods to cure them. As a young adult, he had a surgical procedure to drain his sinuses, which left a small permanent hole alongside his eye and he forever wore eyeglasses to conceal it.

Buddy's childhood bronchial ailments, including fearsome nighttime attacks when the 7-year-old boy could not breathe, brought the Johns to their wits' end and, as a last resort, they took him to Phoenix where the drier climate helped his respiration. The Johns left Lorraine at home with the family servants so she wouldn't miss school. The Johns enjoyed this multi-month trip while staying at the luxurious recently-opened Arizona Biltmore Hotel. They ate at fancy restaurants, rode horses, lounged poolside, and took side trips to the desert and the Alamo in San Antonio. Harry and Elise enjoyed the scenic desert and Buddy loved the pools, hikes, and horses. Due to the arid conditions and low pollen counts, his asthmatic symptoms subsided.

While in Arizona, Buddy and his parents sent notes to Lorraine describing their experiences. When they visited the Grand Canyon, Buddy had ridden two mules named Firecracker and Sparkplug and, after receiving a new cowboy suit, he fed scraps of bread to a mouse he named Jerry. Lorraine responded that she was keeping the fires warm on the home front and thanked Buddy for eating well and drinking milk while reminding him to help his middle-aged parents. After Wisconsin's frost lowered the pollen count, the Johns returned home to hugs, kisses, and dog barks.

The Johns worried about the young Buddy's introverted nature and urged him to become more confident and outgoing. To surmount this problem they encouraged boys such as Bill Miller, to play with him. They also talked to their adult friends and consulted medical and psychiatric doctors. Years later, Buddy told his friend John Rauch that, for a period when he was a teenager, his parents sent him, with their driver, on weekly visits to a Chicago psychiatrist. Unfortunately, these visits did not accomplish their aim of giving Buddy a more gregarious nature.

The Johns cosseted Buddy. For instance, they gave him a black pony named Beauty, which carried him or pulled him in a small cart. Buddy and his Milwaukee friends, such as Ethan and Otto Lemke, Peter SanFillippo, and Paul Wolf, played tag, football, and baseball. At times, Buddy approached the edge of being troublesome. On one occasion he and some pals lobbed a smoke bomb in a crowded streetcar and then scattered before being caught.

Sometimes Buddy's reticent nature caused him difficulties, such as one occasion, when some of the Highland neighborhood lads were gathering to play football on the nearby Concordia College campus and noticed that nobody had brought a ball. Peter SanFilippo, a neighborhood friend, remembered that one of the boys suggested, "Why don't we ask Buddy John to play because he has lots of new balls?" They walked to his house and knocked on his back door. Due to Buddy's many bouts with respiratory problems Elise discouraged his involvement in rough or energetic activities, but this time she acquiesced to his pleadings. He was excited to use his new football helmet, pads, ball, and pants and ran to gather them. The boys were surprised as Buddy stepped out with his new football, pads, spikes, and uniform, whereas, they had regular pants, no pads, and sweatshirts. After a few plays, Bud returned home, leaving the ball.

Buddy was a smart but not brilliant boy who moved from St. Rose Grade School to the exclusive all-male Country Day High School and then to the University of Notre Dame, graduating in 1941. At Country Day, Buddy competed in football, fencing, basketball, and baseball and finished in the middle of his class scholastically. The Johns sent him to Country Day to follow in his maternal cousin Fred Miller's shoes. Buddy's maternal uncles had attended Marquette University High School, which was across the street from St. Rose and near the John's home but, instead, Buddy attended Country Day which was some miles distant on Milwaukee's East Side. Fred Miller attended Country Day because it was highly regarded and near his home. Fred was a star scholar-athlete at Country Day and Notre Dame and Elise was determined that Buddy follow him. Unfortunately for Buddy, he was not as intelligent, motivated, or athletic as his much older cousin. In fairness to Buddy, most anyone would have paled in comparison to Fred.

In September 1937, amid the difficulties of the Great Depression and after spending a wonderful summer sailing on Oconomowoc Lake, Buddy arrived at Notre Dame's Cavanaugh Hall. Sophomore year saw him at Lyons Hall, junior year at Dillon Hall, and senior year at Alumni Hall. His college pal Frank McDonough recalled that, in that era of epidemic destitution, most Americans could not afford college tuition so post-secondary schools, such as Notre Dame, were delighted to have full-tuition paying students such as Buddy in attendance. It was not today's highly selective university.

At Notre Dame, Buddy had a Milwaukee friend, Valentine Blatz of the Blatz Brewery family, who had a personality similar to his. These taciturn daily communicants found opportunities to serve Mass at either the campus-centered Sacred Heart of Jesus main church or one of its many chapels. Soon, due to their serious natures, they got the reputation of being bores. Chuck Bransfield, Buddy's second cousin and fellow Notre Dame student said that Val went so far as to post a note on his dorm-room door outlining the days and hours during which he would be available to entertain guests. Some of the dorm toughs found this notice insulting and sought to intimidate Val. One autumn night these enforcers snuck into Val's room and jumped him, holding his mouth shut and limbs still. Silently they carried him from the dorm and across the campus to St. Mary's Lake into which they threw the panicked student. This incident resulted in the expulsion of these bullies. Before school started, Elise had asked Chuck Bransfield to protect her son, which was the primary reason Buddy did not follow Val into the lake that night. After completing Notre Dame, Val entered an eastern medical school. He died in 1950 from multiple sclerosis.

Buddy and a classmate, Frank McDonough, became friends

and Frank introduced Buddy to boxing. Frank invited Harry, Jr. to exercise with him at the gym where the 1932 Notre Dame graduate and physical education teacher, Dominic "Nappy" Napolitano, was managing the school's boxing program. Nappy took an interest in Buddy and encouraged him to return to work out with the other students.

Boxing became Buddy's salvation. Through this art he changed from a skinny nervous kid to an award-winning pugilist. Buddy relished the smell and atmosphere of the gym while Nappy gave instructive comments and visual demonstrations to the young men. The boxing program provided the second-rate athletes who did not play varsity football or basketball an opportunity to be on a team. Nappy taught Harry, Jr. to keep his elbows tight to his sides and punch straight. Buddy became a boxing aficionado (although years later he viewed it as an immoral sport) and toiled to improve his technique. Frank McDonough remembered that, over summer vacations, Buddy installed a makeshift outdoor boxing ring at his Oconomowoc home in order to spar with friends. Buddy also began to lift weights regularly, which produced a quick, strong, focused man with a good reach, primed to return to Nappy's gym.

During his sophomore and junior years Buddy John participated in the Bengal Bouts, an annual Notre Dame boxing tournament that awarded the winners campus and region-wide recognition. The name Bengal Bouts came about because the money earned from this tournament was sent to Catholic missions in Bengali, India. The winner fought through three eliminations before the final match, held before a large paying crowd at the field house. Buddy's sophomore year saw him lose a decision to Joe Frucci. Buddy succeeded his junior year and won the 155-pound weight class. Through boxing he received his first acclaim as his success was reported in the South Bend and Milwaukee newspapers. During his senior year, Buddy did not fight due to his pugilistic success and his psychological problems, which forced him to concentrate his energies in the classroom. McDonough remarked that due to Buddy John's dedicated regime of sparring and lifting weights he became too effective a boxer and feared injuring other fighters. So with little ado he hung up his gloves and never boxed again except in mock matches with his sons.

Buddy's economic status and relative parental freedom gave him plenty of opportunities to entertain himself and his friends. The summer of 1939 saw Buddy tool around Oconomowoc in a Packard sedan with his cousin Chuck Bransfield and their mutual friend Ray Wise, who in World War II was killed in a submarine. They agreed that they needed to attract young women. They settled on barn dances. With Buddy's deep pockets, they created posters that publicized barn dances and hay rides for a small fee. In Chuck's words:

"We had great camaraderie and fun together and as a social event the dances were a great success. We cast our nets to include everyone who could read our invitations tacked to the trees and telephones in our district. The dances actually played out in the locations available — which were empty schools, barns, etc. In fact we even used one city hall. Beans, franks, beer, and music and a few stolen kisses in the hay wagons — that being the whole objective."

While Notre Dame provided Buddy structure for his life it also was the place where he suffered a severe mental collapse. As an upperclassman, Buddy suffered a severe depression that left his family and Wisconsin friends, who generally overlooked his personality quirks, concerned. One current diagnosis reported in hindsight that he might have suffered from a mood disorder with psychotic features. Buddy's non-communicative funk coincided with a new interest in Catholic spirituality. The Johns wondered whether Buddy's spiritual advisor, Cornelius Hagerty — a priest of the Holy Cross order, had cast a spell over their son or whether Buddy's earlier psychological problems had developed into a psychosis. Stories abound of Harry, Jr., in an attempt to rid himself of his depression, sleeping with painful hair shirts on his dorm-room floor. At home Buddy moved into the chauffeur's quarters, above the garage, and slept on hardwood floors. One cousin, Father Michael Bransfield, was convinced that Buddy developed schizophrenia, another wondered whether, he was addicted to prescription mood-altering pills, others thought that he contracted a debilitating depression, and some believed that his "weak constitution" had come to fruition. Anyway, Buddy never completely shook the mental illness that was partially manifested in obsessive and rigid Catholic spirituality. Mental difficulties and Catholicism became the hallmarks of Buddy's future. From this time forward, Buddy delved into the rigors of the Catholic faith, rejected fun as frivolous, treated family as potential enemies, controlled his loved ones, and occasionally trusted his wealth to con men.

His cousin, Chuck Bransfield, remarked that Buddy was never the same after he returned from Notre Dame. Those suffering from mental illness can have accompanying confusion and physical pain that can, at best, be miserable or, at worst, unbearable. Since Buddy chose not to dull his pain with alcohol or drugs, for relief, he increasingly turned to profound Catholic spirituality, especially devotions to Mary and the Sacred Heart of Jesus. He put a remarkable effort into learning about these devotions, which did not bring him peace, love of self, or love of others. In fact, they had the opposite effect. Regardless, Buddy's mental illnesses did not preclude him from accomplishing many remarkable deeds that most completely healthy people would have been proud of achieving. In 1941, Buddy received a bachelor's degree with a major in philosophy. His grades averaged 85, and he finished *cum laude.*

Another prominent aspect of Buddy's personality was his fits of rage; a trait he shared with his sister, which they inherited from their father. Buddy's mental difficulties severed his relationship with his sister, Lorraine. She suffered from these same peculiarities and after his college breakdown they were forever distant. Although, on January 20, 1941 Buddy, assuredly at his mother's urging, sent Lorraine and her husband Hank a congratulatory telegram for their daughter Karen on her first birthday. Harry Jr.'s relationship with his parents was more complicated, as they could overlook some of his peculiar behavior.

Due to Buddy's chronic suffering from his untreated depression, he developed a strong compassion for sick, disabled or luckless individuals. He would become agitated when others made cruel or snide remarks about transients and would respond, "There but for the grace of God go I." He was supportive of the disabled and infirm, often visiting them at home or in the hospital.

For the second time, the Johns faced a child suffering from an incurable mental illness, as Lorraine already had experienced a severe depression in her mid-teen years. One can imagine their embarrassment at Buddy's heated outbursts and withdrawal, especially from his mother and sister. Any displays of affection after his breakdown were forced and unnatural. Clara's family also had mental problems. Her daughter, Charlotte Miller Blommer, suffered from a progressive life-long depression. Some of Clara's grandchildren suffered from alcoholism and severe schizophrenia.

By early 1930, Fritz, Clara, Emil, and Elise were attempting to settle their mother and Ernest's estates. Lisette had equally distributed her assets among her five children, except for the family mansion at 3200 West Highland Boulevard, which was subject to the right of occupancy and use by her unmarried children. At that time, Emil was the sole child residing at the huge house that was occupied by the family's 59-year-old, long time housekeeper Katherine Dieringer, and her assistants, 31-year old Josephine Calems, and 18-year-old Agnes Sonrig. Certainly, these tolerant servants suffered through Emil's paranoid behavior while he recovered from his extensive gambling jags. The home's atmosphere had deteriorated, thanks to Emil's carousing with unsavory characters, in contrast to the decorum that the staid Lisette and Ernest had maintained. The servants feared answering the door with the probability of thugs, prostitutes, or gamblers appearing to request a conference with the man of the house.[288]

Ernest's will provided for an unequal distribution of his estate, Fritz and Elise each received 1/3 of his proceeds while

Clara and Emil each obtained 1/6. Fritz and Elise were generous with Lisette's jewelry, which was not distributed until after
Ernest's death, dividing it into four parcels, actually providing
Clara and Emil with more than their legal share. Emil, at his
request, received $800 in lieu of the jewelry. Later, he changed
his mind and demanded his share of the precious gems. Fritz
organized the split of jewelry and invited his siblings to a meeting at his office on December 31, 1929. He had the precious
items appraised and then divided into four lots of nearly equal
value. The Millers then, blindly, were to draw pieces of paper
numbered from one to four and then receive the lot of jewelry
corresponding to that number. Since Lisette made Ernest and
Fritz co-executors, with Emil as the alternate, Ernest's death
made Emil a co-executor. After 1925, the brothers split the
mansion's maintenance and taxes, since they both lived there
for part of the year. At this time, Clara and Elise each had their
own homes and families and did not share in the mansion's
costs.[289]

By 1930, Emil was estranged from his siblings for years at
a time, even though they lived in the same city. Among other
reasons, Emil's siblings feared being accosted or kidnapped by
underworld characters trying to collect Emil's sizeable gambling
debts. At this time, Fritz had become so exasperated with Emil's
madcap behavior that he refused to contribute to the house's
maintenance and tax costs. Also, he and his wife, May, had just
built and moved into a mansion in the Washington Highlands.
Regardless, Fritz was still the co-executor of his mother's estate
and was required to share the responsibility of maintaining the
Highland Boulevard house. Recently, however, Emil had been
ordering expensive repairs and improvements to the mansion
without Fritz's knowledge or approval, and he expected Fritz
to cover one-half of the costs. Emil's difficult behavior drove
the usually reticent Fritz into a rage. Fritz, the oldest surviving
sibling, failed to control any of Emil's problematic behavior, as
Ernest had done.[290]

On May 31, 1930, Fritz, in an attempt to break this impasse,
wrote to Emil and recommended that he select an agent to

negotiate with his siblings on the disposition of the Highland Boulevard property and its contents. Fritz noted that the manner in which this matter had been handled, "has brought no results and unless a settlement can be made prior to July, when Clara intends to leave for Europe, it will be late fall [Clara returned in October] before any further negotiations can be entered into."[291] Emil declined. On June 10 of that year, Oscar Treichler, (who was the estate's bookkeeper), on Fritz and Elise's behalf, requested Clara's help in disposing of the house and its contents. The Millers were sufficiently disgusted with Emil that they wanted to sell the mansion and rid themselves of dealing with him. Treichler remarked that it was Fritz's opinion that Emil was making accusations and finding fault with everything, regardless of the facts, in order to further his own interests and force his siblings to make concessions. Additionally, Treichler noted that Emil had exclusive and free use of the Pierce Arrow and Buick automobiles, even though they were owned and maintained by the family business, Oriental Realty.[292]

Finally, Fritz, Clara, and Elise decided on a procedure to dispose of the family mansion and its contents. They offered the property and its contents (except various items on their list) to Emil for $60,000, with the stipulation that they would have the first right to purchase any contents that, later, he might wish to sell. Emil declined this offer in a rude manner.[293] On June 13, Fritz wrote to Emil:

Dear Brother:

Your most carefully prepared letter of more or less distorted facts received. If you have intelligence enough to distinguish between constructive and destructive criticism please apply it, as helpful suggestions are always welcome and I assure you will receive my careful consideration at all times, but hereafter your petty fault finding and nonsensical correspondence will receive only the consideration it merits, because I really owe it to the other members of our family to devote the time I have spent in the past trying to correct your unjust accusations and errors, to the business in an endeavor to produce results which are beneficial to all concerned.

> *It has been my aim in the past to be fair and just in my dealings*
> *with you but you have been most ungrateful and unappreciative.*
> *. .*
>
> *. . .Because I did not wish to be small minded I refused to let Mr.*
> *[Arthur] Kleinboehl take your name off the [brewery] payroll and*
> *you were paid a salary for about three years during which you were*
> *not devoting your time to business but to pleasure, and at the end*
> *of the time E. G. [Ernest G. Miller] took his name and also yours*
> *off the pay roll . . .*[294]

On June 14, before Emil received Fritz's scathing missive, Emil willingly responded to his siblings' request for sundry household items. Despite Emil's self-destructive and anti-social behavior, occasionally, he was capable of lucid thinking, as shown in his correspondence. The Millers had spurred Emil into writing by proposing to him that he hire an agent to negotiate on his behalf. Nevertheless, he was sarcastic in regard to Fritz's request for one of five sets of bed linen that their mother had purchased for her children, "I am glad to give him one set, as I realize he has no place to sleep." Also, Emil accused Fritz of being self-serving, "as most of the things which Fred [Fritz] claims to own are inventoried in mother[']s estate showing clearly that they were not Fred's property. Fred himself made up mother's inventory and had her Will made." Emil made a plea to his siblings, "I personally feel that house and contents should be given to me as a present which would only be a small renumeration [sic] for the many year[']s work I did for Fred [Fritz] and my Sisters and the money I handed to them."[295]

On July 9, 1930, Emil wrote the final existing letter on this matter to Fritz and Elise, who had made an offer to their brother in order to complete the negotiations. (Emil and Clara had made a separate written deal on that same day.) Emil told his siblings, "Of all the cheap tightwads I have ever met in my life, you certainly win the prize. . . The terms outlined in your letter look ridiculous to me and if you, Treichler and [Edwin S.] Mack [their attorney] want to make a 'Kaffee-Klatsch' out of this matter you will have to play alone, as I will not be a party thereto. It appears that you want to get possession of this property just to be dirty to me — not for sentimental reasons at all." Furthermore, he threatened to commence court action, without further notice, if the matter was soon not closed. Emil took this matter to court, but following negotiations, it was settled without a trial. Emil did not buy the mansion. Instead, the Millers donated it to Marquette University in December 1941, which used it to house students in its naval training program. It was unfortunate that the Millers treated each other with such acrimony since one of their father's last wishes was, "Be considerate and kind to each other and remain in peace and unity . . ."[296]

On October 24, 1929, the stock market crashed, which started the national economy's constriction and eventual lengthy depression. Fortunately for the Miller family, the Great Depression helped thin the prohibitionary ranks. The prohibitionists hurt their cause with depression-era politicians who were searching for new tax sources, by fighting any relaxation of the one-half-of-one-percent alcohol limit that the Volstead Act mandated. The Association Against the Prohibition Amendment, which had been formed in 1919, became more powerful after 1926 when a group of wealthy businessmen began to make large contributions to it.

As America inched closer to repeal, the brewers became more excited and overlooked the spreading depression. For instance, the Pabst Brewery in October 1930 began acquiring new brewing equipment and terminating the leases of their tenants at their factory, in anticipation of legal beer. On June 24, 1930, Fritz Miller noted in a letter to his sister, Clara, that he was planning to call a meeting, "in the very near future to discuss the bottling machinery, etc., as I think it is in a rather dilapidated condition and patched up, and if beer should come back the present machinery could not stand the strain, because it would be mostly bottled beer. I think it is very essential to have an understanding about these matters before beer comes back, because I do not want to be blamed for not being prepared for the occasion."[297]

The brewery continued to develop products and, in 1931, rolled out University Club Lager, a non-alcoholic cereal brew. By the middle of 1932, a growing political movement for changing the Volstead Act to legalize 3.2% beer made it appear probable that Congress would support this matter. On March 22, 1933, President Franklin Roosevelt signed the Cullen Harrison Bill legalizing beer with 3.2% of alcohol, which was enacted on one minute after midnight on April 7, 1933. At that moment, the breweries began selling their product in states where it was not prohibited by state laws. On December 5, 1933, the Eighteenth Amendment was repealed by the enactment of the 21st Amendment, with the needed agreement of three quarters of the states.[298]

On May 12, 1933, the Miller High Life Company's stockholders changed its name to the Miller Brewing Company giving them flexibility to market products besides High Life. Diversification of its products and farsighted management decisions allowed Miller Brewery to survive Prohibition. Despite occasional weakening of the Millers' desire to retain the brewery, they made the correct decisions needed to survive the potentially devastating period. By Prohibition's repeal, the Miller name and its quality reputation had remained before the public. In general, the buildings and equipment were maintained in proper working order, and, most importantly, some brewery employees retained their jobs.[299]

15.
THE GREAT DEPRESSION

At one minute past midnight on Friday April 7, 1933, an exuberant crowd at 40th and State Streets cheered as employees from the Miller Brewing Company carted out their first barrels of legal 3.2% beer. There was such a throng that the celebrants parked in the middle of nearby streets and hiked to the party. The Miller family celebrated at the company's headquarters with the brewery's management and close friends. Many years later, Clara and Carl Miller's third-oldest child, Claire Miller McCahey, recalled, "That was a big thing. Oh, my gosh. That was so crowded, the whole brewery was crowded with people. All Milwaukee turned out. And, oh, it was so terrific. . . . It was big doings all night." The brewery choreographed the celebration to achieve the maximum publicity. Employees pushed handcarts of beer barrels into the crowd where they served free cold beer also affectionately known as "barley pop" with sandwiches. There was another party in downtown Milwaukee to which each of the seven local breweries contributed a truckload of beer. Only twenty-two rowdies were arrested there for public drunkenness. These parties were replicated throughout America, wherever breweries existed and state laws permitted. For instance, celebrants jammed Chicago's State Street until sunrise.[300]

Milwaukee historian John Gurda noted that previously, with the return of legal beer on the horizon, "Milwaukee's seven breweries hopped back into production, cooper shops and bottle plants dusted off their equipment, and the city's

1,776 taverns (no longer saloons) were suddenly operating within the law again." With officially permitted beer, eighty-five hundred Milwaukee brewery workers got jobs at $24 to $35 a week that were much welcomed during the Depression. The official Milwaukee party was postponed until April 17, the day after Easter, to appease the city's religious leaders desiring an abstemious Lenten season. At the affair, 15,000 Milwaukeeans jammed the auditorium and consumed hundreds of pounds of food while washing it down with beer. Gurda remarked that the celebration was so successful that Mayor Dan Hoan repeated it on an annual basis until 1941. This renamed and rescheduled Midsummer Festival was a huge success at Milwaukee's lakefront and became the precursor to today's Summerfest that started in 1968.[301]

By Prohibition's end, the Miller's third generation was complete with its youngest member, Harry G. "Buddy" John, Jr., born in December 1919. In fact, twelve of the 34 fourth-generation Millers were already born; Charles "Chuck" Bransfield, born on September 10, 1918, was the first and Buddy's daughter, Jessica Marie John, born on July 1, 1978, was the final fourth-generation Miller. All of the Miller progeny came from Clara and Elise because the Miller males, Ernest, Frederick A. "Fritz", and Emil, remained childless. On April 7, 1933, the third generation included Clara and Carl's children: Loretta Kopmeier, 40; Claire McCahey, 37; Marguerite Bransfield, 31; Frederick Carl Miller, 27; and Charlotte Miller, 23, who was still single. Elise and Harry John's children were Lorraine, 19, and Harry G. "Buddy", Jr., 13.

Despite the Millers' temporary loss of faith in the Miller Brewery in 1926 when they tried to sell it, they retained ownership of their business and continued to operate it during the "noble experiment." On December 5, 1933, Prohibition officially ended, allowing beer with alcohol content higher than 3.2% to be legally brewed. The Millers were determined to continue running the brewery and reaping its financial rewards, as suddenly the future of beer brewing looked bright. In early 1933, Frederick A. "Fritz" Miller was the company's president,

Clara Miller its vice president, Elise John its secretary-treasurer, Walter H. Kraft its general manager and assistant secretary, and the thirty-year veteran, C.H. Hesser, was in charge of sales. Previously, Fritz, Clara, and Elise had banned their brother Emil from any elected corporate position due to his self-destructive behavior. Fritz Miller carried on until November 1937, when Elise assumed the presidency.[302]

As sales boomed, the Millers invested $1 million to modernize the brewery, which was operating at full capacity. The funds likely came from the Miller family, which had withdrawn millions of dollars from the business before 1920. The company purchased a new pure-yeast culture apparatus, for propagating the Dortmund, German strain of single cell organisms, vital to the brewing process. Concurrently, they reclaimed their yeast from a commercial laboratory, where they had "boarded" it since the start of Prohibition. For the fermentation of one barrel of beer, the brewers needed one-half pound of yeast. Master brewer William Eisenbeiss managed this machine of copper and brass that sterilized its tank with hot steam, neutralizing any bacteria, thus creating a sterile environment for the next batch. A pure yeast culture was necessary for brewing beer that would then have the, "flavor, quality and aroma distinct from all others and yet as constant as time."[303]

The Miller Brewing Company had brewed 300,000 barrels in the nine months before Prohibition began in 1920, and vigorously produced 400,536 barrels in 1934, the first full year after the repeal, making it Milwaukee's fourth largest brewery. Miller Brewery's rapid renewal, including construction of new buildings, raised their property taxes from $240,900 in 1932 to $279,600 in 1933, which was remarkable as most Milwaukee-area industrial properties were depreciating due to the lingering depression.[304]

Miller's improvements continued apace from 1932 through 1935. Besides the pure yeast culture apparatus, the brewery saw enhancements to its brewhouse, increasing the brewing capacity and improving the working conditions. The brewing process after Prohibition had changed since the days of Frederick J.

Miller; it was considerably more mechanized, and operated on a larger scale. It began with the millhouse, a building adjacent to the brewhouse where the malt and corn were transferred from rail cars, same as today, to scale hoppers to be weighed. Subsequently, the produce was elevated into flat-bottom bins, each of which held two-and-one-half carloads. The malt was cleaned before it was placed in the bins. After the material was removed from the hampers, it was cleaned again and then moved to the malt scale hopper that held enough for two batches. Next, the material was transported to the six-roller mill where the malt and cornhusks were split, removed from the kernels, and crushed to the consistency of fine grits. At that point, bucket elevators and spiral conveyors transported the crushed grain to the mash tanks for boiling.[305]

After the mashing (boiling) of the malt and corn adjuncts, the brewers used lauter tubs (straining tanks) to separate the wort (soluble matter) from the spent grain (insoluble residue). They then sold it to farmers for nutritious cattle feed. Next, the workers added the hops to the wort roiling in the large brew kettles, giving the finished product a mildly bitter taste and helping to preserve it. Subsequently, the liquid was strained to remove the gritty organic sediment. The next important step was cooling the boiled wort in Miller Brewery's air-conditioned cooler room that was lined with white glazed tiles. This room, with two baudelot coolers, which were a series of pipes that beer flowed over containing a chilling medium, each with a 150-barrel-per-hour capacity, had been completely remodeled to conform "with every requirement of modern science." The ceiling was vaulted above each cooler where a suction fan rapidly exhausted any vapors. The incoming air was filtered so thoroughly that weekly laboratory tests showed 97% to 98% sterility.[306]

The brewers then moved the processing liquid to the main five-story stockhouse or one of the smaller adjacent ones. Stockhouses were often built many stories high to allow gravity to move the product from tank to tank. Also, these buildings were kept nearly sterile, excluding bacteria or wild strains of yeast that could corrupt a batch of beer. These buildings contained numerous 200 to 450-barrel wood and steel tanks. There were twenty-two settling tubs of 350 barrels each and one hundred open fermenters. Pure yeast cultures were put into the cooled wort to begin the slow fermentation process, giving the beer its alcohol and carbon dioxide. After its use, the yeast was washed and separated from impurities and dead cells. It was stored in containers until needed. The brewers used each batch of yeast six times before they propagated a new lot of single-celled organisms from their pure-yeast apparatus. Forty closed-steel fermenters collected the carbon dioxide gas, to be reincorporated later for carbonization. There were 230 wood-and-steel pressurized tanks of various sizes for storage. Beer samples were taken from each lot, after fermentation, to inspect the, "progress of clearing and behavior of each batch brewed."[307]

The final stage in the process occurred in the stockhouse where the brewery produced a stock or batch of the clear liquid. According to Dr. David S. Ryder, Miller Brewing Company's current brewmaster, in this era, during the entire brewing process brewers sampled the product with increasingly sophisticated measuring devices, for instance, to keep control of the levels of sugar and alcohol. Dr. Ryder noted that in Frederick J. Miller's day, the lack of technical advances made the brewer's palate a strategic imperative to ensure that the beer had all the right attributes. The kraeusening process, (adding a small portion of wort to a larger portion of fermented beer), took approximately two weeks, after which the beer was filtered, stored for several weeks, carbonated, and again deposited for at least four weeks. The stockhouse had thirty 350-barrel and thirty-three 100-barrel tanks for lagering (storing) the finished beer. After lagering was completed, the brewers ran the beer through pulp filters to give it its brilliancy. Then the beer was piped to the racking and bottling building to fill wooden kegs and glass bottles.[308]

The Miller Brewing Company used a massive Corliss engine to direct-drive the millhouse equipment and its many air compressors. It also had a coal-fed, 350-kilowatt electrical generator and two 75-kilowatt auxiliary generators in their powerhouse that supplied electrical power to the entire plant. This building also contained pre-Prohibition ammonia compressors that refrigerated various buildings and tanks. In the powerhouse, an automatically-controlled turbine pump delivered 600 gallons of water per minute from a 1,300-foot deep well. By May 1935, increasing beer sales created such an electrical draw that the brewery was compelled to augment its powerhouse.[309]

The brewery's steam heat came from an outdated boiler room, to which railroad cars delivered coal into overhead bins. The coal flowed by force of gravity to men who, by hand, stoked the furnaces. The boiler pumped 210-degree Fahrenheit steam to the boilers. On June 12, 1935, the brewery placed a new $160,000 boiler house into operation with the latest technology in steam plant design and equipment. The new boilers were mechanically, not manually, stoked and the ash-conveying system for removal and disposal system was completely mechanized.[310]

As the "noble experiment" of Prohibition faded, so did Emil Miller. By late 1933, the Miller family scion was bloated, paranoid, and devoid of verve, except when drunk. The endless family lectures and repeated sojourns to expensive private clinics failed to cure his physical and mental ailments. Emil's psychiatrist, Dr. William J. Murphy who claimed to have seen him 400 times, noted that Emil's, "periods of recuperation were progressively longer, until towards the end he was unable to withstand the ravages of his irrational life." It was Dr. Murphy's opinion that Emil was, "mentally unsound and physically infirm," for at least the last ten years of his life. With current drug therapy, Emil might have succeeded in managing his devastating mood swings, the results of alcoholism and probable bi-polar disorder.[311]

Throughout this period, Emil Miller was besieged by creditors who held his gambling I.O.U.s. Oscar Treichler, the West Side Millers' bookkeeper, and Ernest Rahtjen, Emil's personal secretary, negotiated lower payments for Emil, while trying to shelter him from gangsters' collection visits. In November 1933, Emil and his attorneys, Francis X. Swietlik and George A. Burns, successfully petitioned Circuit Judge John C. Kleczka to require Emil's gambling partner, E.E. Cummingham, "to show cause why he should not be restrained from disposing to 'an innocent party' checks signed by Miller, amounting in all to $6,925, so that Miller 'cannot refuse payment and defend himself on the grounds that the checks were not legally obtained.'"[312] In an affidavit, Emil Miller alleged that he lost the funds gambling with Cummings at the Club Madrid roadhouse on West Blue Mound Road, and recalled that the checks were not dated when he signed them. Furthermore, he alleged that the checks were not official because he lost them in an illegal activity, gambling. Eventually, Emil's attorneys recovered his checks from E.E. Cunningham in return for $1,600.[313]

Emil's last year seemed interminable. From January 1, 1934 until November 22, 1934, he spent 181 days out of town, 86 days sick at home, and 50 days in the hospital. His sister, Elise, and her husband, Harry John, had seen him only once in his last six years, as he lived such a lonely and paranoid life when sober. On October 3, 1934, Emil entered St. Joseph Hospital where he stayed until his death, on November 22, of tuberculosis. Surely, no one was surprised by his demise and only his gambling partners wanted the 58-year-old brewer to continue living in that condition. Probably, Emil himself welcomed the end to his tortured life.[314] On November 26, 1934, Emil Paul Miller lay in an open casket with his usually light, puffy face darkened and outlined by a director at the S. F. Peacock & Son Funeral Home. Later that day, Emil's funeral service took place at St. Rose Parish after which, he was buried at the Miller plot in Calvary Cemetery.

Despite Emil's prodigious gambling losses, he left an estate in excess of $4.2 million. His personal property was valued at $3,990,415; his real estate at $164,266; his cash on deposit at the Marshall & Ilsley Bank (now M&I Bank) at $38,791; and his ready money at $10,000. The estate had 11,666 2/3 shares in the Oriental Realty Company valued at $1,458,333, which comprised its largest single security holding. It also held 46 2/3 shares of the Miller Brewing Company that was valued at $15,164. Emil possessed relatively little Miller Brewery stock because most of it was held by the Oriental Realty Company. Emil's estate also contained bonds. Additionally, it held 26 real estate mortgages in Milwaukee, 25 in Chicago, and one each in Miami and Fort Myers.[315]

Emil died without a will so that his estate would be divided equally among his three surviving siblings, Frederick A. "Fritz" Miller, Clara Miller, and Elise John. On December 3, 1934, Fritz Miller, represented by attorney Alexander W. Schutz, filed a petition before Circuit Judge Michael S. Sheridan asking that Oscar Treichler, Carl Miller, and Harry John, Sr., who were chosen by Fritz, Clara, and Elise respectively, be named as administrators. By November 15, 1935, Alexander Schutz had paid approximately $500,000 in estate taxes to the county tax treasurer for Emil's estate. In mid-February 1937, Circuit Judge John Karel imposed a state inheritance tax of $604,626 on the estate. Each of Emil's three siblings would be charged a $202,000 tax on their $1.3 million bequests.[316] The federal taxes totaled $1.4 million but, in December of 1942, the Internal Revenue Service refunded an over-assessment of $186,000.[317]

The administrators of Emil Miller's estate adjudicated a series of legal battles against eleven claimants totaling $65,000, ranging from gambling debts to unpaid medical bills. Claims came from Charles Nelson, a.k.a. Charles Serio, who wanted $11,050 that he said was a gift from Emil. Also, Nelson had a $25,000 joint claim with J.J. Bove. Ben Brooks of Chicago wanted $16,038 from checks issued by Emil in February 1929, that the estate administrators contended were forgeries.[318]

At first, Charles Nelson and J.J. Bove rebuffed any settlement offers and their attorney, James J. Kerwin, pressed ahead for a jury trial to collect $37,050 in check form. The testimony from the trial demonstrated that Nelson was the general manager of Emil's pleasure trips and, then, later paid the bills with Emil's money. These excursions were Emil's constant extravagance and were rife with, "champagne and women entertainers." It was not unusual "for a hotel bill to amount to $1,000 on one trip," testified Ernest Rahtjen, Emil's financial secretary. The estate's administrators counterclaimed that Nelsen and Bove collected $110,877 from Emil, for the food, clothing and shelter worth no more than $10,000 that the "friends" alleged to have supplied to him. They also argued that, in several instances in the years preceding his death, the decedent, "was incompetent and incapable of entering into a contract." They also noted that if Emil intended to give them checks as gifts after his death, they were void for not complying with Wisconsin inheritance laws. At a pre-trial hearing in mid-October Ernest Rahtjen testified that Emil, unlike other wealthy men, was not partial to marble swimming pools, horses or greyhounds, but, instead, relished "night life," spending almost $100,000 a year. This trial's outcome is unknown.[319]

As a final anecdote regarding Emil, the Miller Brewing Company received a letter in early April 1972 from May Aileen Wilson Kingman, of Miami, Florida, claiming to have married Emil in the late 1920s. May Aileen, 73, then destitute and living in a nursing home, wanted money from the Miller family or the Miller Brewery to pay for her medication. She wrote that she had attended one of Emil's north-side Chicago hotel parties and he begged her to marry him. After being alone with him for a couple of days in her Chicago apartment, she agreed. Soon he gave her checks to buy clothes and relinquish her apartment. After their marriage, she said, they were to have circled the world and then announce their union to all. But Emil took ill and needed medical care due to prolonged severe intoxication. His handlers took charge of him and kept him away from Ms. Wilson Kingman, who tried in vain to contact Emil or his family. Her 1972 letter went unanswered.

Over the last years of his life, Emil Miller became a caricature of a drunken gambler. In all likelihood, he used alcohol to self-medicate his probable bipolar disorder. Today, medical treatments can ameliorate some of the worst symptoms of this deadly disease. Fortunately, Emil did not have a wife and children who his behavior would have negatively affected. The few surviving personal accounts of Emil's early life describe a bright, lively person who liked to entertain his family. Emil's legacy, despite his late life collapse, is one of dedication to his father's brewery in combination with imaginative approaches to promoting its product.

Since 1917, Clara and Carl Miller had lived with their children and servants in their fortress-like home on Newberry Boulevard. Both were industrious and, by the mid-1930s, reached their financial goals, allowing themselves a comfortable retirement. They took yearly trips to Western Europe with a few of their progeny at a time. By the end of Prohibition, all of Clara and Carl's children, except Charlotte, were married. Their eldest, Loretta, lived nearby with her husband, Norman Kopmeier, Sr. and their children, Rose Mary, age 14, and Norman, Jr., age 7. Norman Kopmeier, Sr., an owner of the Wisconsin Ice and Coal Company, became related to the Uihleins, who owned the Joseph Schlitz Brewery, when his brother Waldemar married Meta Uihlein. Loretta and Norman Kopmeier proudly connected two traditional Milwaukee businesses, beer and ice. Additionally, the Miller Brewing Company and Wisconsin Ice and Coal, now renamed Hometown, Inc. while delivering bags of ice to gas stations and grocery stores, both survive in industries marked by radical consolidation. Clara's second eldest child, Claire, lived in Chicago with her husband, James Bernard McCahey, Sr., and their five children: Claire, born in 1919; James, Jr., born in 1920; Anita Rose, born in 1923; Frederick, born in 1925; and Carol, born in 1927. James McCahey, Sr. had a long career at the Chicago-based Dunn Coal Company and later served as president of the Chicago Board of Education.

At Prohibition's end, Clara's third child, Marguerite, lived in Chicago with her husband, Michael J. Bransfield II, and four of the five children they would have: Charles "Chuck," (who was Michael's son with his first wife, Anita), born in 1918; Marguerite, born in 1924; Michael, Jr., born in 1929; and Frederick Miller, born in 1930. Joan was born after Prohibition in 1934. Michael J. Bransfield, II worked with his brothers at Michael J. Bransfield & Company, Inc. that was started by their father who, in 1852, had immigrated to Chicago from County Waterford, Ireland. The business sold special assessment bonds from their office in the Loop and also managed an asphalt paving operation. Besides creating a business, the Irish immigrant, Michael J. Bransfield I, served a stint as Chicago's treasurer.[320] Clara's fourth child, Frederick Carl, lived in Milwaukee with his bride, Adele, and their daughter, Claire, born on November 12, 1932, the eldest of their future eight children. The remaining youngsters, Freddy, Loret, Kate, Gail, Carlotta, Adele, and Carl, were born after beer's re-legalization.

At Prohibition's end, Clara and Carl Miller's youngest child, Charlotte, was living with them. On April 25, 1935, she married Bernard Blommer at St. Peter and Paul Catholic Church in Milwaukee. They had a sumptuous wedding, well attended by family and friends. The Blommers, who for years were unable to conceive a child, decided to pursue adopting a baby. Elizabeth was born on December 6, 1939 and, on February 24, 1940, the Blommers adopted her. Following the addition of Elizabeth, the Blommers had two biological children; Marguerite "Margo" born on February 17, 1942, and Mary Claire born on January 4, 1944.[321]

Bernard Blommer, Charlotte's husband, was the son of William and Marie Blommer of Milwaukee. William had started and owned the Blommer Ice Cream Company, which went defunct during the Depression. Soon after, he began working for Ambrosia Chocolate Company, eventually becoming a high-level executive. Ambrosia, which is still in business, produced wholesale chocolate that other companies incorporated in their products. William had three sons, Henry, Bernard "Bern," and Aloysius "Al," who also worked at Ambrosia in the sales department. The three Blommer boys, all graduates of Georgetown University, were ambitious due in part to encouragement from their assertive mother, Marie. After some time, they found any path to high-level management blocked by Ambrosia's owning family and, in 1939, saw fit to leave en masse to found a chocolate company.[322]

In order to keep from embarrassing their father, who was a high-level manager at Ambrosia, the three Blommer sons placed the Blommer Chocolate Company at 600 West Kinzie Street in Chicago. It still prospers in the family's hands, with factories in Chicago; East Greenville, Pennsylvania; and Union City, California. Of the three brothers, Bern alone moved to Chicago, while his two brothers commuted from Milwaukee. Bern's father-in-law, Carl Miller, provided some of the initial capital for the Blommer Chocolate Company with a substantial loan. The company competed with Ambrosia with the same product line. It sold confectionary chocolate syrup to companies such as Nabisco and found its product covering candy bars like O Henry and Baby Ruth.[323]

By her mid-to-late adult years, Clara Miller was able to enjoy her family, traveling, eating well, and attending myriad social functions. Chuck Bransfield remarked that Mama's two great passions were saving money and socializing. She neglected nothing in the social spectrum between christenings and wakes. Also, she was a wonderful gardener and kept her Newberry home and yard filled with verdant plants.

Clara's parsimony went beyond good money management. She believed that, generally, people were over-paid for their work and loathed giving raises. She gave tips of one dime, if at all. She was paranoid that people were trying to steal her money. Chuck Bransfield noted that Clara, in order to save money, used wrapping tissues from fruit for toilet paper, keeping them in a box near the thrones. Carl, who thought that the idea was ludicrous, used regular toilet paper. Chuck also noted that, at restaurants, Mama took items from the table including toothpicks, mints, flora, hard rolls, butter, and celery–any remaining perishable. Also, Clara was known to steal plants for her yard from the public parks and gardens. She regularly reused gifts, even if at times, she forgot to check for the original card. Often she would store the unopened gifts in her attic until the opportunity arose to give them to someone else. It is notable that at this time Clara was one of Milwaukee's wealthiest women. Her granddaughter, Claire Miller Krause, defended her grandmother's behavior noting that, if she had been less thrifty, less wealth would have descended to her children.

Clara was ambitious, encouraging her husband and son in business. From behind the scenes, she greased the path for a substantial part of their success. A side effect of Mrs. Miller's ambitious behavior was a dearth of compassion. Clara, as her father, often was quick to label others' failures as character flaws, such as laziness, whereas, their own success was due to their diligence. Clara was impatient with sickness, despair, depression, or poverty of spirit. Chuck Bransfield wrote that his grandmother never deplored, in fact was pleased by, the fact that she was one of the "haves" in a world of "have nots." To her it was the breaks in the game of life; some were winners, some were losers; some would make it, some would not. He continued, that, in any event, Clara could not see how dividing the fruits of enlightened effort with the unenlightened or indolent was the answer. Clara saw only one real difference in human beings; either they were smart and worked to get ahead or they were dumb loafers. That was the litmus test that worked for her. Chuck concluded that she believed that work by those "without," (wherever they were), would better reduce poverty than all the almsgiving by the producing class. Clara was merciless in her condemnation of her sister Elise and Elise's family. She had no consideration for Lorraine's emotional problems and Buddy's mental illness, choosing to regard them as character flaws.

Chuck Bransfield described his grandmother's manner of dressing in his book, *Mama*:

"Sometimes she came down the stairs slapping things on herself that someone might assume were used bandages. At least the cold Milwaukee climate made her cover herself with solid clothing. . .

"All her ensembles were obsolete. Her uniform-of-the-day for going out in public might include darned silk stockings, shoes molded decades ago and well cracked, a wide garment resembling the skin of a Spad biplane but with less aerodynamic shape, a coat from a scarecrow, and a hat blown from a train window. The garments were clean of course, and shining from the iron, but the net effect would have startled Robinson Crusoe.

"She looked like a fugitive from an overactive volcano. Most of her clothes were from obscure vogues and never the same. She was not, perhaps, the first to attempt to repair silk stockings, but she was the only one to do it with yarn and then wear it in public.

"Her hats looked like they were built by the Wright Brothers.... Her shoes seemed made to fit someone else; they caused her to walk lurchingly, like a land crab in search of grasshoppers. Yet she never fell and no broken hip marred her old age. . . In sum, Mama would not buy new clothes and by law, constitutionally, she could not go naked; the compromise was breathtaking."

Due to the mores of her family and society, Clara did not select any of her daughters for a prominent role at Miller Brewery. The Clara and Carl Miller family was imbued with Old-World convention that precluded leadership positions for females outside of the house. In fact, the Millers promoted their son-in-law, James B. McCahey, Sr., in the family businesses ahead of their daughters. The Miller daughters, capable of handling positions of corporate responsibility, instead, focused on motherhood and supporting their husbands' careers. Clara Miller was a caretaker while serving as a director and an officer of Miller Brewery, by simply taking her turn along with her siblings or, otherwise, occupying a seat to represent her substantial number of shares. Clara would argue that, as a perennial minority shareholder, she had little influence on the brewery's direction. Clara's perpetual minority status was enforced by her obstinate attitude. Elise, on the other hand, easily wielded corporate power aided by her charm and understanding of people. As president, she made independent decisions and used males as advisors.

In 1935 with Fritz Miller as Miller Brewery's president, its sales reached 506,248 barrels. Indeed, during the busy spring and summer brewing period, the brewhouse operated twenty-four hours a day. Certainly, its historic commitment to high standards helped its growth. In 1932, Fritz Miller explained that his family, "always insisted on quality first and promptness in delivery. It is a point of great pride with us that a car of Miller beer was never returned as unsatisfactory. I think it is right to say that this is an unusual record."[324] By 1935, Miller Brewery, in "keeping with the trend for greater scientific control of beer production," built a laboratory and hired a chemist to support its brewmaster, William Eisenbeiss. In 1935 and 1936 the brewery's brands were the Best Milwaukee Beer, Milwaukee, and High Life on draught or in bottles. Besides these labels, it sold Draught Picnic and High Life Draught Picnic beers in large bottles. Picnic beer was not a separately brewed brand, rather it was Miller's regular beer, bottled but not pasteurized, and intended for immediate use at, for example, a picnic. In 1935, a *Milwaukee Journal* consumer analysis survey reported that 49% of greater Milwaukee families purchased beer for home consumption and, of that group, the largest percentage purchased Miller's brands. At this time, Henry C. Mulberger, the brewery's advertising manager and future husband of Lorraine John Mulberger, promoted point-of-sale advertising over other types of advertising such as newspaper, radio, and billboards, which statistics showed had little effect on sales.[325]

The Miller Brewery announced in February 1936 that it was adding a $40,000 canning line to its bottling and keg lines. In 1935, C. Krueger of Newark, New Jersey, became the first brewery to market beer in cans and, in short time, Miller followed suit. Miller Brewery's timely use of the newest technology was one of its strengths. Rarely in its history did Miller develop revolutionizing technology; instead, it quickly co-opted inventions from other breweries, thereby mitigating any long-term gain by their competitors. Additionally, Miller saved the development costs that its largest competitors bore in inventing these technologies. Miller's general manager, W.H. Kraft, the son of John U. Kraft, who in 1891, became Miller Brewery's brewmaster, reported that the equipment, purchased

from the American Can Company, the George J. Meyer Manufacturing Company in Cudahy, the Michael Yundt Company
in Waukesha, and the Alvey Conveyor Company in St. Louis
would output 200 cans a minute. Miller Brewery decided to
employ the American Can flat-top type, then in use at the Pabst
Brewery, instead of the Continental Can Company's cone type,
at that time employed by the Schlitz and Blatz breweries. The
flat-top design eventually won out, as cone-top cans faded into
obscurity. On March 17, 1936, the first cans filled with beer
named Select, featuring a girl in the moon logo printed on a
red can, were placed on the market. In all likelihood, Miller
filled the experimental cans with High Life, but called it Select,
in the event that the canning experiment operation backfired,
thereby salvaging High Life's reputation.[326]

Six-and-a-half months after Miller Brewery's cans hit
store shelves, Kraft reported an expansion program of more
than $250,000 to increase capacity by fifty percent to a 3,000
to 3,500-barrel daily capacity. The additional facilities would
be ready in spring of 1937. This outlay brought the Millers'
total expenditure, since beer's re-legalization, to $1.5 million.
The program called for expenditures in various departments,
"ranging from production to distribution." They were planning
to build a $25,000 warehouse in Cudahy, Wisconsin, to replace
one they were leasing in South Milwaukee. This facility would
handle beer distribution on Milwaukee's South Side as well as
regions further south and west. Brewhouse equipment would
be bought from the Cream City Boiler Company for $75,000.
They had already ordered two automatic pasteurizers at a cost
of $30,000 from the Waukesha-based Michael Yundt Company.
At this same time, they were scheduling to construct a $30,000
bottle-case storage building on the western edge of the brewery.
The last three items were $30,000 of additional rackers (keg
fillers), a $7,000 beer filter, and case-conveyor equipment for
$9,000. The management was contemplating spending an ad-
ditional $45,000 for bottling machines.[327]

In December 1936, the Miller Brewing Company's stockholders reorganized the corporation, which the I.R.S. scruti-

nized to assure that the Millers were not dodging taxes. The stockholders issued 10,000 shares of stock in the new Miller Brewing Company in trade for 1,000 shares of the former Miller Brewing Company. The Oriental Realty Company had owned the old Miller Brewery, except for three shares, one of which Fritz Miller, Clara Miller, and Elise John each owned to qualify as directors. The re-issuing of stock gave the stockholders ample opportunity to gift the numerous new brewery shares equally among their children. Additionally, after Prohibition's demise, Miller Brewery was growing more profitable and it was unreasonable that a smaller company, the Oriental Realty Company, would continue to own a larger flourishing company.[328]

The Millers received stock certificates of the new Miller Brewery in the following percentage; Fritz Miller - 34 4/9% (3,444 4/9 shares), Elise John - 34 4/9% (3,444 4/9 shares), and Clara Miller - 31 1/9% (3,111 1/9 shares). Clara received a lower percentage of stock than either Fritz or Elise because Ernest had given her and Emil less brewery stock in his will than either Fritz or Elise.

Fritz, Clara, and Elise elected themselves to the board of directors. Fritz was chosen as president, Clara as vice president, Elise as secretary/treasurer, and W.H. Kraft as assistant secretary/assistant treasurer. No doubt, Kraft, as the highest-ranking non-family member, did the majority of the tedious corporate work. Often in closely held corporations, such non-family officers receive a pledge of loyalty in return for performing mundane corporate work while the stockholders/officers attend to their personal affairs or enjoy vacations.[329]

In 1935, Elise gifted shares of the old Miller Brewing Company to Buddy and Lorraine's general trusts. When the brewery reorganized, the two trusts each had 500 shares of the new Miller Brewing Company. Elise maintained control of this gifted stock by appointing her reliable bookkeeper, Oscar F. Treichler, as trustee of both trusts. On March 15, 1937, Clara Miller gave each of her five children 500 shares of the new Miller Brewing Company while retaining 611 1/9 shares for herself. Each 500-share block was valued at $150,000. Clara provided this stock to her children a few months before the state legislature amended the gift tax law to increase the surtax and make donors liable for taxes, even on gifts to nonresidents.[330]

At this time, all of the living members of the third generation of the Miller family each owned 500 shares of the new Miller Brewing Company. The two youngest members, Lorraine and Buddy, had them in trust. Until their decision to sell their stock in 1961, Clara Miller's four living daughters never played a significant role in the Miller Brewery. They allowed their brother Fred to make decisions regarding their stock.

In 1937, Carl and Clara decided not to give their grandson, Chuck Bransfield (the son of Anita, their dead daughter), his mother's portion of stock and cash. Instead, they expected him to share in his stepmother Marguerite's fraction. After Chuck's mother died in 1920, his father Michael Bransfield, married Anita's younger sister Marguerite in 1923. Even though Marguerite helped raise Chuck, she never legally adopted him and he did not share in her estate as did her biological children. Chuck later reminisced that he was a difficult child and, as he matured, was an independent thinker. He accepted some of the responsibility for being excluded from his share of his mother's brewery stock.[331]

As with any property transfer, the state government taxed it, which led to a disagreement. The government wanted $53,000 in taxes and Clara's lawyer, George Spohn, argued for payment of $22,000. In mid-April 1941, the state board of tax appeals sided with John H. Leenhouts, the assessor of incomes and demanded payment of the additional $31,000. In December 1938, Clara and Carl also gave each of their five children 250 shares of the Oriental Realty Company, with a total value of $50,000. In 1935, Clara and Carl gave each of their five children $15,000, in 1936, they gave $10,000 to each of their children and in 1936-38, $5,000 to each of their many existing grandchildren.[332]

In 1938, the Miller Brewing Company stock was divided as follows:

Stockholder	Shares	Percentage
Frederick A. "Fritz" Miller	3,444 4/9	34%
Elise K. John	2,444 4/9	24%
Lorraine Mulberger		
(in trust, O. Treichler trustee)	500	5%
Harry G. "Buddy" John, Jr.		
(in trust, O. Treichler trustee)	500	5%
Clara A. Miller	611 1/9	6%

Frederick C. Miller represented the following stockholders:

Frederick C. Miller	500	5%
Loretta Miller Kopmeier	500	5%
Claire Miller McCahey	500	5%
Marguerite Miller Bransfield	500	5%
Charlotte Miller Blommer	500	5%
Total	**10,000**	**99%**

16.
THE THIRD
GENERATION
TAKES OVER

The transfer of the Miller Brewery stock to the third generation of Millers did not have an immediate significant impact on the business's production and marketing. Nevertheless, the new stockholders, in varying degrees, learned their fiduciary responsibilities to the corporation. On November 2, 1937, Fritz Miller, 69, retired as president of Miller Brewing Company yet remained as board chairman. Fritz had served the family and brewery until he saw the inception of the stock transfer to the third generation, which no doubt pleased him. Elise, who had already been the acting primary officer while Fritz incrementally retreated from daily oversight, became president. Fritz's longtime confidant and bookkeeper, Oscar Treichler, was elected vice-president replacing Clara Miller, who was elected as second vice president. W.H. Kraft became secretary/treasurer; and Fabian Bendel - assistant treasurer/assistant treasurer. Treichler was Fritz's choice to represent him. There is no explanation extant regarding Clara's demotion.[333]

In December 1937, Clara, 67, resigned her directorship and corporate officer position, with her son Fred, 31, assuming both of her positions. At this time, Fred also received the proxy to vote his mother's and sisters' stock at the stockholders' meetings. The young Fred was a natural choice to represent his family at the stockholder and board meetings, as he was a born leader. Clara's son had little power after his election, as the West Side Millers still controlled the majority of the outstanding stock, determining that the brewery's management report to them. Fred Miller moved into his mother's office but the responsibilities of his growing brood, the Carl Miller Lumber Company, and civic interests consumed most of his time.[334]

In the mid-1930s, the Miller management encouraged the organization of an independent office-workers' union to pre-empt the American Federation of Labor's unionizing efforts. The AFL took exception to this action and tried to create an affiliated union. Using customary tactics, the Brewer Office Workers' Union, an affiliate of the AFL, brought charges against the brewery before the state labor board. In August 1937, Miller Brewery found itself before Alfred H. Handrich, who acted as examiner for the board, defending against charges of unfair labor practices by the Workers' Union. The union had filed a complaint charging company intimidation and coercion while the company organized the independent office workers' union. Josephine Geiselmann, a Miller office employee, testified that she had applied for membership to the AFL. Some days later, Elise John, Miller's secretary/treasurer, sent her chauffeur to tell Geiselmann that she wanted to speak with her. Later that year, Geiselmann testified that, when she called Mrs. John on the telephone, the executive asked her whether she had attended the union meeting and, upon hearing an affirmative answer, "expressed disappointment."[335]

Attorney Giles Clark, in cross examination of Miss Geiselmann, discovered that when attorney Forrest Rusch, representing the labor board, questioned Geiselmann on facts in the case, he took her to a tavern-restaurant for dinner. They were accompanied by Edward Berg, who was a member of the Office Workers' Union. Attorney Rusch countered that when he met Geiselmann, she was on her way to a meeting and, to save time, they decided to have dinner and, simultaneously, discuss the subject. Additionally, Berg testified that Edward Zander, a 40-year Miller employee, had told him that Clara Miller, the brewery's vice-president, declared that, "the AFL union had to be stopped." Zander disagreed in person, noting that Clara

Miller had asked him, "how the AFL union was going but denied she made statements on desirability of the union."[336]

Many witnesses testified during the multiple-day hearing. Gerald Holtz, who was active in the independent union, testified on adverse examination that he was a friend and former classmate of Elise John's daughter, Lorraine. He continued, "that he occasionally spoke with Mrs. [Elise] John at the plant, and that he was in her home about two weeks before the organization of the independent union." He reported, however, "that the matter of organizing the office workers had never been discussed." Charles J. Reynolds, a director of the Oriental Realty Company, testified on adverse examination that he had told Jack Lewis, a Miller employee, that the existing harmony between employees and the management could be better maintained through an independent union. Reynolds continued that he had spoken with union members and explained that he "felt an independent union was better because it would continue friendly feeling between employer and employee." He also testified that he took no part in forming the unaffiliated union, other than to attend an organizational meeting at the Republican Hotel on May 3. The board's determination is unknown.[337]

While Elise exercised her business acumen at the brewery, her difficult marriage to Harry John soured their lives. They did not marry for love. Elise had found a suitable father for her potential children and Harry wed an affluent socialite allowing him to continue to pursue his youthful hobbies. Marriages of convenience were common, but Elise and Harry were less suited than others to survive one. Acquaintances remembered that for years at a time the couple did not speak with one another. Harry turned to hunting, card playing, and philandering, while Elise found refuge by intensifying the practice of her religion. As they aged, there was meager effort on either of their parts to overlook each other's foibles for the benefit of the marriage. The author believes that with greater exertion, Elise might have mitigated her emotional and sexual withdrawal from Harry, beginning after Buddy was born. Conversely, Harry might have been more patient and loving with Elise during her lengthy depressions.

Elise and Lorraine's life-long depression and Harry G. "Buddy," Jr.'s depression and, possibly, other psychosis, darkened their existence. (There is no surviving evidence of any professional diagnoses regarding the Johns' mental states; rather, the author made these assessments.) Elise's existence was dogged by a moderate depression that left her struggling to enjoy life. Beginning in 1920, she escaped for long periods to the Sacred Heart Sanitarium where the staff controlled the visits of her family and friends. Between late-1945 and mid-1947 she lived there for a total of five months on three visits, no doubt, in part, to escape her husband Harry. Sanitariums were more common in Europe than in the United States. The facility, at 1545 South Layton Boulevard, was opened in 1893 to provide hydrotherapy and physical therapy treatments for patients with chronic physical and mental diseases or, simply, to offer a quiet place for wealthy Milwaukeeans in need of rest.

Part of Lorraine and Buddy's life-long negative self-image resulted from their parents' tortured marriage. Lorraine and Buddy, with their own emotional difficulties, found ways to survive this fractured environment that, in their adult years with no corrective therapy, harmed their jobs, marriages, and lives. Though, as adults, Lorraine and Buddy had spectacular accomplishments, due to their emotional problems, they damaged, as a water buffalo inadvertently tramples foliage underfoot, the people closest to them: spouses, children, and co-workers.

Despite their private problems, the Johns lived lengthy, socially respectable lives. When the boisterous party celebrating beer's return roiled in the street at Miller Brewery, Elise, 52, Harry John, 58, Lorraine, 19, and Buddy, 13, lived on Highland Boulevard. Prohibition's end did not have an immediate significant impact on their lives; instead, they continued living as before, part of Milwaukee's second-tier elite. In no way did their wealth or, for that matter, any of the Millers' affluence, approach the Brew City's highest level. Other divisions among Milwaukee's elite in the 1930s and 1940s included religion, as

Catholics, Protestants, and Jews each socialized at their own clubs and parties. As the Millers and Johns were predominantly Catholic, they hobnobbed with Milwaukee's Catholic elite.

Along with their dogs, Piker and Duke, the Johns lived at both their Highland Boulevard home and Oconomowoc Lake summerhouse in Waukesha County. In 1934, the Johns' net worth was $4.8 million, which in part consisted of $1.4 million in mortgages, $1.2 million in the Miller Brewery and Oriental Realty Company stocks, $1.1 million in properties, and $840,000 in bonds. They kept a Cadillac Coupe, Cadillac Sedan, and Ford Sedan at their Milwaukee home and a Chris Craft, sailboat and an iceboat at their lake home. They also owned two vacant lots on exclusive Lake Drive in Milwaukee and farmland in Arizona for a possible new home.[338]

The Johns' income in 1934 was $107,000 of which $93,000 came from interest. They earned no salary because Harry was not employed and Elise was not yet working at the family businesses. The family's income originated entirely from Elise's investments. Since 1921, when Harry last worked, Elise, the breadwinner, gave her husband a $2,000 monthly dole, which amount no doubt led to many disagreements. Although occasionally, Harry received $5,000 to $10,000 a month.[339]

The Johns rarely cooperated on their finances. Elise brought all of the assets into the marriage and, throughout her life, maintained control of them. At best, Harry served an advisory role. Even so, occasionally Elise allowed Harry to represent her in financial or business matters such as functioning as an executor of her brother Emil's estate and temporarily serving as a director on the Miller Brewing Company's board. Otherwise, whenever an opportunity arose, Elise led.

Harry John's chronic unemployment embarrassed Elise and brought derision from others who valued work. Many of Harry's comrades admired his lifestyle, but Ernest, Fritz, Emil, and Carl Miller scorned him for wasting his gregariousness, intelligence, looks, and energy. Harry was sufficiently sociable and entertaining that his friends unsuccessfully encouraged him to run the governorship of Wisconsin. His chronic poor relationship with the Miller males brought conflicts. During a quarrel with Carl Miller, the volatile Harry choked him before being restrained.[340]

Due to the Johns' wealth, the couple never had to toil for pay. But Milwaukee's culture put a high priority on male employment irrespective of one's financial status. Besides employment, politics and social work were acceptable careers for Milwaukee's Brahmin males; Harry did neither. Instead, he spent his days socializing at clubs, hunting, racing, and womanizing. In Harry's defense, he was kindhearted and performed many private acts of personal charity for family and friends. Additionally, he was a dedicated grandfather to Lorraine's children, Karen and Michael, filling in for their often absent father Henry.

Determined Yankees and Europeans, primarily Germans, created the city of Milwaukee out of marshland. Besides religion, the work ethic may have been these early Milwaukeeans deepest-held belief, making Harry somewhat of an outcast. Many Europeans immigrated to the Americas to escape a system in which the upper class maintained their wealth through inheritance rather than personal effort. Harry's father was an immigrant medical doctor known for his selfless commitment to his patients. Equally, Elise's father, Frederick Miller, and her brother-in-law, Carl Miller, were hard-working immigrants drawn by Milwaukee's financial opportunities.

Elise's growing unhappiness paralleled an increase in her Catholic charitable donations. For example, in 1934, she made mostly small financial gifts to sixty-seven institutions ranging from Milwaukee-area organizations such as St. Rose Congregation, Marquette University, St. Charles Boys' Home, St. John's Institute for the Deaf Mute, St. Joseph's Hospital, and Mount Mary College. She also gave to out-of-state benevolent organizations: St. Benedict Parish in Roundup, Montana; the Indian Mission in Sisseton, South Dakota; Epiphany Apostolic College in Newburgh, New York; Catholic Church Extension Society in Chicago; New Subiaco Abbey in Arkansas, and the Uganda Mission in East Africa. Elise also made various small non-deductible donations that she wrote in a booklet as: "milk for poor; clothes for poor girl; poor boy; groceries for poor family; lumber and old clothes for family; Mrs. Bliefernichts for set of teeth; and the Sacred Heart College in Watertown, Wisconsin for railroad fare for poor boy."[341]

On August 12, 1935, to begin transferring her wealth to her children, Elise set up one trust each, for Lorraine and Buddy, to accept $300,000 in Chicago apartment buildings. These trusts were created by Alexander W. Schutz, the Miller and Johns' attorney, who, from his office in the First Wisconsin National Bank Building, also did substantial work for Miller Brewery. Elise continued to give to her husband and children for their trusts or immediate use. Over the next six years, she would transfer more than $1.1 million. Besides Harry's allowance, Elise gave her children regular stipends. For instance, in 1934, she gave Lorraine a $150 monthly allowance, which climbed to $300 in 1937 and $350 by 1938. Lorraine received her last allowance in January 1939.[342]

In May 1935, Harry John, Sr., pursued plans to build a $150,000 home on two vacant lots they bought for $159,000 at 3452 North Lake Drive in Milwaukee. It is unclear what role Elise took in this undertaking because, years later, she denied any cooperation. This movement toward constructing a house on the Lake Drive property was the second attempt. In 1931, the Johns contracted with the architect, Richard Philip to draw up plans but then cancelled, which cost them $6,250 to settle. In 1935, Harry contracted with the architect, Armin C. Frank, to begin procuring quotations from subcontractors. Soon enough, Frank began receiving mixed signals from the Johns and, finally on July 25, 1935, placed a call to Elise at her Oconomowoc summer home. Mrs. John quashed the notion of building a new house, instead suggesting to Frank that Harry buy an existing one. Just like 1931, the Johns paid $5,000 for unused architectural services. Harry John's loss of face surely angered him. They sold these lots in 1945 for a considerable loss.[343]

The Johns regrouped and, on December 16, 1935, put a $1,000 down payment on a corner lot in Wauwatosa's Wash-

The Miller High Life Girl in the Moon is a revered company icon. She began appearing in Miller ads as an equestrian performer, standing on a High Life beer crate. In 1907 the girl was repositioned on the crescent moon. (Courtesy of the Miller Brewing Company Archives.)

This image is the earliest known photograph of Frederick Miller's Plank Road Brewery, probably in the late 1860s. Note the beer garden on the hill in the background and the rural nature of what is now an urban area. (Courtesy of the Miller Brewing Company Archives.)

This photo is a close-up of Frederick Miller's Plank Road Brewery; notice the steps at the left to the beer garden. The front of the main building has been reconstructed by the Miller Brewing Company and sits on the hill overlooking West State Street (Courtesy of the Miller Brewing Company Archives.)

A teamster with his keg wagon pause in front of the brewery's South Side Milwaukee branch. These wagons were designed to facilitate the lifting of the heavy beer barrels. All of the kegs at this time were made of wood and are now valued collectables, c. 1900. (Courtesy of the Miller Brewing Company Archives.)

Employees of the Fred. Miller Brewing Company gathered in front of the company's office building some time after 1887. This building is now the site of the current Milwaukee brewhouse. The two beautiful F. Miller corner signs would certainly make today's beer memorabilia collectors envious. c. 1890

This photo shows one small section of Miller's caverns as seen in 1968. The caverns are the only remnant of the original Plank Road Brewery. Begun by Charles Best in 1850, they were in use until 1906 when they were replaced by refrigerated buildings. A portion of the caverns was renovated in the early 1950s and is now a part of the brewery tours. (Courtesy of the Miller Brewing Company Archives.)

Miller's regional distribution system is exemplified in this pre-Prohibition photo from Sandusky, Ohio. The local Miller distributor had his office, depot, ice house, and a saloon beside the train tracks where the beer and ice were delivered from Milwaukee. Wagons would then carry the beer to other saloons in his territory. (Courtesy of the Miller Brewing Company Archives.)

This Miller Brewing Company "tied house" in Kenosha, Wisconsin was typical of the establishments owned by breweries before Prohibition. Only Miller products were served at their "tied houses." Notice the sunburst Miller "M" above the doorway. (Courtesy of the Miller Brewing Company Archives.)

LEFT: The Miller brewhouse, constructed in 1886, as it appeared in the 1940s. The six-pointed star above "F. Miller" is a traditional brewing symbol. RIGHT: A glass-lined tank was hoisted into the I house finishing area in 1954. The tank was 43 feet long and held 1,000 barrels of beer. I house was constructed in two stages with the last four floors completed in 1954. (Both photos courtesy of Miller Brewing Company Archives.)

LEFT: Miller's copper brewing kettles in the new Milwaukee brewhouse in 1953. (Courtesy of Miller Brewing Company Archives.) RIGHT: Frederick J. Miller. c. 1875.

LEFT: Maria Ludowika Zepfel Miller, Frederick J. Miller's mother provided vital contributions to her son's success. CENTER: Frederick J. Miller's first wife, Josephine Miller Miller, was an important part of the early brewery's success. (Courtesy of the Miller Brewing Company Archives.) RIGHT: Lisette Gross soon after emigrating from Germany. c. 1849

In this 1867 photo, Lisette Miller, Frederick A. "Fritz" Miller (baby on lap), Frederick J. Miller, Ernest Miller (boy on lap), and Anna Mary "Bebe" Gross (Lisette's aunt and babysitter) pose.

Ernest Miller, Gottfried Gross (Lisette's father), unknown woman (maybe Lisette's mother), Lisette Gross Miller, Clara Miller, Louise Miller, Frederick J. Miller, Frederick A. "Fritz" Miller, Anna Mary "Bebe" Gross (Lisette's aunt), c. 1874. This photograph is the last known image of the exotic-looking Louise Miller, the last member of Frederick J. Miller's first family, who died a year later.

LEFT: Ernest, Clara, and Frederick A. "Fritz" Miller stopped wiggling just long enough for the flash to illuminate them. c. 1874
RIGHT: Emil Miller, c. 1879

LEFT: Brothers Frederick A. "Fritz" and Emil Miller. c. 1885. CENTER: Elise Miller on what is probably her first birthday in 1881. It may have been the first time that she ever wore shoes, which were on the wrong feet. RIGHT: Ernest G. Miller, c. 1883

LEFT: The Miller family home on Miller Lane, behind Miller Brewery, with the widowed Lisette standing on the steps. This structure is still standing. c. 1892. CENTER: Elise Miller, a life-long dedicated Catholic, here holds her First Communion bible wrapped in a rosary. c. 1892. RIGHT: Ernest Miller became a major philanthropist, creating a family tradition that continues unabated. c. 1900.

LEFT: Frederick A. "Fritz" Miller often played the role of Miller family moderator. c. 1895. (Courtesy of Miller Brewing Company Archives.) CENTER: Clara A. Miller. c 1886. RIGHT: Emil Miller in a computer enhanced photo. c. 1902. (Courtesy of the Miller Brewing Company Archives.)

LEFT: Elise Miller. c. 1900.
RIGHT: Clara, Loretta, Claire, Anita, and Carl Miller, 1898

Lisette Miller's house at 3200 West Highland Boulevard under construction in 1900. (Courtesy of the Pabst Mansion Archives.)

LEFT: Emil Miller with his niece Anita Miller. Anita later said that Emil was a fun loving uncle, unlike his more staid brothers. c. 1902. RIGHT: Frederick A., Lisette and Elise Miller John pause in a Victorian garden. c. 1910

LEFT: A unique scenario in which Emil, Clara, Lisette and Elise Miller John stood together. In photos, Clara and Elise never stood side by side. c. 1910. RIGHT: Sisters, Claire and Loretta Miller. c 1910

LEFT: The wedding of Harry John and Elise Miller on June 18, 1912. The photo shows a collection of Millers and Johns, with Harry's brothers scattered behind him. RIGHT: Lisette Gross Miller, c. 1912.

The Miller family at Lisette's Highland Boulevard house in May 1919. Top row, Norman Kopmeier, Sr., Frederick A. "Fritz" Miller, James B. McCahey, Sr., Ernest Miller, Claire Miller McCahey, Harry G. John, Sr.; second row from top, Elise K. Miller John, Mary Josephine Gross (Lisette's sister-in-law), Lisette Gross Miller, May Gibson Miller, Clara Miller Miller; third row from top, Carl Miller, Anita Miller Bransfield, Charles "Chuck" Bransfield, Loretta Miller Kopmeier, Michael Bransfield; bottom row, Frederick C. Miller, Lorraine John, Charlotte Miller.

LEFT: Elise Miller John and Lisette Miller, mother and daughter and best friends, sit beside one another in possibly their last photo together, as Lisette died soon after. c. 1919. RIGHT: Lorraine John, Lisette Gross Miller, and Harry G. "Buddy" John. This is the only known picture of Lisette with her youngest grandchild Buddy, taken months before her death in 1920.

Ernest Miller, who may have been gay, poses with an unknown man in what appears to be California, c. 1915

LEFT: Ernest Miller demonstrating a sense of humor in Miami in 1923, two years before his death. RIGHT: Charlotte Miller in summer 1924.

Fred C. Miller, Claire McCahey, James B. McCahey, Marguerite Bransfield, Norman Kopmeier, Sr., and Carl Miller, in Cuba in March 1929. Being that Prohibition had shut down the production, distribution, and sale of alcoholic beverages in the U.S., Cuba was a nearby destination for wealthy Americans wanting to enjoy the "High Life."

LEFT: Clara A. Miller, who loved flowers, poses beside her Newberry Boulevard home, c. 1935. RIGHT: Frederick A. "Fritz" Miller hiding his glass eye, c. 1935.

Frederick A. "Fritz" Miller and his wife May Miller, c. 1935.

Carl Miller, James B. McCahey, Sr., Byron Vincent Kanaley (Adele Miller's father), Michael Bransfield, Sr., and Frederick C. Miller at what may have been Fred's wedding in 1931.

Standing from left, Marguerite Bransfield, Loretta Kopmeier, Carl Miller; sitting from left, Charlotte Blommer, Clara Miller, and Claire McCahey. c 1940.

In 1955, Loretta Kopmeier, Clara Miller, Gail Miller, Rose Mary Bradford, Claire McCahey, Carlotta Miller, Charlotte Blommer, and Clair Rosenberger observe a plaque and donated stone from the castle in Sigmaringen, Germany where Frederick J. Miller brewed beer.

LEFT: Norman Kopmeier, Sr., (four women with lighter clothes) Loretta Kopmeier, Claire McCahey, Carol McCahey O'Neil and Adele Kanaley Miller at dedication of Stockhouse "F", September 6, 1948. (Courtesy of Miller Brewing Company Archives.)
RIGHT: Frederick C. and his mom, Clara A. Miller, c. 1952.

The Clara and Carl Miller house on East Newberry Boulevard.

LEFT: Loretta Miller Kopmeier, photographed in February 1914, four months after her wedding, was clever, even well into her nineties. RIGHT: Rose Mary, Norman, Sr., Loretta, and Norman Kopmeier, Jr., c. 1928

LEFT: Loretta Miller Kopmeier, c. 1950. RIGHT: Claire Miller McCahey on her wedding day, November 12, 1917.

James B. and Claire McCahey stroll a boardwalk, c. 1948.

Siblings James, Jr., Frederick, and Claire McCahey in their World War II service uniforms.

The second generation of McCaheys: Carol O'Neil, James B. McCahey, Jr., Anita Gray, Frederick McCahey, and Clair O'Neil. c. 1995

TOP LEFT: Marguerite "Muggs" Miller, c. 1922.
TOP RIGHT: Anita Miller Bransfield and her son Charles "Chuck" in the warm months of 1919.
LEFT: Siblings, Chuck and Joan Bransfield smile upon his return from a Japanese prisoner of war camp in 1945.

Marguerite, Chuck, Michael Bransfield, Sr., and James B. McCahey, Sr. welcome Chuck home in 1945.

LEFT: Siblings Michael and Joan Bransfield, "Sr. Michaelina of the Sisters of Mercy," in August 1958. Later, Mike became a Maryknoll priest, serving many years with the working poor in South Korea. RIGHT: Frederick Miller Bransfield and his sister Marguerite in the 1960s.

Siblings, Frederick Miller and Joan Bransfield, c. 2000.

LEFT: Frederick C. Miller at the University of Notre Dame in 1929. RIGHT: Frederick C. Miller and James B. McCahey, Jr., at the Red Arrow Camp in Northern Wisconsin in 1928.

LEFT: Frederick C. Miller on an ice truck handling a set of tongs, c. 1928. RIGHT: On October 9, 1953, Frederick C. Miller, Lorraine John Mulberger, Norman Klug, and Liberace, the late world famed pianist and television star, in the brewery's caves. (Courtesy of Miller Brewing Company Archives.)

Norman Klug, Lorraine John Mulberger, and Frederick C. Miller review an architectural blueprint, c. 1949. (Courtesy of Miller Brewing Company Archives.)

Michael Stoiber, Elise Miller John, Frederick C. Miller, and Adele Kanaley Miller drink High Life at a reception at the Wauwatosa Women's Club in June 1947. Fred had just become the brewery's president.

LEFT: Frederick C. Miller, c. 1953. (Courtesy of Miller Brewing Company Archives.) RIGHT: Frederick C. Miller, Adele Kanaley Miller, and James B. McCahey, Sr., in Arizona on April 5, 1954. Throughout his life, Fred carefully maintained his physique.

The Frederick and Adele Miller Family. Standing, Gail, Kate, Frederick, Jr., Clair, Loret; sitting, Carlotta, Carl, Adele, Frederick, Sr., Adele (daughter). c. 1952. (Courtesy of the Miller Brewing Company Archives.)

LEFT: Charlotte Miller at her wedding on April 25, 1935.
RIGHT: Marguerite, Mary, and Elizabeth with their dad, Bernard Blommer, c. 1949.

LEFT: Charlotte Miller Blommer, c. 1961. RIGHT: The Johns: Lorraine, Harry, Sr., Harry, Jr., and Elise in 1922.

LEFT: Lorraine John holding her brother, Harry, Jr., in 1922. RIGHT: Harry G. John, Sr., and his son Buddy, c. 1924.

LEFT: Harry G. John, Jr., standing atop a rock in Arizona, where he and his parents went to mitigate his asthmatic symptoms. c. 1927. RIGHT: Lorraine John Mulberger at about the time of her 1936 marriage.

Lorraine John and Henry Mulberger's wedding at Oconomowoc Lake on May 16, 1936, which was the social event of the year in the lake region.

Henry and Lorraine Mulberger in the first years after their 1936 marriage. They loved attending dances and Henry was a successful amateur photographer, who developed his own pictures.

LEFT Karen, Lorraine, and Michael Mulberger in approximately 1945. RIGHT: Lorraine John Mulberger in Arizona with one of her thoroughbreds, c. 1980

LEFT: Elise Miller John at the zenith of her authority as the brewery president, c. 1945. (Courtesy of Miller Brewing Company Archives.) RIGHT: Harry G. John, Jr., on his farm near Oconomowoc Lake in approximately 1941.

LEFT: Harry G. John, Jr., at his Town of Summit farm in about 1943. Three years later, he served as president of the Miller Brewing Company. RIGHT: Harry G. John, Jr., and Dr. Donald A. Gallagher ran the de Rancé foundation for many years. Dr. Gallagher was a philosophy professor, Harry and Erica's best man, and their eldest daughter Emily's baptismal sponsor. c. 1950.

Erica Novotny in Rome, where she was born, before marrying Harry John and having nine children. c. 1950.

Harry G. John, Jr., and campers from the Fr. Stephen Youth Camp, c. 1952.

Harry and Erica John on their wedding day on September 22, 1956, in Milwaukee's Holy Cross Church, now renamed St. Vincent Pallotti East.

The Harry and Erica John family photographed in 1981. Standing, Emily, Michael, Bruno, Paula, Henry, and Elise; sitting, Jessica, Timothy, Erica, Harry, Gregory, and Anna Maria Novotny (Erica's mother).

TOP: Pope John Paul II and Harry G. John, Jr., c. 1982. RIGHT: Harry G. John, Jr., who relished Manhattan's excitement, had his picture taken at New York's Waldorf Astoria Hotel in 1977.

In July 2003, Brandon C. John participated in a special tour at the brewery that his great-great grandfather founded.

ington Highlands, a spectacular subdivision created from a Pabst family horse and hop farm. The lot was one block west of Elise's brother Fritz and his wife, May, who in 1930 had built their own spectacular house in the Highlands. Elise was emotionally close to her brother and his wife and decided to live near them instead of living on the East Side close to her estranged sister, Clara. By March 1936, they had completed paying the $20,500 price for the property. The Johns hired the architectural firm of Grasshold and Johnson to design a home and, on August 31, 1936, Elise gave her bookkeeper, Oscar F. Treichler, the authority to pay all of the construction-related invoices. In September, a contractor began digging the foundation and, in early 1937, the Johns moved into their two-story brick home at 6454 Washington Circle.[344]

The house, which still stands, was highlighted with delicately stratified tan and orange sandstone along the corners and front porch. It has a burgundy-tiled roof and leaded-glass square, diamond, oblong, and round window panes. Two stylized stone lions proudly observe visitors from the second story corners of the entryway. A full-size crouching human figure grasps a chain with a lantern over the last step before the porch.

Harry's interest in flowers influenced the interior design. Plants and flowers are integrated into doorknobs, wrought iron doors, pewter panels above fireplaces, wood décor above windows, light sconces and chandeliers, and wall paintings. Along two upper sides of the den are carved, silhouetted, back-lit wooden panels, 30 to 36 inches high, displaying a series of American historical themes.

Apart from its finely crafted walls and floors, the house's dominant feature is its winding, delicately-designed wrought-iron staircase silhouetted against two-story high rear windows. The wooden staircase is adorned with a brass banister decorated with flowing vines and elves hunting or playing a flute. It is in this magnificent space that the Johns placed their tall Christmas trees that so delighted guests. The second-floor bathrooms are exquisitely designed with different tile patterns from ceiling to floor, featuring Crane toilets, sinks, and tubs, augmented with beautifully arranged tile patterns. The Johns' granddaughter, Karen Mulberger Swanson, noted that the Johns had a maid, seamstress, live-in cook, chauffeur, and laundress who came once a week.

The basement was built in the style of a *rathskeller*, or German drinking establishment, with concrete, faux stone, arched walls. Several gargoyles stare out from the pillars. The Johns entertained family and friends at a wooden wet bar that any public tavern would relish. The end of a beer keg extended from the middle of the wooden skirt of the bar with the words *Guzundheit* and Miller High Life stenciled in a circular pattern around a Girl in the Moon insignia.

Lorraine was a determined young woman. While at Marquette University, she was one of the first students to reject mandatory daily Catholic Mass. While Lorraine was rebelling against rules, she also had fun. One fall evening, Lorraine and two friends, Mary Lou Gildea and Betty Kotecki, were in her parents' limousine, on the way to a Marquette College football game when, as a prank, they extracted and then puffed on a corncob pipe full of tobacco, shocking the driver. Life provided Lorraine other opportunities for fun. One summer evening when she was in her late teens, she, and a group of youths, including Buddy and friend Bill Miller, were returning to her Oconomowoc Lake home after attending a Milwaukee professional baseball game, when they found themselves in a Town of Okauchee bar where Lorraine sipped a beer. Unexpectedly, Buddy and his friends created tumult by lighting a stink bomb, emptying the place. They scurried out the front door, making their way home via back roads to avoid the angry patrons. Meanwhile, Bill Miller and Lorraine slipped out of the back door and headed down to Lake Okauchee where they borrowed a boat to row furiously from Okauchee Lake to their home on Oconomowoc Lake. All the while, they giggled about the consequences if the proprietor caught them. They tied up the boat near the Johns' dock, never returning it. Soon enough, Lorraine and Bill got a tongue lashing from Harry John, Sr., for abandoning Buddy and his friends.

In 1934, 21-year-old Lorraine John lived with her parents while struggling to overcome a crippling depression. She had decided against a college degree after temporarily attending Marquette University and the University of Wisconsin in Madison. Besides medical assistance that year, Elise and Harry John gave her various gifts to extricate her from the depression; of the $11,000, $7,300 was in cash, $3,490 was for a new Super Eight Packard Coupe Roadster, painted yellow with sprig green stripes, and $1,000 was for clothes.[345] At any rate, her parents were desperate for a respite, and turned to any means available, some religious. One such source was family friend Brother Lambert Barbier, a Catholic Holy Cross Brother from Watertown, Wisconsin. Brother Lambert knew Henry "Hank" Mulberger, a single intelligent gentleman from an established Watertown, Wisconsin family and asked him to visit Lorraine. Hank came to the John household regularly to speak with the young woman. Soon enough, Lorraine consented to attend social occasions with the young man. Hank's presence corresponded with an improvement in Lorraine's depression and, from that day forward, the Johns were great fans of the Watertown native. Over time, Lorraine and Hank's friendship developed into a betrothal.

Hank, a man with a round face and soft eyes, was born in Watertown on February 27, 1910, to Henry, president of the Bank of Watertown, and Clarabel Shurtleff Mulberger. In 1932, he earned a bachelor's degree in psychology from the University of Wisconsin and in 1933 earned some post-graduate credits. He was an athlete and played on the school's varsity football team. In the 1930s Hank had attended Officer's Training School and, later during World War II, served in the United States Air Corps with distinction.[346] He was a member of the Church of Christian Science, and his thirst for knowledge was boundless. One of his early hobbies included photography and, subsequently, he learned to develop his own film.

Somehow the combination of Hank, a lot of prayers, and a new Cadillac brought Lorraine out of her room. At this time, the Johns, desperate to aid Lorraine, made an appointment at the Mayo Clinic in Rochester, Minnesota, to have her receive a full evaluation. Lorraine's daughter, Karen Swanson, remarked that at first Lorraine balked at the proposal. Finally, she agreed to go, but with Hank Mulberger instead of her parents.

On December 25, 1935, the Johns announced Lorraine and Hank's engagement at a festive "Tom and Jerry" party at their Oconomowoc Lake home. Surrounded with snow and gaily bedecked with Christmas trees and holly, the Johns' home was a perfect setting for the party. They were socially active and customarily gave parties such as this one, named after characters Tom and Jerry Hawthorne from Pierce Egan's *Life in London* that featured a hot drink that was a combination of a toddy and an eggnog.[347]

Norman "Normy" Kopmeier, Jr., Lorraine's 8-year-old cousin, stood at the doorway presenting each guest with a scroll, inscribed with the names of the betrothed. The young couple received the guests in the living room before a tall, red, cellophane Christmas tree. Lorraine wore a metallic cocktail dress with a shoulder corsage of her father's favorite flowers, orchids. Red candles and holly garlands placed about the rooms engendered a holiday flavor. Iceboats, much like the Johns' new one that was reported to be one of the fastest in the area, skimmed across the hardened lake.

Lorraine's marriage to Hank Mulberger on May 16, 1936, at the Johns' Oconomowoc Lake summer home was the area's event of the year. The wedding party, one by one, processed down a stone staircase under a clear sky. After Betty Deuster, the maid of honor, had paraded down the stairs sporting a broad-brimmed white chiffon hat with a spray of lilies-of-the-valley at the front, Lorraine came into view. One newspaper reported that she, unquestionably, was one of Milwaukee's most attractive members of the younger set. Her fine features and dyed blond hair augmented her thin figure that was draped in a long, white chiffon gown. In her right hand, she held a large bouquet of lilies-of-the-valley and a spill of white orchids that almost touched the ground. The nervous bride promenaded down the stone steps, on her father's arm, to Hank's waiting hand. Previously, her dad had planted thousands of tulips that bloomed on cue providing an astonishing multi-hued blanket. At the Oconomowoc Lake Club reception, Harry served fresh fish that had been rushed in from Lake Tomahawk in northern Wisconsin.[348]

Lorraine and Hank postponed having children and instead, for a few years after their marriage, enjoyed life. The dashing couple traveled and took many photographs, including moving pictures, especially of nature. They demonstrated their dancing prowess at parties and balls, at times with the famous bandleader and acquaintance Wayne King. Lorraine and Hank were sufficiently prominent that bands would strike up a version of the 1928 hit *Sweet Lorraine*, by Mitchell Parish and Cliff Burwell, after she entered the ballroom in one of her satin gowns. Lorraine also stayed active with fencing lessons at the Wisconsin Athletic Club, reading, and creative writing. Lorraine's daughter Karen related that her mother learned etching from Dr. George New, a fine Milwaukee artist.

The Johns gave the newlyweds money to build a new home in Elm Grove, an exclusive new suburb west of Milwaukee. After the wedding, the Johns continued helping Lorraine financially. In August of that year, they paid her $13.55 traffic fine. In 1938, Elise gave Lorraine $156,615, comprising $149,500 of Chicago apartments. They also paid $7,115 of her bills, including, in part, $80 to George Watts and Son, Inc. (a store of crystal and fine tableware), $1,475 for a new Cadillac on her birthday, $672 to E.H. Laabs for a coat and other items, and cash.[349]

Hank obtained a private pilot's license in the summer of 1935 and enjoyed flying from Milwaukee to Watertown. On October 9 of that year, Hank crashed his plane into a farmer's field upon leaving Watertown. He explained that his motor failed and the crash left the plane badly damaged. Fortunately, he and a passenger escaped unhurt. On May 5, 1939, Hank was piloting an amphibious plane and rescued three youths from cold Lake Michigan waters where their boat had sunk. They had overturned their catboat during a squall inside the breakwater and floundered for 15 minutes before Hank pulled them into his plane. Hank taxied toward the lakeshore seadrome and saw a Coast Guard boat approaching, to which he then transferred the passengers. Karen remembered that during World War II, her father voluntarily re-enlisted in the U.S. Army Air Force and requested assignment to an aircraft carrier, where he was a flight instructor. Before that, he had a local assignment as head of the Wisconsin Upper-Michigan internal security district. On April 1, 1943, Hank was promoted from first lieutenant to captain. After the war, he served in the Air Force Reserve, from which he retired as a major.[350]

Karen, Elise and Harry John's first grandchild, was born in January 1941 to Lorraine and Hank. Michael was born to the couple in March 1944. The new father saw opportunity wherever he looked. In 1945, he owned H.C. Mulberger, Inc., an advertising agency that performed a significant amount of work for Miller Brewery. At this time, C.A. Mathisson, a popular Miller Brewery advertising executive and later creator of the 1955 Miller family history worked for Mulberger.

Lorraine and Buddy's general trusts dictated that upon them reaching age 21 they would begin receiving annual payments of $5,000. The payments would rise as they aged until they reached 55, when they would receive the entire remaining amount. For unknown reasons, this trust never became very large, capping at about $125,000.[352]

In 1940, Elise and Harry John employed 15 people, inlcuding domestics, office workers, janitors, gardeners and chauffeurs. Many of them worked at the myriad apartment buildings that Elise owned. Among them, Elise paid her long-time cook Rose Eisenmann $1,040. Her housekeeper, Genevieve Stabbe, received $624 while her chauffeur, Clarence Schermeister, was paid $1,560 and her Oconomowoc gardener, Clarence Shannon, received $1,320. All received free room and board.[353]

Elise, as did her siblings, used brewery maintenance workers to perform repairs and errands at her home. For this labor, the brewery sent her invoices. Most of these jobs were superfluous such as purchasing 20 gallons of gasoline and boots, rewinding the starting rope of their boat's engine, repairs in the pantry, and building a cigar cabinet. In April 1938, Miller Brewery charged the Johns $3,508 for beer that it had given them between January 1, 1933, and January 1, 1938. These items were some of the subsidized perks of owning a large, profitable company.[354]

In the 1930s and 1940s, Elise's socializing, donations, and volunteering were increasingly done for the Catholic Church. She was a member of the Happy Death Society, which prayed novenas regularly to St. Joseph the Carpenter, their patron saint, to invoke his intercession for their and others' holy and natural death. Members of this society were afraid of taking their last breath without the inherent knowledge that they, due to their prayer-filled holy life, were destined for heaven. She was also a member of St. Sebastian's Christian Mothers' Society, St. Margaret's Guild, and a twenty-five year associate of the Dominican Rosary Aid Society.

In March 1941, the Johns made the first of several payments totaling $19,239 to purchase the Delafield Butler Dairy Farm, about twenty-five miles west of Milwaukee. In May of that year, Buddy graduated from the University of Notre Dame and immediately moved onto the farm. On this sixty-acre property and on another twenty rented acres, he raised Holstein and Brown Swiss cattle and pigs; he also grew alfalfa and corn. Eschewing modern conveniences, he plowed the fields with black Percheron draft horses. It is unclear whether Buddy lived on the farm to embody the solitary existence of a monk or to dodge the military draft, from which he could have been exempted as the only agricultural worker on the farm. Buddy was not alone, as Fred C. Miller and James B. McCahey, Sr. also owned farms during World War II to augment their family's food rations. Buddy's life-long friend, Bill Miller, said that Buddy wanted to join the Army Air Corps the day after the Japanese attack on Pearl Harbor but was rejected because of his severe asthma and flat feet. In 1945 and 1946 Buddy received physically-unfit rejection notices from the armed forces.[355]

Beginning with a $5,000 gift in 1934, Elise regularly gave significant donations to Buddy. From 1935 to 1938, she gave almost $600,000 in Chicago real estate to his trust. Not all of the donations were intended for her son's extended future. For example, in July 1937, Elise John paid $56.74 to repair his 1934 Packard after he hit a fire hydrant in front of the Miller Brewery.

By 1940, Buddy's general trust was worth $258,000 with $181,000 in Miller Brewery stock and $61,000 in cash. By the end of 1941, Elise had given her son gifts worth $818,000. In 1942, Buddy's general trust had increased to $654,360 after receiving $9,000 from his mother, which included a $5,000 life insurance policy.[356]

In the beginning, Buddy performed much of the tiresome farm work, but soon hired Alfred Koegel, who with his wife and seven children, shared his house, managed the farm, cooked, and cleaned the residence. This change gave him the freedom increasingly to pursue the promotion of his fervent brand of Catholicism, which he inherited from his mother. This gentleman farmer became involved in a Catholic men's group, led by priests, and, with his substantial wealth, made plans to build a Catholic retreat center on his farmland, which was never constructed. Regularly, he traveled to South Bend, Indiana to meet with his college religious advisor, Rev. Cornelius Hagerty, who instructed the young man on Catholic mysticism. Father Hagerty also told Harry, Jr., that worldly wealth hindered his chances of eternal happiness. The priest's teachings troubled the rich young man. In the end, Father Hagerty's teachings convinced Buddy to begin ridding himself of his "burden."[357]

Ever since Buddy John had a mental breakdown at Notre Dame, his mother tried to maintain a reasonable relationship with him. In his early twenties, he began to reject almost everything that his mother represented, except religion. He ceased taking any advice from his family, except from his brother-in-law Hank Mulberger, whom he admired. The young man began ridding himself of his mother's lawyers and bookkeepers, whom he believed did his mother's bidding and were not working in his best interests. He hired the attorneys and brothers, Urban and John Wittig, who had been neighbors at his Highland Boulevard house, to help him give away his assets. They were also partners with their brother Roland in the family law firm.[358]

At this time, it is unclear whether Buddy even thought of marriage or children, (or providing for them), because, at a minimum, his financial decisions would drop him into a lower economic class. His mother's financial advisors, Oscar Treichler and B.H. Protzmann, reluctantly told him that re-designating the beneficiaries of the life insurance policies that he was gifted from his mother to a non-profit institution would be the simplest way to begin transferring his wealth to just causes. At that time, the remainder of his assets, such as income properties and stock, were restricted by trust documents.

In 1945, Harry G. "Buddy" John, Jr., then 25, began to divest himself of his worldly goods in exchange for his eternal salvation. On March 20, 1945, the Equitable Life Insurance Society sent forms to Buddy to sign and then return in order to change the beneficiary of a $50,000 policy, from Lorraine, to the New Melleray (Trappist) Abbey in Peosta, Iowa. Buddy had developed a predilection for contemplative monks from his mother and uncles and, also, from his own life as a farming "monk." In April, Protzmann, a trustee of Buddy's trusts, wrote to the abbey informing them of their good fortune. The New Melleray Abbey's leader, Abbot Albert J. Beston, O.C.S.O., responded happily, noting that, "However, because of innumerable requests for low Masses we could not undertake to offer any great number of low Masses here at the Abbey, but we would see that they were properly taken care of." Buddy was happy to receive the additional grace for his financial donation.[359]

To change the insurance policy's beneficiary, Buddy was required to sign and return various papers, which, as was his custom, he delayed. Harry, Jr., was a chronic procrastinator. In early April, Protzmann prodded Buddy, who was occupied on his farm, to return the papers quickly to him. Finally, Buddy deposited the signed papers at his parents' house on Washington Circle for Protzmann to collect. Elise, curious about the documents, reviewed them after her son had left. Elise John was aghast upon discovering that Buddy had begun ridding himself and, therefore, the Miller family, of their hard-earned wealth, most of which she had just given him.[360]

Decades earlier, Frederick J. and Lisette Miller had inculcated in their children the obligation to perpetuate the family's legacy regardless of personal compunctions. Aside from Emil's period of uncontrolled gambling, the Millers' second generation had fulfilled that duty. In 1945, Elise's son began to expurgate the legacy that the other Millers had maintained. Elise was determined to stop Bud from re-designating his life insurance policy to a non-family entity. At this time, surely she had evidence that her son planned to give away nearly all of his assets, a considerable amount indeed. Rightfully, she could have demanded that he give the money to his sister or her children if he did not want it. Unfortunately for Elise, in her son's mindset, his gifting of money to a family member would not bring him eternal life.

In a memo, Protzmann noted that on April 20, 1945, Elise called him and, "stated that she did not approve of the change in beneficiary to the N.M.A. [New Melleray Abbey] and wants the insurance to go to his [Buddy's] estate so that, in the event of H. Jr.'s death, the money would be available to pay his estate taxes." Next, Elise asked Protzmann to withhold returning the policy to the insurance company and, instead, convince Buddy to change the beneficiary to his own estate. She asked the bookkeeper to refrain from telling her son that his parents knew of this matter, no doubt, fearing his volatile temper.[361] B.H. Protzmann persuaded Harry, Jr., to retract his change of beneficiary, which relieved Elise. Unfortunately, the young man was hurt and angry that he had retreated from pursuing his passionately held goals. Rarely again would he withdraw from following his convictions.[362]

As 1945 passed, Buddy became increasingly focused on purging himself of his steadily amassing wealth. By March 1, 1946, Harry, Jr.'s assets, including his three trusts, were worth approximately $2.5 million. He also was half beneficiary of the $126,000 Harry G. John Family Trust in the event of his father's death.[363]

Harry Jr.'s dispersion of his assets propelled his bookkeepers to warn him of the dire consequences of high tax rates when he died. Everybody concerned tried to dissuade or slow down young Buddy John, figuring that when he aged, he would think differently. His expurgation, besides stocks, bonds, and insurance policies, included farm assets. On May 4, 1946, a priest from the Sacred Heart College in Watertown, Wisconsin, thanked the gentleman farmer for four truckloads of heifers and steers totaling 18,200 pounds that he and his employee had delivered the previous day.[364]

In 1941, Elise earned $224,000, which all came from stock dividends and interest. The following year, she was worth $4.3 million, including cash, savings bonds, her $197,000 Washington Highlands home, investment mortgages and her $91,000 Oconomowoc Lake home. Elise also had nearly 2,444 shares of Miller Brewing Company stock valued at $439,188 and 2,944 shares of the Oriental Realty Company valued at $910,320.[365]

Despite her generosity, in 1945 Elise John still had $4.2 million in assets, including $1.1 million in bonds, $463,000 in mortgages, $404,000 in rental mortgages, $486,000 in cash, $294,000 in residences, 2,942 shares of the Oriental Realty Company worth $975,054, and 2,439 shares of the Miller Brewing Company worth $403,442.[366]

17.
WORLD WAR II AND
A SPECTACULAR FIRE

On Saturday April 9, 1938, a five-story Miller stockhouse, a half-block south of State Street between 38th and 40th streets, caught fire and burned for ninety minutes before firefighters extinguished it. Five employees, who were cleaning metal and wooden vats, escaped safely. Due to the busy brewing season, the stockhouse had 200,000 gallons of lagering beer, which was undamaged. The fire raged between the fifth floor and the roof, burning the shavings and cork used for insulation, because the eighteen-inch concrete floor and firewalls kept it from spreading to the beer vats.[367]

The three-alarm blaze was a show for the 7,000 Milwaukeeans who gathered to see it. "Spectators crowded the bluffs for the best viewpoints and some braved the smoke cloud to line the Wells Street viaduct." Black smoke blew southward across the Wells Street trestle and slowed the streetcar to a snail's crawl. Dense smoke billowed several hundred feet into the air. The flames gave firefighters fits, sweeping out the fifth floor windows leaping 20 feet over the roofline. The fire did $5,000 to $20,000 in damage and, according to Fire Chief Steinkellner, was, "one of the most difficult to fight of any fire in recent years."[368] Even with thirteen hoses spraying on the building, "no stream could be brought to bear directly on the point of the fire's origin." The burning building, surrounded on three sides by bluffs, necessitated that firefighters drag ladders and hoses up the bluffs and destroy wooden fences before they could fight the flames. On the State Street side, the men swarmed over the roofs of adjacent buildings for vantage points from which to ply streams. At one point, the flames started to spread to the adjoining brewhouse before the firefighters doused them. The chief believed that the fire was caused by the improper disposal of a lighted cigarette.[369]

Another fire at the end of June 1940 burned 5,000 to 8,000 empty beer cases at the rear of the brewery that firefighters thought might have been started by spontaneous combustion or a lighted cigarette tossed onto the pile. There were 100,000 cases stored at the rear of the brewery, making a pile 160 feet long, 100 feet wide, and 20 feet high. The men poured water on the flames unceasingly for three hours to extinguish it.[370]

Besides fires, the brewery also occasionally battled political authorities. For example, in December 1938, as part of a John Doe probe, the State of Wisconsin filed charges against Miller Brewery for allegedly breaking laws regarding kept taverns. The state contended that Miller Brewery furnished equipment to taverns through subsidiary corporations. They proposed that Miller had a, "direct financial interest in the equipment and that the equipment was being furnished on the explicit understanding that no rent was to be paid." The law provided a $500 fine for any brewery subsidization of a tavern and could be the basis for revoking a brewery's license. The law was written at Prohibition's end in an effort to preclude the re-establishment of tied houses — saloons owned by breweries and, therefore, exclusive distributors of that business' products. In January 1939, Miller Brewery personnel denied that they had violated laws prohibiting kept taverns. Miller Brewery demurred or objected to the charges, stating that they were, "unreasonable, arbitrary, oppressive and an abuse of process." They continued that the evidence in the four counts was insufficient, "and that the action had not been authorized by the attorney general, the legislature or the governor, as required by law." District Judge Harvey L. Neelen dismissed the state's charges, writing that although the equipment companies supplied equipment to the bars, they made, "no attempt to engage in business for profit."[371]

In the middle of March in 1939, Miller Brewery, for the

first time, launched a national sales campaign. Although Miller beer was available in only 27 states, it launched the campaign in national circulation magazines. It disseminated the details to over 200 distributors and sales representatives at a sales meeting at Milwaukee's Pfister Hotel that surprisingly was the first such gathering since the re-legalization of beer. The one-day affair began with a brewery tour, followed by the meeting at the Pfister Hotel, and finally an evening banquet at the Plankinton Hotel.[372]

During 1941 in the months before the U.S. entered World War II, Miller Brewery continued to sell more beer and improve its physical plant. By that time, it had a capacity of 1 million barrels, twenty-one buildings covering nearly nine square city blocks, and approximately 800 employees. Its distribution network had grown to 40 states, including Alaska and Hawaii, and the Philippine Islands. Besides the popular High Life label, the brewery produced Export, Select, and Muenchener, a dark beer. Bock and Christmas beer were available in season. The brewery also provided guided tours on weekdays.[373]

On December 7, 1941, the Japanese bombed Pearl Harbor, precipitating America's involvement in World War II. As a way to assist in the war effort, in October 1944, the brewery donated $500 to the Los Angeles Community and War Fund and $9,500 to the Milwaukee and Community War Fund. In 1944 Miller Brewery produced 731,470 barrels, placing it fifteenth nationally.[374] Most brewery improvement efforts slowed or were postponed during the war years, due to building restrictions. Other wartime difficulties included loss of employees to the military service and the rationing of malt. In January 1945, the brewery directors discussed a 12 percent cut in malt allotments and decided against changing the beer's formula; instead, they withdrew from certain markets. Fortunately, beer's elevated demand, starting after Prohibition, continued into World War II.[375]

The war effectively ended the Great Depression that had plagued the country since 1929. The booming economy gave Americans more money to spend, some of which flowed to the breweries. The war years were a combination of high demand coupled with limited production capacity due to building restrictions and the rationing of raw materials. The brewery responded by carefully selecting their markets and squeezing the most out of their existing equipment and personnel. Additionally, over time the brewery phased out every label except High Life, its core brand, which simplified its production and marketing efforts, no doubt saving the brewery a considerable sum. The brewers worked around-the-clock making batches of beer that the distributors sold at full price. They also improved their viability by reducing the allotment of kegs and increasing the allotment of bottles that brought them $12 in additional income per barrel.

Throughout this period, the brewery earned handsome profits that allowed the directors to declare per share dividends of $20, or a total of $200,000, in November 1941, $10 per share in December 1941, $15 per share in November 1942, $30 per share in August 1943, $30 per share in November 1943, and $30 per share in November 1944. Together, these dividends were a $13.5-million gain for the brewery's stockholders. The last dividend was taken after 1944's net profit of $750,000. Fred C. Miller had advocated this dividend because he represented his mother and sisters, whose only profits from the brewery were dividends. His sisters pressured him to declare dividends to augment their husbands' incomes. On September 10, 1945, eight days after V-J Day, the directors declared a $20 per share dividend.[376]

Some of the Miller family served in the U.S. military during World War II. The only third-generation member to serve in the armed forces during the conflict was Hank Mulberger, Lorraine's husband, who re-enlisted on his own accord, as he was too old for the draft. At first he served, "in Milwaukee as public relations officer on the staff of Col. [C.J.] Otjen, who was head of the Wisconsin-Upper Michigan internal security district." In March 1943, at his own request, he transferred to an aircraft carrier as an Army Air Corps flight instructor, where he attained the rank of major.[377] Claire McCahey, Clara and Carl

Miller's third child, served the U.S.O. in Chicago by baking pies and cakes. There were various fourth-generation Millers active in the war effort. Anita, Claire McCahey's third child, was a driver in the Red Cross Motor Corps in Chicago. Her future husband, Win Gray, served in the Navy in the Pacific and was at Pearl Harbor when the Japanese struck there in 1941. Captain James B. McCahey, Jr., Claire McCahey's second child, served in Europe as the senior aide-de-camp to Major General Harry J. Collins. Captain McCahey was awarded the bronze star for meritorious operations against the enemy from February 6, 1945 to May 6, 1945. His younger brother Frederick was in the Navy and served in the South Pacific for three years. Robert Bradford, Rose Mary Kopmeier's husband, served for five years in the Army Air Corps, while Rose Mary achieved the rank of lieutenant in the Red Cross motor corps.[378]

Chuck Bransfield was the Miller descendant with the most notable service tenure during World War II, serving in the Navy Air Corps on an aircraft carrier in the Pacific Theater. Bransfield had learned to fly while he was an engineering student at the University of Notre Dame before enlisting in 1939. On September 18, 1943, near the Gilbert Islands, his torpedo bomber, of the 23rd Squadron, flew sorties over the Japanese-held island of Tarawa, despite intense and continuing anti-aircraft fire. On his third run, a shell burst sent it careening toward a rough ocean landing. A later report noted that Chuck skillfully glided to a point four miles south of the hostile base at Tarawa in the Gilbert Islands, executing a difficult cross-wind landing. The report continued that with cool courage and great resourcefulness, Chuck freed his radioman and gunner before releasing the emergency equipment from the plane that sank in less than a minute. Upon plunging into the water, Lieutenant Bransfield recalls that he heard God and his dead mother, Anita Miller Bransfield, calling him to escape the sinking plane and swim to the surface. He complied and, together with his compatriots, inflated a rubber raft and started paddling. His "meritorious achievement" earned him the Navy Air Medal in late 1943.

After drifting for eight days, a food shortage forced the three airmen to risk landing at Makin Island, where, after a month of freedom, the locals turned them over to the enemy. Chuck recalled, "They hauled us before the Jap officers, who took turns beating us with their swords. . . They wanted information about our coming blow in the Gilberts. Thank heaven, we knew nothing of it, so we couldn't tell them anything." They were bound hand and foot by night and under guard by day. Enemy troops were allowed to spit on them and throw rocks at them. His imprisonment was a, "nightmare of systematic torture — beatings with a baseball bat, the water treatment, [water was poured down the prisoners nose and throat causing painful choking], bamboo splinters shoved under fingernails."[379]

He remained a prisoner on the island until the battle of the nearby Tarawa turned in favor of the Americans. Then, he and other prisoners were moved to Tokyo on the Japanese mainland. On the way to the capital city, allied bombers wrecked the sampan he was traveling in, forcing him to spend many months on a Pacific island with his captors waiting for rescue. Later, when bombing became too intense in Tokyo, their guards moved them to Ofuna camp, the Hollywood of Japan, between Yokohama and Tokyo. Among the 100 American prisoners held there was the top Marine Corps ace of the war, Lt. Col. Gregory "Pappy" Boyington, leader of the celebrated Black Sheep Squadron. At this location, the guards would line up the Americans and beat them with baseball bats. According to Chuck Bransfield, "Boyington once took 33 blows on his back without making a sound. He is a tough man and worth a fortune to our morale." Chuck then added, "We thought we'd seen everything until they brought in the first B-29 crews." He resumed, "They shoved bamboo splinters under their fingernails and used the water treatment on them. We could hear their screams all over the camp." Yankee bombing forced another move to an isolated prison camp 250 miles to the north. Here they had little food of any kind, until August 1945, when American B-29s started dropping relief parcels.[380]

With no clear information, Marguerite and Michael Bransfield hoped that their son Chuck was still alive. They, along with his fiancée Vivien O'Neil, believed in Chuck's words before leaving, "Don't ever give up because I'll turn up." Finally, on March 7, 1945, the Bransfields received word when Chuck sent a message through the Japanese media:

> *Dear Mother, Glad to have this opportunity of speaking to you again. The crew and I are safe and in good health. Wish you all a Merry Christmas and a happy New Year. Hope all the family and its friends are well. Keep your mind at ease and we will have a big reunion party when I return. I think of you always and go to Mass each Sunday. Kiss Vivian for me.*
> *Love you all, Chuck. Lt. (J G) Charles M. Bransfield USN.*[381]

During the two years spent in prison camps, Chuck tried to lift the morale of his captured brethren, at one time, promising anyone who was beaten with a bat, a free barrel of Miller High Life. Upon his release on September 4, Miller Brewery president Elise John sent beer to each of these survivors. Pappy Boyington picked up his allotment at the Chicago airport in October 1945.[382]

Meanwhile, in Milwaukee, the brewery complied in October 1944 with an order from the Army's Quartermaster Department to export 15 percent of Miller's total production directly to the troops instead of passing through the distributors. After the war, the brewery settled with the federal government for profits in excess of the legal limit on beer that they had sold to the military. Frederick McCahey, Claire McCahey's youngest son and World War II veteran, noted that these massive beer shipments to the military allowed for shenanigans. For example, the brewery surreptitiously filled beer cans with whiskey before shipping them to units where Miller kin were serving. Whiskey, with its higher alcohol content was, at times, preferable to beer.[383]

On Sunday December 19, 1943, Fritz Miller, the last of Lisette and Frederick Miller's sons, died, leaving his wife

May, and no children. While seated at breakfast at his home at 6300 Washington Circle, the 76-year-old gentleman brewer collapsed and then died, of a heart attack. He had been ailing for some years, but continued his involvement in the business. Two days earlier, he had attended a three-hour business conference at the brewery and, one day before his death, had visited there twice. His visits were honorary, as he had not served nor attended board of directors' meetings since August 1938. Nevertheless, the directors continued to secure his signature on vital documents due to his large number of shares.[384] Funeral services were held at the Ritter Funeral Chapel and he was interred at the Miller family plot in the Calvary Cemetery.

Fritz led a long and purposeful life. As an adolescent, he had the customary indiscretions but, as an adult, walked a straight path. Beginning in 1888, when Fritz took over his father's board position, he flourished as its vice-president under Ernest. Fritz's dedication to the brewery's financial details gave Ernest the liberty to expand the business's sales and capacity. During his tenure, Fritz saw the brewery survive his father's death, the Bismarck expansion debacle, various financial depressions, World War I, Emil Miller's difficulties, and Prohibition. Due to his self-deprecating nature, Fritz was not among Miller's most vibrant presidents, but for decades as a vice-president he helped to unify the brewery's disparate elements. Sadly, the brewery's stockholders and directors did not make any mention of Fritz's passing in the minutes, whereas they occasionally noted the deaths of long-time non-family employees.

Fritz also was a reticent soul and, unlike his nephew Frederick C. Miller, shunned the spotlight. The writer of his obituary in the *Milwaukee Journal* noted that when it came time for photographs at the employee picnics, at the old Miller's Garden, Fritz was nowhere to be seen. He may have been embarrassed by his glass eye and emaciated appearance due to colitis. With no children of his own, Fritz Miller was his family's favorite uncle and granduncle. Just like his brother, Ernest, Fritz was scrupulously honest. No doubt, he did not understand those who bent the truth or lined their pockets at others' expense.

In his later years, he was content to tend his extensive garden at his Nagawicka Lake home.

Throughout his many illnesses, he retained his kind nature. Paul Lewis, a long-time Miller employee said that Fritz, in looks, reminded him of the old John D. Rockefeller. Fritz's great niece Anita McCahey Gray noted that he put people at ease with his sweet smile. Fritz was an ardent Catholic and supported many Catholic causes. He started at St. Joseph Parish where he was baptized, secondly, he joined St. Rose Parish where he was married, and thirdly, after moving to Wauwatosa's Washington Highlands in the 1920s, he established himself at St. Sebastian Parish from where he was buried.

After Fritz's death May Miller withdrew from contact with her husband's family and moved out of their grandiose homes. On October 16, 1970, she died of cancer while living at the Shorecrest Hotel on Milwaukee's East Side. Her October 17, 1970, *Milwaukee Sentinel* obituary noted that the 90-year-old May had been a member of the Milwaukee Athletic Club and the Wisconsin Club. She was buried beside Fritz.

Fritz named Oscar Treichler, his bookkeeper, who benefited by $10,000 from the will, as the estate's executor, with Elise and Buddy as the alternates. The $6.9 million estate included $1.2 million in real estate, mortgages, and cash. Of the portion in stocks, the estate held 3,444 4/9 shares of Miller Brewing Company worth $1 million and 3,444 4/9 shares of the Oriental Realty Company worth $861,111. The estate's federal taxes were $2.6 million and the state taxes were $513,204.[385]

Fritz Miller's last will and testament that he created on December 30, 1938, mirrored those of his mother and Ernest. His munificence was manifest in the dissemination of his estate among his family members and charitable organizations. For instance, Fritz furnished five gifts of $1,000 each to his mother's cousins and $56,000 to Catholic institutions such as, St. Charles Boys' Home, St. Vincent de Paul Society, Children's Hospital Association, St Aemilian's Orphan Asylum, and St. Francis Seminary. He added additional money specifically earmarked for poor students and patients at St. Francis Seminary and

St. Joseph Hospital respectively. The two largest charitable bequests were $350,000 each to the Missionary Association of Catholic Women and the Jesuit Seminary Aid Association of Gesu Church. Fritz also gave $25,000 in currency to his wife May, "to use as she may see fit, in making gifts to my or our employees, and former employees, and employees or former employees of the Miller Brewing Company and the Oriental Realty Company."[386]

Fritz gave his 63-year-old wife 300 shares of Miller Brewing Company stock, one-half of his personal belongings (his sister Elise inherited the other half), $200,000 in cash, and the Nagawicka Lake property and improvements. May's benefits totaled $504,000. Fritz also provided May with $100,000 to fulfill their prenuptial agreement signed on October 31, 1912. May Miller also profited from a $330,000 trust fund that Fritz created, on January 7, 1938, comprising securities and $25,000 in cash. The currency remained intact until Fritz's death, after which, John H. Leenhouts, Milwaukee's assessor of incomes, taxed it on the basis of $25,000 cash, amounting to $425. May objected to being taxed based on the actual $25,000 when her husband had established this fund eight years previously. She claimed that she should be taxed on only $17,031 because his life expectancy, by actuarial tables, was only eight years. May appealed her case to the Wisconsin Board of Appeals, which upheld Leenhouts. Undaunted, May Miller took her case to the U.S. Supreme Court, where she lost.[387]

Fritz Miller largely bypassed his sisters, Clara and Elise, in his will. He only gave one half of his personal belongings to Elise and nothing to Clara. On the other hand, he gave Clara's children 444 4/9 shares of the Miller Brewing Company. If any of his nieces and nephews had died by the time of his death, then their shares would pass to their children. In this way, Anita Miller Bransfield's only child, Chuck Bransfield, received his mother's 74 2/27 shares, unlike in 1937, when his grandmother, Clara Miller, failed to give him his dead mother's share of her brewery stock. Interestingly, at the time Chuck inherited 75 shares of the Miller Brewing Company, he was a prisoner of war on a Japanese-held island. Since the executors did not know whether he was alive, his share of Fritz's estate remained in limbo. It was not until a time after Chuck's release that his father, Michael Bransfield, informed him that he might have a piece of the estate. Today, Chuck believes that if his father had not enlightened him of his inheritance, he might never have received it.

Fritz's nephew, Buddy John received the largest bequest, from Fritz's estate, in the form of 2,400 shares of the Miller Brewing Company. Fritz's will created two testamentary trusts with Oscar Treichler as their trustee, one for Lorraine John Mulberger, to receive her 300 brewery shares, and the other for Harry G. "Buddy" John, Jr. to receive his brewery stock and other residual assets. To be assured of keeping the stock in the family, on December 27, 1943, Buddy signed his last will and testament bequeathing all of his assets to his sister Lorraine. Finally, Fritz gave one-half of his estate's residue to Clara's children and the other half to Elise's. Altogether Bud received $1.95 million from his uncle and Lorraine got $1.3 million. Clara's children, Loretta Kopmeier, Claire McCahey, Marguerite Bransfield, Fred C. Miller, and Charlotte Blommer each received $517,000.[388]

To recap the history of Fritz's brewery ownership, at his father's death in 1888, the five Miller siblings garnered a one-fifth share in the brewery. At the time of his brother Ernest's death in 1925, he and Elise inherited a somewhat larger portion of Ernest's stock than Clara and Emil. Since Emil died intestate in 1934, Fritz received one-third of his brewery shares, which brought him to 3,444 4/9 shares or slightly over one-third of the Miller Brewing Company's 10,000 shares of outstanding stock. Because Fritz had no children, his sisters' families earnestly competed for his brewery stock. For instance, the Johns watched jealously, from their home one block away, as Elise's nephew, Fred C. Miller, sporting a full-length raccoon coat, occasionally visited Fritz's Wauwatosa house. They were convinced that Fred C. Miller was lobbying his uncle for his brewery stock.[389]

On December 30, 1938, Fritz had determined the dissemination of his estate. In all likelihood, except for the witnesses, who were his bookkeepers, the brewer remained discrete regarding the future dispersal of his estate. In fact, his wife May might not have known about his plans until after his death. The alleged secrecy stemmed from his decision to bequeath most of his Miller Brewing Company stock to his nephew, Buddy John. If May and Fritz's relatives had known his plans, they might have made his last years miserable with their jealousy. As it was, May remained perturbed with Buddy until her death in 1970. In 1938, Fritz was happily married, had two sisters, and seven nieces and nephews; regardless, he chose his youngest nephew to receive the majority of his treasured stock. Fritz did not give his shares to Buddy based on the young man's accomplishments or personality; rather, Buddy inherited the stock because he was Fritz's favorite sister's son. If Fritz had given his stock to May, she might have willed it to her biological family as she did with her estate in her will of August 24, 1960; therefore, it would have left the Miller family.

Clara Miller and her family felt slighted regarding Fritz's unequal division. They rationalized that Fritz gave Elise's family the lion's share of his Miller stock because he pitied her due to her husband's chronic unemployment, whereas, Carl Miller was a successful businessman. Regardless, the breach between the West Side and East Side Millers, which began in 1888, had again been exposed at Fritz's death. Simply put, Fritz did not like Clara and her husband. The estate's unequal distribution further alienated the sisters; reportedly, they remained estranged for decades. For the foreseeable future, the East Side Millers would continue as minority stockholders in their family's brewery.

With the war's end more certain in every Allied advance, in September 1944, the Miller Brewery's directors, Elise John, Oscar Treichler, and Fred C. Miller, hired a brewery architect, Harold S. Ellington, to study the feasibility of building a new stockhouse to give the brewery additional storage and fermentation space. Ellington, based on a 700,000 projected yearly barrel capacity, planned to take six months to survey the "physical properties in order to bring the various operations of the brewery into better balance" before presenting a proposal.[390]

Milwaukee consulting engineer, Lawrence E. Peterson, presented a proposal to the directors for improving the bottling and beer storage facilities. The directors wanted a strategy in place, so that when the war's construction restrictions were lifted they could immediately begin expanding their facilities to meet the high current and future demand. Peterson determined that a complete rehabilitation of the physical plant would cost approximately $900,000; $400,000 for improving the bottling house facilities for bottling, capping, and labeling and $500,000 for a new stockhouse for lagering the beer. With the war's termination in September 1945, a month later, the directors ordered Peterson to draw up plans immediately for the new stockhouse and then procure construction estimates. His fee would be 5% of the cost of constructing this building. On March 19, 1946, the ceremonial first shovelful of ground was dug from the hillside just south of State Street, marking the genesis of the brewery's massive construction expansion.[391]

The new beer storage building, stockhouse F, was to be constructed atop the limestone bluff south of State and 40th streets. The commanding six-story building would rest above the cave system that Fred J. Miller, the brewery's founder, had used to lager his beer and alongside the grass-covered foundation of the old beer garden. The stockhouse, with a 180-by-96 foot footprint, would be completely air-conditioned and insulated. The brewery would construct it of structural steel and reinforced concrete floors. Concrete fermenting tanks would be on the two upper floors, "with the remaining four containing large glass lined steel tanks." The stockhouse would be equipped with 148 tanks and have a capacity of 3.6 million gallons.[392]

At the end of 1945 and the beginning of 1946, Fred C. Miller, who had been a brewery board member and officer since December 30, 1937, suddenly took a larger role in the brewery's affairs. He met with planning engineers, made motions at the board meetings, and a surviving memo demonstrates that he was intimately involved with the company's finances. His increased boldness mirrored a decline in Elise John and Oscar Treichler's vigor due to their encroaching old age. Additionally, various non-family high-level managers resigned at about this time, giving Fred the opportunity to help select their replacements. His vivaciousness, added to Elise and Treichler's decreasing vitality, gave him the edge in finding replacements, who then regarded Fred Miller as their protégé. For example, on October 23, 1945, Frank Huber became secretary and general manager as well as maintaining the position of general sales manager. Edward W. Huber, (who was no relation to Frank), the master brewer, general superintendent, and production manager was chosen as treasurer.[393] Certainly, Fred Miller was behind their advancements. Elise John turned 66 in March 1946, had missed some board meetings, and knew that the Miller Brewing Company's near future would be demanding, which led her to seriously consider retirement. At this time, Elise was spending months at a time living at the Sacred Heart Sanitarium where she entertained visitors, including brewery officials. Meanwhile, Oscar Treichler, who had worked for the Miller Brewery and its controlling family since 1904, resigned from the brewery as director and first vice-president effective November 2, 1945.[394]

Continuing his planning for the post-war era, on February 12, 1945, Fred C. Miller invited Mr. C.A. Mathisson, of the Henry C. Mulberger Agency, to address the board regarding a post-war advertising program. On March 6, 1946, Miller Brewery paid Henry Mulberger $5,000, out of a total of $15,000, to film a sound movie, in color, of their entire operations. It is unclear whether this project was ever completed as no copy is known to exist.[395]

In the first four months of 1946, the brewery earned $409,291 in profits compared to $364,397 from the same period in 1945. The April 1945 profits were $88,714 compared to the April 1946 profits of $127,111, an increase of $38,397.[396] Wartime restrictions had not been lifted, which diminished the malt supply by 30%, leading to a reduction of 28% in beer production. Most of the increased profits stemmed from allocating more beer for bottling than kegs and also eliminating workers' overtime hours.[397]

By December 31, 1945, the Miller Brewing Company had $8.8 million in total assets that in part was composed of $4 million in cash and marketable securities, $338,000 in product–finished and in process, $294,000 in raw materials, $208,000 in miscellaneous supplies, $184,000 in revenue stamps, $378,000 in tavern fixtures, and $1.333 million in plant and equipment. In that same year it earned $772,000. In 1946, the brewery assets had increased by $1.2 million, totaling $10 million by the end of the year. Its 1946 profits were $1.5 million, almost double those of the previous year. The large number of returning soldiers and the diminution of wartime rationing of their raw materials guaranteed its robust profitability. The brewery was bullish on future sales and, in 1946, invested $1.1 million in plant and equipment improvements. In December of that same year, the brewery used 78,000 bushels of malt, 971,000 pounds of grits, 32,000 pounds of hops, and 9,000 pounds of soybeans. The grit or corn and soybeans was used as an adjunct to the malt in order to make the beer lighter and clearer for America's palates.[398]

Sometime in early 1946, Elise decided to relinquish her Miller board and officer positions, effective at the annual May stockholders' meeting, though she retained her stock ownership. With her impending retirement and Oscar Treichler's prior departure, Elise needed to fill two board and officer vacancies. Also on April 22, 1946, Treichler resigned from Lorraine and Bud's testamentary trusts, which respectively had 300 shares and 2,400 shares of Miller Brewing stock. Fritz Miller's will stipulated that Elise should succeed Treichler should he resign. Moreover, Elise owned 2,434 shares in her own name, which gave her control over 51 percent of the 10,000 outstanding shares; enough stock to single-handedly pick the next directors and officers.[399] This rare condition had not existed since 1887, when Fred J. Miller alone chose the brewery's original board; otherwise, the stockholders by necessity cooperatively selected the positions.

Excluding females, there were two candidates in the family, Buddy John and his cousin, Frederick C. Miller, who already was a director and second vice president. It is unfortunate that no women were seriously considered, such as Lorraine Mulberger or Clara Miller's daughters, because Elise had proven the success of female leadership. In fact, no woman has served as president of the Miller Brewing Company since Elise resigned her position in 1946. No doubt, Frederick lobbied his aunt for the presidency. He was the choice of his immediate family and, likely, the brewery's employees. Frederick had been building his experience as brewery board member and officer since December 30, 1937, serving with his *Tante* Elise and Oscar Treichler.

Harry, Jr., had shown no interest in working at the brewery, instead isolating himself at his farm while pursuing profound Catholic mysticism. He had not taken any business courses at Notre Dame and knew little or nothing of running a company short of his uninspired farming venture. Due to his considerable wealth, he lacked the financial incentive to make the farm a profitable enterprise. Subsequent to World War II, Buddy used the farm as a veneer to cover his true passion of promoting his brand of extreme Catholic spirituality. When asked what he did for a living, he replied "farmer" to escape the embarrassment that his father experienced of a lifetime of not working. Bud had lived at the farm but not had worked there since approximately 1943, when he hired a family to live there and perform the daily chores. Nevertheless, he regularly dressed in overalls and rubber boots to promote himself as an authentic dirt farmer hardly connected to his wealthy parents living in the Washington Highlands.

To most observers the decision was clear; but Elise had other intentions. She would use the presidency of the Miller Brewing Company to bring Buddy back from the farm. Elise was convinced that, if her son came to Milwaukee daily to sit in the president's chair, he would develop a passion for Miller

Brewery and reconnect with his family.

People were shocked at Elise's decision, figuring that Fred Miller was the better choice. In order to procure Fred's compliance, Elise certainly told her nephew that she was going to give Buddy one year to rehabilitate himself or she would replace him with Fred. Otherwise, it was inconceivable that Fred would have supported his neophyte cousin as his new boss.

Next, Elise began a concerted effort to convince the reticent Buddy to accept a directorship and then presidency. In an odd scenario, Elise recruited the brewery's next president from an eighty-acre farm in the Town of Summit to lead the business into one of its most dynamic periods. Miller Brewery's future vice-president, John F. Savage, remembered Elise soliciting his cooperation, as a new associate house attorney, to convince Buddy to accept the presidency. Finally, Harry, Jr., acquiesced to serve. Elise also chose her 71-year-old estranged husband, Harry John, Sr., as a director at the likely urging of Lorraine and Buddy.[400]

Elise's next step was to appoint 26-year-old Buddy John president before the annual stockholder meeting, scheduled for May 22, 1946, to give him the advantage of being re-elected instead of simply being elected. Toward that end, on May 3, Elise and Fred held a special directors' meeting during which they elected Bud to fill Oscar Treichler's vacated board position.

In 1946, the Miller Brewing Company's ownership was as follows:

Stockholder	Shares	Percentage
May F. Miller	300	3%
Clara A. Miller	611 1/9	6%
Loretta Miller Kopmeier	574 2/27	5.7%
Claire Miller McCahey	574 2/27	5.7%
Marguerite Miller Bransfield	574 2/27	5.7%
Frederick C. Miller	574 2/27	5.7%
Charlotte Miller Blommer	574 2/27	5.7%
Charles M. Bransfield	74 2/27	0.7%

Stockholder	Shares	Percentage
Elise K. John	2,435 4/9	24%
Henry C. Mulberger		
(in trust for Elise K. John)	1	0%
B. H. Protzmann		
(in trust for Elise K. John)	1	0%
Harry G. John, Sr.	5	0.1%
Lorraine Mulberger	1	0%
Harry G. [Buddy] John, Jr.	1	0%
Lorraine, General Trust	500	5%
Lorraine, Testamentary Trust	300	3%
Buddy, General Trust	500	5%
Buddy, Testamentary Trust	2,400	24%
Total	**10,000**	**100%**

At this time, the Johns controlled the Miller Brewing Company with 6,144 4/9 shares; the Clara Miller family was a minority shareholder with 3,555 5/9 shares; and May Miller had 300 shares. The majority stockholders could elect the directors and officers without considering the minority shareholders' wishes, thereby, setting the business's direction.

Nineteen days later, the stockholders held their annual meeting with the following persons present: Charles M. "Chuck" Bransfield (the only family attendee still living), Elise K. John, Harry G. "Buddy John, Jr., Harry G. John, Sr., Loretta Kopmeier, Claire Miller McCahey, May F. Miller, Clara A. Miller, Frederick C. Miller, Lorraine John Mulberger, B.H. Protzmann (in trust for Elise K. John). Marguerite Miller Bransfield and Charlotte Miller Blommer were absent but, previously, had given their proxies to their brother, Fred. Henry C. Mulberger was also absent but had not signed a proxy for his single share. His absence was due to his estrangement from his wife Lorraine. Elise, corporation president, ran the meeting and Frank Huber, corporate secretary, recorded the minutes. The stockholders unanimously elected the following directors:

Bud, who was nominated by Harry and seconded by Elise John. Forty-year-old Fred C. Miller, who was nominated by Harry, Sr. and seconded by Buddy. Harry, Sr., was nominated by Elise John and seconded by Bud. A discussion followed during which May Miller, Fritz Miller's widow, recommended that an unbiased businessman augment the board of directors. She was free to say this, as she was biologically unrelated to the current candidates and did not mind offending anybody. Fred recommended the Hubers, an idea that was dropped due to Elise's opposition.[401]

Directors Harry G. "Buddy" John, Jr., Harry G. John, Sr., and Frederick C. Miller met after the Miller Brewing Company's stockholder meeting on May 22, 1946. Fred was the acting chairman of the meeting because he was the highest-ranking existing corporate officer. Under new business, Harry John, Sr. stated that he was concerned about black market activities in the brewing industry. He continued that Miller Brewery, "should show its willingness in the past and in the future to cooperate with the United States Government by doing everything in its power to prevent such practices on the part of its distributors." He proposed the writing of a letter to all of the company's distributors to "engage only in legitimate practices with all their accounts," an idea that was unanimously accepted.[402]

Another order of business was the selection of face brick for the imminent construction of stockhouse F that was the first building of Miller's impressive post-war growth. The board agreed with a Mr. Kurth, a brick expert of the W.H. Pipkorn Company, that a product manufactured by the Metropolitan Paving Brick Company of Bessemer, Pennsylvania, was the best choice. The board meeting was then adjourned until May 27, at which time the directors elected the officers. Harry G. "Buddy" John, Jr. was chosen as president, Harry G. John, Sr., as vice president, Fred C. Miller as second vice president, Frank Huber as secretary, and Edward W. Huber as treasurer. The top officers were to be paid $1,000 monthly.[403]

The last order of business was Fred C. Miller's proposed resolution that was unanimously adopted, providing the directors' regret that Elise John had decided not to seek reelection as a director. Fred suggested that Elsie's experience and sincere interest in the affairs of the brewery made her a highly valued leader in the company's growth and success. The resolution continued: "The Board wishes to express its deep gratitude for a long, loyal and significant service to the Miller Brewing Company, its warm appreciation of an enjoyed personal, as well as business, association, and directs that a copy of this testimonial be sent to Mrs. John with the fervent wishes of each member for many years of health and happiness in which to enjoy the leisure she has so richly earned."[404]

The year 1946 ended with Elise's resignation and Fred C. Miller's ascendancy, yet the 26-year-old Buddy John was occupying the president's chair and Harry John, Sr., was holding the vice-presidency. It remained to be seen how long this scenario would continue. Subsequently, the brewery was preparing for vigorous growth. The American economy was vibrant as the returning veterans built homes and bought new automobiles. These citizens were laying the groundwork for the Miller Brewing Company's extended prodigious growth.

18.

THE BRIEF REIGN OF HARRY JOHN

On May 27, 1946, 26-year-old Harry G. "Buddy" John, Jr., began his tenure, as the initial third-generation Miller family member to serve as president of the Miller Brewing Company. Bud also served on the board of directors, with his father, Harry G. John, Sr., and first cousin, Frederick C. Miller. Regularly, Bud drove to the corporate offices, at 4002 West State Street, from his Town of Summit dairy farm, where he continued to perform selected daily chores. Simply stated, Bud was a caretaker president, in place to fulfill Wisconsin's legal requirement for an officer of that title. Since the end of 1945, Frederick C. Miller, the brewery's second vice-president, had controlled the brewery's overall direction along with its daily activities. As the brewery's primary titular officer, Buddy maintained the status quo; he attended every board meeting. He lacked the confidence to further his own ideas and for the most part supported Fred's resolutions. At the bi-weekly board meetings, he spoke infrequently. Otherwise, he would have exposed his lack of business training.

In Bud's thinking, he was serving a power greater than his mother, Elise K. John, the corporation's majority stockholder. At this time, Harry, Jr., was increasingly estranged from his parents and sister, though especially his mother. His spiritual boss did not care how he dressed. In fact, the humbler he appeared and behaved, the more dutiful he was. Occasionally, to spite his mom, he arrived at Miller's State Street headquarters in coveralls and mud-caked farm boots, which ironically would have befitted the first decades of Miller Brewery's existence in the rural township of Wauwatosa. No doubt Fred J. Miller, the brewery's founder, sported similar outfits at sundry business conferences.

Buddy John's election as president coincided with a period of stockholder enthusiasm for a $5.5 million plan to boost the brewery's production facilities by 25% to 30%. The owners intended to capitalize on the post-war boom in beer consumption and, while becoming a national brewer, jump ahead of many of their competitors. They proposed to construct a $500,000 six-story stockhouse, a bottling house, a brewhouse, and finally a $200,000 administration building. Bluntly said, they were going to recreate the brewery.[405]

The driving force behind the plan to enlarge the brewery was a member of Miller Brewery's board of directors, its second vice president, and *de facto* leader, Frederick C. Miller, who, on December 30, 1937, had become formally associated with the business. Fred was also a grandson of the brewery's founder, Frederick J. Miller. The former college football star, with boundless energy, carried on the blueprint that he had originated under the presidency of his *Tante* Elise, which lasted from 1937 to 1946. Besides owning his own stock, Fred held the stock proxies of his mother, Clara, and his sisters, Loretta, Claire, Marguerite, and Charlotte, and nephew Chuck Bransfield, equaling 2,981 13/27 shares out of 10,000. More importantly, he enjoyed the backing of his Aunt Elise, who owned or controlled most of the remainder of the shares. Since she was retired from her directorship and officer's position, no doubt, Fred regularly gave her updates on his plans at her home or at the Sacred Heart Sanitarium, where she often resided. The sanitarium, at 1545 South Layton Boulevard, provided hydrotherapy and physical therapy treatments for patients with chronic physical and mental diseases or, as in Elise's case, just offered a peaceful living place.

The intellectual origin of Fred Miller's bullish attitude toward Miller Brewery is unclear. There are no records extant detailing his sources of brewing and business information. As an educated *mensch*, no doubt he read various local and national news publications along with local and national brewery journals. Also, he had the successful histories of other large breweries to follow, such as Anheuser-Busch, Joseph Schlitz, and Pabst. Also, Fred was influenced by his father, Carl, a businessman with noteworthy experience in the United States, Europe, and Africa. The erudite Carl, even in his later years, while running his businesses in Wisconsin, Arizona, Michigan, and Florida, was trading currency and bonds in Germany. Ironically, the talented businessman, Fred, was more parochial than his cultured father. Fred's escapes were fishing trips in Michigan's Upper Peninsula, instead of steaming across the Atlantic on European vacations as his parents and sisters often did.

Fred's personality and the era in which he worked provide clues to his motivations. His primary inspiration for promulgating the brewery came from his loyalty to his mother, Clara, and her father Frederick J. Miller, the brewery's founder. Even though the beer baron died in 1888, eighteen years before Fred C. Miller was born, his grandson emulated him. For example, in the early 1950s, after being asked why he opposed building another brewery on one of the coasts, to save shipping costs, Fred responded that Milwaukee was good enough for his grandfather and, therefore, was good enough for him.[406]

Besides his tendency to promote tirelessly anything in which he was involved, Fred exploited the economic potential of the U.S. following World War II. Fred surmised that the momentum of increased beer consumption following Prohibition's demise would continue and expanded the brewery's capacity to meet it. To his credit, he expanded Miller Brewery more aggressively than did other breweries while utilizing a solid marketing and publicity department. To explain further, as the anti-alcohol forces increasingly dried up state after state in 1915 and 1916, breweries diversified their product line, introducing offerings such as malt syrup, instead of investing in their alcoholic beer production. Following the difficult eras of Prohibition, the Great Depression, and the grain and construction restrictions of World War II, every large brewery was ripe for expansion. Also, the demand increased from 1915 to 1945 as America's population grew from the infusion of beer-drinking European immigrants. When the federal government lifted the World War II grain restrictions, Fred grasped the opportunity for Miller Brewery's volcanic growth.

Harry G. John, Sr., a director and corporate vice-president, was more vocal than his son at the board meetings, making assorted resolutions, some of which carried. Harry exerted his independence from his authoritative nephew, Fred, occasionally by encouraging the board to make decisions that Fred, rightfully, wanted settled at the management level. Regardless, overall, Fred Miller enjoyed support from the older and younger Johns for his initiatives. Despite his bravado, Harry, Sr., lacked self-assurance and could not ignore criticism. At a board meeting on June 18, 1946, he reported that Jerry Purtell, a brewery employee, previously had made various derogatory remarks about him and his son in the presence of fellow workers. Harry made a motion that Purtell, "be requested to offer his resignation as an employee of the Company for this showing of disloyalty." Buddy seconded this motion. After a discussion, the corporate secretary, Frank Huber, and, house attorney, John F. Savage, noted that they would discuss the matter with Purtell and, subsequently, report back to the board, an action that mollified the father and son. Such an episode should have been handled in a separate conference, instead of a board meeting, and demonstrated that Fred Miller and the two Mr. Johns rarely spoke outside of the boardroom.[407]

Bud's ascendancy to the presidency of Miller Brewery did not check his divestiture of personal assets, which remained between $1 and $2 million. Ironically, and to Buddy's consternation, due to the brewery's success, his net worth continued to rise despite his significant charitable contributions. He believed that his wealth would preclude him, after death, from entering the kingdom of God, making him donate ever more fervently. His mother's plan to curb his compulsive philanthropy while weaning him from the farm was failing. In 1946, Buddy began to donate regularly to Catholic contemplative orders and other

Catholic institutions. Among them were Our Lady of the Valley Abbey in Rhode Island ($24,000), New Mellery Abbey in Iowa ($15,000) and Poor Clares in New York City, Chicago and Rockford, Illinois ($3,000). He also made five gifts of $1,000 each to Carmelite convents throughout the U.S.[408]

Buddy John looked into selling the 2,400 shares of Miller Brewery stock in his testamentary trust and then donating the proceeds to charitable organizations. He broached the subject with the managers of his Uncle Fred A. Miller's estate and Elise K. John's assets, Oscar Treichler and B.H. (Bertram Henry) Protzmann, who tried to dissuade him. Protzmann explained to Bud that his tax burden would be $44,261 if he sold the 2,400 shares. This amount would be in addition to a $203,461 tax payment on the shares due to the Wisconsin Department of Revenue and the I.R.S., increasing the stock's value from $400 to $600 per share. When John told his parents of his plans to sell his stock, his mother vehemently opposed the idea and, as trustee of his money, prevented it.[409]

Elise looked for help in curbing Bud's substantial philanthropic activities. On August 7, 1946, she called one of Bud's advisors, J. [Joseph] Peter Grace, Jr., chief executive officer, of the W.R. Grace & Company Corporation in New York City (a multinational chemical, mining, and shipping company) to encourage him to change Buddy's mind. (In 1966, the W.R. Grace Company, under Peter's control, bought a substantial share of the Miller Brewing Company from Lorraine Mulberger, Bud John's sister.) Peter continually solicited funds for contemplative Catholic orders, and Bud's burgeoning philanthropy caught his eye. Harry, Jr. and Peter had a nascent friendship based on a strict adherence to the Catholic faith, profitable investments, and a concern for contemplative orders. Peter's younger brother Michael, also a major contributor to Catholic contemplative orders, had attended the University of Notre Dame with his long-time friend, Buddy.

Elise complained to Peter Grace that her son wanted to donate all of his assets, especially any proceeds from a sale of his Miller Brewing Company stock, to the Catholic contemplative Trappists. Elise continued that, despite her opposition and the objections of Treichler and Protzmann, Harry Jr. was determined to follow through with his plan. Elise warned that she had "given away" the presidency and her board position but she was determined not to "give away" her stock. Ultimately, she implored Grace not to report this conversation to her son.[410]

Peter responded that, previously, he thought that Elise was in agreement with Bud's actions, no doubt, based on Harry Jr.'s conversations. Grace was unmoved by Elise's plea because he wanted Harry, Jr. to continue donating his assets. Peter skirted her concerns then changed the subject, recommending that Bud marry and have children. He noted that Bud had already missed an opportunity with one woman, but that he was dating another fine lady with whom he should marry and live "decently." In conclusion, he complained that Wally Muenzuer [Bud's Milwaukee friend] had his vocation to the priesthood but he should leave Harry, Jr. alone.[411]

In mid-October 1946, Peter Grace wrote to Bud John at his farm, regarding Harry Jr.'s interest in aiding Cistercian nuns, also known as Trappists, at the Abbey of Our Lady of the Valley in Valley Falls, Rhode Island. Earlier, Bud had made an oral pledge of $125,000 to a Cistercian fundraiser, Brother Leo, for the monastery, backed by 2,400 shares of Miller stock in his testamentary trust. It was to be paid in five years when it matured, giving Harry Jr. unfettered access to the assets. (Brother Leo was born Roderick Gregory on August 10, 1917 and currently lives at St. Joseph's Abbey in Spencer, Massachusetts.) At that time, Elise was the trustee and, therefore could block Bud's intention. Charles Quarles of the law firm of Line, Spooner and Quarles, now Quarles and Brady, assisted Harry, Jr. in formulating an eleven-year repayment plan. Unbeknownst to his mother, the bank would use Bud's oral pledge as collateral and give the Trappists a promissory note. Brother Leo, who wanted the money before five years, used Grace as an East Coast fundraising contact and financial consultant. Grace, to help Brother Leo procure the money sooner, instructed Buddy to use a Wisconsin bank instead of a New York one for a loan, "against a personal note and an assignment of your interest in the major trust." Peter wrote that, "it would be simpler for you to borrow this money against an assignment by you of an interest in the Trust in a Wisconsin bank where they are acquainted with your fine Brewery business and where your family's financial standing and reputation are well known." To ease some of Harry Jr.'s fears, the New York executive offered to pay the interest on the five-year loan. Peter Grace concluded:

"One last thought — I don't know, of course, just what your future plans are, but if you do plan on giving away a lot of money and I understand that you are contemplating the creation of a Trust — why not consider three possible moves:

"1) Definitely establish the Trust outside of Wisconsin so that any gift the Trust makes will not be taxable by the state of Wisconsin.

"2) Possibly consider establishing residence now outside of the state of Wisconsin so that any income that you receive from your trusts, your interest in the brewery or other interests will be available to you to give away without Wisconsin state gift taxes.

"3) Definitely consider moving out of the state of Wisconsin after you have come into all of your money, taking your money with you so that you may be free to give all of it away if you wish without the impediments of the Wisconsin state tax. In this case, I presume that you can move to and from states within the United States with your money in your pocket without any state impediments."

Grace concluded, Bud, "rest assured that we are all working for the same purpose."

By early October 1946, Harry John, Jr. had solicited the legal services of brothers and attorneys, Urban R. and John A. Wittig, to assist him in his mission. It was at this point, that Bud, using the law firms of Line, Spooner and Quarles and Wittig and Wittig, while seeking the advice of Peter Grace, had retreated from his mother's influence and advisors. On the other hand, Harry, Jr.'s sister, Lorraine Mulberger, continued to use her mother's advisors as her own. For decades,

Elise and the Miller Brewing Company had used attorneys Alexander W. Schutz and Edwin S. Mack, among others, for legal advice. Additionally, Bud dissociated his financial affairs from Oscar Treichler and B.H. Protzmann who had served three generations of Millers; Lisette Miller, Elise Miller John and her brothers, and Lorraine Mulberger. The last Miller to completely separate from the family was Harry Jr.'s aunt, Clara Miller, who in 1890, sought her own financial and legal advisors apart from her siblings and her mother, Lisette.

In December 1946, Harry John, Jr. gave his first donations, totaling $1,100, to de Rancé, Inc., a private foundation that he had organized on October 23, 1946, with himself, John Wittig, and Urban Wittig, as trustees who were akin to stockholders at a for-profit corporation. Years later, Buddy spelled out his personal motivation for the foundation: "It has been my wish to advance, insofar as I am able, the cause of Christianity in general and Catholicism in particular. I would like to help to make the U.S.A. a more Christian nation. . . ."[412]

The Wittigs, who were approximately Bud and Lorraine's ages, had lived one house away from Elise and Harry John on Highland Boulevard and were partners with their brother Lawrence in the family law firm. Another brother, Roland A. Wittig, who assisted in Bud's endeavors, worked for Dun and Bradstreet. The de Rancé foundation was named after Trappist Armand Jean de Rancé the 17th-Century abbot of the monastery at La Trappe, France, who founded the Cistercians of the Strict Observance, popularly known as Trappists. "De Rancé, a wealthy French noble, gave his fortune to the abbey, joined the order and led a reform so rigorous in diet and religious practices that the average life span of a monk, after entering La Trappe, was eight years."[413] The first meeting of de Rancé's trustees was on November 4 of that year, at the Wittigs' law office, at 135 West Wells Street in downtown Milwaukee. At that time, nobody foresaw that de Rancé would by the mid 1970s become the world's largest Catholic foundation.

At first, de Rancé was a non-profit corporation, without any assets, created to accept Bud's Miller Brewing stock. It was not until December 1952 that de Rancé was endowed with 2,400 shares of stock of the Miller Brewing Company, as that time marked the maturation of the trust that Buddy received from his Uncle Fritz. In 1953, he gave 190 shares followed by another 310 shares in 1955, which together with the 1952 gift, totaled 2,900 shares. The foundation would exist only during his lifetime because a deed of gift specified that, upon his death, its assets would pass to the Catholic Archdiocese of Milwaukee. At that time, Bud was single, without children, and did not want to bequeath his assets to his niece and nephew, Karen and Michael Mulberger, despite the fact that he had received the majority of his assets from his childless Uncle Fritz. Bud did not create the foundation for charitable reasons, because he could and did make personal donations. His primary reason for originating this non-profit corporation was to escape the substantial capital gains taxes, which he would incur upon selling his stock for cash to grant to Catholic causes. (Additionally, the foundation would not be charged gift taxes when Bud donated the assets.) At this time, it was clear that the brewery stock was worth considerably more than the $450 per share price that the family and taxing authorities had established for Fritz Miller's estate in 1945. Earnings and dividends had raised the stock's value from $1,000 to $1,200 per share. If Harry, Jr. had kept the stock in his name and then sold it, regardless of his intention to donate the proceeds, he would have incurred a tax liability of at least several hundred thousand dollars.

In December 1951, Bud became the sole beneficiary of his testamentary trust. On June 5, 1952, Bud donated 2,400 shares of the Miller Brewing Company to his testamentary trust, equaling approximately $4.8 million, to the de Rancé foundation. Due to the corporation's tax-exempt status, Bud escaped any federal or state gift taxes.[414]

On Monday, September 9, 1946, Bud's cousin, Fred C. Miller, suffered the first of three accidents in private airplanes. Earlier, he had convinced the University of Notre Dame head coach Frank Leahy to allow two players, stand-out Terry

Brennan, 19, and Frank Kosikowski, 20, to fly with him to Milwaukee to give a speech. Fred had piloted the plane into a rainstorm and, near Chicago, became disoriented. He looked in vain for the LaPorte, Indiana, airport and, upon running out of gas, belly landed in a plowed field, one and a half miles west of the LaPorte runway. The passengers were physically unscathed, though the plane suffered $1,000 in damage. Two days later, the resilient Fred attended a Miller board meeting where the directors, besides discussing the impending start of construction of the new stockhouse, then named "F," declared a $20 per share dividend.[415]

Years later, on September 9, 1950, Fred C. Miller had a second serious small plane accident in an amphibious Gruman Widgeon. During the wintertime, Fred landed his other plane, a Cessna 175, on a frozen Pabst Family Farm field near his lake home. To accomplish this feat, he kept his car at the airport and shuttled himself back and forth to work. In regard to the marine accident, Miller, who was alone, landed his Widgeon airplane on Oconomowoc Lake, and unfortunately fractured one of the pontoons. Luckily the plane stayed upright. He unbuckled his safety belt, grabbed his brief case, opened the door, and blithely stepped outside onto the only working pontoon. Fred's family, who lived on the lake, stood at the shoreline watching their father's struggles.

August "Augie" Uihlein Pabst III, a member of the Pabst and Joseph Schlitz Brewing families, (whose own father had died in a small-plane crash while he was a child), was a long-time fellow lake resident whose family was fast friends with the Millers and witnessed the incident. In time, Augie noted that Fred Miller was relieved to see his friend Lee Posselt speeding toward him in a fishing boat. As it approached, Miller leaned out on the wing that was still afloat and put his weight on it, as a counter balance, to keep the pontoon-less wing from sinking further. Unfortunately, both Fred and Lee's efforts were in vain as the plane slowly sank under Oconomowoc's waves. Regardless, the stylish Miller, sporting a tailored suit and two-tone wing-tip shoes, arrived on shore dry as an autumn leaf.

Fred's aviation incidents aside, the Miller families maintained substantial assets as the brewery continued to prosper. For example, on December 31, 1946, Elise John's net worth was $3.8 million, composed in part of 2,437 4/9 shares in the Miller Brewing Company worth $403,111, 1,942 4/9 shares in the Oriental Realty Company worth $643,565, $1 million in bonds, $626,000 in cash, $445,000 in mortgages, $363,000 in rental properties, and $393,000 in two personal residences. That year, Elise gave $8,000 to her husband, $50,000 to her financial advisor Oscar Treichler, $1,089 to her granddaughter, Karen Mulberger, and $1,222 to her grandson, Michael Mulberger. Also, Elise gave both Lorraine and Harry, Jr., 500 shares of Oriental Realty Company, worth $165,744 each. At this time, she gave her husband five shares of the Miller Brewing Company and Lorraine and Buddy one share each so they could serve as directors of the brewery, as noted in the bylaws.[416]

On January 9, 1947, Circuit Judge Allen D. Young granted Elise's daughter Lorraine and Hank Mulberger a divorce in the Waukesha County courthouse. Their personal shortcomings, together with Hank's time away during World War II, caused their marriage to falter, eleven years after their exquisite May wedding on Oconomowoc Lake. Lorraine filed for the divorce, although she was spurred on by Hank's desire to marry another woman. Hank Mulberger did not contest the filing and called the separation "friendly." Lorraine testified that, after her husband came home from the war, "there wasn't room for him in their 15 room Elm Grove home." Karen mentions that her mother severely mourned the loss of her husband for a year after the divorce. Subsequently, Hank lived with the Johns, his in-laws, before moving into the Elks Club. Hank's attorney, Col. C.J. Otjen also served as his superior officer during part of his military service. The judge granted Lorraine full custody of 6-year-old Karen and 2-year-old Michael. Court testimony established that Hank had an annual income of $7,000 and Lorraine Mulberger had, "an independent income." The judge granted Lorraine her home, while determining that she give Hank $10,000 to satisfy his share in the property.[417]

After the divorce, Hank Mulberger's contact with Miller Brewery was limited, as Lorraine would not suffer his continued involvement with her company. By September 1947, Hank was ordered to turn over all of his materials pertaining to the Miller Brewing account to the Chicago-based Frank Nahser Company. Frank Nahser, who was an advertising executive, was Fred C. Miller's wife's brother-in-law. By October 7, 1947, Hank complied. The brilliant Henry Mulberger had been intimately involved with Miller Brewery in an important era in its history. He helped to modernize and make Miller's advertising department national in scope. After all, the brewery had to sell the millions of bottles of beer that it was beginning to produce in its updated buildings.

On Saturday, January 24, 1948, before leaving the Midwest, Hank married Peggy Fiebrantz in Winnetka, Illinois. Before departing, Hank sold his Luscomb airplane, bought a house trailer and traveled 10,000 miles before settling in Colorado Springs, Colorado. Soon thereafter, he founded and served as president of the Atomic Research Corporation, which manufactured Geiger counters during the uranium boom of the 1950s. Years later, Hank reminisced: "Our company was the first in the nation to have the word 'atomic' in a firm. That was even before the Atomic Energy Commission." He then founded and served as president of Alpine Labs, Ltd., manufacturing and selling ultraviolet lights. In 1959, he began to work for the Raytheon Corporation as its regional corporation-marketing manager for the western states until his retirement in 1982.[418]

In early 1947, there were rumors that the Miller Brewing Company was for sale, distressing Fred C. Miller. On March 9, a shaken Fred Miller spoke publicly of the probable sale of the Miller Brewing Company. As the brewery's most active and visible officer, he was its public face, even though he was merely its second vice president. At that time, he denied reports that the business had already been sold to the City Ice and Fuel Company of Chicago, which owned the Pilsner Brewery in Cleveland and the American Brewery in New Orleans and

Miami. Nevertheless, in refuting the "sure" sale, he mentioned another "possible deal." He explained, "It is not with any outside [Wisconsin] concern. But the deal, if made, is months away. Talk of a deal with City Ice is idle gossip." Subsequently, an elusive Elise John added that she did not believe any agreement with City Ice had been made, although she had heard some "talk about it." She confirmed that "nothing definite" had been decided in regard to selling the brewery.[419]

Oscar Treichler, former Miller Brewery executive and the John family's long-time confidant and bookkeeper, was the family's secret negotiator, with the blessings of Harry, Elise, Lorraine, and Bud John. As early as January 11, 1946, Treichler noted that he had an inquiry from both Chicago and New York regarding purchasing the brewery. Later in that year, Treichler, "had advised the John family, 'as sound business under existing conditions and for tax reasons,' to sell the stock for $1,200 or more a share. From numerous inquiries concerning the sale of the stock it was apparent that it could be sold for more than $1,000 a share." At first, Canadian Breweries, Ltd., of Toronto offered Treichler $800 a share for the combined Johns' stock amounting to 6,144 4/9 shares, which he declined. Subsequently, he negotiated with Milwaukee brewing executive Charles McKeown, who acted as a broker. Treichler reported, "An option was offered to the John family to permit the McKeown interests 20 days in which to purchase the John block of stock for approximately $1,342 a share but Elise K. John refused to enter into the option."[420]

Buddy provided much of the John family's impetus for marketing their Miller stock. Furthermore, Elise and Harry John were becoming elderly and Lorraine, a single mother of two children, had meager interest in the brewery. No doubt, Fred had argued fervently with Elise to keep the brewery, realizing that a sale certainly would have ended his employment as new owners would have installed their own management group. Fred was bullish on Miller's future and, in due course, convinced Elise that the burgeoning investment would have a decades-long significant return for her grandchildren, Karen and Michael. At this time, Harry, Jr., was still single and without children. Finally, Elise quashed any stock sale while assuring Fred of her support for his leadership. Bud was irritated at his mother's reversal and undertook to change her mind.

With Elise's solid backing, Fred Miller confronted Vice-President Harry John, Sr., on his role in marketing the stock. At an April 22, 1947, board meeting, Fred indignantly asserted that Harry, Sr., had shown personnel from the Pabst and Hamm's breweries through Miller's facilities in order to sell the company. Fred Miller knew that the publicity of a probable sale and the tours of competitive brewers could undermine employee enthusiasm for the ongoing expansion. An annoyed Fred remarked that he wanted to speak, "on record as definitely opposed to allowing a competitor to view this plant without the permission of the Board of Directors, for any purpose whatsoever." To reiterate his point, on May 1, 1947, at a dinner for Charles Hesser, Sr., Miller's retiring western sales manager, Fred noted that, "The Miller Brewing Co. definitely will not be sold. . . it will definitely remain in the Miller family."[421] Frederick Miller's outburst flustered Harry, Sr., who did not endorse the minutes as written and never attended another board meeting.

On Tuesday, May 6, 1947, at 3:27 p.m., an earthquake centered in the Milwaukee area shook Miller's buildings, foreshadowing upcoming ownership struggles. Buddy mistakenly believed that a truck had careened into the brewery's headquarters. The first recorded earthquake in Milwaukee history lasted 4/10th of a second. It rattled dishes, made chairs tremble, and cracked walls but did not damage building structures. Many frightened people, unsure about what had happened, ran out of their homes and businesses and then milled in the streets dreading more quakes. Miller attorney John Savage remembers running into a bathroom, at the old headquarters, where he saw Buddy, and together they rushed outside.[422]

With the earthquake's thrill behind them, on May 12, 1947, Buddy John and Fred Miller directed the brewery's legal department to take action against an independent refrigerator salesman, Michael T. Stoiber, to collect a $110 overdue account.

Miller attorney John Savage broached the matter with Stoiber, who said haughtily, that he would "take up" the issue with a "higher source" (Elise John) at the brewery, who would end all discussions of the matter.[423]

Harry, Bud, and Fred Miller disdained Michael Stoiber, who met Elise John in 1936 and, with a convincing nature, eventually became her confidant. By the mid-1940s, the aging matron was suffering from diabetes and hypertension, while feeling estranged from her husband and son, which gave Stoiber the opportunity to manipulate her. Ultimately, he obtained control over her financial, legal, and personal affairs. According to Stoiber, in April 1947, "After going into detail of all the headaches which were involved from a personal standpoint and from business I was asked directly from Mrs. John if I would please take over due to the fact that she is going crazy, she can't take it any more. I told her point blank that I would take over, that I would drop my business and give the best efforts as to my ability to run said Miller Brewing Company."[424]

Before Stoiber's intrusion into Elise's life, he had been selling or renting refrigeration equipment to taverns and individuals to chill beer. Each time that he placed equipment in an establishment, he procured a contract to supply Miller beer to them. Stoiber, who was born in 1899, had a cozy relationship with Miller's city sales manager, Frank Rystrom, who "gave Stoiber tips on taverns which required refrigeration." Stoiber was determined to start a relationship with Elise and even visited, "her local parish priest, Father [Otto A.] Haertle of St. Sebastians in order to influence her." On December 28, 1945, Stoiber wrote to a Miller manager unsuccessfully requesting a job in return for providing the brewery with his accounts and loans. Eighteen months later, Stoiber would finagle his way into Miller's second position.[425]

Over the succeeding days in May 1947, Stoiber discussed his unpaid balance with his "higher source," who besides forgiving his debt, gave him one share of her Miller Brewing Company stock and then nominated him for its board of directors. The brewery's bylaws indicated that any director must own at least one share. Fred Miller was beside himself upon discovering that Stoiber had conned Elise out of one share of her Miller stock. Immediately, he asked Frank Huber to investigate any police record that Stoiber might have and whether the scoundrel was actually ever in the refrigerator and fixture business.[426] To avoid a potential conflict of interest, Stoiber noted, in an abbreviated letter to the Miller Brewing Company management, that he had sold his refrigeration business, M.T. Stoiber Co., prior to becoming a stockholder. This turn of events, from accused deadbeat to Miller stockholder and board member, may be unprecedented in Milwaukee's rich brewing history.

Over this period, Stoiber had developed a close relationship with Lorraine, counseling her on personal and financial matters, eventually becoming her confidant. Lorraine, who was recently divorced and raising Karen and Michael, was susceptible to Stoiber's wiles. Also, Lorraine believed her mother's misguided assessment of the scoundrel. Stoiber's July 28, 1948 letter to Lorraine demonstrated his inappropriate intrusion into her life. As a precursor to this missive, Lorraine had complained to Stoiber about various physical ailments. Stoiber wrote about her spending and health:

"... *At this time I am reconstructing the balance you have in your account so that if (and I am spelling IF with capital letters) you will be needing additional money, I will if possible arrange an advance to you on the lots which you have purchased. I would suggest that you retrench yourself on your buying sprees. Call me if I can be of further assistance to you. Best regards.*

"*Yours very truly,*

"*M. T. Stoiber.*

"*P. S. As per my telephone conversation with you in regard to having a thorough examination made, I am not only insisting, but demanding, that you give me an analysis of your report. Do not be alarmed—I know how you feel and the only way you can find out what is wrong is by consulting doctors. If they cannot help you, you can call on Dr. Stoiber.*"

Prone to overstatement, Stoiber credited himself for introducing Attorney Norman Klug to Elise and the brewery. In early 1944, Stoiber and Klug were neighbors and Stoiber had used the lawyer's services to collect a claim in his refrigeration business. Then, the salesman introduced Klug to Mrs. John, after which, the lawyer began to consult for the *grand dame* and the brewery. Stoiber explained Klug's growing involvement with Elise, who wanted him to help her with "difficulties she was encountering with both sides of the family. . . [I] Told him [Klug] also that it's gone as far as Mrs. John cannot [can] take it and she asked me who I could recommend to take over due to the fact that there was nothing but constant fighting at the brewery and with the families." Stoiber described some of the first interaction between Klug and Elise John. Beforehand, Klug had billed Elise $500 for her legal fees, which she found, "rather exorbitant" but would pay nevertheless. She gave Klug an envelope with cash, but the lawyer found only four $100 bills in it and reported it to Stoiber, who told him, "No, Norm, Mrs. John is not built that way, but I will take this matter up with her . . ." Klug in turn said to Stoiber, "Let her keep that $100." Stoiber retorted, "No, Norm, I will not tolerate any talk from you making reference that Mrs. John deliberately held out $100. When we had this second meeting Mrs. John gave him an envelope with that $100 in and what her statement to Klug was I can not recall but there was plenty [of] sarcasm in it to the extent that this was not done purposely."[427]

Some weeks before the May 28, 1947 stockholder meeting, Fred Miller and Harry John, Jr. grudgingly arranged a compromise board consisting of them and B.H. Protzmann, Elise's accountant. Bud trusted Protzmann, a long-time family employee, and Fred believed that he could make constructive independent decisions. Fred accepted Bud's continued presence in a reduced role but, without a doubt, wanted his Uncle Harry John, Sr. removed. Stoiber disapproved of the compromise board and, as Elise's mouthpiece, scrapped it. Also, to save his job and find someone to reduce Fred's authority, Harry, Jr. tried to hire a general manager to run the brewery's daily operations. He interviewed Rudy Zimmermann, "an acknowledged competent brewery man," with the notion to employ him, but Fred and Elise blocked the hiring.[428]

In the last days before the meeting, Elise settled on the new board. She concluded that her one-year experiment, with Buddy as president and Harry, Sr. as vice-president, had failed and would not re-elect them as directors and officers. Elise adhered to her promise to her nephew Fred, of the preceding year, by backing his presidency. Some family members were displeased. According to Stoiber, "Mrs. Mulberger did not like the idea of Fred Miller going in as president due to the fact that she hated him venomously but after a course of [Stoiber] talking and conversing with her she finally ceded the point."[429] Elise did not implicitly trust Fred, so she determined that Lorraine and Stoiber would serve alongside him as directors and officers. If she had completely trusted her nephew, she would have allowed him to name one or two friendly directors. The 2,400 shares in Bud's testamentary trust, 300 shares in Lorraine's testamentary trust, and her 2,360 shares gave Elise ownership of or trusteeship over more than 50% of the stock. Once again, Elise single-handedly chose the board of directors and, except for Fred, selected members based on their loyalty to her rather than their business acumen.

In anticipation of her absence from the May stockholder meeting, Elise John gave her daughter and Stoiber a proxy to vote her stock at any Miller Brewing Company meeting. Concurrently, Elise gave Lorraine a proxy to vote the 2,400 shares of Miller stock in Buddy's testamentary trust. Harry John, Sr., and Protzmann, as trustees of the 500 share general trusts of Lorraine Mulberger and Bud John, gave the siblings proxies to vote their shares.[430]

The May 28 meeting portended to be contentious because Bud John ignored the "writing on the wall." Bud's myopia did not originate from ignorance because, in many ways, he was a bright man. Instead, it stemmed from his mental disorder. Whenever he felt severely threatened, he would "circle the wagons" instead of exploring novel solutions. He perpetrated this behavior when confronted with threats, both actual and imaginary, the remainder of his life, which brought him considerable troubles. Ironically for a world-class philanthropist, his perception that someone would steal his money was the primary precipitator for him to become hyper-possessive. Of course, as often is the case, one loses the very ingredient that one overprotects. Bud's life became a routine of his protecting his assets from those who he feared would take them, often, paradoxically, his closest family members. Since Harry, Jr. was incapable of compromising with his mother, he was doomed to forfeit any role at the brewery. Simply explained, Elise wanted her son to cease expurgating his assets. On the other hand, Bud saw his position as righteous and believed that his mother would retreat and, once again, name him a director and president. In all likelihood, this episode represented the first time ever that Elise had denied one of her son's wishes.

In his defense, Buddy had attended every board meeting and studied brewing. For example, he read the 1946 book, *The Practical Brewer*, by the Master Brewers' Association of America to gain an overview of the brewing process. Also, during his term as president, the brewery's sales increased rapidly. The profits were remarkable, $1.5 million in 1946 and $2.1 million in 1947. The beer sales had grown from 635,002 barrels in 1946 to a record-setting 805,215 barrels in 1947. Furthermore, the massive building program had commenced under his reign, even though Fred Miller had provided the planning and impetus for it. In fact, Harry John, Jr. probably holds the record, among Miller's presidents, for his overall average of success during his reign. How could Bud do better than aping his mother, an accomplished president who also successfully delegated her authority? He allowed Fred to run the brewery, rarely interfering in his directives. As explained, Elise removed Bud for personal rather than business reasons.[431]

At 2:00 p.m. on May 28, 1947, the stockholders' meeting commenced at the corporation's headquarters at 4002 West State Street. Ignoring the impending storm, the composed

27-year-old president Harry G. "Bud" John, Jr. opened the meeting, with his personal attorneys, Frank Donohue, Urban Wittig and John Wittig in attendance. Harry John, Sr., who was absent, was loath to attend since his confrontation with his nephew the previous month. On the other hand, Elise, who was also not present, was so afraid of Buddy's and her husband Harry's temper that, during this time, she spent two weeks, under an assumed name, at the Edgewater Beach Hotel in Chicago, with Phyllis Engelhardt, her confidant and cousin. Another version had Klug and Stoiber sending Elise to the Chicago hotel because she was "unpredictable" and might have reinstated Bud.[432]

After Buddy opened the meeting, John Savage, Miller's associate house attorney, read the roll call and proxy votes. In anticipation of legal action, Hillard Viets, a court reporter, re-coded the verbiage. Eunice Hilgendorf, a secretary of the Miller brewing Company was also present. Fred Miller held proxies for his mother Clara Miller, and his sisters; Loretta Kopmeier, Claire McCahey, Marguerite Bransfield, and Charlotte Blommer, who were absent. Chuck Bransfield, Fred Miller's nephew, was in attendance. May Miller, Fritz Miller's widow, was there, as was Lorraine Mulberger; Norman Klug, who was newly employed as Miller's general counsel; B.H. Protzmann as a trustee of Buddy's stock; and Mike Stoiber, as a stockholder.[433]

After the attendees spoke their name for the record, Fred Miller objected to the presence of Harry Jr.'s attorneys because they were not stockholders. Buddy snorted, "I think that is out of order. Their capacity is my representative." Thereafter, Miller registered an objection to having non-stockholders at the meeting. At that moment, Harry, Jr.'s three attorneys stood to leave, to which Fred interjected, "Before you do that—sit down, a minute, Urb.—I will bring it to a vote of the stockholders. I don't want to take that course of my own volition, I mean, because I don't represent the majority." After a quick discussion between Miller and Norman Klug, the three lawyers quietly departed. Fred then turned to the brewery president noting drolly, "I have no objection, Bud, if you want to have an attorney representing you, but I don't think it is necessary to have three in the meeting."[434]

Harry, Jr., filled the next few minutes questioning the legality of various proxies, to stall the inevitable vote that would conclude his tenure as a director and, thereafter, president. Bud had changed his thinking since April of the previous year, when his mother strained to convince him to accept the job. Now, a team of horses could not separate him from his title. Next, Harry, Jr., Fred, John Savage, and Norman Klug discussed the legal complexities of these proxies. Everyone else sat mutely, fearing Buddy's reaction when he would realize that the last path to retaining the presidency had closed. All the while, there were averted eyes, clicking fingernails, and moistened armpits among those unaccustomed to attending board meetings, especially contentious ones. It was especially difficult for Bud's sister, 33-year-old Lorraine, and 28-year-old cousin, Chuck Bransfield, who, until the onset of Bud's mental illness in his college years, had shared innumerable delightful experiences with him. Lorraine surely anticipated that her vote would preclude, forever, any chance of a meaningful relationship with her brother.[435]

In a last-gasp quixotic effort to retain power, Harry, Jr., objected to the proxy for Lorraine's testamentary trust. (Note Bud's forewarning of family lawsuits that, eventually, became his *modus operandi*.) "I have–I have competent legal opinion on such general proxies, that such general proxies are not quite in order. I think in the light of this opinion, and also to avoid litigation in the family, and in order to give further study to this proxy, I hereby adjourn this meeting until the 28th of June of this year. The meeting is hereby adjourned." Fred Miller quickly intervened, "I object to any adjournment." Bud interposed, "The meeting is hereby adjourned," then rose and strode out of the room.[436]

Everybody else remained seated and, immediately, Klug, then Miller, declared that the meeting would continue, while noting Bud's objection to the proxy of the testamentary trust. Klug explained the legality of Lorraine's testamentary proxy and, afterwards, announced that Fred would run the meeting as highest reigning officer present. He also said that Harry John, Jr., had failed to call for a stockholders' vote before announcing an adjournment over an objection. Then, Klug made a motion, which was approved, to elect Fred, in absence of the president, as chairman of the meeting. Afterwards, May Miller made a motion to accept the minutes from the previous year and Chuck Bransfield seconded it.[437]

The next order of business was the election, with 6,792 out of 10,000 outstanding shares, of Fred Miller, Lorraine Mulberger, and Michael Stoiber as corporate directors or as Bud called them sarcastically; the "football player," the "divorcee," and the "tavern service man." The relieved stockholders quickly moved through the last business and, thirty-five minutes after the meeting began, Fred adjourned the meeting. A subsequent annual board meeting saw the election of Fred Miller as president, Lorraine Mulberger as first vice-president, Norman Klug as second vice-president, Frank Huber as secretary, and Michael Stoiber as treasurer. It was the first time in Miller Brewery's history that the directors and officers had not been elected with a unanimous vote. They drew no compensation for their directorships or officer positions. Fred Miller and Michael Stoiber were named co-executive managers and given $12,000 yearly salaries and $12,000 annual expense accounts. Norman R. Klug became general counsel and received the same compensation as Miller. Monthly, Lorraine received $1,000 for her services.[438]

After his election as Miller Brewing Company's president, Fred remained loyal to his *alma mater*, the University of Notre Dame. For ten years in the 1940s and early 1950s, every Wednesday and then on game day, he would fly to South Bend, Indiana or to the away-game locations voluntarily to instruct the tackles under his friend Coach Frank Leahy. For this effort and many others, in 1950, his alma mater named him "man of the year." Frederick Miller Bransfield, Fred Miller's nephew, said that his uncle's personality was so expansive that many people, including the Notre Dame contingent, thought that he was Miller Brewing Company's sole owner. Of course, his last name added to the perception. Fred was a living billboard ballyhooing the brewery. He inspired others by his dedication to Notre Dame, especially the players. He also helped recruit Wisconsin boys for the football team. Jack Swanson, Lorraine's son-in-law, author, and sport enthusiast, recalled an incident involving football great Alan Ameche. In 1950, Fred Miller was determined to recruit this Kenosha, Wisconsin athlete to Notre Dame, of course competing against the in-state power, the University of Wisconsin. Due in part to Fred's persuasive skills, Ameche had agreed to join the Irish. This announcement caused a great stir among Wisconsin's fan base and sundry angry alumni began to make plans to organize a boycott of Miller Brewery's products. They became sufficiently vociferous that Fred reneged on his support for Ameche, who then attended Wisconsin. This star, nicknamed "the Horse," set numerous records as fullback at the University of Wisconsin and won the Heisman Trophy. He went on to play six years with the Baltimore Colts of the National Football League.

South Bend sports writer Joe Doyle wrote of Fred's willingness to accept high risk in order to accomplish his coaching goals. Ignoring an early November, 1953, blizzard, Fred and Adele Miller, Mr. And Mrs. Fritz Wilson, Dr. and Mrs. N.C. Johns, and the wife of Notre Dame's athletic director, Ed "Moose" Krause, were determined to attend the Notre Dame-Penn State game. They left Milwaukee in a Miller Brewery plane but rough weather forced them to land in Pittsburgh where they transferred to a car. Unfortunately, a state trooper had barricaded the road due to hazardous conditions that had stalled trucks, cars, and busses. Fred defied the odds, pulled aside the barricade, and demanded that Fritz drive forward. Soon, the road was so jammed with stalled vehicles that Fritz would not continue. In the article, Dr. Johns remembers that Fred said, "What do you mean we can't get through. Get out of there, I'll drive." After taking the wheel, he drove wildly, around cars, trucks, on the shoulder, through rest areas—hardly slow-ing down a bit. The windshield was so foggy that he could not clearly see the road, until he opened up the side windows, nearly freezing the passengers. They arrived in Philadelphia in time for Mass and breakfast with the team at the Hotel Warwick.

Fred enjoyed the good life, which showed in his stylish clothes. He wore tailored suits, wing-tipped shoes, and owned a full-length raccoon coat. Fred compulsively either played or promoted sports. As an adult he swam, golfed, snow and water-skied, lifted weights, and played squash, tennis, handball, and racquetball. He stayed physically fit by jogging, lifting weights, playing ball games, and eating well. He treasured his physique and, at Florida beaches, gladly posed for snapshots in his swimming suit.

His nephew, Chuck Bransfield, noted that Fred and Adele held many gatherings at their Oconomowoc Lake house. He was the clan hero and is still lionized by his descendents and relatives, many of whom are named for him. To help them during the food-rationing period during World War II, Fred bought a farm on the Rock River, forty miles west of Milwaukee. He may also have purchased the farm to avoid the draft, as farmers were excluded from military service due to their importance to the war effort. In all likelihood Fred Miller would not have been drafted because of his advancing age. His daughter, Claire Miller Krause, mentioned that the produce from the farm was for personal use only, not brewery use. Occasionally, Fred would bring his mother to the farm and give her carriage rides. In late summer and fall, Claire and her mother enjoyed canning fruits and vegetables in the farmhouse basement.

One of Fred's weaknesses was his penchant for risky behavior, especially regarding motorized vehicles. In early July 1954, he was arrested in Oconto, Wisconsin, for speeding and operating a motorized vehicle with an expired driver's license. At the time of the arrest, he had been driving with Adele and their daughter, Claire, and her husband John Rosenberger to their property on Craig Lake in Michigan's Upper Peninsula. Fred owned this land and a rustic cabin for a getaway retreat. Along with his many accomplishments, he was also an avid outdoorsman. Oconto County traffic officer Crosby Whitcomb said that Fred had been traveling 70 miles per hour in a 45-mile-per-hour zone and, additionally, his license had been expired since April 10, 1950. Days later, Fred was represented in court by Oconto attorney Harold W. Krueger, who was determined to fight the $53 fine. There was confusion when Officer Whitcomb told a Milwaukee reporter that the "Fred Miller" that he had arrested was a retired employee of the Rahr Brewery. The *Journal* article explained that Whitcomb reported that he had been confused about the defendant's identity but, eventually, explained that Fred Miller did not want any publicity from the arrest. Fred denied any effort to squash news of the arrest. "I didn't speak more than five words to the man," Miller declared.[439]

Fred was a remarkable force in Milwaukee. From the current Milwaukee Repertory Theater, to the Braves professional baseball club coming to Milwaukee, he used his persona to promote causes. Along with his business successes, he was a civic giant bringing energy, money, and publicity to numerous Milwaukee organizations. In 1947, he belonged to nearly a dozen organizations such as the Milwaukee Athletic Club, Wisconsin Club, Town Club, and Oconomowoc Lake Club, demonstrating his inability to say "no." One may use the word compulsive to describe Fred. His family suffered from his absence, as one cannot be fully committed to all endeavors. Fortunately for Miller Brewery, it was the object of much of his relentless behavior. He fulfilled every wish his mother had for him and, until his death, remained a dutiful son. Years later, Fred's sister Claire Miller McCahey remarked that he was well known for his generosity to the poor; at Christmas he always made a big donation. He was loquacious and loved to be among people, at times singing with them. He was recognized around town; seemingly, every waiter in Milwaukee knew him. He also was a dedicated Catholic. In 1952, Pope Pius XII named him Knight of St. Gregory in recognition of his work as chairman of the fund drive to build the new 500-bed St. Aemilian's Orphanage in Milwaukee.

Bud was devastated by his removal from Miller Brewery's hierarchy by all of his adult Miller relatives except his father. For some months afterwards, while filled with rage and then depression, he tried to recapture his brewery authority by badgering his mother. Harry, Elise, and Lorraine were concerned that Buddy, in this crisis, might hurt himself or others. Bud's family knew that he kept guns at his farm but also knew that he had never used them inappropriately. Nevertheless, these urban folks were frightened at the thought of the combination of Harry Jr.'s temper and firearms. Supposedly, they obtained a report from a psychiatrist, without Bud's knowledge, on his physical and mental state. Reportedly, Harry, Sr. accompanied his son to a psychiatrist, who introduced himself as a general practitioner to hoodwink Bud.[440]

At this time, supposedly, Elise asked Fred Miller, Michael Stoiber, and Norman Klug to appear before Milwaukee County District Attorney Bill McCauley to have Bud declared legally insane and temporarily committed to a mental institution.[441] Allegedly, the three brewery executives, as a favor to Elise, hired psychiatrists to watch Bud, "without his knowledge and they [doctors] are of the opinion that, if he is not incompetent, at least he needs treatment." Reportedly there was, "a meeting between Mrs. Elise John, Mrs. Mulberger, and Dr. Jefferson in which Dr. Jefferson expressed the opinion that Harry John Jr.'s mental condition would deteriorate as time goes on and that, unfortunately, he would attack those to whom he owes the most." These executives alleged Bud's incompetence was based on his, "statement in the lobby of the MAC [Milwaukee Athletic Club] that F.M. [Fred Miller] and Klug and MTS [Stoiber] were crooks; were mismanaging the brewery." Also they believed that Harry Jr. needed treatment because he had accused his mother of incompetence. Bill McCauley refused to act, citing insufficient evidence. Regardless, somehow Elise prevailed and, from August 29 through September 8, 1947, Bud convalesced voluntarily at the Austen Riggs Foundation, a psychiatric hospital in Stockbridge, Massachusetts.[442] To Elise's credit, she worked in Bud's best interests, as he had overreacted to his removal from the brewery job that, at first, he had spurned.

Despite the trials of the John family, the brewery progressed. Following the May 1947 shareholder meeting, Stoiber declared that, every morning, Miller, Klug, and he held hour-long sessions to, "grasp any and all details which came up or may come up for the following day." Lorraine, as Miller director and officer, attended board meetings and kept informed with daily hour-long conversations with Fred and Norman, when she stayed at home with her children. Of course, she alone was raising young Karen and Michael after their father had departed for Colorado. Nevertheless, the departure of Harry and Bud John did not guarantee a pacific executive team, as jealousy abounded while Fred established his hegemony over operations and Stoiber and Klug jostled for second place. At that time, Frederick C. Miller supported Klug and Elise backed Stoiber. The former refrigerator salesman, who later facilely fabricated stories, noted that, after every meeting, Klug told him privately, "I do not trust Fred Miller. He will double cross us at the first chance he gets." Again, our storyteller responded, "Let's not form conclusions. Lets find out and see what he is made of." To which Klug answered, "I am just telling you, I do not trust him." Stoiber noted, "This I would say kept up every day and more so after every directors meeting . . ." [443] To Fred Miller's credit, he remained above Stoiber's machinations.

Stoiber's slyness caused him increasing problems at the brewery. In May 1948, he informed Klug, "let me tell you for the last time it is none of your goddam business what I do after working hours, and what authority have you got to tell Mrs. Mulberger that I never go to bed before three or four o'clock in the morning. That our lights are always lit and that we are always running parties to that hour." Klug countered, "Mike gee! I did not mean anything by this but you can rest assured I will not tell Mrs. Mulberger anything from here on in." [444]

The 41-year-old Fred Miller's first official statement, as Miller's president, reiterated his earlier statements, "Contrary to many rumors, the Miller Brewing Co. has not and will not be sold, but will remain under the sole control of the heirs of the original founder." In order to boost employee morale, on Saturday August 2, 1947, Fred hosted a buffet supper for its more than 750 workers in the main garage. Fred explained that the party was, "an expression of the strong feeling of unity between executives and the office and plant employees." He then introduced John H. Heiden, a maintenance superintendent who began employment in 1901, as the oldest employee still working.[445]

For reasons that are unclear, in early June 1947, the newly elected Fred Miller fired Frank Huber, Miller's general manager. Frank, who had worked at the brewery since December 1, 1941, declined to comment on the reasons for his departure. After his discharge, Huber plied Bud's legal team with scurrilous stories of Stoiber, Miller, and Lorraine. On June 15, Edward T. "Jiggs" Donohue took over as secretary and general manager at $15,000 a year. On January 12, 1948, Fred discharged Donohue by eliminating the general manager position and turning the duties over to the board of directors, or in other words—Fred himself. Denying any conflict between the board and Donohue, Stoiber, speaking for the brewery, remarked that the three-person board has proved to be so active that a general manager is unnecessary. Subsequently, Donohue also helped Bud's legal maneuverings.[446]

On July 15, 1947, Fred celebrated the completion of a document that every stockholder signed except Bud, Harry, Sr., and May Miller. In part it read, "Whereas, rumors have been circulated from time to time that the said company was about to be sold, which rumors injuriously affected the interest of said company and the stockholders thereof, and whereas, the undersigned holders of a majority of the stock of said company are of the opinion that it will be for the best interests of said company and the stockholders thereof, not to sell control of said company outside of the family, but to continue to operate it for the best interests of said stockholders and said company . . ." The instrument gave Fred Miller, Lorraine Mulberger, and Michael Stoiber ten-year contracts as directors. Also, it specified that if Fred Miller were found incapable of serving, his brother in law, James B. McCahey, Sr., would replace him.[447] The four-page document gave Fred Miller a long-term vote of confidence by the majority of the stockholders, to progress with the brewery's expansion. Regardless, in February 1949, due to Bud's attorney challenging the validity of the long-term contracts, the brewery board voided them.

After the May meetings, Elise found little harmony at home, as her husband and son created increasing disquiet for her. In her last years, this woman, who had sacrificed so much for her family, the brewery, and society, longed for domestic peace. On July 18, 1947, after suffering a major stroke, she entered the Sanitarium — as she had many times before — never to live anywhere else again. She found comfort among the nuns who tended to her every need, such as her great defender, Sister M. Walditrudis Miller, O.S.F.[448]

As Elise recuperated from her stroke, Harry, Sr., Lorraine, Bud, Stoiber, Fred, and Klug jockeyed for her favor. Miller Brewery's general manager, Edward Huber, heard Stoiber pronounce, "We have her on ice at the sanitarium and apparently [he] . . . used the phrase 'on ice' frequently in regard to Mrs. John's being at the sanitarium." In order to keep the contentious Harry and Bud at bay, Michael Stoiber and Lorraine hired a private detective, Ed Prohaska of the firm Prohaska and Bauschek, to guard her door. At this time, Bud was harrying his mother to allow him to sell the Miller stock in his testamentary trust, reinstate him as director and president, and give him a major portion of her remaining 2,434 shares of Miller stock. Reportedly on August 7, Bud visited his mom, visibly upsetting her and raising her blood pressure by sixty points. Another time, Prohaska denied Harry, Jr. and his attorney, John "Jack" Wittig's, visitation, "by stepping into his path and blocking his moving towards his mother's room."[449]

Bud's legal team reported that Norman Klug and Michael Stoiber had hired Ed Prohaska to collect damaging personal information on Fred Miller, Harry John, Sr. and Bud John in order to blackmail them or disparage them to Elise. Presumably, Stoiber kept a black book, with the detective's findings on the three men, though its existence has never been substantiated. Frank Huber, a Miller executive, and Lubin Pelkey, Miller Brewing Company Company's chief counsel, reported that they each had seen the volume several times, which contained salacious stories of Fred Miller and Harry John, Sr. The information on Bud was merely mundane.[450] After Michael Stoiber died, Bud wanted to break into his house during the funeral to remove this mysterious black book. Fortunately, his wife, Erica Novotny John, dissuaded him.

In the few months after the May stockholders' meeting, the air was rife with stories of subterfuge. On August 8, reportedly, Lorraine had recruited her second cousin, Norman "Normy" Kopmeier, Jr., (the son of Loretta Kopmeier, Fred's oldest sister), to spy on Bud. In return for "information as to the actions and whereabouts" of Bud, Normy was to receive $1,000 a week and a car. Also, reportedly, Normy owed his Uncle Fred Miller $250 for services rendered, for which Fred held a note. Norman Kopmeier, Sr. refused to settle his son's obligation stating that it would be against the "interest of his wife." In exchange for forgiving the loan, theoretically, Fred wanted a five-year proxy of their Miller stock from Norman and his sister, Rose Mary Kopmeier Bradford. One preposterous rumor held that Lorraine might remarry and then install her new husband as brewery president. At this time, Lorraine did not have enough stock to accomplish it. Another anecdote from Bud's legal team had Michael Stoiber offering Fred Miller either $1,000 or $10,000 to apprise Elise John of Stoiber's "good work" at Miller Brewery.[451]

Some of the edginess among Fred Miller, Lorraine, and Harry, Jr., stemmed from their anticipation of Elise's impending donation of her stock to her children. Fred C. Miller knew that his tenure as president might be abridged if Bud got significantly more stock than Lorraine. Over the past few months, Lorraine and Harry, Jr. had been lobbying their mother for a major share. The suspicious siblings accused one another of trying to steal their mother's assets. They each had informants at the hospice who secretly reported on Elise's guests. Each time Lorraine visited her mother at the Sanitarium, it evoked waves of jealousy in Bud and, likewise, for Lorraine, the few times that her brother could see his Mom.

On August 24, 1947, Elise gave all of her Miller stock, 2,434 shares, to Lorraine. Magnanimously, Elise, beforehand, had paid all of her children's substantial gift taxes. To understand her kindness, if she provided Lorraine with a $500,000 gift and the taxes were $150,000, Elise's assets decreased by $650,000 to net the $500,000 contribution. Elise declared $450 a share or $1,095,500 total in her gift tax return. The Wisconsin Department of Taxation disagreed, putting the price per share at $1,000, which dramatically increased Elise's tax burden. She gave nothing to Bud who, in her eyes, had been disloyal to her. Elise objected to her son disposing of the assets that his ancestors had earned. Regardless of Elise's thoughts in 1947, she may have had an oral agreement with her brother Frederick A. "Fritz" Miller, in 1938, for him to give the lion's share of his Miller Brewery stock to Bud with the notion that, years later, she would confer the majority of her stock to Lorraine. In this way, eventually the two siblings would have roughly equal amounts of stock, which is in fact what occurred.[452]

On August 13, 1947, Elise asked, "Stoiber to take care of all of my personal affairs, including financial matters. In all such matters which may arise, he has full authority to pass final judgment." The fact that Elise had a husband and two grown children and yet gave the power of attorney to someone else, demonstrated the Johns' internal estrangement. Soon after receiving this extraordinary coup, Stoiber traipsed into Elise's business office, at the First Wisconsin Bank Building at 735 North Water Street, to assume control. The business office also supervised the estate of Fritz Miller, who had died in 1943. The avuncular Oscar Treichler ran the show. The tall, slender, aging man was a lenient supervisor, who had reached his zenith in the late 1930s under Fritz Miller. The two of them had an intimate working relationship that concluded with Treichler representing Fritz on the board of Miller Brewery. After Fritz died in December 1943, Treichler managed his estate and Elise's finances. Working for Treichler were B.H. Protzmann and Walter Charles Lemke, both C.P.A.s; Attorney E.D. Fitzpatrick; Joyce Meinicke, assistant bookkeeper; and a secretary.

The office, in room 1107, had a wooden door with an opaque glass upper section, painted with the relatively small names "Frederick A. Miller" and below "Elise K. John". Many years earlier, the staff had done the personal financial work for Lisette and Ernest Miller. Elise's sister, Clara Miller, always maintained her own financial and legal staff. The walls, paneled with dark wood, reflected the somber atmosphere of 1940s Milwaukee. Oscar Treichler occupied the only private office and the mountain of documents was stored in a walk-in vault. Besides managing Fritz and Elise's multi-million dollar assets, it also oversaw many of the Millers' apartment buildings in Milwaukee, Illinois, and Florida. Tenants would come to the eleventh floor to pay their rent over the waist-high swinging door. In the same building, the Miller-owned Oriental Realty Company was on the twelfth floor and Alexander Schutz, the brewery's attorney, worked on the fourteenth floor.[453]

Upon Stoiber's asserting his new authority over Elise John's business office, he ordered an audit of the books from the CPA firm of John G. Conley, which discovered that there were tens of thousands of dollars in untracked cash transactions. Stoiber immediately blamed Treichler, whom Elise had discharged on August 6. Treichler's departure sharply decreased his income as, in recent years, Elise had been gifting him $50,000 on top of his normal salary. Subsequently, Stoiber received this yearly gift. Protzmann and Joyce Meinicke departed the office with Treichler to continue to manage Fritz's estate. Protzmann blamed his subsequent case of tuberculosis on Stoiber's actions because after he, Treichler, and Meinicke left their First Wisconsin office, they rented a poorly heated storefront on North 27th Street, where he became sick. This illness led to Protzmann's quarantine in the tuberculosis sanitarium at the county grounds and then early death in Arizona. Protzmann wrote to Elise that, "after faithfully, loyally and honestly serving you for twenty years, you have allowed someone [Stoiber] to take over the position I have earned for myself after these twenty years of service." He continued, "The fact that you received my services through the best years of my life also seemed to make no difference to you. The fact that I stayed with you throughout the war years when I was receiving offers to work elsewhere, but did not, makes no difference to you. You have allowed someone else to play into your confidence and would allow him to make an office boy out of me. I tell you this to let you know how unfair you have been and that is the reason for my resigning."[454]

Lemke stayed to collaborate with Stoiber against his old boss and co-worker. Soon thereafter, Stoiber brought in Treichler and Protzmann, who was then living in Arizona, for questioning after threatening to use the legal system against them. Eventually, the parties concluded that Treichler ran the Millers' affairs with outdated accounting methods that improperly tracked the debits and credits. Additionally, Elise and Harry John, Sr. liked using cash instead of checks. In the mid-1940s, Joyce Meinicke once counted 70 one-thousand dollar bills that eventually found their way into Elise and Harry's hands. Elise liked giving cash donations to family, friends, and charitable causes. Harry did likewise but additionally used cash to carry on clandestine relationships with females.[455]

John "Jack" Savage, Miller's assistant corporate counsel, remembers the early phase of Fred Miller's presidency. Fred Miller, whom Jack holds in the highest regard, was an everyman's president. Fred disregarded his reserved parking spot, instead randomly placing his car with the other employees' vehicles. At the time Fred became president, according to Savage, the brewery had suffered a long period of neglect, as World War I, Prohibition, the Depression, and World War II restricted the brewery's sales and, therefore, ability to improve its facilities. Part of the problem included the past three presidents, Fritz Miller, Elise John, and Buddy John, none of whom were energetic organizers. Fred C. Miller would methodically review one area after another of the brewery's facilities with an eye to improve them. He began with the headquarters that was built before the turn of the century and was an embarrassment to use for entertaining guests. Jack mentioned that the exposed radiators were painted so sloppily that paint drips were solidified like stalactites.

In late 1947 and early 1948, to make way for Miller's new brewhouse, the brewery consolidated their corporate offices, on the northwest corner of 40th and State Streets, in an annex at the rear of the old administration building. Then in August 1947, a construction crew razed it. Miller's rush to construct citadels of brewing efficiency destroyed various historical gems, such as the administration building, which had survived since 1881, during Frederick J. Miller's tenure. With today's sensitivity, this brick and stone treasure would have been moved for future generations to enjoy. As it is, the administration building, where generations of Millers made both constructive and destructive decisions, exists only in photographs.

Since October 1946, when the brewery began building stockhouse F, plans dictated construction of a bottling house and an 188,000-gallon a day capacity brewhouse. The bottling house, of reinforced concrete construction, would be two stories tall, 160 feet wide and 270 feet long. The new bottling house, together with the old one, would have a daily combined capacity of 1.4 million bottles. In September 1947, the brewery began construction on both projects.[456]

In August 1947, Fred Miller proclaimed, "When this program has been completed—our expectations for that are about Jan. 1, 1949—the total output of our company will be well more than one million barrels annually," up from 800,000 barrels. He continued, "And I believe it may be said without exaggeration that our facilities will rank with the best." Fred C. Miller remarked that the expansion would add approximately 300 new jobs on top of the 750 existing employees. In 1947 and 1948, as the $5.5 million brewhouse, stockhouse, and bottling house were being fabricated, the brewery management added to its plans another stockhouse, brewhouse, granary, and a bottling house capable of filling 2 million bottles a day.[457]

At this same time, Fred had to handle potentially catastrophic matters. For example, at minutes before noon on Friday, December 19, 1947, a two-alarm fire raced up 90 feet of wooden scaffolding on the nearly completed stockhouse. There were no injuries among the 150 workers putting the finishing touches on the interior and the damages were approximately $35,000 including some smudges on the outside wall. Four days later, around 6:30 a.m., a fire struck Miller's pitch house causing $2,000 in damages. In the structure, "where beer cans and metal barrels are keglined, 100 gallon kettles of synthetic resin are cooked over gas burners." A pot boiled over and the spilled material caught fire, which the firemen extinguished in ten minutes with chemical foam.[458]

On December 11, 1947 at a Miller board meeting, Fred and Lorraine sat silently as Stoiber read a letter from Elise John, dated December 9, 1947. It beseeched them to redeem 2,400 shares of Miller stock in Bud's testamentary trust. Elise, acting in her capacity as the trust's sole trustee, stipulated that Lorraine would have the opportunity to purchase sufficient stock to procure a majority position. At that time, Lorraine had 3,235 4/9 shares of the 10,000 outstanding shares of Miller stock. The remainder, except Buddy's 2,400 shares in his testamentary trust, equaled 4,364 15/27 shares. In order to maintain a majority of the shares, Lorraine would need to buy 1,130 shares of Buddy's testamentary trust stock, thus leaving 1,270 shares for the brewery to redeem.[459]

To help understand the issues, it is worthwhile to realize that Bud John's testamentary trust provided him with an annual payment of $10,000 for eight years after the death in 1943 of his uncle, Fritz Miller. At that time, the trust was to terminate and the principal given to him, on Harry Jr.'s thirty-second birthday, December 19, 1951. On April 22, 1946, Treichler resigned as trustee of Bud's testamentary trust and, in a prearranged transfer, was replaced by Elise. At the time of Fritz's death, the 2,400 shares of brewery stock were appraised at $450 per share or $1,080,000 total.[460]

On about June 22, 1947, before Elise's redemption request and one month after Bud's removal as brewery president, Elise, Lorraine, and Klug met with Bud and offered him $450 per share for his Miller shares in his testamentary trust. Elise, as had her siblings, strove to keep the Miller Brewing Company family owned. They asked Harry, Jr. to sell this stock to either Elise or Lorraine, which he refused. Buddy knew from earlier marketing efforts that the brewery stock was worth $1,000 to $1,200 a share. They argued that since he wanted to give the stock sale proceeds to charitable causes, he could just as easily sell it to them at a lower price "and not to a stranger."

After Stoiber finished the letter, Fred Miller remarked that it was the fiduciary duty of the president and the board to purchase the stock as reasonably as possible. Stoiber responded that Elise John wanted $450 per share, "the price at which the stock was appraised by both the State and Federal governments in the estate of Fred A. [Fritz] Miller." Miller responded that Alexander Schutz, the executor and attorney for Fritz's estate, "and most of the heirs had vigorously protested this valuation, and had contended that the stock was actually worth $400 per share." Fred said that heirs desired a lower valuation to pay less tax. Stoiber reported that Mrs. John insisted upon $450 per share and, "wanted it understood that her offer to the company was with the understanding that if the brewery elected to purchase the stock, the stock was to be retired so that it could not be available for re-issue."[461]

Fred Miller complained that, "in view of the large expansion and balancing program presently being conducted, with a proportionately large demand on the finance of the company, from a financial standpoint it was an inopportune time for the company to expend $571,500 to purchase this stock. He further stated that he realized, however, that it had always been the policy of the stockholders to keep the stockholdings within the family insofar as possible, and that certainly it was desirable to keep control of the company within the family as it had been ever since his grandfather established the company in 1855."[462]

With Lorraine and Michael Stoiber supporting the redemption, Frederick C. Miller had little choice in the Johns' internecine battle that had spilled into brewery business. Fred had grown accustomed to directing the brewery while the Johns squabbled, effectively ignoring them unless it directly affected the brewery. Fred Miller Bransfield remembers his uncle's looks of exasperation upon hearing more news of the Johns' sparring. Fred also successfully balanced the wishes of his immediate family: his mother, wife, sisters and their husbands. Regardless, the board redeemed 1,270 shares of Harry, Jr.'s Miller Brewing Company stock at $450 per share, with the said stock being, "retired and not reissued." Furthermore, the stockholders reduced the number of outstanding shares from 10,000 to 8,730 in the articles of incorporation.[463]

Harry, Jr. vigorously opposed the redemption of his stock. On December 30, 1947, he received a legal opinion from the respected law firm of Lines, Spooner & Quarles noting that, after a thorough examination of the brewery's documents, the brewery was being sufficiently well run so Bud would fail if he sued the current management team for malfeasance. On the other hand, it was their, ". . .opinion that the transfer was made to Miller Brewing Company for grossly less than the fair market value of the stock and we recommend that action be taken to set aside the transfer of stock on the following alternative grounds: a) Gross misuse of trust powers in bad faith; b) Fraud; c) Undue influence of the trustee." Also, "We further recommend that action be taken to remove the trustee [Elise John] of the testamentary trust."[464]

At this time, Bud was steaming about Stoiber's increasing influence over his mother and sister. The ex-Miller president mistakenly believed that his condition would improve if Stoiber left. On rare occasions, Harry, Jr. verbally attacked Stoiber, hoping to intimidate him. In early January 1948, Elise John insisted that her son apologize to Stoiber for his outburst toward him in late 1947. Bud's attorneys, the Wittigs, recommended against a written apology presuming that Stoiber would never sue Elise's son.[465] Bud's attorney, Louis Quarles, wrote to John Wittig, on January 13, 1948 that, "Klug has called again and is quite insistent that the apology matter be settled this week. I told him that Harry had been on the farm and we had trouble getting him, but that we wouldn't give an apology, certainly not in that form, unless we got a letter from Stoiber evidencing that on its acceptance the matter was closed and would not again be raised. I told him that we would want to be sure that no suit would be predicated on what had heretofore transpired. Of course, if Harry should be indiscreet enough to do things of that sort again, that would stand on its own feet." What follows are two letters of apology that Bud wrote but may not have mailed.

January 22, 1948

Mr. Stoiber:
Dear Sir:
Over the past year I feel I have been maneuvered out of the Miller Brewing Co., have been ousted as an officer and director and have been barred from visiting my mother. Naturally, all of this has bothered me a great deal, has worried me much, and when I met with you some weeks ago at the Milwaukee Athletic Club, I guess I lost my temper and may have been sharp and ungentlemanly in my remarks to you.

I regret this exceedingly, and feel you have an apology due you. Hence, I hereby apologize to you.

I know that you would not use this apology, but, so there will be no misunderstanding between us, I predicate my apology upon the condition that its acceptance closes all past actions or remarks.

Will you kindly so indicate, and it is understood that this letter shall never be used in any litigation by you.

Very truly yours,
Harry John, Jr..

The second letter reads:

January   1948

Mr. Stoiber,
I have called you a crook and a thief and made disparaging
remarks concerning your business ability. I hereby apologize to you,
and acknowledge that these statements had no basis in fact.
I also herewith apologize for any ungentlemanly conduct towards
you at Sacred Heart Sanitarium on January 5, 1948.

Harry G. John, Jr.

On January 26, 1948, after Elise John refused to rescind the
stock sale and redemption, Bud filed a complaint in circuit court
against his mother, sister, Norman Klug, Michael Stoiber, and
the Miller Brewing Company demanding a return of the Miller
stock to his testamentary trust. The founder of the Miller Brewing Company, Fred J. Miller's last words, "Be considerate and
kind to each other and remain in peace and unity," were falling
on deaf ears. Harry, Jr., did not name his cousin Frederick C.
Miller in the suit, due in all likelihood to Fred's resistance to
the stock sale. At that time, Stoiber remarked that there would
be no comment by Elise John, himself, or the brewery. Elise
was so shocked and hurt by her son's lawsuit against her that
on January 27, 1948 she wrote,
       "Mr. Harry G. John, Jr. I hereby demand you to stay away
from me hereafter. May God be your judge."[466]
       The Wittigs contended that Elise had sold Buddy's shares
for $450 a share even though outside parties had offered more
that $1,000 a share. Moreover, "by disposing of John's 2,400
shares of stock, he was eliminated from possible control of the
Miller Brewing Company." Also, "For a number of years past,
and more especially since the death of the said Fred A. [Fritz]
Miller in 1943, there has been considerable ill feeling between
the Harry G. John, jr. [Sr.] family and the Carl Miller family,
which latter family owns a substantial minority interest in the
Miller Brewing Co... The 2,400 shares in the Harry G. John, Jr.

testamentary trust represents control of the Miller Brewing Co. as between the two families." Bud charged that on December 11, 1947 Elise John, "in conspiracy with all other defendants in this action. . .made the above offer fraudulently and in bad faith, and in mismanagement of her trust." The action asked that the transfer be set aside and that any of the stock purchased by the company and Lorraine Mulberger from Bud's trust be ordered returned to the trust.[467]

On February 23, 1948, Elise wrote to Bud,

Dear Harry:

I have been deeply hurt by the court action which you commenced against me on account of the sale of your brewery stock. You repeatedly said that the business was being mismanaged and that your invest-ment was in danger and you constantly insisted that the stock be sold, although I always assured you that your fears were groundless. I under the circumstances decided to do anything I could to relieve you of all worry and therefore sold the stock at a fair & reasonable price. After the stock was sold you apparently changed your mind on the advice of others and now claim that I fraudulently disposed of your stock. You have no idea how this untrue charge has affected me. For years I have tried to satisfy your wishes. Since 1940 I have given you money and property worth more than a million dollars and now you charge me with fraud. I have always acted for your interests. Now you have chosen to be guided by others who don't have the interest in your welfare, that your mother has. You have made your decisions. In view of it I have requested Lorraine and the brewery to co-operate with me to place the stock back in trust and they are ready to do so.

Bud prevailed. On April 8, 1948, Elise resigned as trustee from Bud's testamentary trust, with him replacing her two days later. Additionally, Lorraine and the brewery returned the stock to the trust. George A. Affeldt, Elise's attorney, expressed that Harry, Jr. stipulated the dismissal of the fraud charges was agreed upon before Elise resigned. The only remaining issue, before Circuit Court Judge Michael S. Sheridan, was Elise's final accounting of her trusteeship. In December 1948, the opposing parties settled the case without prejudice with each party paying their respective legal costs.[468]

In mid-December 1948, in the days before the settlement of Bud's lawsuit, Elise wrote but never mailed a letter to her son:

> *Dear Bud:-*
>
> *I received your letter and thank you for your congratulations to my birthday. Regarding business of the brewery which you speak of I cannot do any now I first have to regain my health which I have tried to get back since six months. The brewery is in fine working order & I have good honest men. I want you to send a letter of apology to Mr. M. Stoiber on account of the way you have treated him because he has done wonders for our business and for you; also for Mr. N. Klug who is a good lawyer. I am not near well[,] well hoping you will think this over & don't listen to other people who are looking out for themselves not for you. I have to stop now. And Lorraine has been a good sister to you only looking out for your good & meant it well.*
>
> *Sincerely, Mother.*
>
> *Your action of your sueing [sic] me almost killed me & and I can never forget it after all I have done for you.*[469]

Now that Bud had direct control of 2,400 shares of Miller stock in his testamentary trust, he wanted to create a new voting majority. Previously, Fred, representing the East Side Millers, and Elise had formed a controlling percentage of the stock but, since August 1947, Fred had created an effective majority by cooperating with Lorraine. Harry Jr.'s primary motive in cooperating with Fred was to oust Lorraine, who he, unfairly, held in low regard. (Bud's paranoia caused him to distrust those who were closest to him, such as his mother and sister.) Bud's secondary motive was to gain a hand in controlling the brewery, which he had been denied since May 1947. Bud wrote to Fred in March 1948, after conversing with John A. "Jack" Puelicher, the president of the Marshall & Ilsley Bank and Fred's confidant, a draft of which follows:

> *Hello Fred —*
> *Good Mr. Puelicher and I had a little talk today. Mr. Puelicher is a wise man. He said this –*
> *In view of these facts, you and I:*
> *1)　are past friends*
> *2)　we are cousins*
> *3)　we are Catholics and N. D. [Notre Dame] graduates*
> *4)　we are unavoidably associated in business*
> *5)　we have a responsibility to resolve the strife rampant in our family for the past generation*
> *(If we fail in this we will be jeopardizing our chances for a peaceful death, and for that matter for a beautiful life, for we'll have to live together many more years. It isn't going to help your reputation any, or mine either, to continue this strife. And it will not help the Catholic Church any.)*
> *In view of these facts, said Mr. Puelicher, we ought to forget the past, and work out a basis for a friendly and profitable relationship for the future. Along with many others I admire you and wish to be your friend. Perhaps we can meet with Mr. Puelicher some day.*
> *Sincerely*
> *Bud*[470]

Some weeks later, Fred responded to Bud's missive:

> *April 13, 1948*
> *Dear Bud:*
> *This letter is in answer to yours of March 25.*
> *I assume that your purpose in asking for a meeting is to discuss your future relation with the company since I hardly think that you would be seeking a meeting for social purposes. I lived through an experience of about a year during which you were associated with the management of the company. The experience was neither pleasant nor conducive to the company's welfare. I was cooperative and friendly with you both socially and during business hours at that time but there was never any return of that spirit. Since then you*

have made derogatory and untrue statements about the brewery and its management. My ambitions for the growth and future success of the company go far beyond personal gain. The traditions that my grandfather so courageously started and that my uncles developed are far more important to me. For these reasons, and others, any attempt by you through a conference with me to work out a position for yourself with the brewery would be a waste of time.

If what you have in mind is some combination of your stock and mine to constitute a majority interest, it would be useless for us to discuss this. I am personally satisfied with my present working arrangement with Lorraine under which the brewery is being run successfully and for the best interests of all the stockholders. However, Lorraine and I will meet with you sometime if you wish.

Yours truly,
Fred [signed][471]

19.
POST-WAR
EXPANSION

On Thursday September 16, 1948, the brewery dedicated stockhouse F, a $3 million cornerstone of its massive expansion program, to Frederick J. Miller the brewery's founder. The event was attended by Frederick C. Miller's mother Clara, wife Adele, children, sisters and Aunt Elise John, other family members, and various civic leaders, totaling 100 people. The building, which was begun in March 1946, was, "a monument to the integrity of our product," according to Fred C. Miller. The structure that topped off 170 feet above State Street, was the first piece completed of Miller's $8.5 million construction effort. Fred added, "today Miller Brewing Co. is the leader in an industry where quality is foremost." Subsequently, the crowd filed down to the Miller Inn for a luncheon.[472]

By mid-July 1949 the brewery completed the triumvirate of new buildings that had risen in cost from $5.5 million to over $25 million. Uniquely, the Miller Brewing Company built these buildings out of the earnings, instead of bank loans. Their only foray into debt was a $500,000 loan from the Oriental Realty Company that the brewery repaid within a year in 1947. Stockhouse F, the brewhouse, and the bottling house fulfilled Fred Miller's vision of a modern, efficient brewery. The brewery trumpeted the event in a special four-color insert in the *Milwaukee Journal*. Fred C. Miller, together with the 51-year-old architectural engineer, Lawrence E. Peterson, wanted, "to give Milwaukee something unique, something that would stamp the Miller firm as the most modern in the brewing industry." The dedication of the brewhouse and bottling house, featuring Governor Oscar Rennebohm and Mayor Frank P. Zeidler, was followed by a buffet luncheon with music by the Miller High Life Band under the direction of Edwin Schmidt. Fred Miller's oldest son, 15-year-old Frederick C. "Freddy" Miller, Jr., unveiled a plaque on the brewhouse honoring the founder's wife Lisette Miller.[473]

Three daily tours brought visitors through the gleaming edifices that were covered on the inside with easy-to-clean white tiles, giving them a hospital-like appearance. The three uniformly designed buildings featured innumerable burnt-orange bricks that demonstrated Miller Brewery's capacity to organize hundreds of construction workers to place the blocks into a monolith, much like Egypt's pyramids. For example, stockhouse F has over one million bricks. Visitors might believe themselves insignificant in comparison to Miller's corporate strength. One thinks: If they can build these magnificent buildings, they must be capable of other great achievements. After looking up the featureless sides of the three towers, one is expected to genuflect in honor. It is unclear whether Fred Miller desired this effect, but there is no warmth or old-world charm in these new edifices.[474]

Whatever their commercial success, these three structures, including the next addition, stockhouse I, as seen after more than fifty years, are artistic failures. They fall short of engendering the warmth or German culture of traditional breweries. Of course, the same could be said about most new brewery buildings. Historical Bavarian breweries had the dual purposes of producing items for consumption while entertaining guests. Breweries, though production facilities, traditionally entertained an enormous number of visitors expecting the warmth of *der sternewirth,* or beer hall, replete with paintings of bulbous cherubs clasping steins of frothy, spilling fermented liquid. Miller's numerous visitors continue in this tradition. Miller Brewery's novel "cathedrals" fail to engender *gemuetlichkeit* in their guests. Fred J. Miller's existing 1886 brewhouse embodies this dual purpose in contrast to the 1949 monstrosities. Currently, the Milwaukee-based Miller Brewery struggles to preserve its historic buildings, such as the old brewhouse, refrigeration building, garage (formerly the stables), and Gettelman Brewery, with their architectural flourishes, that have secondary and tertiary uses and give the brewery its grace.

On February 27, 1949, 86-year-old Carl A. Miller, Fred C. Miller's father, died at Sacred Heart Sanitarium where he had resided for some time. The silver-haired immigrant, who originally had six children, left five children, 23 grandchildren, and seven great-grandchildren. He lay in state at the Feerick Funeral Home and, afterwards, was buried at the Miller plot at Calvary Cemetery. He had been a member of the Milwaukee Athletic Club, the Wisconsin Club, and St. Robert's Holy Name Society. Besides his ownership of the Carl Miller Lumber Company in Milwaukee and the Carl Miller (real estate) Company in Florida, he owned a holding company for residential properties. At one time, Carl owned over $250,000 worth of stock in the German company I.G. Farben. After World War II, supposedly he sent more than $100,000 to an architect friend in Bern, Switzerland to distribute to his needy German relatives.[475]

Carl lived life fully. Certainly, his trek to Victoria Falls in southern Africa, before he was married, was the climax of his adventurous traveling. After marriage and children, his risky trips were relegated to imaginary voyages in his well-stocked library. Nevertheless, he traveled extensively in the U.S. and Europe. Late in life, he pursued intellectual interests such as studying Italian. During his last five years, he read the works in the original French of the novelist Alexandre Dumas Sr. He also explored German philosophers Friedrich Nietzsche and Arthur Schopenhauer.

At 2:45 p.m. on February 22, 1949, five days before his Dad died, Fred Miller carried out what he had waited twenty-one months to do, fire Michael T. Stoiber. After considerable preparation, Fred Miller, Lorraine Mulberger, and Norman Klug invited Stoiber to a meeting at the brewery to provide evidence why he should resign before 2 p.m. the next day or be fired. Miller and Stoiber's ex-friend, Klug, read a list of the former refrigerator salesman's peccadilloes, many which involved insubordination. Stoiber was resolute, as he first looked Miller and then Klug in the eye while they, alternately, read the charges. Lorraine remained silent during the ordeal. A month earlier, on January 19, 1949, Lorraine released Stoiber as her financial advisor and agent, which gave Fred the opportunity to move against the flawed brewery officer. It had been Elise and then Lorraine who kept Stoiber employed at the brewery. Stoiber challenged his detractors as Klug read the first charge, "Look, cut out your window dressing. Come to the point. What are your charges, and I'll tell you quick what is going to happen. That is all I want. You are making an accusation here, all three of you."[476]

Karen Mulberger Swanson reported that she was at her mom's Oconomowoc Lake home when Fred C. Miller, Norman Klug, and Lorraine Mulberger set a trap for Stoiber. Karen remembers that two private detectives had hid a microphone in some curtains where Lorraine generally received Stoiber. Previously, Lorraine had invited the former refrigerator salesman to her house under the false pretense of querying him about her finances. Earlier Fred Miller and Norman Klug had prepared various questions for Lorraine to ask in order to best trap Stoiber. While Lorraine entertained Mike Stoiber Karen was peering over the upstairs railing. Simultaneously, the private dicks hid in the basement. Fred Miller later confronted Stoiber with the taped conversation, in which Stoiber likely denigrated Fred and Norman, but was unable to use it legally due to obtaining it improperly.

At the meeting to fire him, to his credit Stoiber was tenacious. The charges were serious, yet Miller, Klug, and Mulberger declined to pursue a criminal case against him, as he remained Elise's confidant. At this time, they merely wanted him to "evaporate." Mike Stoiber knew what was going to happen at this meeting and yet, unlike Buddy John at the May 28, 1947 Miller board meeting, did not bring a lawyer. The gravest charges involved soliciting bribes from vendors and stating to brewery employees that, soon, he was going to be replacing Fred as president. Other matters involved Stoiber appearing at the September 16, 1948 dedication of stockhouse I, "under the influence of alcohol during business hours and in view of our employees," and telling Elise John that he, "was entirely responsible for the success of the building program, that Fred was never present, and that I [Klug] was too dumb, and that as a result the entire burden rested on your [Stoiber] shoulders." Miller warned Stoiber that if he did not resign immediately he, Miller, would report the charges to Elise. Stoiber was uncooperative, "All these answers will be answered by my attorney–will be answered by my attorney, and I will challenge every one of these answers. That is all." With that said, Miller demanded that Stoiber leave the keys to his desk, office, and the front door. Then, Stoiber snapped at a question from Klug, "I am not talking, not at all. I am not talking." Later he added, "I am challenging these statements you have made, collectively. It is just a shame, that is all I have got to say. I will challenge them. That is my ultimatum, and put that down."[477]

At the end of July, Stoiber filed a $204,500 lawsuit against the Miller Brewing Company alleging that he was fired, "wrongfully and without cause or justification." Stoiber employed Attorney Ray T. McCann, who was also Elise John's lawyer. Four years later, in 1953, McCann represented the Blatz Brewing Company in an action against the Milwaukee Brewers' Association of which Fred C. Miller was the president. Stoiber reported that he had a ten-year contract with the Miller Brewing Company, signed by president Fred Miller and then secretary Edward T. Donohue, beginning on August 1, 1947 for $12,000 a year salary and an equal amount for annual expenses. He also claimed $500 for his February salary. The Brewery responded that Stoiber was "dishonest, disloyal and insubordinate" and that he committed " illegal transactions and acts of misconduct." Additionally, he proposed schemes to individual officers for the replacement of other officers and for the perpetuation of himself in office while trying to get other officers to cooperate with him in those plans. The brewery also charged that Stoiber, on numerous occasions, misrepresented the policies and determinations of the board and officers to the employees, "thereby causing uncertainly among the subordinate executive employees as to their duties and anxiety concerning their tenure." It also claimed that Stoiber had entered into negotiations with another person to form a partnership to operate a distributorship of Miller's products for his own profit. Finally, they accused Stoiber of misrepresenting the company's business in a speech.[478]

Lorraine and Bud's representatives used the opportunity of Stoiber's departure to promote a rapprochement between the siblings. Bud's representative, Urban Wittig, opined, "Ain't it reason enuf & time for the family to get together & have a reconciliation." On May 20, 1949, Lorraine and Bud agreed, in principle, to support each other's policies at the Miller Brewing Company and Oriental Realty Company. Bud agreed to swap his stock in the Miller Brewing Company for Lorraine's stock in the Oriental Realty Company. Lorraine agreed to trade her Oriental stock for Bud's Miller stock, which would give Lorraine control of the Miller Brewing Company and Bud the same at the Oriental Company. This deal floundered, though Bud received sufficient of Lorraine's proxy votes to select Oriental Realty's board of directors, who promptly excised Fred Miller from that corporation. Someone reported to Harry, Jr., who was enjoying his revenge that, at the Oriental Realty board meeting, Fred took the news with aplomb.

At the end of November, Circuit Judge August E. Braun dismissed Stoiber's financial claim, remarking that since Stoiber and two other directors had voted for each other, the ten-year contract was invalid. The judge, "held that directors are trustees for stockholders and cited precedents that such voting was contrary to public interest." Nevertheless, Stoiber won the next round in early April 1950, when the state Supreme Court overturned Judge Braun's decision explaining that the case must be argued on its merits. The parties finally settled out of court for a $50,000 payment to Stoiber for missed back wages.[479]

In July 1949, Fred Miller addressed an issue that would pursue him until the end of his tenure; the idea of building another brewing center. Fred maintained a consistently negative position toward this matter. He explained, "Our workers recognize that Milwaukee has more shipping brewers than elsewhere in the country and consequently that their employment security is safe as long as Milwaukee can continue to compete in all national beer markets." He explained further, alluding to current labor relations, "There are several other large beer producing centers whose markets are strictly local. They don't have competition in marketing around the country. As long as management and labor here recognize that, the future of the breweries in Milwaukee is unlimited." Fred's nephew, Chuck Bransfield worked at the brewery at this time and was a strong advocate of building a satellite brewery. He had numerous run-ins with his uncle on the matter, eventually leaving the brewery in frustration. He believed that Fred's ideas were wrong and that he relied too strongly on his grandfather's dictates. Chuck noted that Fred believed that part of the brewery's success stemmed from the good local water, but Chuck explained that with current filtering technology, water quality was irrelevant.[480]

Nevertheless, Fred had a magical touch regarding the Miller Brewing Company. For instance, in 1945 its sales were 729,000 barrels, in 1946 – 644,000, in 1947 – 806,000, in 1948 – 911,000, in 1949 – 1,330,000, in 1950 – 2,105,000, and, in 1951 – 2,681,500. During this period, the brewery leapfrogged from 16th to eighth place nationally among America's brewers. It planned construction of a new administration building and a third stock house, bringing the cost of the building program begun in 1946 to $25 million. At the end of January 1951, Miller opened a refurbished guest center in the Miller Inn. Brooks Stevens, the famous industrial designer and relative of Fred Miller's sister, Loretta Kopmeier, did the interior design. A collection of 100 steins purchased from the U.S. and Europe graced the first-floor Stein Hall. Two second-floor spaces, named the High Life Room and the Champaign Room, each held fifty people. This beautifully designed building interior is the terminal of the popular brewery tour, where guests can sample sundry Miller products. Next, they built an administration building that was also designed by Brooks Stevens. On the northeast corner of 40th and State Streets, the construction of the new administration building of glass, brick, and concrete, necessitated cutting into a bluff just east of the structure.[481]

In 1951, Fred Miller earned $66,975, consisting of a $24,000 salary, a $37,600 bonus, and $5,375 in expenses. Norman Klug earned $47,260, consisting of a salary, bonus, and expenses. Lorraine earned $30,000, with $12,000 in salary and $18,000 in bonuses. In 1952, Fred's total earnings were $75,195, with Klug and Lorraine's remaining static. In 1951, the Miller Brewery, at Fred's request, purchased a Lockheed Ventura plane for $50,000 and then spent $190,000 to convert the machine into Miller's corporate airplane. In 1953, the brewery spent $115,000 to build a hanger, in order to store it, at Milwaukee's Mitchell Field.[482]

On May 23, 1951, Fred Miller's nephew, Norman J. Kopmeier, Jr., was found dead in his Phoenix apartment. The 26-year-old-son of Loretta and Norman Kopmeier had moved to Arizona, two years previously, for its drier weather due to his problems with asthma and a rheumatic heart. The man, who was single and without children, was the first of Frederick and Lisette's thirty-four grandchildren to die. He had attended Milwaukee's Country Day School and Cleveland's John Carroll University. He left his mother, Loretta Kopmeier, father, Norman Kopmeier, Sr., and married sister, Rose Mary Kopmeier Bradford.[483]

In May 1952, the shares of Miller Brewing Company were so divided:

Stockholder	Shares	Percentage
Clara A. Miller	611 1/9	6.1%
Loretta Miller Kopmeier	574 2/27	5.7%
Frederick C. Miller	574 2/27	5.7%
Claire Miller McCahey	574 2/27	5.7%
Marguerite Miller Bransfield	574 2/27	5.7%
Charlotte Miller Blommer	574 2/27	5.7%

Stockholder	Shares	Percentage
Harry G. John, Sr.	5	0%
May F. Miller	300	3%
Charles M. Bransfield	74 2/27	.07%
Harry G. John, Jr.	2,599	26%
Harry G. John, Jr., et al Trustees General Trust	302	3%
Norman R. Klug	2	0%
Michael T. Stoiber	1	0%
Norman R. Klug Trustee for Karen Mulberger	500	5%
Norman R. Klug Trustee for Michael Mulberger	500	5%
Lorraine John Mulberger	1,785 4/9	18%
Lorraine John Mulberger et al Trustees General Trust	450	5%
Total	**10,000**	**100%**

20.
HARRY JOHN
MOVES ON

Since his removal in 1947, Harry John, Jr. relentlessly badgered his mother on personal and business matters. Finally, the supervisor of the Sacred Heart Sanitarium, Dr. H.H. Blanchard, wrote Bud expressing that, "Mrs. John gets very nervous when she attempts to discuss business thus I am asking that you not try to discuss any business with her and that you take up anything that you have in that line with the office."[484] Besides badgering his mother throughout this period, Bud continued his philanthropic work at his de Rancé foundation, while, simultaneously, pursuing his interests in the Catholic Church. In 1950 he visited Rome during the Holy Year, as his Uncle Ernest had done in 1925. His father saw him; Donald Gallagher, his associate on the de Rancé board; and a religious brother, leave from Milwaukee's nascent Mitchell Field. As an afterthought, he brought a $34 camera but soon discovered that it was insufficient for the job. While there, he bought a fine German camera and took hundreds of 35-millimeter color transparencies. Upon returning to Milwaukee, he created, "the Sacred Pictures Company and had 220,000 copies of the best 15 pictures lithographed and mounted." (Since its inception, this company, renamed Blue Mound Graphics, Inc., publishes religious calendars nationally from its location on Milwaukee's West Side and is run by this book's author.) Regrettably, "he felt he had been limited both by his equipment and his admittedly amateur ability as an amateur photographer." He made adjustments, and returned to Europe, "to do the job with expert skill and the best technological equipment available."[485]

In May 1952, thirty-two-year-old Buddy took a second trip to Italy and Spain. Bud's four-month mission was to capture the artwork of the great masters and lesser masters of that era in famous galleries but also in obscure monasteries and churches, many of which were unknown except locally. He planned to capture their images on color film, "and bring them back to Milwaukee for lithographing and mass distribution to the people of the United States and other countries." Bud reported that they would be distributed in the U.S. and foreign countries at a reasonable price, "to those who are devoted to Christ and to His saints, and also to those who wish to familiarize themselves with the religious, artistic and cultural history of the Western world."[486]

In Naples, Italy, Harry, Jr., along with professional photographers Arthur Pohlman and Harvey Kiefer; printing plate expert Paul Mueller; and print mounter Norman Jaques, collected their six-ton truck outfitted with six sleeping bunks and quantities of food. It also carried 8-by-10-inch view cameras and, "1,500 pieces of 8-by-10 color film from which reproductions can be made with maximum effect." Additionally, the truck stocked 175 rolls of 35-millimeter color film for making projection pictures. Aluminum scaffolding and lighting equipment was also in the truck's inventory. To power the lighting equipment, wherever there was insufficient electricity Bud brought two 2,500-watt electric generators.[487]

"Poor lighting, the result of poverty, is one of the major tragedies of these countries," Harry, Jr., explained to a reporter. "Look at that," he continued while picking up a reproduction of a sculpture in Avila, Spain, showing Jesus at the scourging pillar. "You are probably seeing it better than anyone in the world, even the people of Avila." Bud continued, "When you go into a church or shrine over there and light up a work like this to take a picture, the people gather crying out as though they had never seen it before. When you turn off the lights, there is a great sigh." Bud used this opportunity to further explain his actions. "I may be putting an awful lot of money into this, but I think people are hungry for pictures like these. Contemporary religious art is either too sentimental or else so abstract it's almost fantastic. There is no strength in it, no food for the soul. But pictures like these can go anywhere in the world and have meaning, without translation."[488]

Bud expounded: "When people have seen St. Peter's Basilica and visited the art galleries, they think they've seen it all, but it's only the beginning. There are things of great beauty off in the little mountain towns and out-of-the-way villages. But many of them have never been photographed, even in black and white, much less color. Year after year, some of them are deteriorating and all of them may be destroyed — if war comes."[489]

It was on this trip that Bud met his future wife, Erika Paula Novotny, who was going to school to become a Red Cross nurse. Erika, who later anglicized her name to Erica, was 13 years younger than Harry. She was the child of two Viennese immigrants to Rome, where she was born. Erica's father, Karl, was a dentist by trade and a diplomat by avocation, who headed the Austrian expatriates in Rome. Erica remembers, as a child, charming Christmases at the Austrian embassy. Erica's mother, Anna Maria, taught German to the people of Rome and was a particularly determined person, who, during World War II, personally challenged the occupying Germans on their treatment of the citizens of Rome. Erica shared a devotion for the Catholic Church with Harry, Jr. that she augmented with a solid background in the classics. She knew German, Italian, English, French, Greek, and Latin by the time she met her future husband.

Erica arrived in the U.S. on Friday January 13, 1955 on the spectacular steamship *Andrea Doria* that, in July 1956, sank outside New York City's harbor. Erica came to study at New York's Columbia University where she had been accepted. Bud's requests for her to come to Milwaukee temporarily to help him with his calendar business, instead of studying, paid off for him when she traveled there. Erica remained in Milwaukee, eventually becoming engaged to Harry.

Between 1950 and 1952 while suffering from diabetes, Elise had suffered a series of strokes that slowly diminished her ability to function physically and mentally. Regardless, she maintained a pleasing life at the sanitarium. On March 21, 1950, Mrs. John was in the sanitarium's dining hall marking her seventieth birthday with family and friends, who sat at a large U-shaped table. Her 9-year-old granddaughter Karen Mulberger Swanson sat at her side and remembered, at one point during the meal, when the septuagenarian stood, with her beautiful and warm smile present on her wide face, and began to sing Harry Dacre's 1892 hit;

Daisy, Daisy,
Give me your answer, do.
I'm half crazy,
All for the love of you!
It won't be a stylish marriage,
I can't afford a carriage,
But you'll look sweet,
On the seat,
Of a bicycle built for two!

Upon completing the final note, her well-wishers rose and cheered.

According to Karen Swanson, by early 1952, Elise was bed-ridden and breathing with the help of oxygen tubes. When she was especially ill a priest came and gave her extreme unction, which, in Catholic doctrine, along with the holy oil and prayers, gave her a clear path to heaven. Elise's mental condition was a matter of ongoing concern, as the matron had a net worth in excess of $1 million. Due to Elise's continued reliance on the difficult Mike Stoiber, her husband and children looked for ways to regain her confidence or, at a minimum, control over her finances. On June 16, 1952, Harry, Sr., and his daughter Lorraine successfully petitioned Milwaukee County Circuit Judge M.S. Sheridan to have Elise declared incompetent, due to her brain damage from strokes. The Marshall & Ilsley

Bank was appointed as her special administrator, effectively ending Stoiber's grip over her assets.[490] On August 3, 1952, at the Sanitarium the 72-year-old Elise breathed her last, finally discovering whether her novenas for a happy death succeeded. On August 7, her friend Bishop Roman Atkielski celebrated her funeral at St. Sebastian Parish after which she was interred in the Miller Family plot at the Calvary Cemetery.

Fred Miller, who respected his aunt remembered her thus, "In her quiet manner, distinguished by the absence of fanfare and publicity, Mrs. John all her life gave tremendous assistance to charitable organizations in America. Although an efficient business woman, Mrs. John never lost sight of the less important, but more personal human traits of Miller employees."[491]

Elise left an estate of $2.4 million including one share of the Miller Brewing Company, $925,000 in government securities, $467,000 in real estate, $631,294 of stock in the Oriental Realty Company. She named her "friend and advisor" Michael Stoiber as the executor of her will and trustee of her estate while leaving him $300,000. According to her will created on August 12, 1949, her estate left her husband $1,000 a month stipend with the remainder of the income being split equally between Lorraine and Bud. Twenty years after Elise's death, the estate's corpus would be given to the Milwaukee Catholic Home for the Aged at 2301 East Bradford Avenue. The gift was to be used to build an addition to its existing structure and be named the Elise K. John Home for the Aged. Also, Elise denoted various moderate bequests, for instance; $5,000 for each of her grandchildren Karen and Michael Mulberger, $5,000 for the University of Notre Dame, $3,000 for the Sacred Heart College in Watertown, Wisconsin, $1,000 for the Carmelite Fathers of the Holy Hill, $1,000 for the Milwaukee Archdiocese for perpetual care for the Miller family plot at Calvary Cemetery, and $500 for the Milwaukee Misericordia Hospital.[492]

Elise's estate, though substantial, was small compared to what she had gifted to her husband and children over the years. Elise's financial manager, Michael Stoiber, computed what Elise had provided to her family beginning in 1926. Harry John, Sr.

received $2,026,697 from Elise. In addition to the gifts, since their marriage, she had been responsible for half of Harry's bad investments equaling several hundred thousand dollars. Since Harry had not worked since 1921, the yearly cash stipend that Elise gave him equaled $12,000 to $50,000. Harry loved Cadillacs and, late in his life, bragged that he had owned 33 of the expensive cars. Over the years, Lorraine received $7,413,010. The plurality consisted of $2.4 million in Miller stock from her mother that Stoiber had valued at $1,000 per share. The value also stemmed from Elise's payment of $907,502 in Lorraine's gift taxes. Another $881,425 came from a trust from Lorraine's uncle, Fred A. "Fritz" Miller. In 1948, Elise had gifted her $38,900 Oconomowoc summer home to Lorraine. Buddy John received $5,733,805 in value from his mother and Uncle Fritz. As with Lorraine, the vast plurality came from his Miller stock. His mother remunerated his substantial gift taxes, farm, and cash.[493]

By August 8, Harry John and his daughter, Lorraine Mulberger, had filed a protest to the will. The petition alleged that the document was, "an instrument purporting to be a will including a bequest of $300,000 to Michael Stoiber which was found among Mrs. John's effects." The petitioners denied that this instrument was a valid will and were contesting its probate thereof. They argued that Stoiber had exercised undue influence over Mrs. John. By February 1953, the suit was settled with Stoiber resigning as executor of the estate in return for receiving $200,000.[494]

In conjunction with Elise's death and Stoiber's removal as executor, there were other related legal matters to settle. For instance, in 1949 Elise had paid Lorraine two payments totaling $31,817 in cash for her daughter to pay gift taxes on $121,000, which in turn was a payment of gift taxes for a gift of over $1 million. The legal question was whether the $31,817 payment was a loan or gift. Of course, if it was a loan then Lorraine was expected to repay the estate. Bud contended that the payments were loans and Stoiber testified likewise. He reported that, "Mrs. John asked him to draw a promissory note from Mrs.

Mulberger to her mother in that amount. He said he did not know if Mrs. Mulberger signed the note or where it was now." Lorraine retorted that Stoiber's testimony was the first time that she had ever heard of any promissory note. At that time, a note was not among the records that the Marine National Exchange Bank, the estates' new executor, possessed. The $31,817 was provided to Lorraine in two parts and she testified that $20,000 was a gift from her mother to her and the other $11,817 was paid directly by her mother to the tax authorities. Lorraine said that she remembered the $20,000 gift since Stoiber became angry with her because she had "gone over his head" to her mother to get the money. Lorraine concluded, "Mother never made us pay gift taxes on anything; my brother or me."[495]

In early December 1949, Fred C. Miller assumed the presidency of the Milwaukee Brewers' Association. In August 1953, the Miller Brewery cave museum was completed, using about one-third of the original caves and today is a fascinating stop on the public brewery tour. On February 9, 1953 the Miller Brewery paid Finn, Tollkuehn & Smith of Chicago as part of the effort and expense of Miller Brewery, "in trying to get a Major League baseball franchise for Milwaukee, which finally was accomplished in bringing the Boston Braves to Milwaukee, with all the valuable good will to the brewery and increase of sales, from public recognition of the brewery's promotion of this popular civic and sports achievement."[496]

Fred C. Miller had a unique tenure as Miller Brewing Company's president. He had great vision and focus that allowed him to dramatically boost the brewery's production, sales, and profits. Besides running the brewery, he managed the Carl Miller Lumber Company and two other family businesses. He was a flurry of activity. The life-long Republican belonged to a broad array of organizations for which the brewery paid the fees, for example, the Milwaukee Athletic Club, the Milwaukee Club, the Wisconsin Club, the Serra Club, the Oconomowoc Lake Club, the Country Day Alumni Association, the Notre Dame Club of Milwaukee, the Kova Club in Phoenix, and the

Arizona Country Club. He enjoyed dining with his wife Adele at the historic Red Circle Inn in Delafield. Also Fred traveled extensively; on one such trip in February 1953, Fred and Adele flew from Phoenix to Tucson, to Miami, to San Juan, Puerto Rico, to St. Thomas, to San Juan, to New Orleans, to Dallas, and to Phoenix.[497]

In February 1953, *Fortune* Magazine ran an extensive and favorable article on the Miller Brewing Company, which motivated Fred to order 9,300 copies to send to Miller's distributors and suppliers.[498] To help beer production, Fred strained to fashion a family atmosphere among the brewery workers. For instance, each morning his secretary gave him the names of each employee whose birthday fell on that day and, when possible, Fred would call that employee. Long-time Miller manager George Vespalec remembers Fred enthusiastically waving to employees, and calling out their names, as he drove on State Street. Also, once a month, each department head joined Fred in a bull session where everyone was invited to discuss ongoing problems. These sessions lasted as long as anyone had something to say. Fred bragged, "We have a Christian family spirit in this organization, which I wouldn't trade for anything else we've accomplished."[499]

The Miller Brewing Company was divided into four groupings; production, sales, administration, and industrial relations. The heads of each grouping would make daily written reports, copies of which were distributed to all officers. Each night, Fred Miller and Klug would study the reports at their respective homes and then in the mornings compare ideas. Miller's and Klug's offices, in the new administration building, were adjoined with a connecting conference room. Klug remarked, "It was Fred's idea to save us time because we spent so much time together going over company matters."[500] With Fred's frenetic schedule apart from Miller Brewery, it was clear that Norman Klug had a considerable say in the brewery's daily activities.

21.
DISASTER HITS:
A CRIPPLING STRIKE
AND A PLANE CRASH

Employee relations were not always serene. The longest period of brewing cessation in Milwaukee since Prohibition occurred in mid-1953, when 7,100 area brewery employees struck for 76 days. Local 9 of the C.I.O. United Brewery Workers' Union struck on May 14, 1953, to coincide with the year's heaviest beer production and sales, therefore causing the greatest financial damage to the six Milwaukee breweries: Miller, Pabst, Schlitz, Blatz, Gettelman, and Independent. The shut-down gave operational breweries in other regions a golden opportunity to seize market share from the inactive ones. The union was advocating for a thirty-five-hour work-week for all of its employees, increased hourly rate, paid lunch, and full health insurance coverage. The striking workers were without pay during the work stoppage, as the union did not have a strike fund. At this time, many of them sought employment elsewhere to maintain their families. When the workers walked out, supervisors completed the beer's fermentation process and then refrigerated it. This beer was held for immediate bottling the moment that the strike ended. Otherwise, all bottling ceased. Since the union had given a twenty-day notice before striking, the breweries had made plans to minimize any spoilage. Miller's managers traveled between buildings in underground passageways to escape the jeers of the picketing workers.[501]

The work stoppage and its accompanying difficulties posed one of Fred's toughest predicaments. As president of the Milwaukee Brewery Association, Fred Miller was central to providing a unified front against the union's demands. Ultimately, the Blatz Brewery broke ranks with their compatriots in the Milwaukee Brewery Association, making an independent deal with the union. Immediately the remaining five breweries, "were then forced into settling immediately themselves or being put in the competitively untenable position of staying shut while Blatz produced beer. They chose to settle." Later, a vindictive Fred excised Blatz from the Association, which commenced a lawsuit for its reinstatement. Fred had resisted settling with the union and had even threatened to move the construction of a planned Miller bottling plant to another state without unions. The 76-day strike ended on Tuesday July 28, 1953 at 11:25 p.m. when the rank and file voted to approve the union management's recommended offer. Gettelman and Independent were regional breweries compared to the four national companies, to whom the union gave concessions based on their smaller scope. The union gained a paid half-hour lunch, a $.20 per-hour across-the-board pay increase, a pension plan, an increase in shift differentials, and a health and welfare plan.

On July 27, the news of the pending end of the strike was overshadowed by the enthusiasm of the signing of the compromise armistice that halted the Korean Conflict, giving Milwaukeeans two reasons to celebrate. The workers anticipated an affirmative vote on the proposal, so at the moment the strike order was rescinded, the breweries restarted production. At 11:25 p.m., when the strike ended, the first bottlehouse workers, "donned their clean white overalls and pitched in to work." Miller's first trucks left the dock at 7 a.m., on July 29, and the first train car left the same place at 6:20 p.m. that day. Long before the employment office opened at 8 a.m., "men waited in a line that wound beyond the building and up the hill. Throughout the day four to five hundred men crowded into the employment lobby."[502]

With the strike behind them, Miller Brewery turned to other matters. Rapid growth caused occasional problems for them. A miscalculation regarding bottles cost the corporation a $237,584 loss in 1953. Previously Miller had purchased all unbreakable bottles until mid-century, at which time they began supplementing them with breakable or non-returnable bottles. The materials purchaser did not manage the transition properly and the brewery ended up with an excess of 5 million cases of breakable bottles, which it stored in a Butler warehouse under a tarpaper covering. Eventually this covering became saturated with water, causing a deterioration of the "mountains of cases stacked there." The result was an avalanche of broken bottles. The workers did not remove them for fear of being buried by the unsteady pile so they bulldozed large parts of the mess.[503] Fred Miller offered an alternative explanation. "During the World War II and the post-war shortage of steel for cans, bottles were purchased for beer normally sold in cans. When cans were again available, these bottles became surplus and were stored from time to time in different locations and finally on outdoor premises at Butler. Because of the rising demand for canned beer, these surplus bottles were not used within the time expected and because of exposure to freezing the glass tended to crystalize [sic] and they otherwise deteriorated due to other exposure. The cost of sorting and salvaging was an unwarranted expenditure and it was decided to junk them and to charge off and deduct the amount at which they were carried on the books."[504]

Previous to the May 1953 Miller stockholder meeting, Buddy wrote to his cousin Fred, asking him to provide Bud with a representative on the board due to his controlling 29% of the outstanding stock. Of course, Fred denied the request if for no other reason than Bud had been challenging Fred's brewery management, especially his expense account.[505] At the May 26, 1954 Miller stockholders' meeting John A. Wittig, representing Bud John, nominated Bud for a board position, in opposition to Lorraine. Fred pointed out that his cousin's, ". . . judgment was so poor that you were represented today by people who had sued the brewery or the Miller family on four different occasions. You lost the election 7,092 to 2,901, seven shares not voting." Wittig refrained from voting for Fred Miller and nominated Judge Otto H. Breidenbach, formerly Circuit Court Judge, in opposition to Norman Klug. Judge Breidenbach lost by 7,092 to 2,902.[506]

At this same meeting, "Fred reported on the building program that they have spent approximately fifty million dollars and there is still about four million dollars committed, and the program is to wind up within the next year." Wittig told Buddy that, "Fred reported that in 1952 they sold over three million barrels, but due to the strike in 1953, sold only 2,100,000 in 1953. For the first four months of this year they have sold 630,000 barrels, which if projected for the balance of the year at the same rate, would give them 1,900,000 barrels which would be well under last year's figure." Wittig continued, "He stated they are fighting to get the market back and that all of the large Milwaukee brewers are behind in their 1954 sales as compared to 1953, stating the following figures as the deficit this year: Miller Brewing Company- 28%, Blatz Brewing Company- 34%, Pabst Brewing Company- 32%, and Schlitz Brewing Company- 32%."[507]

On June 4, 1954, Norman Kopmeier, Sr. died after a long illness. He was the husband of Loretta Miller Kopmeier, Clara and Carl Miller's eldest child. His death was attributed to high blood pressure and a subsequent stroke. Norman had been ill since 1951, which coincided with the death of his only son, Norman, Jr. Besides Loretta, Norman was survived by his daughter, Rose Mary Kopmeier Bradford and her four children. He was known for his "genial disposition and his hearty love of life." Norman was a leading Catholic layman and in 1948, due to his work on behalf of Catholic charities, had been named a Knight of St. Gregory the Great by Pope Pius XII. Until he took ill, he was a daily communicant. The seventy-four-year-old gentleman expired as president of the Wisconsin Ice and Coal Company, a position that he had held for thirty-one years. Kopmeier began working at the company in 1897 as an ice route supervisor. He began loading ice wagons at 3:30 a.m. and did not finish until 10 p.m. when the last man had completed his deliveries and checked in.[508]

On December 17, 1954, Frederick C. Miller, Sr. and his oldest son Frederick C. "Freddy" Miller, Jr., and pilot Joseph Laird and co-pilot Paul Laird who were brothers, died in a crash of a small Miller Brewing Company plane three-quarters of a mile north of Milwaukee's Mitchell Field. They were departing at 5:07 p.m. in a twin-engine Lockheed B-34 Ventura for a hunting trip to Portage la Prairie, near Winnipeg, Canada. The 20-year-old Freddy, Jr. was a third-year honor student in liberal arts at Notre Dame. The 48-year-old Fred was the only passenger who outlived the crash. Even though he was badly burned, had a broken right leg, and had internal injuries, he remained conscious and was taken by ambulance to the local Johnston Emergency Hospital, where he died five hours later. Fred, Sr., had been thrown or crawled 20 to 30 feet away from the burning plane. Roy Piorier and George E. Hagen, airport neighbors, apparently were the first people to reach the crash site. Piorier, a Schlitz truck driver, used his jacket to smother the flames on Fred. At that moment, Fred shouted, "For God's sake, there are three others in the plane." Hagen said that after Miller said that there were three others on the plane, he fell back and lay quietly. Hagen explained, "He must have passed out." Many Milwaukeeans still vividly remember the event and a neighbor recalls that the light covering of melted snow created a ring around the crash site.[509]

The weekend previous to the crash, Fred had attended a retreat, with his ten-year old son Carl, the Laird brothers, and several business associates, at the Redemptorist Seminary at Oconomowoc Lake. The morning of the crash, he and Adele had awakened before dawn, at their Oconomowoc Lake home, and then attended 6:30 a.m. Mass at Oconomowoc's St. Jerome Parish. The last thing Fred, Jr., did before leaving Notre Dame's campus to drive to Milwaukee for the hunting trip was attend Mass and receive Holy Communion. This calamity devastated the Millers, Milwaukee, and the Notre Dame football community. His family still discusses some of its unusual circumstances.[510]

On March 17, 1955, the Civil Aeronautics Board released its Accident Investigation Report, noting that Joseph Laird had done everything within his power to avoid the crash. Joseph Laird had been employed by the brewery as a pilot since 1947 and his brother had been employed for nearly five years. They both had received all of their expected training and licenses. The board determined that the crash was caused by a broken crankshaft due to fatigue in the left engine. A power lessening in the right engine prevented normal single-engine performance. "This condition together with the fact that the aircraft was overloaded for single-engine performance resulted in the loss of control."

On December 19, the wake, with open caskets holding wrapped corpses to hide much of the burns, took place at the Millers' Oconomowoc Lake house. At 10 a.m. on December 20, Father G.E. McGinnity, the pastor of St. Jerome's in Oconomowoc, (the Miller's home parish), celebrated Fred and Freddy Miller's requiem high Mass at Milwaukee's Gesu Church, which was filled to capacity. Adele requested that there be no eulogies for her husband and son, as she said that only God should be praised in church. Milwaukee Archbishop Albert G. Meyer gave the final absolution, assisted by Father Theodore Hesburgh, Notre Dame's president. Afterward, they were buried in the Miller Family plot at Calvary Cemetery. The Laird Brothers' Mass was held at Wauwatosa's Christ King Church, and they were then buried in Milwaukee's Holy Cross Cemetery.

Fred was a compulsive achiever with an astonishing list of accomplishments. He enjoyed engaging in risky behavior that could have injured or killed him many times before his final crash. He married a beautiful, well-educated Chicago woman and, together, they brought eight healthy children into the world. He experienced success in business, sports, hobbies, fundraising, traveling, and promoting Milwaukee. He was a director of the Milwaukee County Society for Mental Health and the Milwaukee Boys' Club. In the 1950s, he was a director of the Green Bay Packers, and was in part responsible for bringing the Hawks professional basketball and Braves baseball teams to Milwaukee. Never again would a Miller Brewery president embody that office the way Fred Miller did. He "wore" the position as a sheep wears its wool. For thousands of people, Fred Miller was the Miller Brewing Company. He remains an iconic figure in the present-day Miller Brewing Company.

His multitude of energetic pursuits made his balancing act between family and professional lives a difficult one. In the early 1950s, these difficulties took their toll and Adele took the children, for months at a time, to live in Florida and Arizona. Many of his children only discovered their father's successes after his death.

22.
DECLINE OF THE FAMILY ERA

O n Monday December 20, 1954, three days after Frederick
C. Miller's death, Lorraine Mulberger and Norman Klug,
constituting the Miller Brewing Company's board of directors,
elected Klug as president. Previously, he was the business's vice-
president/secretary and general counsel. In the past, owing to
Fred's immersion in myriad other interests, Klug had run the
brewery's daily operations. Unbelievably, Fred Miller treated
the brewery's presidency as a part-time job; Klug would not
be so blessed.

At this same time, Lorraine was elected vice-president/trea-
surer and Miller brewmaster Edward W. Huber was chosen
vice-president in charge of production and secretary, assuming
Fred's position on the board of directors. Lorraine decided not
to pursue the presidency. Unlike her brother Harry, Lorraine
had the sagacity to realize that she was not suited for the position. Her wisdom led to the election of the first non-Miller
family member ever to be president.[511]

In the period before Fred hired him in 1947, Norman Klug
was an outside legal counsel for Miller Brewery. As a member of
the law partnership of Timlin, Dean and Klug, he had also done
personal legal work for Elise John and former Miller officer
Michael Stoiber. Born in Milwaukee in 1905, Klug attended
Washington High School and Marquette University where he
had earned a law degree in 1927. From 1928 to 1930, he served
as a state assemblyman, as a Progressive Republican; and, from
1939 to 1947, was a Town of Milwaukee police judge.[512]

Miller Brewing Company's assistant legal counsel at that

time, John Savage, remarked that, due to Klug's nervous nature, at first he doubted that Norman would be a successful president. After Klug logged some time in the office, Savage saw Klug relax and perform admirably. His associates described him as a man with a quick legal mind, "a sort of take-charge guy."[513] Immediately after accepting the presidency, Klug announced that he foresaw no changes in policy, explaining that he and Miller always had the same approach to brewing. Nevertheless, he had the regrettable task of following in Fred Miller's footsteps, where any significant directional changes would have been discouraged by the stockholders.

At this same time, the officers released a joint statement, "It was Mr. Miller's wish that the policies and high standards of the company be a continuing policy. The present splendid, well knit and carefully selected organization, functioning with highly qualified and experienced men, is a tribute to Mr. Miller's vision and organization ability. Fred Miller's belief was that a leader is measured by his ability to create an organization that would continue to function with effectiveness regardless of the absence of any one or more men."[514]

In late December 1954, Klug argued in defense of Lorraine Mulberger, the brewery's primary stockholder and vice-president, against Harry John's admonitions. "Mrs. Mulberger has taken quite an active part in the affairs of the brewery, attending almost all of the executive meetings and following every administrative detail with the closest attention. She's probably been more active in the management than many people have realized," he said. At the executive committee meetings Lorraine's primary interests were production, building, advertising, and employee relations. When she was not present, she was, "in almost daily contact with other officials." Another brewery document noted that besides her major interests—her children, her home, and the brewery—she also was an active gardener and read everything from financial reports to fiction. Throughout her life, Lorraine maintained a love of art and created many oil paintings. She also wrote prose, poetry, and a few radio scripts.[515]

Soon after the funeral, Frederick Miller's widow, Adele, withdrew to mourn, while her daughters, Clair Rosenberger and Loret Miller, represented her at the myriad events memorializing her husband. Nine months later, she took her six youngest children to Rome, where, for eight months, everybody lived in a convent. In the Eternal City, the children attended school, while Adele visited the city's abundant churches.

Frederick C. Miller's estate was valued at $2,179,392 and was split between Adele and their seven surviving children. Each of Fred's children received $88,000 from the estate, a paltry sum considering the effort their father had put into the brewery and the resulting success. The bulk of his holdings were 574 shares of the Miller Brewing Company valued at $1,047,685. He also held 4,420 shares in the Carl Miller Lumber Company valued at $482,400. The estate's federal taxes were $322,874 and state taxes — $147,641.[516]

Sadly, Fred Miller died just two weeks before the Miller Brewing Company's long-planned 100th anniversary year, 1955. It was on September 25, 1855, that the founder, Frederick J. Miller, began to prepare the first batch of beer. Norman Klug, in a tribute to Fred, pursued the celebration as planned. The first event was a national sales meeting at the end of January, peppered with stars of stage and screen. The distributors saw a color movie funded by Miller Brewery called *With This Ring*, a loose retelling of Miller Brewery's history, beginning with the founder's experiences in Sigmaringen, Germany. The next major event was the brewery's sponsorship of the Professional Golfers' Association Miller High Life Open in Milwaukee in July, featuring a $35,000 prize stake. Also, the brewery built a three-sided replica of the original Frederick Miller's Plank Road Brewery that today stands on a bluff immediately east of the Miller Inn.[517]

Fred's departure from the brewery destabilized the habitual stockholder alliances. One of Fred's under-appreciated talents was a capacity to forge alliances with disparate parties. He accomplished this task with two successive major stockholders, Elise John and Lorraine Mulberger, creating a majority position to maintain his authority. This cooperation between one member of the West Side Millers, Lorraine, with the complete membership of the East Side Millers was a rare occurrence in the family's recent history. Another feat, no less tricky, was keeping his mother and sisters supportive of his leadership. Though Clara, an unswerving admirer of her son Fred, enforced unanimity among her daughters.

Frederick C. Miller's brother-in-law, James B. McCahey, Sr., stepped into a leadership role among the East Side Millers, created by Fred's death. This 67-year-old Chicagoan, Claire McCahey's husband, was the eldest male in Clara Miller's family, as Carl Miller, Fred C. Miller, Norman Kopmeier, Sr., and Michael J. Bransfield were already dead by 1955. The only other East Side Miller male still living in the generation directly below Clara was her son-in-law, Bernard Blommer, who was enmeshed, along with his two brothers, in their chocolate business in Chicago. Unfortunately, Clara Miller's family discounted female leadership in business, thereby eliminating various capable female family members. Jim McCahey had been slated for authority in 1947 as the replacement for Fred Miller on the board, should he fail to serve. However, this ascension plan was discounted long before Fred died, as Miller Brewery gravitated toward professional guidance, away from familial oversight.

Fred's death brought the East Side Millers into direct contact with Lorraine, a relationship that was doomed to fail. In fact, Clara Miller's descendents' inability to cooperate with Lorraine eventually led to their decision, in 1961, to sell their stock. Nevertheless, the intervening years saw shifting alliances among the three voting blocks; Lorraine Mulberger and her two children, Clara Miller and her descendants, and the de Rancé foundation controlled by Harry John, Jr., its founder and most dynamic trustee.

Lorraine John Mulberger was reluctant to speak publicly, even in small professional groups, despite being quite amicable with her immediate friends and family. To Fred Miller's credit, he formed a successful working relationship with her. This union was especially remarkable considering that Lorraine would complain privately about his arrogant nature and devotion to the Catholic Church, from which she was estranged. Occasionally, Fred trifled with her serious nature. On one occasion Fred convinced his cousin that she could purchase "heaven insurance" for money, which she discounted, thinking that it was another flaw of his fidelity to the Catholic faith. Norman Klug continued in Fred's shoes, developing a close relationship with Lorraine, eventually becoming her financial counselor. Lorraine trusted Norman, in part, possibly because he was Lutheran, not Catholic, as were the Millers.

Unlike Fred Miller and Norman Klug, James McCahey failed to form a constructive relationship with Lorraine, as she considered him a bossy Chicagoan ignorant of the nuances of Milwaukee's social structure. There might be some truth to this view because McCahey was used to the turbulent Chicago political scene, serving as president of the Chicago Board of Education from 1933 to 1947, among other political positions. Conversely, McCahey thought of his second cousin as an aloof *prima donna*, ignorant of the business and political world. Fred Miller had the advantage over his brother-in-law, Jim McCahey, of growing up in Milwaukee and having numerous points of contact with Lorraine, including a life-long relationship with her mother, Elise. McCahey, on the other hand, only came to Milwaukee for social and business visits because his family and busy work schedule occupied him in Chicago.

A year after Fred's death, his mother Clara; his wife Adele; his four sisters, Loretta Kopmeier, Claire McCahey, Marguerite Bransfield, and Charlotte Blommer; and Chuck Bransfield, formed a voting trust on December 27, 1955 with their combined 2,980 13/27 shares of Miller Brewing stock. They chose Carl A. Schmitt, long-time Miller family friend and employee of the Oriental Realty Company, as its trustee. This legal instrument unified their votes, providing the maximum influence at stockholders' meetings. Since none of these people were involved in the brewery's management, the trust removed some of their fiduciary duties, decreasing their time-consuming oversight.

On Sunday January 8, 1956, the eighty-one-year-old Harry G. John, Sr. died at St. Joseph Hospital after a three-week battle with the complications of diabetes. The Feerick Funeral Home supervised Harry's funeral at the Trinity Evangelical Lutheran Church and then buried him at the Catholic Calvary Cemetery, beside his wife Elise who had died in 1952. At first, the Milwaukee Archdiocese balked at Harry's burial in the Catholic Calvary Cemetery because he was not a baptized Catholic, except, while he was in a coma on his deathbed, Buddy had him informally baptized.

Harry, Sr. was a prolific flower gardener, known for growing orchids in spectacular garden plots at his Wauwatosa property and in a greenhouse on his Oconomowoc Lake property. Claire Miller Krause, Harry's grandniece, reminisced that he owned peacocks that strolled among the flowers at his lake property, adding to the enchantment. In April 1950, anonymously, he placed a newspaper advertisement promoting a flower show at the Mitchell Park Conservatory where he was a familiar figure consulting with employees about cultivating orchids. After being discovered, Harry explained, "I am deeply interested in flowers. I believe that if more people would take time to enjoy them, they would become better acquainted with each other. It doesn't take money to enjoy this world."[518]

Harry's sister-in-law and Elise's sister, Clara Anna Miller, was outspoken to a fault, usually disregarding what others thought of her. Until her death at age 87, she refused to surrender to tragedy, age, illness, or diminished mental ability. Her eldest grandchild, Charles "Chuck" Miller Bransfield, said that she had a way of compelling attention that was sometimes sweet and sometimes bitter, but it could never be ignored. At her brother-in-law, Harry G. John Sr.'s 1956 funeral, Bill Miller, (no relation,) overheard the eighty-six-year-old Clara bellow at her escort, "Don't tell me what to do. Nobody tells me what to do."

The iron-willed Clara, though demanding, loved and nurtured her children and grandchildren. Chuck noted that she was matriarchal; not by political mandate but by strength of will, energy, and mind. He wrote that his grandmother knew no fear of anything on earth. She respected and protected her husband, children, and close friends but could be significantly less accommodating to others. She believed that the world owed her a good living and complained mightily if it was not immediately forthcoming. She had little patience for her sister, Elise, and Elise's family. Their temperate lifestyle, compared to her hard-driving personality, and Lorraine and Buddy's mental problems, gave her plenty of reasons to denigrate them privately. She was hardly empathetic. To her family and friends, though, Clara had a gregarious personality that kept them entertained.

On March 21, 1957, Clara died in a coach car (as Chuck remarked, it was cheaper than a parlor car) of the Florida East Coast Railroad Company, between St. Augustine and Jacksonville, while returning from a vacation at the Old Flamingo Hotel in Miami Beach. She had traveled to Florida for her annual vacation even though, at the time, she was critically ill with pneumonia. For a short period, she had been treated at Miami Beach's St. Francis Hospital. Her funeral was held at SS. Peter and Paul Parish, after which, she was interred in the Miller plot at Calvary Cemetery between her son and husband. Lying supine between her two favorite men, her ebullient spirit rests.

Clara Miller left an estate of $2.2 million; including 9,000 shares of the Carl Miller Lumber Company valued at $1 million; 610 shares of the Miller Brewing Company worth $753,487; life insurance worth $102,240; gifts made between 1956 and 1957 of $180,594; cash of $76,137; a $60,000 home on Newberry Boulevard that previously she had left to St. Mary's Hospital; and $11,000 in personal effects. Her executors were her daughters, Loretta and Claire, while the noted local attorney Herb Hirschboeck handled the estate's probate. Clara made $12,000 in bequests to Catholic churches and charities. She left $1,000 each to the parishes of Holy Cross, St. Robert, and St. Rose of Lima; Miseracordia Hospital; the Little Sisters of the Poor; St. Vincent's infant asylum; the Catholic Home for the Aged; and St. Aemilian's Orphanage. She gave $2,000 each to SS. Peter and Paul Parish and St. Charles Home for Boys. Shortly before her death, Clara had given $50,000 to Adele Miller and her adult daughters, besides giving $6,000 each to her other 21 grandchildren. In 1948, the Millers had given each grandchild $5,000, in 1949, $7,000 each, in 1951 and 1952, $5,000 each, in 1955, 1956, and 1957, $3,000 each. Clara gave Chuck Bransfield, the only son of her dead daughter Anita, $75,000, and then divided the remainder of her estate into separate trusts that she had created, on July 15, 1949, for her five other children or their descendants.[519]

At the May 23, 1956 Miller Brewery stockholders' meeting, Attorney Herbert C. Hirschboeck replaced Lorraine Mulberger on the board of directors. Hirschboeck represented the trust of the East Side Millers, owners of one-third of the brewery's stock. Since Fred Miller's death in December 1954, the East Side Millers had no voice on the board, as Norman Klug was firmly in Lorraine's camp and Ed Huber, in turn, was in Klug's employ. The cherubic Hirschboeck, a founding member of the Whyte, Hirschboeck, Minahan, Harding & Harland law firm, was Fred Miller's long-time friend, even standing up at his wedding. Hirschboeck was also one of the few people, along with Carl Schmitt of Oriental Realty and John "Jack" Savage, Miller Brewery's assistant legal counsel, who was trusted by all the branches of the Miller family. Therefore, Hirschboeck was the natural choice for a board position and the vice-presidency. Certainly, Herbert did not leave his law practice, instead providing a minimum of his time to the brewery. Lorraine was named chairman of Miller Brewery's board, an honorary position, to mitigate the loss of her other titles. Lorraine was the third consecutive Miller family woman in this position following Elise John and Clara Miller.[520]

Since May 1947, Harry John, Jr. had been excluded by the majority of the stockholders from having a voice in Miller Brewery's management in person or by proxy. Many people believed that his absence benefited the company. In control of roughly one-third of Miller stock through his trusteeship at the de Rancé foundation, Harry was livid at this situation. Nevertheless, his position was partially self-imposed, as he could have cooperated with the existing successful managers. Harry remained busy during this period; for instance, he took two productive photographic voyages to Western Europe, which led to him creating a nation-wide calendar publishing company, Sacred Pictures Company (now Blue Mound Graphics, Inc.).

In 1953, Harry John and James Rogge, a maintenance engineer at St. Anthony Hospital, started Fr. Stephen's Youth Center, Inc., an outgrowth of their involvement in Milwaukee's growing black community. The gentlemen, members of the Catholic St. Vincent de Paul Society, assisted numerous re-cently-arrived black southerners, who came to Milwaukee in search of work. Bud visited these poor families, providing them with food, clothes, or merely companionship. His wife Erica John later explained that Buddy, to demonstrate his humility to the host family, always accepted an offered glass of water regardless of the vessel's cleanliness. Such symbolic behavior was significant for this man who was almost phobic regarding germs.

Fr. Stephen's Youth Center was named for Father Stephen Eckert, O.F.M. Cap., "champion of the colored people," who founded St. Benedict the Moor Mission for black Milwau-keeans. Harry founded this day camp for Milwaukee's poor black children, providing meals, education, entertainment, and two prayer services. In 1959, the center was serving 450 children daily for free. Bud, through the de Rancé foundation, paid all the camp's bills. Buddy, who also worked at the camp, explained its genesis:

"As a member of the St. Vincent de Paul Society, I became acquainted with the dire plight of the colored citizens of Mil-waukee. A summer day camp for colored children was started with both volunteer help and paid employees. It provides wholesome summer recreation within a religious atmosphere. A winter, weekly youth center was started. I also financed substantial costs of clothing, school bills and medical services for Negro children."[521]

Besides Bud's desire to promote his faith, he also understood the importance of charity. He described the concern of the 30 staff members for the children, "by pointing out their awareness of the children's standard of living, which many people would find unendurable." He noted that, "Some of the children at the camp may already have suffered more harshness than some people know in an entire lifetime." This quotation elucidates Harry's substantial inner pain, due to his own depression that allowed him to empathize with the physical and psychological suffering of others.[522]

At first, Fr. Stephen's Camp was located at St. Benedict Parish on 10th and State Streets, but soon after, it moved to Blessed Martin de Porres Parish at 7th and Galena Streets on Milwaukee's North Side. The camp admitted all children, although ninety percent of them were black. Bud, whose wife Erica also worked at the camp, commented, "To observe these hundreds of little ones, Catholic and Non-Catholic, white, Negro, Mexican and Indian — their heads bowed before the living presence of God and all speaking to Jesus in their hearts with their own words, is to be deeply moved and to be convinced that, apart from other practical good aspects of the camp, here is an act of religion whose eternal value can hardly be overestimated." Many of the staff, including numerous seminarians, went on to live in service to others, often through civil disobedience. For example, James Groppi, the diocesan priest who led open-housing marches in the 1960s, was a seminarian who volunteered at the camp. He was involved with a regrettable incident as a staff member in August 1957, when a school bus he had been driving rolled over four camp children camping at the Kettle Moraine State Forest, twenty-five miles west of Milwaukee. They were taken to Waukesha Memorial Hospital for treatment of their non-life threatening injuries. After Groppi left the priesthood, he was a bus driver for Milwaukee County, even becoming president of the local union.[523]

During his exile from Miller Brewery, 36-year-old Harry

married 24-year-old Erica Paula Novotny, on September 22, 1956, at Holy Cross Parish, now St. Vincent Pallotti Parish's east campus. The Johns had an interracial ceremony with one each white and black best men, Donald A. Gallagher and Eugene McCrary respectively. The couple was preceded down the aisle by fifteen black children from Fr. Stephen's Center. In the 1950s it was rare for an upper-class white couple to have a mixed-race wedding party. The Johns honeymooned in Egg Harbor in Door County, Wisconsin and, eventually, had nine children; Emily born on June 16, 1957; Timothy on March 22, 1959; Paula on February 17, 1961; Henry on July 6, 1962; Bruno on October 6, 1963; Gregory on January 3, 1967; Michael on May 7, 1968; Elise on June 11, 1970; and Jessica Marie on July 1, 1978.

In May 1957, Harry seized on an opportunity to change his status as a minority stockholder at the Miller Brewing Company by creating an alliance with the East Side Millers, who were represented by Jim McCahey. Harry supported Jim McCahey's election to the board and as vice-president in place of Miller brewmaster Edward Huber. Concurrently, McCahey was occupied at the Carl Miller Lumber Company and the Oriental Realty Company, sorting out their ownership and management, which had become unsettled when Fred C. Miller died. McCahey noted that many years ago, Ernest Miller "asked me to give up my Chicago business and home and take a principal management position in the brewery. As long ago as that I declined a job in the family company."

Jim continued, "Two years ago, I was asked by various interests in the family to become a director of the Miller Brewing Company. I declined this honor at the time explaining that at my age one does not look for or welcome such responsibilities.... However, dissatisfaction of substantial stockholders continued and, shortly before the stockholders' meeting of last May, I was again asked to become a director and was assured sufficient votes to be elected."[524]

Jim, in collaboration with Harry, saw his objectives as a Miller Brewery director to be: Representation on the board of all major factions of stockholders, termination of the practice of having administrative officers in control of the board and thus in effect approving their own acts, and liberalization of the dividend policy. Regarding the dividends, McCahey explained, "One of our largest stockholders is a Roman Catholic charitable corporation which had never received a donation from the Miller Brewing Company during the many years of its existence. . . . Its interest, as I have stated before, was in the achievement of larger dividends and in some participation equivalent to the salary heretofore paid to the favored stockholder [Lorraine Mulberger]."[525]

Jim took a sincere interest in his job at Miller Brewery, trusting Harry and seeking to fulfill his wishes. He was ignorant of the fact that Harry John was using him to accomplish his short-term goals. At any rate, Jim McCahey, as did Harry, wanted Lorraine excised from any role in the brewery's management. Jim gleefully forced the termination of Lorraine's salary on July 8 because, in his opinion, she was acting as a director and not an officer; in other words, she was putting insufficient time in at the office. To demonstrate his good faith, at that time, Jim promptly resigned his office and salary. Harry's newfound friendship with Jim McCahey chilled Lorraine Mulberger and Norman Klug, who knew that Bud's penultimate goal was their removal from the brewery. Bud, though at times magnanimous to strangers, had a pitiable capacity for forgiveness toward his family and remembered the humiliation of being removed from the Miller presidency in 1947 and, in part, blamed Lorraine and Norman for it.

Bud's cooperation with the East Side Millers had its desired effect, scaring his sister Lorraine into forging an alliance with him. It is unclear why Harry decided to sever his temporary relationship with the East Side Millers and establish a legal bond with his only sibling, since either alliance would have given him a majority. It's likely that Jim McCahey had difficulty keeping his relatives in line, whereas, Lorraine exercised hegemony over her own and her children's stock. Regardless, on

July 15, 1957, Lorraine and Bud reached an agreement, through their lawyers, "to pool their voting interests for a period ending July 1, 1963." The voting trust, similar to the one the East Side Millers created in 1955, combined the voting interests of Lorraine and her children with the de Rancé foundation. All Miller stockholders were encouraged to sign the agreement but only Harry and Lorraine participated. This newfound cooperation, representing approximately 60% of the voting stock, effectively precluded any future representation by the East Side Millers and soon terminated James McCahey's tenure as a director and officer of the Miller Brewing Company.

Lorraine and Bud each nominated two representatives to the board with a fifth mutually agreed upon. To ease future tension, the John siblings decided that, "neither Harry John, Jr., nor Lorraine John Mulberger will be elected to the Board of Directors of the aforesaid brewery during the life of this Agreement, nor will they be elected as officers nor participate actively in the management of the aforesaid brewery." This agreement, besides ending the hands-on involvement of the East Side Millers, saw the last direct participation of any member of the Miller family in the brewery's management. Lorraine proposed Norman R. Klug and Edward W. Huber, Harry proposed Charles W. Miller and John A. Wittig, and they jointly proposed Louis Quarles. Charles Miller, unrelated to any of the Miller Brewery family, was chairman of the Department of Marketing in the College of Business Administration at Marquette University. John Wittig was an attorney and trustee of the de Rancé foundation. Louis Quarles, of the firm Quarles, Herriott & Clemons (now Quarles and Brady), was a respected attorney who had done considerable work for Harry G. John, Jr. Miller Attorney Jack Savage later wrote, "Mr. Charles Miller then expressed his introduction to Harry John through Father O'Donnell [the President of Marquette University] and the work he had done with Mr. John and for de Rancé to establish sound business principles in trying to protect the capital investment." Quickly, Harry and Erica John became quite friendly with Charles Miller and his wife, even selecting them in 1959 as godparents of their son Tim.[526]

On July 12, 1957, the Miller Brewing Company stockholders held a special meeting for the declared reason of amending its by-laws. Instead, its main purpose was to effectuate the new voting alliance between Lorraine and Buddy, thereby removing Jim McCahey. A majority of the stockholders planned to provide: for directors' fees, that directors need not be stockholders, that the board be increased to five, and that the entire board be elected by stockholders. Furthermore, if James B. McCahey, Sr. could, "be induced to resign," his resignation would be accepted.[527]

James McCahey, Sr., was averse to abdicate power before his one-year term expired. Regardless, he knew that his future tenure was blocked by the burgeoning cooperation between the John siblings. Before leaving, McCahey objected: "In view of this impending humiliation and personal insult, I feel that I cannot approve the motions made at this time [increasing the board to five].

"This special meeting to remove me is an unusual step in view of the fact that the changes which have been made were for the benefit of all the stockholders . . . This meeting is exceptionally unusual when you consider that the stockholder [Harry John] who originally asked me to become a director, and whose every stated immediate aim has been won, takes part in such a proceeding."[528]

Harry was unsympathetic, likely considering Jim McCahey's removal as partial settlement for his own exclusion in 1947.

To exemplify the newfound cooperation between Lorraine and Harry, the Miller Brewing Company made a $5,000 donation to de Rancé, Inc. in early July 1957. The voting trust agreement between the Lorraine Mulberger family and de Rancé, which would remain in effect until July 1, 1963, appointed the Marshall & Ilsley Bank as trustee. The bank was a natural choice, as it had been involved with Miller family trusts for some years. It would hold title to the stock certificates while providing receipts to the shareholder. The trustee could either vote the shares at stockholder and board meetings or use a proxy. Still, the M&I Bank was obligated to provide germane information to the participating stockholders, giving them the opportunity to offer their opinion on voting matters.[529]

As was Harry's *modus operandi*, he failed at maintaining long-term relationships. He was paranoid about people who were emotionally close to him; afraid that they would steal his money. This human frailty caused ruptures in almost all of his extended business and personal relationships. After enjoying a flourishing affiliation with the Wittig Brothers, Roland, John A. "Jack," and Urban R., he fabricated reasons to extricate them from his related organizations, Blue Mound Graphics, Fr. Stephen's Youth Center, de Rancé, Inc., and of course, the Miller Brewing Company, as his representative. Like most of his associates who were suddenly rejected, the Wittigs did not understand the reasons behind their removal. To them, Harry was enigmatic or as some whispered, crazy.

On April 21, 1958, Harry John opened de Rancé's annual trustee's meeting, with himself, John Wittig, Roland Wittig, and Donald Gallagher present. Donald Gallagher was a philosophy professor at Marquette University whom Bud had selected to de Rancé's board. Harry had been enthused with Gallagher's devotion to the Catholic Church coupled with his profound intellect. Gallagher had accompanied Harry to Rome on his 1950 pilgrimage. Donald Gallagher's wife, Idella, was also a philosophy professor, who later worked alongside her husband at the foundation. The Johns liked the Gallaghers enough to select them as their eldest child, Emily's, baptismal sponsors. Nevertheless, Harry noted Donald's, "business and financial experience were more meager even than mine."

An associate remembered: "Well, Don, I thought was a loveable character. He was a professional philosopher. He had great credentials in an obscure field. He was very kind. He was extremely loyal to Harry, and he saved him from embarrassment in his problems with the Wittigs. As a person, wonderful. As to his knowledge in business, I think in his business approach he lived on Cloud Nine. Now this is not bad. He was a teacher. He was not a businessman."[530]

After opening the April 1958 meeting, which Gallagher recorded as secretary, Harry, expressed "keen disappointment in the failure of Trustee John Wittig to promote the interests of de Rancé at the MBC [Miller Brewing Company] in the past year by expending little or no time or effort in his capacity as assistant MBC secretary. The President pointed out that this first official position at MBC for a representative of de Rancé was the first fruit (along with the MBC directorship of de Rancé agent Charles Miller) of the Voting Trust Agreement entered into by de Rancé the previous July. It appeared these unprecedented blessings (after so many years of humiliation and forced exile from MBC affairs) might be the first in a series bestowed by Almighty God (most probably in answer to the prayers of contemplative communities aided by de Rancé in past years) whereby de Rancé might gain more and more influence and prestige at MBC and thereby be in a better position to improve MBC efficiency, increase profits and cause larger profits to be paid — thereby making more money available for the cause of Christ (de Rancé being completely dependent upon MBC dividends for its source of income)."

After a discussion, Harry asked John Wittig to resign as Miller Brewery's assistant secretary, while simultaneously withdrawing his name from nomination for director and officer from de Rancé, Inc.[531]

Harry's assault on John Wittig brought a legal response from Jack and Roland Wittig, who attempted to dismiss Harry from the de Rancé foundation. After a short period, a settlement ensued; for $20,000 the Wittigs resigned their posts as directors of Blue Mound Graphics (Harry's publishing company), de Rancé, and Fr. Stephen's Youth Center. Furthermore, Herb Hirschboeck replaced Jack at the Miller Brewing Company. The expulsion of the Wittigs was unfortunate because they were fervent believers in Bud's dreams, standing beside him during his legal battles. In fact, for a period before she married Harry, Erica John lived with John Wittig and his wife Mary. They were integral, though compensated, partners in establishing de Rancé, Blue Mound Graphics, and Fr. Stephen's

Youth Center. Donald Gallagher and Charles Miller took the Wittigs' places at the foundation. Harry and Donald were the sole trustees, giving them equal authority concerning the foundation's management. In reality, Gallagher perennially deferred to Bud, providing Harry unrivalled control over the foundation and its assets.[532]

23.
CALIFORNIA
EXPANSION

Despite the machinations on Miller Brewery's board of directors, the company prospered. It paid total dividends in 1957 of $800,000, in 1958 and 1959 - $1 million, in 1960 and 1962 - $1.2 million. As time passed, Klug disregarded Fred Miller's notion of maintaining only one plant and actively searched for a location in California to brew High Life to decrease shipping costs to this huge market. He also knew that, eventually, they would need southern and eastern brewing facilities. In 1956 and 1957, Miller's management made inspections of several breweries, "with a view to acquisition." On the other hand, there was a proposal for the Falstaff Brewing Corporation of St. Louis to acquire Miller Brewery by merger, but Peter Grace recommended against the deal, due to his perception of a potential anti-trust issue. His recommendation helped to kill the deal. Eventually, Klug discovered an opportunity to purchase the plant of the San Francisco Burgermeister Brewing Corporation. Miller Brewery's management felt that the acquisition was critical to Miller's future on the West Coast. In 1960, Klug prepared to make an $11 million bid for it.[533]

Miller Brewery member of the board of directors Louis Quarles explained that: "At the annual meeting of stockholders held on May 25, 1960, at the insistence of certain members of the Carl Miller family group, it was agreed that there would be no acquisition of other breweries without first presenting the same to the stockholders, although stockholder action was not required under Wisconsin law." Miller director Herb Hirschboeck then reported that members of the Carl Miller family were, "gravely concerned that such expansion [the Burgermeister purchase] involves further commitment of earnings to larger capital investment and diminished liquidity of assets."[534]

After Norman Klug made an offer to purchase Burgermeister, he submitted it to the Miller stockholders; Lorraine and de Rancé supported the acquisition, with the East Side Millers being less enthusiastic. The bid's submission to the stockholders caused a three-day delay, giving the Joseph Schlitz Brewery a chance to intervene, outbidding Miller. Miller Brewery sued Burgermeister for failing to give it time for due diligence. "In the course of the litigation that followed, the Miller Executive Committee offered $12 million in settlement of the Burgermeister litigation and in payment for the assets of the brewery. This increase in price from $11 million to $12 million was frowned upon by certain members of the Carl Miller family group."[535]

On August 24, 1961, Miller was offered the same chance as Schlitz to buy the Burgermeister Brewery but, "Owing to the feelings of certain members of the Carl Miller family," Klug decided against making an offer, allowing Schlitz to buy it. Hirschboeck believed that, "The insistence of members of this group that any acquisition of another brewery be submitted to prior vote of the stockholders has indicated to him that such members of the group lack the confidence which the majority of stockholders have in the management's program and policies."[536]

While Miller Brewery was reviewing its alternatives regarding the Burgermeister acquisition, on January 14, 1961, it purchased its neighbor, the Gettelman Brewing Company, for something over $1 million. This regional brewery was just four blocks west of Miller Brewery. While the two breweries had similar beginnings and were somewhat comparable until the mid-1940s, at that time Miller Brewery's massive expansion sent its sales skyrocketing past Gettelman. By 1960, Miller sold 2.4 million barrels and Gettelman's sold 132,285 barrels. Thomas and Frederick Gettelman were on friendly terms with the Millers, especially the late Frederick C. Miller, easing the transaction. Miller Brewery wanted Gettelman's popularly-priced brands, Milwaukee's Best and $1000 Beer, to augment its premium High Life. In March 1966, a Miller officer reported that this acquisition was made solely for the purpose of retaining Wisconsin distributors and was not intended to meet future demands that an increasing population would impose upon the company. In 1970, Gettelman's facilities were shuttered, as Miller Brewery moved all of its production into its own facilities. The company razed some of Gettelman's buildings. Currently Miller uses the remaining two buildings for storage and the grounds to park its trucks.

This period also saw interest in the three major blocks of Miller stockholders to sell their stock either to outside interests or, in Lorraine and Harry's case, to each other. One of the perennial difficulties for Lorraine Mulberger, the East Side Millers, and Norman Klug, was that Harry regularly changed his mind in order to keep them unsure of his intentions. One moment he wanted to sell de Rancé's Miller Brewery stock and the next, buy Lorraine's shares. Harry's flip flopping, coupled with his chronic procrastination, frustrated potential associations.

Another item in Bud's bag of tricks was feigning ignorance. Customarily, he would ask professionals simple-sounding questions, pretending a lack of knowledge that often led them to characterize him as dim-witted. Bud bolstered this façade by keeping his black hair closely cropped and dressing in lose-fitting drab clothes that often had wear holes in the elbows. Bud's business associates, friends, and adversaries habitually underestimated him, paying dearly for it. Harry John was misunderstood; much like President Harry Truman, whose plainspoken Missouri style was mistaken for ignorance by East Coast sophisticates.

Harry John also gave people the impression of being an ascetic by living far below his social class. For example, after he married Erica in 1956, they moved into the rear area of his calendar publishing concern at 76th and Blue Mound Road, where a wall separated the printing presses from their living quarters. While most of Harry's relatives lived in luxurious homes, often with second lake "cottages," he lived more like the ascetics who he idolized. His one-room "home" had a bed and two cribs in the open, below a factory-like suspended ceiling. It was here where Harry and Erica welcomed some of Milwaukee's highest social class and numerous missionary priests beseeching financial grants. After Emily and Timothy were born, in 1960 Erica finally persuaded her millionaire husband, in part due to an absent occupancy permit, to move, sight unseen, into a nearby two-bedroom apartment.

Harry's self-portrayal as ignorant was a pretense, as he was a voracious reader of the most complicated financial material available, besides literature on Catholic spirituality, American history, architecture, and classical art. He also studied dictionaries, challenging himself to learn every word. Moreover, Bud knew German and taught himself Italian and some Spanish. As an illustration, in the mid-1970s, his son Tim remembers collecting his father, along with some of his siblings from the airport after they returned from Europe. As Harry drove the car home, Tim turned to speak to Paula, in hushed Spanish, a language that they had studied in high school and were convinced that their father did not know. Tim asked Paula, "Is Dad still acting like a jerk?" Before Paula could respond, Harry sharply slapped Tim on the thigh, demonstrating his obvious understanding. Tim, unhurt, was flummoxed at his father's acute hearing and surprising command of a new language.

Harry's substantial knowledge of business was entirely self-taught, as he had studied philosophy at the University of Notre Dame and his own father, Harry John, Sr., had little business acumen. Bud's long-time attorney, John P. Miller, called him brilliant, with a spectacular memory, even while appearing inattentive. John Miller added that Bud was a man with undying faith in his convictions allowing him to accomplish great things, while also somewhat blinding him. Nevertheless, a Miller Brewery associate of Harry had a different view of his business sense, "He thought with his heart in business, or in facts as they should be instead of the facts as they existed. This is a bad trait. . . If I had a sum of money and wanted a return on it, I would not ask Harry's advice."[537]

On January 29, 1960, the West Side Millers renewed their voting trust, increasing the brewery's board to seven. Lorraine's choices were Miller president Norman Klug, Miller brewmaster Edward Huber, and M&I Bank president John Puelicher. Harry chose Marquette business professor Charles Miller, Attorney Herbert Hirschboeck, and New York businessman J. Peter Grace; their combined choice was attorney Louis Quarles. The East Side Millers also saw Hirschboeck as their representative because he maintained a close relationship with Fred Miller's widow, Adele, among other members of their family.[538]

Since 1945, Harry had maintained a constructive relationship with the gravelly-voiced J. Peter Grace, president of the multi-national Manhattan-based W.R. Grace Corporation. Grace was Buddy's highest-ranking business acquaintance. In approximately 1961, Grace's directorships included the W.R. Grace Company, Grace Lines, Kennecott Copper, First National City Bank, Magnavox, Atlantic Mutual Insurance Company, Centennial Insurance Company, Stone and Webster, Ingersoll Rand, Deering Milliken, and Emigrant Industrial Savings Bank. Bud remarked that, "he had a towering reputation in the field of business and finance." Harry, and Miller board members Norman Klug and Charles Miller were impressed with Grace's ability to find solutions to prickly problems without creating enemies. Charles Miller later described Klug's impression of the New York impresario: "Well, he said that he was absolutely a genius, a business genius in this age. That his holdings extended all over the world and that he had put together this company and was the most capable businessman in the world, he felt, at that time."[539]

Though Grace's speech was littered with foul words and his manner was gruff at times, he maintained constructive relationships with Harry and Lorraine and the brewery's management. Grace successfully played both sides of the fence, at one time privately bragging to Klug that he, "was now going to play rough with Bud to keep him from hurting himself. . ."[540] Occasionally, Grace would fly to Milwaukee's Mitchell Field on his corporate plane to attend meetings of Miller Brewery and de Rancé boards and then, after returning to New York, reinforce his ideas with phone calls and letters. Other times, Norman Klug and Charles Miller would fly to New York, Chicago or elsewhere, to meet with Grace for his insight.

Peter Grace was Harry John's business confidant, providing him with free advice on financial matters at the de Rancé foundation. Grace agreed to serve as the foundation's treasurer beginning on June 20, 1960. The New Yorker did not perform the perfunctory duties of a treasurer; instead, as he explained, "It was a title, as I understood it, that Mr. John conferred on me to give him the right to call me at home on weekends or late at night saying, 'Now, you are the treasurer of de Rancé, so I'm calling you.' "[541] Peter and Harry shared the same worldview, believing in reinforcing the orthodox wing of the Catholic Church against a perceived left-wing attack. Like many Americans, Harry John was convinced that there was a worldwide atheistic radical conspiracy, emanating from Moscow, intent on destroying American culture and the Catholic Church. At this time, the American Catholic Church was undergoing the same cultural revolution as was the country itself. There was a broad contentious debate on socialism's role in the church while priests and nuns in droves reentered the lay world. Despite Harry and Peter's unity of thought concerning the Catholic Church, the New York *mensch* had the additional fiduciary duty of propelling the W.R. Grace Corporation toward financial success. Concurrently, Buddy was enmeshed in promoting de Rancé's interests. It was these apparently divergent corporate interests that, in time, caused a cleavage in their relationship.

On October 31, 1960, Peter Grace wrote to Miller Brewery's management, expressing his interest in buying their assets, business, and property for $24 million in cash. He wrote that, "It is the essence of this transaction that it be closed prior to January 1, 1961." He also wanted Miller's interest in the San Francisco Burgermeister Brewing Corporation that was in flux. At the same time, de Rancé's board voted in favor of the

Grace buyout. They agreed that the Grace deal would provide the foundation with $10.5 to $11 million in cash, annually affording them $550,000 to $600,000 in income. At that time, for reasons unknown, the sale did not come to fruition.

The East Side Miller family was composed of six clans. The Milwaukee-based Loretta Kopmeier was the eldest of Clara and Carl Millers' children. By 1961, her husband Norman, Sr. and her son, Norman, Jr. had died and her last child, Rose Mary, was married to Robert Bradford. The only surviving child of Clara Miller's second eldest daughter, Anita, who had died in 1920, was Chuck Bransfield, who was married to Vivian and living in Florida. Clara's third child was Chicago-based Claire McCahey, who was married to James, Sr. Their five children were all married. The fourth child was Chicago-based Marguerite Bransfield, a widow, who had four children one of whom was married. The fifth child was the deceased Fred C. Miller, whose widow, Adele, was married to Clarence C. Christiansen and living in the Milwaukee area. Some of her seven children were married. The youngest of Clara's children was Charlotte Blommer, who lived with her husband Bernard and three daughters, one married, in the Chicago area.

By spring 1961, the East Side Millers began to unite around a plan to sell their stock to the Miller Brewery, also known as a stock redemption. Jim McCahey, Sr., who was still smarting from being involuntarily relieved of his duties at the brewery, promoted it to his wife and sisters-in-law. Together with May Miller, Frederick A. Miller's widow, they controlled approximately 38% of the outstanding shares. Until her death in early 1957, Clara Miller had kept her descendants supportive of the Miller management. Her loyalty toward her father's brewery precluded her children from seriously considering selling their stock. After her death, some of her children and their spouses displayed their opposition to the brewery's expansion, believing that it would reduce their dividends. Despite having independent income from careers, all of the Millers had come to rely on the brewery's ample dividends for an elevated lifestyle that they really wanted.

Earlier, individually, the East Side Millers found scant interest for their shares in the marketplace. Selling a minority interest can be difficult, as a new buyer might face the identical difficulties from which the seller suffered. Additionally, each share of Miller Brewery stock was valued at $2,000 to $4,000, making it too costly for average investors to buy. In 1959, the East Side Millers had tried to sell their stock to the brewery, "However, owing to the tax obstacles, it could not be done at that time." Herb C. Hirschboeck, a Miller board member since May 1956 and the principal representative of the East Side Millers, noted that they were, "concerned about the absence of a market for their stock or voting trust interests in Miller Brewing Company. This group represents a little more than 33% [apart from May Miller] of the total outstanding stock of the corporation, but has not the voting power to elect any member of the Board of Directors nor to prevail in any matters submitted to stockholders for vote."[542]

Miller president, Norman Klug, noted on March 29, 1961, that Jim and Claire McCahey were, "committed to liquidation, which is not the objective of a majority of the share holders [of Clara's descendents]." Klug noted that Marguerite Bransfield was also committed to liquidation but he did not know the position of her sisters, Loretta Kopmeier and Charlotte Blommer. Adele Miller represented her husband's shares and generally followed the advice of her long-time friend Herb Hirschboeck. Chuck Bransfield wanted to keep his shares. Chuck's brother, Fred Miller Bransfield, was diametrically opposed to selling the stock, as he accurately understood its extraordinary earnings potential, but despite a valiant effort was unable to sway his mother, aunts, and uncles.[543]

Another factor of the East Side Millers deciding to sell their brewery stock was their growing dislike of Norman Klug, the company's president. The idyllic relationship that Klug shared with Fred C. Miller did not necessarily transfer to Fred's family. Klug did not always acquiesce to the demands of Fred C. Miller's widow, Adele, and Fred's sisters. Klug strengthened his presidency by keeping Lorraine happy and not the East Side Millers. He fired Loretta Kopmeier's son-in-law Robert Bradford and withdrew job offers and favors to other of the East Side Millers. Many of the them grew to hate Klug.

Louis Quarles, who was Harry's attorney and a Miller director beginning on January 28, 1960, reported:

"There has been a general opposition by these members of the Carl Miller family to Miller's proceeding into the market by way of acquisition of other breweries or diversification to other industries and to vertical expansion. There has been further interest in the Carl Miller family in participating in management rather than having the company run by professional management, as is desired by Mrs. Mulberger and de Rancé, Inc. Certain members of the Carl Miller family have also desired to involve themselves in the company's purchase of supplies, etc. Disagreements have also been experienced regarding Miller's plant expansion, its research program, its development or failure to develop new brands of beer, its fiscal policies, its personnel policies, its purchases and practically all other aspects of management."[544]

Hirschboeck explained:

"Some members of the Clara Miller Family Group are gravely concerned that such expansion [the Burgermeister Brewing Corporation bid] involves further commitment of earnings to larger capital investment and diminished liquidity of assets." He maintained, "Mr. Charles W. Miller, who is also a trustee of De Rancé, Inc., is aware of the concern of the Clara Miller Family Group under the circumstances. . . Mr. Miller has stated to me that he would support redemption by the corporation of the stock of the Clara Miller Family Group, or a substantial part of it, with liquid funds now held by the corporation before they are invested in acquisition of other breweries. His proposal is intended to allow the Clara Miller Family Group to withdraw its investment from the corporation at a value, while not approaching book value, would still be as high as could be obtained by a division of shares and a public offering of its holdings by the Group. The redemption price which he has proposed is $3,940 per share."

Hirschboeck continued:

"He considers it necessary to have an answer within a few weeks, since he has the responsibility of financial planning for the management, including provision of funds for anticipated acquisition of one or more breweries. Once a large financial commitment is made for such an acquisition, it will not be possible for the suggested redemption to be made, since funds will not be available for such acquisition and redemption at the same time."[545]

The Miller Brewery management was compelled to redeem the stock of the East Side Millers due to their exclusion from the management's board and inability to sell its stock for a reasonable price in the open market. In effect, the brewery's management and majority shareholders were obligated to convert the stock of the East Side Millers for cash, an equitable swap of assets.

To provide a measure of harmony, in November 1961, Klug and Charles Miller, respectively Miller's president and treasurer, understanding that the redemption of the East Side Millers' stock was a forgone conclusion, tried to arrange a stock equalization plan between Lorraine and de Rancé. To accomplish this goal, the foundation would have had to purchase some of Lorraine's shares. Jack Savage reported that, "He [Klug] pointed to the fact that when the understanding was originally reached [for the equalization plan] he was under the mistaken impression that de Rancé was controlled by Charles W. Miller and J. Peter Grace, who were knowledgeable about business matters. It now appears that it is controlled by Mr. John, who lacks business knowledge and judgment, and he would be very concerned about entering into an agreement with de Rancé under those circumstances."[546]

Klug was under the false impression that Charley Miller and Grace comprised two of the three trustees of de Rancé, with Bud being the third. In reality, Harry and Donald Gallagher were the trustees and Grace was their advisor. The brewery president believed that Gallagher would not vote independently, thereby giving Bud two sure votes to control the foundation's assets, the Miller Brewery stock. Klug convinced Lorraine that this idea was not in her best interests, and it foundered. Klug wrote, ". . . I didn't want to have Bud dictate de Rancé's policies and indirectly exercise a 50% share in the Miller Brewing Company affairs since apparently he could block whatever we desired to do, and for that reason I thought it best that the Mulbergers should not sign a Voting Trust Agreement."[547] Bud later wrote that he was averse to the plan because he would end up with an equal power sharing arrangement, whereas, he wanted control of the brewery.

Bud was unsure of his position regarding the redemption of the East Side Millers' stock. He solicited counsel from myriad people, trying to discern its effect on de Rancé. He discovered that if the stock was redeemed, de Rancé's share would grow from 29% to 47.21% of the outstanding shares and the value per share would grow from $5,056 to $5,657, giving the foundation $16,405,300 in assets.[548]

It was difficult to coordinate the interests of the East Side Millers. "Mr. Hirschboeck had his problems; there were estates to be settled and eighteen people to be satisfied." On December 13, 1961, the Miller Brewing Company's board of directors voted affirmatively to redeem the stock of the East Side Millers and May Miller, who was Fred A. Miller's widow. Lorraine supported it and, at first, Harry opposed it, though he eventually agreed to the proposal. The directors who supported the resolution were Lorraine's representatives, Norman Klug, Edward Huber, and John Puelicher; and Harry's representative Herbert Hirschboeck. The independent representative Louis Quarles abstained. The opponents were Harry's representatives Charles Miller and J.P. Grace, though they personally supported it. Klug later wrote, "He [J. Peter Grace] said he never again wanted to be in the position that he found himself in at our last meeting, when he had to vote contrary to his best business judgment." The brewery president added that, "Mr. Grace then announced that he would advise the Directors that if they voted for the resolution, it was likely that injunction proceedings [by Harry] would be started the following day."[549] After the affirmative vote, Klug, Charlie Miller, and Jack Savage sought signatures from all of the stockholders to cement the deal.

As was his custom, Harry John waffled on the issue of the stock redemption. Initially, he forbade his representatives on the board of Miller Brewery to support it but, later, signed the document approving it. He used this opportunity to create the maximum irritation for everyone concerned, if for no other reason than to fluster some of Milwaukee's top lawyers and businessmen. Bud enjoyed his "moment in the sun," as the brewery needed his full cooperation as a major stockholder in order to redeem any stock. The matter was made more complex because of Norman Klug and Harry's mutual hatred. Klug, unlike Peter Grace and Charley Miller, was unable to deal successfully with Bud. Klug saw Bud as a threat, looming on the horizon, who he believed, given the chance, would reverse any of his accomplishments at the brewery.

At the time of the stock redemption, Klug wrote:

"When I returned from lunch on December 13th about 1:30 p.m., there was a call from Lorraine. She advised that Bud had called her approximately ten minutes previously and stated that Charles Miller was a stallion who has to be controlled. He stated that he knew nothing of this agreement, but that he had called Miller Bransfield [Marguerite Bransfield's son] who advised him that he knew about the proposed redemption some three months ago. He [Bud] stated that they had never hired a lawyer and that he needs another week to look over the situation, and if the company went ahead at this time, he would sue. He said, 'Think of Charlie doing this behind my back.' "[550]

After Bud discovered that Louis Quarles had personally favored the redemption, Bud released him as de Rancé's attorney and hired Kenneth K. Luce, of the law firm Michael, Best & Friedrich, who also taught at Marquette's Law School. Presently Harry and Gallagher elected Luce as a foundation director and its secretary. Luce continued his association with de Rancé until January 1967, at which time Bud and Gallagher fired him from the foundation and as their representative at the brewery. Bud believed that Luce had become overly independent in his thinking as a member of Miller's board of directors; instead he wanted Luce to reflect his views. Nevertheless, Bud extolled Luce's virtues unlike other of his firings: "This action is by no means intended as a reflection on your character or talent—both of which we hold in high esteem. Moreover, we thank you sincerely for the effort and time you have devoted to the work since you began here with us on January 25, 1962. . . We will pray for your health and prosperity, and if there is anything we can ever do to help you, please do not fail to let us know."[551] Bud lamented, in 1962, that de Rancé's past two firms of attorneys were now the 'opposition' attorneys [Louis Quarles and Herb Hirschboeck] and it was difficult to find a lawyer of the necessary moral and technical quality in a short time.

On June 19, Jack Savage wrote:

"Mr. John stated that Mr. Miller and Mr. Grace had attempted to pressure him [Mr. John] into signing and that he was 'off of' Mr. Miller forever. Mr. John wanted an injunction. Mr. Luce [de Rancé, Inc.'s new attorney] discussed the matter with Mr. John for three hours and persuaded him not to sue. He further spent a full day with Mr. John explaining that it was to Mr. John's advantage to sign the proposed agreements and go through with the deal."[552]

Charley Miller dismissed Harry's personal attacks while continually reaching out to him. Finally, the tall, balding, ever jovial Charles Miller procured Bud's signature on the redemption documents. On December 19, 1961, the Miller Brewing Company redeemed the stock of the East Side Millers and May Miller for $3,940 per share in cash. "He [Kenneth Luce] then volunteered that, with the prospects of the company, the stock should be worth considerably more than $3,940 a share. Mr. Luce threw out the suggestion that the company may want to buy the de Rancé shares for $12,000,000 but volunteered . . . that the stock would be worth considerably more than that. . . In the course of the discussion, Mr. Luce made the remark that the company 'got them pretty cheap,' referring to the redemption of the Carl Miller stock."[553]

As was his custom with past friends and business associates, Bud turned against Charley Miller, who, in 1957, had joined Miller's board of directors as Bud's representative and then, in March 1960, had become the brewery's treasurer. Harry abhorred Charley Miller's increasing involvement at the brewery, disappointed that he had supported the redemption and stock equalization plans. In fact, Charles had initiated the negotiations of redemption between the East Side Millers and the brewery. Bud maintained that his employees or representatives should be dedicated to him and his causes, discounting split loyalties. Apparently, Charley was drawn to the advancement, as a moth to light, including remuneration, at the brewery in contrast to his lower-paid full-time position at Marquette University and part-time work at de Rancé. For example, in 1960, the brewery paid Charles Miller $11,883 and by 1962 — $53,100. Charley become Norman Klug's employee rather than Harry's minion. Charley was intimately involved with coordinating the stock redemption, though, seemingly without Harry's knowledge. Bud charged that Charles Miller's entire action in this matter had been, "surreptitious, arbitrary, disobedient, rebellious, impetuous, grossly imprudent, narrow minded, disloyal, and vain." Bud asserted that Charles had said that, "de Rancé strongly desired that all of the Clara Miller Family leave the Miller Brewery roster of stockholders—implying a kind of latent hostility for this family as a whole." At this time, Klug assured Charley Miller, "that whatever happened would not affect Charles personally in his relations with the Miller Brewing Company, and his job at our company was not dependent upon a satisfactory agreement between de Rancé and the Mulbergers."[554]

On January 23, 1962, during a two-hour meeting at the de Rancé offices, Harry John and Don Gallagher asked for and received Charles Miller's resignation as director and secretary of de Rancé, Inc. On his resignation note he wrote in pencil, "I do this with much regret. I will write you my reasons later." Klug wrote that at this meeting that:

". . . [Charles Miller] indicated that Bud was disappointed that the east side Millers were bought out, even though at a fair and satisfactory price arrangement, because while they were stockholders, he could always threaten to deal with them against Lorraine and so obtain his objectives. Charlie also indicated nothing short of the complete domination of the company [Miller Brewery] was sought by Bud, and this would ruin the company in his opinion. For these and other reasons he resigned. I expressed the opinion that while I refrained from advising him on whether or not to resign, I was happy that he did because it was becoming increasingly difficult for him to do that which was right for the company and comply with Bud's requests."

Charley Miller's departure from the brewery did not end his relationship with Bud, as the two of them, despite further difficulties, remained respectful of each other.[555] Charley and his wife maintained their relationship with Bud's oldest son, Tim, who was their godson, sending him expensive books as gifts every Christmas.

After Charles Miller resigned, Bud wrote to Grace, announcing his reelection as de Rancé's treasurer and advisory member. He then inscribed, "Peter, I hope and pray that you can get out here quickly in order to lend us your business wisdom, your commanding presence, and, above all, your moral power to help De R. solve its problems outside of court!" It was difficult to see how Harry and Peter maintained a productive relationship over this period because Harry wanted Grace to buy Lorraine's stock for de Rancé, whereas, Grace wanted to purchase all of the outstanding shares for the W.R. Grace Corporation — clearly divergent intentions.[556]

Thinking that they were doing Bud a favor, in October 1963, Norman Klug and Charlie Miller made an offer to de Rancé's trustees to redeem their 2,900 shares of Miller stock for a ten-year $12 million unsecured note; in other words, the debt would rank on an equal basis with other creditors. The price per share was $4,965.[557] Harry rejected it, noting that his research demonstrated that the Miller stock was worth much more than that. Bud had the good sense to seek qualified advisors who provided him with valuable information. He never relied on only one person or organization for advice, often playing one advisor off against another.

As the years passed, Miller Brewery prospered, increasing the value of its stock. For example, in 1953 the brewery sold 2.1 million barrels of beer and by 1965 — 3.7 million. The somewhat secretive Klug wrote that on February 20, 1965, Bud called him at home and requested a Miller Brewing Company financial statement to help him contemplate a stock sale offer. "I told Bud I would not send him the long form, and after my last experience with him, I considered him neither businesslike nor gentlemanly. He said I'm not a saint you know. I told him that he had established that fact to my complete satisfaction."[558]

Peter Grace continued to make purchase offers to Harry and Lorraine, at one time intoning to Bud: "I have not only your best interests at heart but also de Rancé's and even more so, the Church's—and certainly no one has tried to help the Church more than you have during your lifetime...As you know, Miller Brewing Company has 6,144.5 shares outstanding. De Rancé owns 2,900 of these shares, or 47.2%...I think that you are wrong to call this peanuts, Harry, and I feel you should give every consideration to taking this deal for de Rancé and the Church, which you are supporting so generously...You keep saying that three times peanuts is still peanuts."[559]

Harry John frustrated and antagonized Norm Klug, causing Miller's president to research ways to excise de Rancé from the roll of Miller stockholders. For instance he lobbied Lorraine Mulberger and Peter Grace to acquire the foundation's interests. Klug complained to Louis Quarles on April 8, 1965 that ". . .it appears that all of our considerations are under the cloud of that which for want of a better word might be termed Bud's 'instability'... Bud's 'instability' manifested itself when on the one hand he admitted the Grace offer was a fair one [Grace had recently offered $51 million for all of the Miller stock] (and certainly the interest factor was favorable to him since he would have to realize $30 ½ million at 4% to obtain an equivalent income of $1,230,000), and nevertheless he would not make up his mind either to accept or reject it. . ." Klug explained further: "In addition, he [Harry] is tricky and deceptive, whether he is taking corporate papers without permission, or whether he is telling Lorraine on March 26 that he is desirous of helping her, and within the next week trying to make a fast $5-15 million by trying to buy her stock without telling her that he has what appears to him a better offer." Klug continued, noting that to the ordinary man, a collapse of a sale to Grace would seem extremely unlikely, "but we know Bud is not the ordinary man, and he is convinced 'God wants him to work slowly.'" Klug concluded: "To sell a 52.3% interest in a corporation of this size to a single stockholder would be extremely difficult. When you couple this with a 47% minority stockholder with Bud's demonstrated 'instability', it would be highly unlikely. . . Independent of personal or other considerations, it seems to me at this point that the Mulberger interests would best be served by a sale to Grace."[560]

By May 14, 1965, despite Klug's prodding, Lorraine had decided against accepting Grace's offer. Grace asked Klug, "to what did I attribute Lorraine's unwillingness to sell, and I indicated that I felt she was willing to sell but didn't go along when Bud refused. He said, 'You mean blood is thicker than water,' and I replied I felt that had a great deal to do with it." Lorraine and Harry's blood was not always so viscous. On June 24, 1965, Harry and Donald Gallagher visited Lorraine's home on Oconomowoc Lake to discuss Miller stock, as they never spoke about anything personal, but she refused to see them. Their relationship was so poor that most of Harry's nine children never even met their aunt, even though she lived until 1998. Lorraine was afraid to see Buddy without Klug or a lawyer present for fear of his badgering her. She declined to subject herself to the wear and tear of another fruitless discussion. She felt that he always became insulting. She sent word to her brother that she was too busy to talk to them since the heating contractors were present, ripping out the old furnace. She did not go out until a half hour after they left.[561]

One of Harry's continuing disappointments was his difficulty in procuring adequate financial information from Miller Brewery, in order to value de Rancé's stock. The corporation was obligated to provide stockholders some data but it was an ongoing disagreement between Bud and Klug on how much was reasonable. Harry relished requesting information that he said was necessary for him to decide whether or not to sell de Rancé's stock. Klug was reluctant to provide Bud with material that the philanthropist might use against him.

On May 26, Harry John and de Rancé attorney Herb Hirschboeck arrived at Miller Brewery, to procure financial information, and, as planned, Klug, Charley Miller, and Louis Quarles received them. After some uncomfortable discussion, Klug mentioned that the brewery had already supplied sufficient information to an accounting firm that had done an audit for de Rancé. Klug reported that, "Bud then demanded that we give him the material today, and I indicated that it might take us several days to get it together. Bud became agitated and said, 'Don't give me that crap.' I told him that we would give him the information as soon as we got it together." Klug relented, providing Bud and Hirschboeck the 1964 audited financial report.[562]

After Charles Miller had taken Bud and Herb through a comparison of the short and long form 1964 audited report in Norman Klug's office, Bud continued to peruse it for some time, ignoring everyone else. Harry enjoyed this tactic in an attempt to establish a superior status. Presently, Klug suggested that if he wanted to continue reading the audit report, he and Hirschboeck could retire to Charles Miller's office. Instead, Bud deadpanned, 'It's quite comfortable here.' Klug then mentioned that while he might be comfortable here, "I had work to do and had already explained the crucial situation we found ourselves in connection with a possible strike, and expressed the feeling that I ought to be permitted to pursue the business at hand since it was up to the stockholders' interest that I do so. Finally at the suggestion of Mr. Hirschboeck, Bud agreed to continue his reading in Mr. Miller's office."[563]

Lorraine wanted to diminish the tension between herself and Bud by purchasing de Rancé's stock, therefore eliminating their final reason to communicate. On April 29, 1965, Lorraine called Harry and said, "I must do something. Will you sell to the brewery? How much do you want? I will instruct Norm to show you what you want to see and to let you use the MBC [Miller Brewery] photocopier. I just bought a $110,000 farm for Michael [her son] and had to pay a $110,000 gift tax."

The negotiations continued. Charley Miller noted that Harry John and Donald Gallagher came to his house on June 22, 1965:

"Between much small talk Harry stated that he had great difficulty in making up his mind — first, to sell and second, at what price. The more he asked for advice, the more confused and complex the matter seemed to be. As yet he had not been able to see clearly what course of action to take. Unfortunately the Lord had not yet pointed out what he should do. Therefore, until it became clear in his mind through this help, he could not act with conviction. He next wanted to know why Lorraine wished to buy his stock and how many offers she had besides Grace's. I told him on the first question I thought she wished to be helpful to him by offering a premium for de Rancé stock. On the second question I understood she had two offers for her majority stock but whether this included or excluded Grace I did not know."[564]

Charley Miller continued:

"I also told him I thought both he and his sister should sell their interest, assuming a fair price could be attained, and that the sale should be made to a third party such as Grace or by selling to the public. In any event, I did not believe it was best to sell to each other. It would not seem prudent to me for either to have all their funds invested in one single enterprise. Harry replied that he agreed but that the 'when' to sell wasn't clear because the company was doing so well and that very year the value of the stock was increasing."[565]

On June 25, 1965, while Lorraine and Norman Klug were meeting at the Wisconsin Club, she reported that Bud had called her on June 23 and halfway through the conversation she discovered that Gallagher was on an extension. Subsequently, Klug wrote about Lorraine's description of the conversation noting that:

"She then said that the trouble with him was that he couldn't make up his mind. She told him that she had offered him the Grace deal, and he claimed he didn't know that. She pointed out that she not only offered him the Grace deal, but 5% in addition, and he still couldn't make up his mind."[566]

On September 1, 1965, Norman Klug met with Lorraine Mulberger at the Wisconsin Club, where he again urged her to sell her brewery stock, pointing out that she should not have 'all her eggs in one basket' and that she should not be concerning herself with these matters. Her reply was, "It doesn't worry me. In fact, I enjoy it. What do you think I want to do–rot?" With that she walked into the dining room with a sly smile.[567]

On February 16, 1966, J. Peter Grace wrote to Bud:

"We have gone around and around the Mulberry bush for years now on this Miller Brewing situation. I am unhappy the way you have been stuck with a de Rancé income of around $375,000 a year, particularly at a time when the active apostolate of the Church is in such dire need, particularly in Latin America...This is your decision and not mine. I am merely an agent or a catalyst who will make it possible for you to greatly increase your charitable giving, if you wish to. In the first place I wouldn't think of offering you any less proportionately for your 47% that I would offer for the 53%, i.e., I would never try to take advantage of your minority position."

On May 1, 1966, Miller Brewery purchased a brewing plant in Azusa, California, for $8 million. The plant, built in 1948, had a 600,000-barrel capacity before Miller increased it to one million barrels after a $3 million remodeling effort. In October 1966, it began brewing Miller High Life that shipped the first week in November 1966, to California, Arizona, New Mexico,

Nevada, Utah, Oregon, Washington, Idaho, Alaska, and Hawaii. At the March 23, 1966, Miller stockholders' meeting, an official explained: "Accordingly, we looked to the West Coast where we believe the greatest increase in population will occur in the next five years. In addition, this is the most distant point to which we ship in the United States and the most expensive point to which we ship. From a time standpoint, the return of containers from this area provides the longest lag, requiring us to invest more for half-barrels, at $30.00 apiece, than we should like to."[568]

Harry was hurt by Grace's apparent self-interest. Harry explained:

". . .Mr. Grace's incessant disparagement of MBC [Miller Brewery] – his portrayal of its dismal competitive posture as a one-town brewery [one brand, High Life] and his false and hyperbolic estimates of its expansion needs, $60-120 million – were calculated to and did install in our minds considerable insecurity and even anxiety as to the wisdom of fulfilling our intent [buying Lorraine Mulberger's shares]. After all, we had sought out Mr. Grace because, as my sister put it, he was a businessman genius, the most capable businessman in the world. Especially because of our own lack of business experience, his negative evaluations of MBC were impossible for us to ignore."[569]

Finally, Bud's disagreements with Peter Grace, regarding de Rancé's Miller Brewery stock, had reached the breaking point. Bud had demanded that Peter use every opportunity to purchase Lorraine's stock for de Rancé. There is no evidence that Peter ever tried to follow Harry's command. Interestingly, Harry was surprised that Grace acted in the best interests of the W.R. Grace Company instead of the foundation. Unbeknownst to Harry, his act of bringing Peter Grace to Miller Brewery as his representative was equivalent to asking a finch to safeguard thistle seeds. On February 14, 1966, at de Rancé's offices at 324 North 76th Street, in the presence of trustee Donald A. Gallagher, Father Patrick Peyton (this crusading priest, a close friend of both Harry John and Peter Grace, was internationally known for his Family Prayer, Family Rosary, and Family Theater Programs), and Thomas E. Hanigan, (vice-president of the W.R. Grace & Co.), Harry fired Peter as treasurer of the foundation. Harry's behavior was adolescent, as he tried to embarrass Grace in front of his associates. Instead, Bud could have handled this matter privately. Practically speaking, Peter may have been pleased by this event, as he was strictly a volunteer at the foundation, though Harry allowed him to choose recipients for 7% of the total grants.

The pugnacious Grace, of course, was unimpressed with Harry's maneuver and, until their deaths; they maintained a grudging respect for each other. Erica John remembers that Peter Grace retained an interest in helping Bud or Erica whenever possible. From time to time in the late 1970s and early 1980s, Peter provided Bud with the use of his corporate jet to fly to various American locations.

In early 1966, the Miller Brewing Company had 10,000 shares with 6,144 4/9 validly issued and outstanding. The shares were divided as follows;

Stockholder	Shares	Percentage
Lorraine Mullberger	1,786 4/9	29%
Karen Swanson Trust	500	8%
Mike Henry Mulberger Trust	500	8%
Lorraine Mulberger General Trust	450	7%
Henry Mulberger	2.5	0%
Karen Swanson	2.5	0%
Clark & Co.	1	0%
de Rancé	2,900	47%
Harry G. John, Jr.	1	0%
Michael Stoiber	1	0%
Total	**6,144 4/9**	**99%**

On July 25, 1966, Lorraine signed an agreement to sell her and her children's Miller stock to W.R. Grace. On that day, Lorraine, certainly with Klug's assistance, wrote to her brother:

Dear Bud,

Over the years I have tried to work some equitable agreement with you on the operation of the Miller Brewing Company. This has not proven successful despite the fact that I maintained your nominees on our Board of Directors after the expiration of the Voting Trust Agreement and after I had the majority control of stock. I am also concerned with the problem of my estate and leaving it in such condition that my family will not be placed in jeopardy because of inheritance taxes. In an effort to accomplish this objective, under date of May 14, 1965, I, by letter, offered to pay you a premium of 5% over the appraised value of your stock, one appraiser to be appointed by each of us, and they to appoint a third. When you refused to sell, even at a premium, we attempted at the last Annual Meeting to split the stock 500 to 1 in order to enable either of us to make a public offering, should we so desire. Your vote defeated this move. Under the circumstances, I have given the W. R. Grace & Co. an option to buy my stock with the understanding that they will offer to purchase your stock at a proportionately relative price. I feel that I have done everything possible to work with you and will continue to follow this Christian attitude, but I cannot permit your indecision to jeopardize my own future and that of my children.

Sincerely,
Lorraine [signed]

On September 22, 1966, the Grace Corporation consummated the sale of 3,241 4/9 shares of Lorraine and her children's stock for $36 million in cash and stock in the Grace Company. W.R. Grace paid Lorraine $18,069,000 in cash and a little over $15 million in Grace common stock, 402,801 shares at $37.50 per share. The federal taxing authorities took $7.7 million and the state — $3.1 million. At that time, Norman Klug issued the statement: "The management of Miller Brewing Co. views this change of partial stock ownership with complete approval and enthusiasm. It assures the stability and continued successful operation of the company." J. Peter Grace said, "We are proud to join forces with the Miller Brewing Co. Its business was founded in 1855 and the W. R. Grace & Co. business was founded a year earlier. . . Miller will be a subsidiary of W. R. Grace & Co. and will be included in its consumer products group."[570]

Miller came under the control of J. Peter Grace, chief executive officer of the W.R. Grace & Company Corporation, an operation with approximately $500 million in assets. His paternal grandfather and company's namesake, William Russell Grace, had founded it. In 1966, the company was primarily in the chemical business. It also owned a steamship line, half of an airline, and a candy and confectionary business. It also owned the Ambrosia Chocolate Company in Milwaukee. In Latin America, it had some paper operations, some trading, and some mining operations.[571]

Lorraine had been loyal to Miller Brewery throughout her long association with it. Lorraine never spoke publicly, leaving it to others, such as Norman Klug. After the sale, she felt the liberty, for the first time in her life, to expound on her feelings about the brewery. Lorraine was never comfortable with the intricacies of brewing, yet performed admirably supporting decisions that propelled the business forward. Nevertheless, for some time, she had been ill at ease promoting consumption of an alcoholic drink.

Lorraine explained that she had sold her interest in the Miller Brewing Company for religious purposes, even though she had not broached the matter in any of the negotiations. She told a reporter that "the brewery was not the will of God for me." In a way she may have been apologizing to her ancestors for selling the control of the brewery that they had toiled to build and retain. She said that she put the matter "in his hands" and that the sale was "the will of God."[572]

For five years, Lorraine had been attending, but had not yet joined, the Waukesha Bible Church, where Rev. William Pederson was the shepherd. In an interview together with the pastor, Lorraine mentioned that "the religious motivation that prompted her to sell her interests in the brewery began about five years ago." She had been awaiting the opportunity to sell the stock. She said that she had received other offers besides the one she accepted. The reticent Lorraine spoke briefly to a reporter, quoting Romans 14:13 to explain her reason for selling, "Let us not therefore judge one another any more; but judge this rather, that no man put a stumbling block or an occasion to fall in his brother's way." Rev. Pederson noted that Lorraine had told him of her plan to sell her Miller stock. He explained that there was nothing in the church constitution against drinking. Nevertheless, Lorraine's son, Michael Mulberger, noted that his mother did not currently drink and that she disliked the use of alcoholic beverages. Karen Mulberger Swanson noted that, previous to her joining Rev. Pederson's conservative church, her mother enjoyed an occasional Miller High Life. Karen continued noting that her mom thought that the misuse of alcohol could lead to problem drinking, car accidents, and familial problems and did not want to negatively contribute to others' well being. Lorraine had experienced the painful side of alcohol use in her father, Harry John, Sr., and husband, Henry Mulberger. Pastor Pederson continued that Lorraine had made her decision, "based upon her understanding of the teachings of the Scriptures and her personal convictions."[573]

On October 28, 1966, Miller Brewing Company acquired a brewing plant in Fort Worth, Texas, from the Carling Brewing Company for $5.5 million. The plant and equipment, which had a 300,000-barrel capacity, was expanded to 800,000 barrels by a two-year $6 million construction project.[574] This purchase gave Miller, which already had a production plant in California, a new one in the South, providing them with lower shipping costs to those regions.

On October 24, 1966, Norman Klug died of a heart attack at Columbia Hospital. Previously, in late April, he was taken to this same hospital by a fire department rescue squad, after collapsing in his home. He had been hospitalized since the previous Saturday, upon returning from a board of directors' meeting of the U.S. Brewers Association, of which he was chairman, in Boca Raton, Florida. Since December of the previous year, he had been hospitalized for fifteen weeks for a heart ailment. He was buried in the Pine Lawn Cemetery following funeral services at Divinity-Divine Charity Evangelical Lutheran Church in Whitefish Bay. Norman was survived by his wife, Florence, and son, Thomas Norman, currently an attorney in Milwaukee. Klug's pallbearers, which demonstrated his dedication to the Miller Brewing Company, were among others, Edward Huber, Miller brewmaster; John Savage, Miller vice-president and secretary; Charles W. Miller; Louis Quarles, private attorney; John A. Puelicher, president of M & I Bank; J. Peter Grace; Kenneth K. Luce; and Edward J. O'Donnell, S.J., [president of Marquette University].[575]

Norman Klug was a tremendous asset to the Miller Brewing Company. While lacking Fred C. Miller's panache and commanding presence, he did everything else that Fred would have expected. Klug dedicated his life to the brewery and its fortunes, as its first president without any stock. In a manner of speaking, he ranks with Fred J. Miller, the brewery's founder, and Ernest Miller, his son, as the hardest working chief executives to that time. He was quoted in *Miller High-Lites*, an employee publication, in early 1965, upon returning from an extensive fact-finding tour of the Far East with 26 other businessmen, sponsored by *Time* magazine, "It is defeatist to evade responsibility by questioning the worth of one's action, no matter how small it might necessarily seem to be. The important thing is that we make the effort, that we make a start." Norman gave, "willingly of his time and his abilities to numerous programs and causes that he believed were of benefit to his community, his state and his country."[576]

Klug gave of his time and energy to benefit the brewing industry as a whole by serving a president of the U.S. Brewers Association. Following that, he was elected chairman of its board of directors in 1965 and 1966. He also served for many years as president of the Wisconsin State Brewers Association. In 1957, he was chairman of the United Way and, in 1964, was named chairman of the newly organized Board of Regents of Marquette University. His activities extended into many more local organizations and clubs.[577]

Despite his continual battle with Harry John, who was in control of 47% of Miller Brewery's stock, Norman Klug remained focused on improving the company. He engineered the increase of the brewery's sales from 2.1 million barrels in 1953, the year before Fred Miller died, to 4.15 million barrels in 1966. Miller Brewery's net earnings jumped from $1.5 million in 1954 to $8.3 million in 1966. He accomplished it without the *gravitas* bestowed upon presidents who were major stockholders or members of the founding family. Several years before he died he noted: "The future of our (brewing) industry is bound to the future of our country, which to my way of thinking is almost limitless. I don't see how you can hold a country like ours down, with all the potential it has for development."[578]

Within a week after Norman Klug's death, Peter Grace chose Charles W. Miller, 58, as the chief executive officer of the Miller Brewing Company. In 1965, Charley, the Detroit native, had left Miller Brewery to become vice-president of the consumer products group of W.R. Grace & Co., before returning as the brewery's new leader. Charley received a B. S. in business from Marquette University in 1948, a Master's degree in economics from the University of Minnesota in 1950, and then earned a Ph.D. in business administration from Minnesota in 1952. While Charley Miller was named chief executive officer, Jack Savage was named executive vice-president. Savage had joined Miller Brewery in 1946, becoming general counsel in 1956, secretary in 1957, and vice-president in 1964. Jack currently lives at the Milwaukee Catholic Home and, at approximately age 93, retains a delightful personality and a sharp memory for the many events in Miller Brewery's history in which he participated or witnessed.[579]

Three months after assuming the brewery's top position, Charles Miller expounded on some of his thoughts. He noted that, "Our set of principles and philosophy of the past have proven successful. Quality has been the cornerstone of the foundation of this company. We have stubbornly adhered to a strict rule of only using the finest of ingredients and the best of craftsmanship. . . Our marketing department is very optimistic and they are hoping that we can continue the trend that has been going for us in the last three years. We feel that 1967 will be another record year."[580]

As far as Harry John was concerned, the treatment of de Rancé, Inc., as a minority shareholder, at the Miller Brewing Company, had not changed since W.R. Grace assumed control. He still felt the need to lobby or threaten the management to attend to de Rancé's needs. Harry wanted the brewery to supply ample dividends to the foundation for its grants. Bud desired ever more money to fund his activist causes. Over the decades, he was compelled to support various Catholic causes. For instance, in the mid-1940s and early 1950s, besides providing considerable sums to existing contemplative monasteries and convents, he funded seven Trappist Foundations that each supported the establishment of another monastery. For this devotion, Harry's actions are under-appreciated, as monks, meditative by nature, believe that that they can improve and bring salvation to the world through prayer and work, making self-promotion difficult. Although on April 6, 1967, Father Stephen Mary Boylan of the Carthusian Foundation in Arlington, Vermont, gushed: "In the whole wide world, there is assuredly not a layman who is devoted to the purely contemplative Orders in the truly heroic degree that you are, so you abundantly deserve the continuous stream of Graces and blessings and temporal favors that being a Member brings to you and your family."

Ultimately, Erica John remembers that Bud told her that contemplative orders can only absorb so much money, so he looked for other causes to fund. In the 1950s and 1960s, Harry subsidized a small Catholic movement devoted to promoting a devotion to the Sacred Heart of Jesus. It was one of numerous Catholic devotional groups, who toiled to increase the awareness of the greater church to its beliefs, expecting that the church would become energized and save more souls. Harry attended weekly meetings on the Sacred Heart of Jesus and traveled worldwide for de Rancé-funded meetings.

In the 1960s, Harry John became intrigued by Patrick Peyton and his worldwide crusades to promote the love of the Blessed Virgin Mary through daily recitations of the rosary. At this same time, de Rancé funded myriad mission projects on American Indian reservations, in the Philippines, Chile, Brazil, Ecuador, India, and Ghana. For example, Donald Gallagher, during a trip to South America came upon Brooklyn native Rev. John Halligan, S.J., who was assisting shoeshine boys in Quito, Ecuador. Eventually, Fr. Halligan's work became a movement, known as the Working Boys' Center, and grew into two campuses in Quito, aided in large part by de Rancé's funding, catering to the physical and spiritual needs of entire impoverished families. Martha Cecelia John, a sister of Marco Cabezas, one of the original shoeshine boys that Fr. Halligan assisted, came to study in Milwaukee. She lived with Patricia and James Parks. Patricia, the sibling of Sister Miguel Conway, a co-director of the Working Boys' Center, hosted Fr. Halligan during his Milwaukee fundraising trips. Over time, Patricia and Erica John became friends, which led to them introducing Martha to Harry and Erica's son, Tim, the author of this book. Later, Martha and Tim dated, eventually marrying and raising three children.

The 1970s saw Bud delve into the anti-abortion movement, in due course becoming a major funder of the crusade. Harry augmented his promotion of the movement by displaying posters of aborted fetuses in de Rancé's halls, which his daughter Paula judiciously removed. Ultimately, in the late 1970s and early 1980s Bud began to create a nationwide Catholic media empire, incorporating radio and television.

It was to fund these myriad causes that Harry wanted substantial dividends and, until de Rancé sold its stock in the Miller Brewing Company in 1970, brewery dividends were the foundation's only income. De Rancé's demands did not always meet Miller Brewery's direction, as noted, on March 22, 1967, when a brewery official remarked, ". . .we must envision a program of 5 to 10 years—of new construction—greater marketing effort—all of which will require the infusion of substantial capital." Such talk scared Bud, who wanted to withdraw the brewery's cash for de Rancé's grants instead of further brewery development.[581]

After Grace bought Lorraine's interest in Miller Brewery, Harry demanded that the brewery maintain the voting trust that had been established between Lorraine Mulberger and de Rancé, giving the foundation the right to name three directors; increasing the brewery's dividends; and copying the brewery's minutes, tax returns, budgets, among other documents. A brewery officer responded that de Rancé would be unable to select directors because the voting trust between Lorraine and Harry had expired in 1963. He also noted that minority shareholders had no right to choose directors, unless provided that opportunity by the majority interests. Furthermore, he asserted that their, "dividend policy is the prerogative of the Board of Directors." Finally, all other corporate documents, besides the regular reports to stockholders such as the annual report, would not be provided, but relevant documents would be available on site for Harry to examine. Miller vice-president Jack Savage provided such documents as he saw necessary and nothing more. Charley Miller notified Harry that he could not, as he did on April 25, 1967, "drop in unannounced and demand to inspect records and make copies thereof."[582]

Harry doggedly continued his quixotic efforts to influence Miller Brewery's board of directors. Each annual stockholder meeting saw him parade to the brewery's corporate offices with Donald Gallagher and an attorney, sometimes John P. Miller, in a futile attempt to be elected to the board of directors. One such trip saw Harry John, Donald Gallagher, and John Miller driving to the brewery while Gallagher expounded on Bud's brewing ancestry. John Miller remembers that, presently, Harry wheeled the car around and headed to the Miller family plot at the nearby Calvary Cemetery, exclaiming that they should look to his ancestors for inspiration for their imminent board meeting. For a period, the intrepid men stood silently, with heads bowed, before the graves of Frederick J. Miller and his two wives, Josephine and Lisette, Fred's three sons Ernest;

Frederick A. "Fritz", and Emil. Also at this site were the graves of Bud's aunt, Clara Miller, and her husband Carl and their son Fred C. and grandson, Freddy. Finally, two stones were inscribed with the names of Buddy's parents, Elise K. John and Harry G. John, Sr.

24.
THE BREWERY'S
LATER YEARS

Peter Grace grew frustrated with Harry John's reticence to sell him de Rancé's shares of the Miller Brewing Company, representing 47% ownership. In early May 1969, Peter told the board of directors at the W.R. Grace & Company that, "this holding would not be sold to us." Soon after, Harry John reported that, "he is interested in selling the stock and that Grace has failed to say he was unable to complete the purchase, at Grace's price." Grace described his frustration: "If you have 53% and one stockholder holding 47%, you probably will be more careful in the ways the company is operated. If you don't own it completely and use profits to develop the business, or borrow the money to expand, it's a restricted situation. The other holder can question what you're doing. We feel we should have 100% owned domestic subsidiaries." Later, one Grace executive noted: "At the time of the purchase, we expected to acquire the remaining 47% interest in Miller. However, in the intervening period we concluded that this holding would not be sold to us. This situation, we feel is undesirable as it handicaps development of the full potential of this business."[583]

Peter became impatient and looked to unload Grace's 53% of Miller's stock. In early May 1969, the company came close to consummating a deal with PepsiCo for $120 million in cash and notes. Peter said that he could not break down the cash and notes to be paid by PepsiCo but, "It's a full $120 million, not wallpaper or potato chips," referring to the types of securities that had been used in some acquisitions. Grace defended the large profit that the Grace Company would realize, $84 million, noting "It's a fair price for a company which has done well in the last three years. I don't think it was too high a premium. He explained, "We have no interest in other brewers. We had a jewel in Miller and wouldn't take less. We're unhappy about leaving the business and deeply regret we had to sell it."[584]

The sale of Miller Brewing Company to PepsiCo collapsed and, immediately, on June 12, 1969, Peter Grace lined up Philip Morris, Inc. as the next buyer, for $130 million in cash. The additional $10 million and the cash-only offer made this deal an improvement over PepsiCo's offer. The sale to Philip Morris followed by one day after the breakdown of negotiations aimed at selling Miller to PepsiCo, Inc. Officials from the soda company were reportedly dismayed by the failure of their negotiations. "They thought the purchase was all but completed until last week when it became apparent that Grace wanted to back out." PepsiCo. sued the W.R. Grace Company and Philip Morris, alleging fraud, conspiracy and breach of contract. At the end of 1969, a federal court dismissed the suit, deciding that no contract existed between W.R. Grace and PepsiCo.[585]

Philip Morris was the nation's 147th largest industrial concern in the county, with sales of $1.02 billion in 1968 and profits of $48.9 million. The cigarette manufacturer made Marlboro, Benson & Hedges, Parliament, Virginia Slims, Alpine, and Philip Morris cigarettes. It also produced Clark chewing gum, Personna razor blades, surgical blades, and a variety of industrial operations around the world. It was a major producer of adhesives and chemicals for the textile industry. Joseph F. Cullman, III, Philip Morris's chairman from 1957 to 1978, explained his company's interest in acquiring Miller Brewery in his autobiography, *I'm a Lucky Guy*. He noted that they, "believed marketing techniques developed for cigarettes could be transformed to beer. . . Both products are low priced, processed from agricultural commodities, and packaged by expensive equipment; they are advertised in a similar fashion. Moreover as George Weissman [Cullman's successor] put it, 'Your beer drinker and your cigarette smoker are often the same guy.' "[586]

Grace's sale of their Miller stock to Philip Morris incensed Harry John. He believed that Peter had misused his confidence, as de Rancé's representative on the brewery's board to enrich his own company. Even though it was nearly three years since Grace purchased Lorraine Mulberger's stock, it was Grace's $94 million profit by selling this same stock to Philip Morris that compelled Bud to sue Peter Grace and the W.R. Grace Company. Since Bud had asked Peter to buy Lorraine's stock for the foundation, he believed that the large profit that the W.R. Grace Company earned, by all rights, belonged to de Rancé, Inc.

Harry hired the New York law firm Pomerantz Levy Haudek & Block to attempt to recover the $97 million in profit that W.R. Grace realized when it sold its 53% interest in the Miller Brewing Company. Harry, "proposed to show that Grace Co. gained the profit in suit through misuse and betrayal of Mr. Grace's fiduciary relation to plaintiff." Harry reported that, early on, Grace was aware that he had fiduciary duties at three associated organizations, the W.R. Grace Co., the Miller Brewing Company, and de Rancé. Harry continued, "His sensitivity to his patent conflicts of interest evaporated, when self-interest triumphed over fiduciary duty." After hearings, depositions, and investigations, in August 1974, de Rancé settled for $6.4 million, which Peter Grace probably regarded as a donation to the foundation. De Rancé's Milwaukee attorney, John P. Miller, remembers that Harry insisted that everyone in his legal camp agree that the settlement be regarded as an actual triumph instead of the closure of a nuisance suit.[587]

In July 1969, Harry John became concerned by hearings in the U.S. House of Representatives Foundations subcommittee that showed privately held tax-exempt foundations, such as de Rancé, Inc.'s 47% of Miller Brewery, had major holdings in large corporations. Rep. Wright Patman (D-Tex.), chairman of the house foundations' subcommittee, made public a report showing that 154 of 647 foundations under study, including de Rancé and five others in Wisconsin, held sizeable amounts of stock in 313 corporations. "The report to the parent House

Select Small Business Committee singled out the Miller Brewing Co. as one of the nationally known that had "substantial" links with tax free foundations." Patman said that his bill limiting foundations holdings to no more than 3% of a company's shares, "would make it more difficult for our millionaires to bypass the tax collector by handing their intact estates over to tax free, captive foundations." Patman had authored a bill, then before the House Ways and Means Committee, that attempted to limit a foundation holding in stock to 20% to 35% of its value. His bill also provided for a 20% tax on the gross income of foundations and would require that all of their net income be disbursed annually for the purposes for which they were organized. This populist bill did not pass, but it demonstrated a movement to limit the power of rich people to create foundations and thereby evade taxes.[588]

Patman criticized many of the big foundations for accumulating too much of their unspent income. De Rancé's stock in the Miller Brewing Company was valued at $5.2 million when the gift of the stock was made in the early 1950s. In 1966, it had a market value of $19.3 million, in 1967 — $30 million, and then, based on the deal with Philip Morris, approximately $100 million. A reporter for the *Milwaukee Journal* noted that Patman's criticism did not seem to apply to de Rancé because in 1967 its charitable donations totaled $311,550, which had come from $471,250 in dividends from the Miller Brewery. "In one year there were 44 recipients, ranging from the Archdiocese of the Port-of-Spain, Trinidad, to the Archdiocese of Oslo, Norway, to Catholic University in Puerto Rico, to St. Peter's Mission in India. The contributions ranged in size from $150 to the Redemptorist Fathers in Wisconsin to $45,000 to the Family Rosary in California [Father Patrick Peyton's organization]."[589]

At the end of July 1970, Harry John decided to sell de Rancé's holdings in the Miller Brewing Company, representing 47% of the outstanding stock, for $97 million. The pressure of Congressional hearings and his desire to provide more funding to his Catholic interests, tied with Philip Morris's liberal offer, provided Harry with the impetus finally to sell. The purchase of 2,900 shares, out of 6,100 total outstanding, gave Philip Morris ownership of 100% of the brewery's stock. The price contained $25 million in cash and $72 million in subordinated notes payable in 12 years. The notes were subordinated to other debt, such as bank loans. To explain their interest in Miller, Philip Morris reported that Miller Brewing Company's sales in 1970 were expected to be approximately $200 million. The brewery's sales had doubled in the last ten years, reaching a record 5 million barrels in 1969. At this same time, Miller Brewery announced that besides its plants in Azusa, California and Fort Worth, Texas, they were planning to build a brewery in Pittston, Pennsylvania, that would be ready to brew beer by 1973.[590]

Harry John explained that, "Various people have been trying to buy this block of Miller stock ever since 1960. I've had seven offers in the last eight years. Each one was a little better that the one before. Grace was one of them but its price was only about half of what I thought the stock was worth."[591] Harry received kudos on his deal. John Wittig, a founding de Rancé trustee wrote, "You certainly did well in hanging on to the stock." A New York attorney fawned, "...I want to reiterate my congratulations to you for the exceptionally favorable transaction which you have concluded in the face of unusually adverse market conditions."

Harry maintained his typical demeanor during the sales process. Bud's attorney, John P. Miller, noted that one day when executives and lawyers from Philip Morris, Miller Brewery, and de Rancé were at the brewery's headquarters to hammer out the fine points of the sale, Harry excused himself from the room. Time passed while the parties made small talk. Over time, they stopped chatting, wondering where Harry was. After an hour and a half, John Miller left to look for Bud, who, he soon found photocopying Miller Brewery's minutes, especially 1946 and 1947 when he was president. As usual, Harry John enjoyed making important people wait for his own projects.

Harry's sale of de Rancé's 2,900 shares, including his one

personal share, was the termination of the Miller family's association with the Miller Brewing Company. Many years earlier, the Millers could not have foreseen this end to their involvement; Frederick J. Miller's grandson selling the stock for a considerable sum. Harry John, the man who gave most of his stock away in the 1950s ended up holding it longer than anyone else. The $97 million, minus the fees, boosted de Rancé, Inc. into reportedly the richest Catholic foundation in the world. Quietly, Harry John would disperse millions of dollars around the world educating, feeding, healing multitudes of people.

After the final purchase of stock from de Rancé, Inc., a private foundation, Philip Morris was free to move the company forward as it saw fit. During the next decade they orchestrated an expansion unprecedented in American brewing history. Philip Morris began a gradual replacement of the former management and, in 1971; John A. Murphy of Philip Morris International was named CEO. Philip Morris brought an approach to beer marketing that had served them well in selling cigarettes — dividing the domestic beer market into segments, producing new products for those segments, and promoting them with gusto.

One of their achievements was strengthening sales of Miller High Life, then the company's largest selling brand. The beer underwent a mild reformulation, but its advertising was markedly changed. Instead of emphasizing its upscale aura, new Miller advertising promoted the theme of everyday male beer drinkers being rewarded with a High Life at the end of a day's work. "Miller Time," introduced in 1971, entered the language as an expression for "the time to relax." Changes were made in the structure of the sales network, and sales in cans were also emphasized. High Life reached its all-time peak in 1979.

The next step was even more inspired. Miller Brewing Company purchased the Meister Brau Lite brand from a bankrupt Chicago brewer. One source stated that the Lite purchase was mentioned by Philip Morris representatives at the time that they closed the deal for the de Rancé stock. The idea of a light beer was not new, but it had not been successfully marketed to American males and suffered from a less than macho image. Somewhat by accident, Miller's ad agency began using athletes and celebrities in humorous television spots, and then continued when their success became apparent. The first Miller Lite commercial was shot in July 1973 and the brand was rolled out nationally in 1975 with the advertising slogan, "Lite Beer from Miller. Everything You Always Wanted In a Beer — and Less." Further ads included the "Tastes Great-Less Filling" chant.

It was the right presentation at the right time for a light beer; the results were astounding. Miller's sales exploded: Annual barrelage rose from 6.9 million in 1973 to 24.2 million in 1977. By 1978 Miller was the nation's second largest brewer, rising from the fifth position just five years earlier. Its operating revenues in 1978 were $1.8 billion, up from $276 million in 1973; employment increased from 2,574 in 1973 to 10,199 in 1978. By 1982 its barrelage was 39.3 million, which was approximately 22 percent of the domestic beer market.

Through 1978 Philip Morris had put $850 million into Miller, not including the cost of the acquisition. While other brewers resented the intrusion of tobacco profits into their business, it was apparent to all that Philip Morris was getting spectacular results. The increasing sales necessitated the construction of new breweries. Before the Miller family's stock was sold to Philip Morris, breweries in Azusa, California, and Fort Worth, Texas, had been acquired and brought on line. The first new brewery to open was in Fulton, New York, in 1976, followed by another in Eden, North Carolina, in 1978 and Albany, Georgia, in 1980. Later in 1980 the Azusa, California, brewery was replaced by a new facility in Irwindale, California. A Miller archives photo from its construction shows California Governor Jerry Brown as a speaker, foreshadowing a later visit to Irwindale by present-day California Governor Arnold Schwarzenegger.

Industry leader Anheuser-Busch was not about to surrender its position without a fight, and mounted a variety of marketing counteroffensives against Miller. The Milwaukee brewery narrowed the gap somewhat, but was never able to wrest the top position from the St. Louis brewery.

Miller opened a new tour center to welcome visitors to its Milwaukee brewery in 1977; this facility is still in use after subsequent renovation and expansion. New corporate offices were also completed that year in Milwaukee, located along Highland Boulevard on the hillcrest overlooking the brewery.

In the 1980s Miller introduced the Milwaukee's Best brand nationally as a sub-premium, or economy beer. It had been obtained from Gettelman Brewery with the 1961 acquisition and remains an important part of the Miller portfolio of beers. Miller Genuine Draft was introduced in 1986 and it has endured. Today, it and Miller Lite are the company's premier premium brands. Genuine Draft is not heat-pasteurized as are other beers; instead it is brewed using a cold filtered process. Sharps, a non-alcohol brew, was introduced nationally in 1989 and is part of the Miller portfolio today. Some of the other Miller introductions of the 1980s and 1990s did not survive. In 1987 the Jacob Leinenkugel Brewing Company of Chippewa Falls, Wisconsin, a brewer of craft beers distributed in the Upper Midwest, became an operating unit of Miller.

The selling of beer changed in ways that earlier brewers might not recognize. Miller Brewing Company had begun to target African Americans as consumers in the 1960s and continued to expand its efforts to attract them. Furthermore, it sought to reach out to Hispanic beer drinkers and to other groups. Alcohol awareness and education programs became part of brewers' efforts to encourage responsible consumption, prevent underage access, and reduce drunk driving. Recycling and waste reduction programs sought to reduce shipments to landfills.

The 1990s were a more difficult decade for Miller as barrelage remained the same at the end of the decade as at the beginning. Anheuser-Busch Brewing did not remain static and its lead over second-place Miller Brewing Company increased. The decade had a considerable amount of activity for Miller, nevertheless. A brewery that had been mothballed for a decade was brought on line in Trenton, Ohio in 1991. Three years later the brewery in Fulton, New York was closed. The Plank Road Brewery name, harkening back to Frederick J. Miller's first brewery, was revived as a small division of Miller and used for brewing Icehouse and Red Dog beers. There was substantial realignment in the whole brewing industry, and when the game of musical brands ended, Miller acquired the Hamm's Beer and Olde English 800 Malt Liquor names from the Pabst Brewing Co. and the Northwest craft brewer's name of Henry Weinhard from Stroh's. Also, Miller became a contract brewer for Pabst. Miller also acquired the Tumwater, Washington brewery from Pabst and operated it for four years before closing the facility in 2003. Baseball fans benefited from Miller largesse in 1996 as the company assisted the Milwaukee Brewers baseball club with a $42 million contribution (over 20 years) towards their new stadium, to be called Miller Park.

By 2002 Anheuser-Busch dominated the domestic beer market with a 51 percent share, while Miller was in second place with 19 percent. Philip Morris was under increasing attack in its core tobacco business and sought to diversify itself further. As a result, Miller represented only 4 percent of Philip Morris revenues.

The latest chapter in Miller Brewing Company history began in July 2002 when it was purchased from Philip Morris by South African Breweries. The latter company had a dominant position in South Africa and was also prominent throughout southern Africa. After investment restrictions from the apartheid era ended, the firm began a rapid program of acquisitions within developing nations in Asia and Africa, and in Eastern European countries. A new company called SABMiller plc was formed, based in London. It is one of the largest brewers in the world, with a strong brewing presence in 40 countries across four continents. Philip Morris retained a one-third interest in the new firm and agreed to restraints on any stock sales for three years.

After careful study, SABMiller began to move to revive the Miller brands. Norman Adami, chairman/managing director of SAB in South Africa, was named president of the Miller Brewing Company in January 2003. In a closing of the circle, Adami was the first Miller president since company founder Frederick J. Miller to be born outside the United States.

Adami announced a three-year turnaround plan. It positioned Miller as the "able challenger," ready to engage the dominant Anheuser-Busch. The plan focused on four points, which of themselves comprise a commentary on the areas in which Miller needed substantial improvement: 1) becoming "...a market-driven company that leads a market-driven distribution network with market-driven brands"; 2) improving relationships with distributors; 3) reviving the company's competitive spirit; 4) capitalizing on the fact that Miller was now part of a company that focused on beer.

The plan to revive sagging Miller brands began with the largest, Miller Lite. Results from the first year were quite successful, and surprising, as declining brands are very difficult to turn upward. As of this writing, Miller Brewing Company continues to push forward on its historic undertaking to rejuvenate and strengthen the company. A difficult task, to be sure, but perhaps not more difficult than the one undertaken 150 years earlier by an equally determined Milwaukee brewer, Frederick J. Miller.

EPILOGUE

For three generations, the Miller family controlled the Miller Brewing Company; from Frederick and Josephine Miller's purchase of the Plank Road Brewery in 1855 to Harry G. John, Jr.'s sale of his single share to Philip Morris in 1970, along with the sale of 47% of brewery stock held by de Rancé, Inc., which spelled the end of the family's involvement in the business.

Due to talent, hard work, self-control, and luck, the Millers succeeded where thousands of other brewery families failed. The talent was made up of ample native intelligence, an ability to focus, and the knack for hiring capable employees. The hard work is self-evident. The Millers generally displayed financial self-control by not withdrawing from the brewery and spending on themselves more than a reasonable amount of money and, therefore, not handicapping the growing business. The luck included Frederick J. Miller's being born into a rich merchant family in Germany; buying a brewery in the beer-rich tradition of the Milwaukee area; and the brewery early on not being one of the nation's largest beer makers and, therefore, escaping the attention of the suitors wanting to buy the stock. On the other hand, the Blatz Brewery was purchased by an English syndicate in the 1890s and no longer exists. Many other breweries went down that same road. The Miller Brewing Company remained independent until 1966, when the W.R. Grace Corporation purchased 53% of the business. Until that time, the family used their instincts, along with their considerable intelligence, to steer the business through devastating eras, such as Prohibition, that shuttered most breweries.

The Miller family brought grace to Milwaukee and a devotion to their Catholic faith. They also were obstinate which, occasionally caused familial difficulties. Additionally, there was a bevy of competent female Millers who ran the brewery.

Presidents Lisette Miller, Clara Miller, and Elise John, and vice-president Lorraine Mulberger all successfully served the brewery, a tradition that, unfortunately, has not been continued by subsequent owners.

After 1970, the family of Clara and Carl Miller could no longer be called East Side Millers as they mostly had moved away from Milwaukee by then. The fourth generation generally married well and lived financially successful lives, even though many of the fourth and fifth generation members spent more money than they earned and dropped out of the wealthy class into the middle or working class. Despite Anita Miller Bransfield and Fred C. Miller's untimely deaths, the rest of Clara's children lived relatively long, productive lives. Of Clara and Carl Miller's children, Marguerite died on July 10, 1975, Charlotte on February 16, 1976, Loretta on March 2, 1990, and Claire lived three days longer, dying on March 5.

Clara's descendents maintained a tradition of providing service to the Catholic Church and the greater community. Two of Marguerite Bransfield's children joined religious orders. Her son Michael served many years as a Maryknoll priest in South Korea, occasionally irritating the government as he fought for the Christian ideal of workers' rights. Her daughter Joan, Sister Michaelina, became a member of the Sisters of Mercy. She dedicated her life to Catholic primary education until her recent retirement. Several of Fred C. Miller's children followed their father's dedication to public service. Loret Miller Ruppe (1936-1996) served from 1981 to 1989 as director of the Peace Corps and served from 1989 to 1993 as U.S. Ambassador to Norway. Carlotta Miller Johnson became a religious sister and spent many years in Tanzania in service to the poor. Adele Kanaley Miller joined her sister Carlotta as a lay missionary in Tanzania. Gail Miller Wray has spent much of her later adult life promoting recycling and conservation in Milwaukee and Washington, D.C. Fred C. Miller's widow, Adele, over the years, became an honored political activist, concentrating her efforts and resources on the cause of world peace.

In 1970, Lorraine moved permanently to Phoenix, Arizona

but lived in Santa Fe, New Mexico during the hot summers. Karen Swanson mentioned that her mother loved the mountains and never tired of painting them. Lorraine funded a ranch for troubled boys in northern Arizona and bought a house for unwed mothers in her work with Right to Life. She supported Teen Challenge, a Christian ministry to gang members and poor drug addicted teens. Lorraine aided many charitable causes and often was beseeched by Christian missionaries seeking funding for their endeavors. For a hobby she raised prize-winning Arabian horses. On October 12, 1998, Lorraine died at age 85 in Paradise Valley, Arizona, after a three-year illness while retaining her mental acuity and spiritual depth to the end. On October 24, she was buried in the Miller Family plot in Milwaukee's Calvary Cemetery.

Lorraine's daughter, Karen Mulberger Swanson, purchased a Victorian house on Oconomowoc Lake and, together with her husband Jack, provided a stable home for numerous troubled teens. The Swansons helped and prayed with these youths while raising five of their own children. They have also hosted ecumenical charismatic prayer meetings for forty years, simultaneously helping countless people with the power of healing prayer.

After selling de Rancé's brewery stock, the foundation enjoyed a massive influx of cash, which Harry G. John, Jr., distributed to his causes worldwide. Eventually, he named his wife Erica as a director, but maintained Donald Gallagher as the only other trustee beside himself. In the late 1970s and early 1980s, Harry began to fund his last cause, the establishment of a nationwide Catholic network of television and radio stations. The last endeavor was his grandest and most expensive, but in October 1984, it led to his ouster from the foundation by his wife Erica and Donald Gallagher. After a lengthy trial a Circuit Court judge upheld the ouster.

His last years, from October 1984 until his death from a massive stroke on December 21, 1992, were filled with a divorce, lawsuits, and counter lawsuits, with Harry dying soon after his last appeal was denied. His glorious funeral celebration was held at Gesu Parish, the same place where Harry's cousin, Fred C. Miller, had been honored after his death in December 1954. Harry was buried at the Miller Plot at Calvary Cemetery. His daughter Emily maintained the family tradition of interest in religious matters by earning a doctorate in theology, and went on to teach and ultimately provide fundraising services for numerous Catholic organizations.

Afterword

The Continuing Saga of Harry G. John, Jr.
and the de Rancé Foundation

Written by James Ewens

The curious reader might wonder, "What happened to Harry G, John, Jr. (and his family, and de Rancé, Inc.) after the sale of the Miller Brewing Company stock to Phillip Morris for $97 million?" The brief answer is, "Many things."

The rapid growth of the foundation's activities can be seen in these figures: In 1970 de Rancé awarded grants totaling $455,000. During the next five years the foundation averaged $6.6 million in yearly grants, including $10.9 million in 1975. In the final weeks of 1972 over $5.4 million in grants were approved, included a record setting $2,185,000 being awarded at the December 21st meeting. By the end of the decade de Rancé had dispersed $75 million in grants with $51 million of that total occurring between 1975-1979.

Erica John became the third member of the board in January 1971 and remained in that capacity, with Dr. Donald A. Gallagher, until its close in 1992. In 1975 the John family numbered eight children, ranging in age from 7-18, with a ninth arriving in June 1978. Erica John was, first and foremost, a parent but she also found time to travel alone, or with Harry and the Gallaghers to many of the conferences, symposia, and international meetings that were sponsored by universities, religious orders, and highly placed Vatican officials.

During these years conservative clerics, laity, and religious began to exercise increasing amounts of influence over Harry John, convincing him that the forces of liberal Catholicism unleashed by the Second Vatican Council (1964-67) needed to be curtained and opposed. Some of the people were active in the international Institute of the Heart of Jesus (I.I.H.J.) that began in 1973 and, within, a few years, was receiving yearly grants of $2-3 million. Others, including groups opposing liberation theology in Latin America and those in support of right to life and natural family planning groups also received grants on a regular basis.

It is difficult to summarize in this short space all of the small and large charities that de Rancé supported during these years, with grants averaging $27,000 a piece. These gifts, oftentimes, made the difference between smaller groups getting started—or staying in business—across the country and the world. Additional charities that received major grants included the small, conservative Cardinal Newman College in St. Louis, Mount Senario College in Ladysmith, Wisconsin, a film entitled *Messiah,* directed by the noted Italian Roberto Rossellini, a second film on of the life of Mother Teresa, and the various scientific investigations into the authenticity of the Shroud of Turin in Italy.

In the early 1980s Harry John became increasingly focused on the possibilities for shaping Catholic perceptions in the U.S. through the use of radio and TV stations. In a letter he wrote in February 1981, later dubbed the "Sleeping Giant" text, Harry said:

"It has been said the Catholic Church in the U.S. is a sleeping giant; if this is true, then the magnificent 18,000 diocesan parish system might be termed a sleeping giant. But could we not find one more giant in the enormous potential impact of a full-blown Catholic TV network?"

Harry quickly moved to establish a TV network, "to achieve a substantial and continuing Catholic presence on national TV and to identify the criteria for authentic Catholic Christian TV programming." Purchase of stations in Texas and California, along with production studios in a half dozen cities in the U.S. and Europe, resulted in the expenditures of ten of millions of dollars over the course of two years. This expansion happened to coincide with the foundation's assets increasing from $116 million in early 1981 to a high of $188 million by June 1982.

A statement made by Harry John in April 1981, during a tense discussion about the pending purchase of Channel 46 TV station in Los Angeles, proved to be a prescient warning of what might occur at de Rancé if the board approved this purchase:

"If we approve this purchase de Rancé will be faced with an enormous emergency situation, including planning, the production of programs, etc. For a time much of de Rancé's efforts would be devoted to this undertaking."

Three years later the full scope of this dire warning was being finalized at the foundation. Despite numerous efforts by Erica John and Donald Gallagher to slow Harry John's expenditure of funds on these television station and studios, he persisted in lavish outlays of money—as much as $2 million a week in the first six months of 1984—to pursue his dream of becoming "God's banker to the world." He also secretly invested a major portion of his own assets, along with some of de Rancé's funds, to finance deep sea salvage of ships laden with gold that sank in the ocean in the early 1900s.

By July 1984 the foundation's assets had decreased to $99 million, a drop of $50 million since January. Almost all of this money had been loaned to meet the escalating expenses of the television stations and productions coordinated by Santa Fe Communications. The speeding electronic train that had been wildly careening out of control came to a crashing halt on October 5, 1984 with a single resolution being approved at de Rancé:

We, being all the Directors of de Rancé, Inc. now legally able to act as such, Harry G. John having been suspended as a director by order of Milwaukee County Circuit Court on October 5, 1984, hereby waive notice of a meeting of the Board to be held at noon, October 5, 1984, at the offices of Smith & O'Neil in Milwaukee, Wisconsin.
Signed Erica P. John and Donald A. Gallagher.

Erica John had felt compelled to take legal action when

Harry refused to accept the concerns and votes of the de Rancé directors, his ordering other employees to pay bills that had not been approved by the board, and his extensive expenditures in deep sea salvage operations and the television studios. The court case, titled John versus John, commenced in April 1886, with the plaintiffs, Erica John and Don Gallagher, receiving a resounding victory on all counts in Judge Michael Barron's 28 page decision given on August 21, 1886. Barron's landmark decision makes frequent references to the "fraud, malfeasance, self-dealing, cross trading, conflicts of interest and perjury," that Harry John had engaged in for many years, both as president of the de Rancé foundation and in his testimony during the four months of the trial. The judge's key conclusion was the issuance of a permanent injunction removing Harry John from the foundation he had founded—and funded—during the past 38 years.

Newspaper coverage of the trial was extensive, both locally and nationally, with Erica John being quoted in the *Milwaukee Journal* when the trial ended, "A victory? It's a tragedy." The last four years of her life had been an ordeal, the two years since she and Gallagher filed the lawsuit in an attempt to stop her husband's reckless spending, and the two years before that during which they attempted unsuccessfully, to change his behavior without taking legal action.

As might be expected, given the issues and sums of money involved, this decision was followed by many years of appeals, along with 24 additional lawsuits (19 of them filed by Harry John) that resulted from the initial case. When all the appeals were exhausted—including the possibility of the case being reviewed by the U.S. Supreme Court — Judge Barron's ruling was upheld and Harry John never again retuned to the de Rancé board.

More could be written about what happened with the sea salvage efforts that Harry John had spent millions of dollars on, the changes that occurred in the family during these years, and the final outcomes of the court cases and the foundation. Suffice it to say that when Harry John died on December 19, 1992, a week after suffering a stroke, a great number of people from all segments of society and all areas of the Catholic Church came to his funeral, held at Gesu Parish Church in Milwaukee.

Paul Wilkes, in his October 1993 article in *Milwaukee Magazine* entitled "Saint and Scoundrel," described the people who attended the service in this way:

"There were teenage Vietnamese Dominican novices with simple wooded crucifixes around their necks and Schoenstaat nuns in starched headpieces, black Carthusian monks in coarse brown robes and liberal Jesuits in sports clothes, liberation theologians and those unwavering in their allegiance to the Vatican. Members of Milwaukee's wealthiest family stood amidst maids and janitors, Cistercian abbots, native Americans, former drug addicts, the past and the present homeless. All had come to say goodbye."

By the time of Harry John's death, at age 73, the de Rancé foundation had been terminated, with the remaining $70 million in assets being placed in a new non-profit organization, the Archdiocese of Milwaukee Supporting Fund (AMS), that continues to provide substantial grants to qualifying organizations in the diocese as this publication goes to press.

Erica John is president of the organization, with her daughter Paula John as the second member of the board and the current Archbishop of Milwaukee as the third member. Timothy John continues to publish religious calendars from the same building where his father first began the Sacred Pictures Company in 1952 and his brother Bruno John, the president of Santa Fe Communications, continues to produce films in English and Spanish for church groups across the country and the world.

NOTES

[1]Gunnar Mickelsen, "When Milwaukee Meant 'Beer' – Magic of Milwaukee's Art Led Frederick Miller to Menomonee Valley," *Milwaukee Sentinel*, section D, January 24, 1932, 6-1.

[2]C.A. Mathisson, ed, *The Miller Family History,* (Milwaukee, 1967), 9. (The Miller Brewery, sponsor of this project, hired advertising executive C. A. Mathisson to oversee it. This project was begun over a decade earlier and was worked on by serious students of history on both sides of the Atlantic Ocean. They put their notes, copies of the original documents, and writing into three-ring binders and gave copies of them to various family members while keeping some for themselves.) Andrew J. Aikens and Lewis A. Proctor, eds. *Men of Progress - Wisconsin (Milwaukee: The Evening Wisconsin Company, 1897)* 394.

[3]Mathisson, 9.
Aikens and Proctor, 394.

[4]Mathisson, 17.

[5]*One Hundred Years of Brewing: A Complete History of the Progress Made in the Art, Science, and Industry of Brewing in the World, Particularly during the 19th Century,* (Chicago: H. S. Rich and Co., Supplement to the Western Brewer, 1903), 86. Henry T. Garvey, "Master Brewer Huber Perfectionist," *Milwaukee Sentinel,* part G, April 17, 1955, 10.

[6]Mathisson, 18.

[7]Ibid, 17.

[8]Ibid., 18,19, 23.

[9]Ibid.

[10]*Sigmaringen Official Gazette,* November 12, 1849. (Included in Mathisson's Miller Family History work.)

[11]"Barley Bree. [Beer], A History of the Great Industry in which Milwaukee Leads the World," *Milwaukee Sentinel,* July 24, 1881.

[12]Mathisson, 22.

[13]Frederick J. Miller letter to his landlord, the Princely Revenue Office, June 4, 1851. (Translated copy in the Miller Brewing Company [MBCo] Archives.)

[14]Mathisson, 22.

[15]Ibid., 42.

[16]"Cholera Plague Failed to Stop Miller from Starting His Brewery in 1855," *Milwaukee Journal,* March 3, 1940.
"Fred. Miller Brewing Co." *Milwaukee Sentinel,* July 31, 1892, 7-1.

[17]Mickelsen.
"Cholera Plague Failed to Stop Miller," *Milwaukee Journal,* March 3,

1940.

George Ehret, *Twenty-Five Years of Brewing*, (New York City, 1891), 42.

[18]Mickelsen.

"Cholera Plague Failed to Stop Miller," *Milwaukee Journal*, March 3, 1940.

[19]Harry H. Anderson and Frederick I. Olson, *Milwaukee: At the Gathering of the Waters* (Milwaukee County Historical Society, 1981), 10 to 23.

[20]Anderson and Olson, 23.

[21]Thomas C. Cochran, *The Pabst Brewing Company, The History of an American Business* (New York City University Press, 1948), 27.

Ries Behling, "Bricks and Mortar," Miller High Life News Flash, February, 1955, 21, (MBCo Archives).

[22]Cochran, 3, 4.

[23]*History of Milwaukee, Wisconsin Illustrated Volume ll*, (Chicago: The Western Historical Company, A. T. Andreas, proprietor, 1881). 1458, 1459,

Milwaukee County Register of Deeds, Deed 28-7, April 30, 1849.

[24]Clara A. Miller, recorded and transcribed interview, March 17, 1949, 1, (MBCo Archives).

[25]Ralph M. Aderman, ed., "Trading Post to Metropolis: Milwaukee County's First 150 Years," (Milwaukee County Historical Society, 1987), 330, 332, and 333.

[26]Ibid.

[27]Milwaukee County Register of Deeds, mortgage 38-16, October 14, 1850.

Milwaukee County Register of Deeds, Deed 33-131, January 1, 1851.

Town of Wauwatosa Tax Records held at the Milwaukee County Historical Society.

[28]1850 U.S. Census, the City of Milwaukee and the Town of Wauwatosa (A copy of this census is kept at the Milwaukee County Historical Society.)

[29]Cochran, 31.

Wisconsin Banner, April 1, 1851.

[30]Milwaukee County Register of Deeds, deed 38-392, December 29, 1853.

Milwaukee County Register of Deeds, deed 44-441, December 31, 1853.

[31]*Milwaukee Sentinel*, May 8, 1854, 1-5, 3-1.

Milwaukee County Register of Deeds, deed 43-239, May 27, 1854.

Frederick J. Miller July, 1879 letter to his German relatives.

[32]*Milwaukee Sentinel*, May 8, 1854, 3-1.

Miller Brewery Company Time Line. (This undated document, without an author noted, was compiled, over many years, by various individuals including Jeffrey T. Waalkes in the Miller Brewing Company's communications department. The information was culled from articles, company documents, and articles from internal publications.)

[33]Milwaukee County Register of Deeds, mortgages 27-279, 27-277, November 29, 1854.

[34]Milwaukee County Register of Deeds, mortgage 30-447, July 30, 1855.

"Fred Miller, Brewer and Maltster," *Industrial History of Milw.*, E. E. Barton Publisher, Reference 7, pages 195-196, 1886. There are reports that the Millers purchased a brewery that had lain fallow for one year. The evidence does not support this story. Fred Miller may have promoted this version, so his efforts to resurrect the brewery would appear more impressive. Milwaukee County Register of Deeds, mortgage 52-520, June 11, 1856.

[35]*The Evening Wisconsin Men of Progress*, (Milwaukee, 1897), 128.

[36]Frederick J. Miller financial records written in his hand, original at the Miller Brewing Company Archives, September 25, 1855, (translated from German in February 2003).

[37]Frederick J. Miller financial records written in his hand.

[38]Ibid.

[39]Aderman, 24.

Cochran, 55.

"Barley Bree. [Beer], A History of the Great Industry in which Milwaukee Leads the World," Milwaukee Sentinel, July 24, 1881.

Frederick J. Miller financial records written in his hand.

[40]Frederick J. Miller letter written in approximately early 1886.

[41]1860 United States Census.

Cochran, 43-44.

[42]The North State Brewers' Cooperative web site, August 28, 2003, (http://www.umich.edu/~nsbc/).

Frederick Miller financial records written in his hand.

[43]Cochran, 13.

"Barley Bree. [Beer], A History of the Great Industry," Milwaukee Sentinel, July 24, 1881.

[44]Cochran, 14-15.

The North State Brewers' Cooperative web site, August 28, 2003, (http://www.umich.edu/~nsbc/).

[45]"Yeast Is Yeast, and Yet Brewer's Yeast Is Fussy," *Milwaukee Journal*, sports – market, February 5, 1933, 5-3

[46]Cochran, 16,17, 111,112.

[47]Ibid.

[48]Ibid., 18.

[49]MBCo Time Line.

[50]St. Joseph Parish records in Wauwatosa, Wisconsin.

[51]1860 U.S. census.

[52]MBCo Time Line.

Clipping from Fred Miller's scrapbook, June 15, 1861 (MBCo Ar-

The Miller Beer Barons 409

chives).

Clara A. Miller, recorded and transcribed interview, March 17, 1949, 2.

[53]MBCo Time Line.

Clipping from Fred Miller's scrapbook, June 15, 1861.

Clara A. Miller, recorded and transcribed interview, March 17, 1949, 2.

[54]*Milwaukee Sentinel,* April 27, 1857 3-1.

"Saloon Broken Into," *Milwaukee Sentinel,* February 2, 1858, 1-3.

[55]Fred Miller letter to his relatives in Germany, July 1879.

[56]St. Joseph Parish Centenary Booklet, Wauwatosa, Wisconsin, 1956.

[57]Raphael Noteware Hamilton, "The Story of Marquette University," (Milwaukee, Marquette University press, 1953)

Marquette University 1883 and 1884 College Catalogues.

Dr. Thomas Jablonsky, Professor of History at Marquette University and author of an ongoing history of that school, interview on May 20, 2004.

[58]*Milwaukee Sentinel,* March 10, 1973, 4-1.

[59]Ibid., September 20, 1873, 8-2.

[60]Joseph G. Fellner, (c 1950s) Mr. Fred Miller's German Scrap Book, 18. (The author reviewed and translated the contents of Fred Miller's scrapbook, which contained news clippings primarily in German. This particular article appeared in the mid 1870s but has no newspaper name or date.)

[61]October 22, 1855 Declaration of John P. Engelhardt's Intention to Become a U.S. citizen, original kept at the Milwaukee County Historical Society.

[62]Ibid.

[63]Andreas, 1463.

Frederick J. Miller letter to his relatives in Germany July 1879.

[64]Miller-Engelhardt Employment Contract dated October 29, 1881, (MBCo Archives).

[65]Henry Anthony Engelhardt Will and Probate Papers dated April 4, 1883 stored at the Milwaukee County Courthouse.

[66]"The Amount of Malt Beverages Made in Milw. in 1867," *Milwaukee Sentinel,* January 21,1868, 1-5.

MBCo Time Line.

Andreas, 1463.

"Brewers Protection Insurance Company," *Milwaukee Sentinel* March 17, 1869, 1-3.

"Fred Miller Brewing Company," *Milwaukee Sentinel* July 31, 1892, 7-1.

[67]Article from Frederick J. Miller's scrapbook.

[68]*Milwaukee Sentinel,* May 11, 1873, 8-2.

MBCo Time Line.

[69]*Milwaukee Sentinel,* June 12, 1875, 8-2.

Ibid., September 20, 1875, 8-2.

Newspaper article from Frederick J. Miller's scrapbook.

[70]Mortgage filed against F. Miller and Wife on October 13, 1877, Vol. 123, p. 621, # 10691, Milwaukee County Register of Deeds, located in the basement of the Milwaukee County Courthouse.

[71]Frederick J. Miller letter to his German relatives, July 1879.

[72]*Milwaukee Sentinel,* December 11, 1885, 3-5, December 12, 1885, 3-3, and January 21, 1886, 3-3.

[73]Frederick J. Miller letter to his German relatives July 1879.

(ad), *Milwaukee Sentinel,* February 26, 1882 (This advertising also ran daily in March 1882.).

MBCo Time Line.

Wayne L. Kroll, "Badger Brewers: Past and Present," (Jefferson, WI, 1976), 75.

[74]*Milwaukee Sentinel,* May 18, 1866, 1-6.

[75]*Milwaukee Sentinel,* June 7, 1867, 1-6.

[76]Frederick J. Miller letter to his German relatives, July 1879.

[77]*Milwaukee Sentinel,* May 12, 1883.

Ibid., August 2, 1884, 3-3.

[78]Fred Miller letter to his German relatives, July 1879.

Milwaukee Sentinel, February 15, 1876, 8-3.

[79]Frederick J. Miller letter to his German relatives, July 1879.

[80]*Milwaukee Sentinel,* November 19, 1880, 8-2.

"Milwaukee," *Milwaukee Sentinel,* November 20, 1880.

[81]MBCo Time Line.

[82]*Milwaukee Sentinel,* September 3, 1879.

Andreas, 1463.

Milwaukee Sentinel, January 21, 1881, 2-2.

MBCo Time Line.

[83]"Independence Day," *Milwaukee Sentinel,* July 4, 1881, 6-4.

"Fred Miller, Brewer and Maltster," *Industrial History of Milw.,* E. E. Barton Publisher, Reference 7, pages 195-196, 1886.

Milwaukee Sentinel, February 21, 1880, 8-4.

Ibid., July 12, 1880 8-1.

Ibid., October 4, 1883, 5-2.

Ibid., May 21, 1878.

Mickelsen.

[84]*Milwaukee Sentinel,* May 31, 1881, 10-4.

[85]Ibid., May 20, 1884, 3-2.

MBCo Time Line.

Fred Miller, Brewer and Maltster, Reference 7, 195-196, 1886.

Milwaukee Sentinel, April 3, 1873, 8-3.

[86]Cochran, 303-304.

[87]Wisconsin Title Service Company, Abstract of Title, Lot 22 in Block 7 in Addition Number 5, Wellauer Park, undated [c. 1970s].

[88]Frank E. Vyzralek, March 25, 1988 letter from his Great Plains

Research organization in Bismarck, North Dakota, to MBCo researcher Darlene Waterstreet.

[89]Annual Statement of the MBCo, September 1, 1884, (A typewritten copy is kept in the MBCo Archives.)

Bismarck Weekly Tribune, June 20, 1884, 3.

Ibid., July 18, 1884, 8.

Ibid., August 8, 1884, 8.

[90]Ibid., September 5, 1884, 16.

Ibid., October 10, 1884, 8.

[91]Ibid.

Ibid., May 7, 1886, 3.

[92]*Milwaukee Sentinel* October 12, 1886, 3-3.

Behling.

Schwarz, Julius J. "Continuous Improvement Features Miller Brewery," (Brewery Age, May 1, 1935.)

[93]Louis Hirsch letter, July 24, 1887.

[94]Frederick J. Miller undated letter written before just April 7, 1886.

[95]Ibid.

[96]Ibid.

[97]Milwaukee Brewing Company letters, October, 23 1886, (MBCo Archives).

Frederick J. Miller letter, November 3, 1886, (MBCo Archives).

[98]Frederick J. Miller letter, August 11, 1886, (MBCo Archives).

[99]"Fred Miller, Brewer, Dead," *Milwaukee Journal,* December 20, 1943, 1.

Mickelsen, 6-1.

[100]*Milwaukee Journal,* July 15, 1887, 1.

Ibid., August 26, 1887, 3.

Ibid., September 15, 1887, 3.

[101]Sanborn Fire Insurance Map dated July 1888, copy obtained from the MBCo Archives.

Kroll, 4.

[102]Fred J. Miller letter to Carl Miller, November 3, 1886, (John and Donna Brandt Collection in Hartford, Wisconsin).

[103]Carl A. Miller letter to Clara A. Miller December 18, 1892 (John and Donna Brandt Collection).

[104]Cochran, 273.

[105]Ibid., 276-278.

[106]Ibid., 279-282.

Letter from Frederick J. Miller to Carl Miller, November 3, 1886, (John and Donna Brandt Collection).

[107]Cochran, 279-282.

"Left as One Man: Walk-Out of the Employees in the Breweries," *Milwaukee Sentinel,* May 2, 1886, 1-7.

[108](ad), *Milwaukee Journal,* April 29, 1887, 4-3.

"To Ignore the Union," *Milwaukee Sentinel,* November 24, 1887, 3-4.

Cochran, 286-289.

[109]MBCo Time Line.

"Death of Fred Miller.," *Evening Wisconsin,* June 11, 1888, 3-1.

Cochran, 107, 109.

[110]Frederick J. Miller Last Will and Testament, February 8, 1888, (Copy at the MBCo Archives.)

[111]MBCo corporate minutes held at their headquarters, (The author personally reviewed them on August 26, 2003).

Milwaukee Sentinel, April 29, 1887, 4-6.

[112]MBCo corporate minutes.

[113]Ibid.

Frederick J. Miller Last Will and Testament.

[114]Mickelsen.

[115]*Evening Wisconsin,* June 11, 1888, 3-1.

[116]"Miller Plant Is Still Run By Family," *Milwaukee Sentinel,* April 7, 1933, 8-1.

Frederick J. Miller letter dated June 2, 1888.

[117]"Death of Fred Miller," *Evening Wisconsin,* June 11, 1888 3-1.

"Large Sums Bequeathed," *Milwaukee Sentinel,* July 8, 1888 1-1.

[118]Ibid.

[119]*Milwaukee Sentinel,* December 15, 1889 3-2.

Ibid., December 20, 1889, 3-4.

[120]J. V. Quarles, Attorney at Quarles, Spence, and Quarles, June 16, 1918, (Letter to Fred Miller Heirs, Inc. summing up their corporate history due to a tax claim by the United States Government. Author's collection).

[121]Frederick J. Miller letter in German to family and friends, June 2, 1888. (The original letter's location and translator is unknown.)

[122]MBCo corporate minutes. (The author reviewed the minutes at the corporation's headquarters on August 26, 2003.)

[123]"Fred. Miller Brewing Co." *Milwaukee Sentinel,* July 31, 1892, 7-1.

[124]Thomas C. Cochran, *The Pabst Brewing Company: The History of an American Business* (New York, New York University Press, 1948), 151-152.

[125]*Bismarck Weekly Tribune,* July 1, 1888, 1.

Ibid., September 30, 1888, 1.

Fred Miller letter to family and friends, June 2, 1888.

[126]Frank E. Vyzralek, *Dakota Brewed: A History of the Brewing Industry in North Dakota, 1868-1965,* 1986 (Unpublished manuscript without page numbers authored by North Dakota historian Frank E. Vyzralek.)

[127]Vyzralek.

[128]Frank E. Vyzralek, March 25, 1988 letter from his Great Plains Research organization to MBCo researcher Darlene Waterstreet.

Vyzralek, *Dakota Brewed.*

Bismarck Daily Tribune, June 8, 1889, 3.

[129]Ibid., October 4, 1889, 3.

[130]Ibid.

[131]Miller Brewing Company Time Line. (This undated document, without an author noted, was compiled, over many years, by various individuals including Jeffrey T. Waalkes in Miller Brewing Company's communications department. The information was gleaned from articles, company documents, and articles from internal publications.)

Ries Behling, "Bricks and Mortar," *Miller High Life News Flash*, February 1955, 21, (MBCo Archives).

[132]*1889 Milwaukee Sentinel Illustrated Annual Review*, advertisement, 82.

"New Enterprises at Tomahawk," *Milwaukee Sentinel*, March 14, 1889, 8-1.

[133]"Fred Miller Brewing Co.," *Milwaukee Sentinel*, July 31, 1892, 7-1. MBCo Time Line.

[134]"Fred Miller Brewing Co.," *Milwaukee Sentinel*, July 31, 1892, 7-1. MBCo Time Line.

"Miller Plant Is Still Run By Family," *Milwaukee Sentinel*, April 7, 1933, 8-1.

[135]MBCo Time Line.

Behling.

Tice Nichols, MBCo historian, The author gleaned this information from Nichol's presentation to MBCo employees on July 22, 2003.

[136]Behling.

Milwaukee Sentinel, February 28, 1890, 3-3.

MBCo Time Line.

[137]MBCo Time Line.

Behling.

[138]Edward H. Vogel, Jr. et al. *The Practical Brewer: A Manual for the Brewing Industry*, (St. Louis, Master Brewers Association of America, 1946), 41.

[139]Ibid., 30, 62.

[140]Ibid., 112.

[141]"Miller Home to Be Palatial," *Milwaukee Sentinel*, October 6, 1901, 4-2.

[142]"Built in 1901 for $100,000, Miller Mansion Being Razed," *Milwaukee Journal*, home section, April 3, 1966, 4-3.

[143]Charles "Chuck" Miller Bransfield, (Carl Miller's grandson), Telephonic interview on October 24, 2000.

[144]Carl A. Miller correspondence to his then girlfriend Clara A. Miller. Information taken from many letters. (John and Donna Brandt Collection in Hartford, Wisconsin.)

[145]Letter from Carl Miller to Clara Miller, September 21, 1889, # 107. (John and Donna Brandt Collection.)

[146]Letter from Carl Miller to Clara Miller, October 31, 1889, # 48. (John and Donna Brandt Collection.)

[147]"Carl A. Miller Funeral Set For Tomorrow," paper unknown, March 1, 1949.

Letter from Carl Miller to Clara Miller, December 10, 1889, # 20. (John and Donna Brandt Collection.)

[148]"Miller Brewing Co. President Is Colorful Figure," *Milwaukee Journal,* July 19, 1949, special advertising supplement, 2.

Robert DuFour, "All-American for God," *The Reign of the Sacred Heart,* May 1957, 5.

[149]Clara Miller 1958 U.S. Estate Tax Return, (MBCo Archives).

[150]"There were Many Fires," *Milwaukee Sentinel,* July 5, 1891.

MBCo Time Line.

[151]"Fred. Miller Brewing Co.," *Milwaukee Sentinel,* July 31, 1892, 7-1.

MBCo Time Line.

MBCo corporate minutes.

[152]Ibid.

[153]*Milwaukee Sentinel,* February 28, 1890, 3-3.

MBCo Time Line.

[154]"Fred. Miller Brewing Co.," *Milwaukee Sentinel,* July 31, 1892, 7-1.

"The Book of Milwaukee," (The Evening Wisconsin Company, Milwaukee, 1901), 109.

Miller, Lisette, letter to Commissioner of Internal Revenue, June 24, 1920. (MBCo Archives.)

[155]"Fred. Miller Brewing Co.," *Milwaukee Sentinel,* July 31, 1892, 7-1.

"The Book of Milwaukee."

[156]MBCo Time Line.

Claire Miller McCahey, "The Miller Family and their Brewery: A Granddaughter Remembers," (Kenosha, WI, 1970s) 37. (MBCo Archives.) (Claire McCahey was Frederick and Lisette Miller's third oldest grandchild and knew her grandmother well. Professor John Neuenschawander, a history teacher from Carthage College, created this unpublished manuscript from four tape-recorded interviews with the subject and notes from Mrs. McCahey's son, James, who interviewed his mother several times.) (MBCo historian Tice Nichols has researched this matter and had no success finding a cigar company in New Orleans with the High Life name or brand.)

[157]Advertising, *Milwaukee Daily Gazette,* May 13, 1913, 3.

[158]MBCo Time Line.

[159]Tice Nichols, MBCo historian, as told to the author on September 24, 2003.

Milwaukee Sentinel insert, July 20, 1949.

MBCo four-page "Interesting Facts" pamphlet, March 10, 1941. (MBCo archives).

[160]MBCo Communications Department, Corporate Affairs Division, (Fall 1991), 8.

[161]Gunnar Mickelsen, "When Milwaukee Meant 'Beer' – Magic of Milwaukee's Art Led Frederick Miller to Menomonee Valley," *Milwaukee*

Sentinel, section D, January 24, 1932, 6-1.

[162]MBCo Time Line.

MBCo four-page "Interesting Facts" pamphlet.

[163]*The Commercial History of Wisconsin,* Miller Brewing Company history, Adams & Thompson Publishers, 1910.

[164]Cochran, 123.

Carl H. Miller, *Breweries of Cleveland,* Schnitzelbank Press, Cleveland, 1998.

[165]Wayne L. Kroll, *Badger Brewers: Past and Present,* (Jefferson, WI, 1976), 1-7.

[166]Kroll, 1-6.

[167]"Miller Brewing Company," *Milwaukee Journal,* February 17, 1906.

The Commercial History of Wisconsin.

[168]John F. Savage, MBCo Inter-Office Correspondence, August 3, 1949, 3.

[169]MBCo Time Line.

[170]MBCo Profit and Loss statements kept in Elise John's 1937 Federal Income Tax Return, (Author's collection.)

[171]"Miller Brewing Company to Put up New Building," *Milwaukee Journal,* May 24, 1914 12-5.

[172]"Does Slavery Exist in Milwaukee?" *Milwaukee Sentinel,* August 7, 1916 7-8.

[173]Charles "Chuck" Bransfield interview, 2002.

[174]MBCo Head Ledger, September 1, 1887 to September 1, 1892, ice account, (MBCo archives.)

[175]*Milwaukee Journal,* July 15, 1945.

"The Book of Milwaukee," 109.

[176]Original documents for the Power of Attorney and Codicil are at the MBCo Archives.

[177]Cochran, 302-324.

[178]Ibid.

[179]*The Columbia Encyclopedia,* Sixth Edition, Copyright © 2002 Columbia University Press (Obtained from the internet).

Cochran.

[180]Ibid.

[181]Ibid.

[182]"Fred. Miller Brewing Co.," *Milwaukee Sentinel,* July 31, 1892, 7-1.

[183]Ibid.

[184]Cochran.

[185]Ralph M. Alderman, ed. *Trading Post to Metropolis: Milwaukee County's First 150 Years* (Milwaukee County Historical Society, 1987), 262.

[186]"Big Saengerfest to Begin Today," *Milwaukee Sentinel,* July 28, 1904, 1-5.

John Gurda, *The Making of Milwaukee,* (The Milwaukee County Historical Society, 1999), 141.

[187]Gurda, 237.

[188]Cochran.

Telephone interview with Charles "Chuck" Bransfield, May 30, 2000.

[189]*Milwaukee Journal,* June 7, 1916.

[190]Copy of letter found at the *Milwaukee Journal Sentinel* Archives, December 15, 1916.

[191]Oliver Carlson, *Brisbane: A Candid Biography,* (New York: Stackpole Sons, 1937) 219.

[192]"Tell Why Beer Makers Bought Newspapers," *Milwaukee Journal,* September 20, 1918, 1-1.

[193]"Miller Says Loan Was Given to Brisbane to Save Brewing Trade," *Evening Wisconsin,* September 20, 1918, 1-2.

[194]"Tell Why Beer Makers Bought Newspapers," *Milwaukee Journal,* September 20, 1918, 1-1.1

"Miller Says Loan Was Given to Brisbane to Save Brewing Trade," *Evening Wisconsin,* September 20, 1918, 1-2.

[195]Ibid.

[196]Mickelsen.

"Miller Plant Is Still Run By Family," Milwaukee Sentinel, April 7, 1933, 8-1.

"Cholera Plague Failed to Stop Miller From Starting His Brewery in 1855," Milwaukee Journal, March 3, 1940.

[197]Cochran.

[198]John Gurda, The Making of Milwaukee, (Milwaukee County Historical Society, 1999), 238.

[199]Ibid., 238-239.

"History of Alcohol Prohibition," National Commission on Marihuana and Drug Abuse, http://www.druglibrary.org./schaffer/LIBRARY/studies/nc/nc2a.htm, (This section of the Commission's report is based in large part on a paper prepared by Jane Lang McGrew, an attorney from Washington, D.C.), September 17, 2003.

[200]Gurda

Cocktail, Speakeasy, information garnered from the internet at http://hotwired.wired.com/cocktail/archive/links/nc/_speakeasy.html, September 16, 2003.

[201]Inventory of Lisette Miller's estate, July 15, 1921, (author's collection).

Videotape of tour of Clara and Carl Miller's Newberry home in the early 1990s, Adele Miller O'Shaughnessy, Fred C. Miller's wife, remembered the actual winemaking apparatus. Mark D. Kelly, Adele's grand nephew recorded the tape.

Information told to author by James Guardalabene, the Monte Carlo's owner's grandson, May 2002.

Information told to Erica John, Harry John's daughter-in-law, by her husband Harry John, Jr. in the 1960s.

202Consumer Price Index 1913-2003, Federal Reserve Bank of Minneapolis, Accessed at http://minneapolisfed.org/research/data/us/calc/hist1913.cfm on February 20, 2003.

Lisette Miller municipal, state, and federal 1913-1920 income tax returns, (MBCo archives.)

203Invoices from Lisette Miller's doctors, 1920 and 1921, (author's collection).

Claire Miller McCahey, "The Miller Family and their Brewery: A Granddaughter Remembers," (Kenosha, WI, 1970s) 37. (Claire Miller McCahey was Frederick and Lisette Miller's third oldest grandchild and knew her grandmother well. Professor John Neuenschawander, a history teacher from Carthage College, created this unpublished manuscript from four tape-recorded interviews with the subject and notes from Mrs. McCahey's son, James, who interviewed his mother several times.)

Invoice from the John Zimmermann Company, who manufactured Lisette Miller's headstone, October 23, 1920, (author's collection).

204"Children Get Bulk of Miller Estate; Value Is $450,000," *Milwaukee Journal,* August 19, 1920, local 1-2.

Lisette Miller codicil to her Will, executed on December 29, 1919. (MBCo Archives).

205"Children Get Bulk of Miller Estate; Value Is $450,000."

Lisette Miller codicil to her Will.

Lisette Miller Estate correspondence to Sophia Meyer Estate, August 1, 1921.

206Correspondence from Charles S. Rogers of the Internal Revenue Service of the Treasury Department to Fred Miller Heirs, Inc., May 20, 1924, (author's collection).

207MBCo payroll records.

208Correspondence from Charles S. Rogers of the Internal Revenue Service of the Treasury Department to Fred Miller Heirs, Inc., May 20, 1924.

1926 Fred Miller Heirs, Inc. Federal, State, and Municipal tax returns, (author's collection).

1925 Fred Miller Heirs, Inc. Wisconsin Corporate Income Tax Return.

Papers of Ernest Miller's Estate, (kept in the Milw. County Court House Register of Deeds Office.)

209Telephone interview with Milwaukee historian Dr. Frederick I. Olson on August 8, 2003 by the author. (Dr. Olson was an expert in Milwaukee history. He was the executive director of the Milwaukee Humanities Program and professor of history at the University of Wisconsin in Milwaukee. Also, he served as the acting dean of its college of Letters and Science and chairman of the Department of History.)

Charles S. Rogers of the Internal Revenue Service of the Treasury Department correspondence to Fred Miller Heirs, Inc., May 20, 1924.

The Fred Miller Heirs, Inc. Report on Distribution of Assets as of November 30, 1926, (It was prepared by the Price, Waterhouse & Company Accounting Firm, author's collection.)

[210]Mimeographed and handwritten September 15, 1920 notes with A. L. Kleinboehl, a high-ranking MBCo employee's initials after the words "Miller Brewing Company." (author's collection).

[211]Report from the Oriental Realty Corporation listing the shareholders of record as of March 13, 1950.

"Show Building Will Be Sold, Miller Realty Firm to Liquidate Big Real Estate Holdings," Article on approximately February 19, 1955, newspaper unknown, (author's clipping file).

[212]MBCo corporate minutes held at its headquarters, special stockholders' meeting on June 28, 1897. (The author reviewed them on August 26, 2003.)

[213]Thomas C. Cochran, The Pabst Brewing Company, The History of an American Business (New York, New York University Press, 1948), 196.

[214]Ibid., 198.

[215]Carl A. Schmitt, general manager, corporate secretary, and treasury of Oriental Realty, letter to the corporation's shareholders on December 20, 1955, (MBCo Archives).

"Show Building Will Be Sold, Miller Realty Firm to Liquidate Big Real Estate Holdings," Article on approximately February 19, 1955, newspaper unknown, (author's clipping file).

[216]MBCo corporate minutes held at its headquarters, special stockholders' meeting on January 26, 1898.

MBCo corporate minutes, special stockholders' meetings on April 4, 1905 and May 5, 1909.

[217]Elise K. John 1927 Federal Income Tax Return (author's collection).

[218]Ries Behling, "Prohibition 1920-1933: Hundreds of Miller Employees Kept Brewing Kettles Humming as Production Switched from Suds to Soda," *Miller High Life News Flash,* Milw., April 1, 1955, 19-20.

Milo Guarantee from the Milo Beverage Company, which was a subsidiary of the Miller Brewing Company, E. Rahtjen was the assistant secretary, March 26, 1917.

[219]Behling.

[220]Ibid.

[221]Ibid.

MBCo Time Line.

[222]Cochran, 336.

Gurda, 238.

[223]Behling.

Leonard Jurgensen, telephone interview on July 28, 2003. (Mr. Jurgenson is a long-time expert on historical Milwaukee breweries and is an accomplished Jos. Schlitz Brewing Company memorabilia collector.)

[224]Behling.

MBCo corporate minutes.

[225]Ibid.

Behling.

MBCo Time Line.

[226]Behling.

MBCo Time Line.

[227]Behling.

MBCo Time Line.

MBCo corporate minutes held at its headquarters, special stockholders' meeting on January 26, 1898.

Elise K. John 1927 Federal Income Tax Return. (Oscar Treichler was arguing for lower taxes on Elise's income and mailed copies of MBC financial records to the Internal Revenue Service. The author had access to only partial financial records from 1908 until 1927.)

[228]Ernest Miller letter to Carl Miller, September, 1925. (author's collection.)

[229]Ibid.

[230]Ibid.

[231]"Ernest Miller, Brewer, Dies," Milwaukee Sentinel, September 22, 1925, 1-3.

[232]Ernest G. Miller 1913 to 1924 municipal, state, and federal income tax returns, (MBCo archives.)

[233]"Ernest Miller, Brewer, Dies," Milwaukee Journal, local, September 22, 1925, 17-2.

[234]"School for Colored Children Dedicated, E. G. Miller Honored," *Catholic Herald*, Sept. 10, 1925, 2-6.

[235]Ibid.

[236]"Ernest Miller, Brewer, Dies," Milwaukee Sentinel, September 22, 1925, 1-3.

[237]Ernest G. Miller Last Will and Testament, September 8, 1924, (The Original is kept at the Office of Probate Records at the Milwaukee County Court House.)

[238]Ibid.

Charles "Chuck" Bransfield, Clara Miller's grandson's oral interview.

[239]Ernest G. Miller Estate papers, (The Originals are kept at the Office of Probate Records at the Milwaukee County Court House.)

"Charity Gets $800,500 Gift – Miller's Will Includes $500,000 Bequest for St. Francis," *Milwaukee Journal*, October 24, 1925, 1-3.

"Miller Estate Tax $374,000 – Brewer Aids Catholic Charities Out of 4 Million Total," *Milwaukee Journal*, September 2, 1927, 1-4.

[240]MBCo corporate minutes held at its headquarters, special stockholders' meeting on November 28, 1925.

[241]Ibid.

[242]Ibid.

[243]Ibid.

[244]Ibid.

[245]Ibid.

[246]MBCo corporate minutes held at its headquarters, special stockholders' meeting on January 28, 1926.

[247]MBCo corporate minutes.

[248]Ibid.

[249]Behling.

MBCo Time Line.

MBCo corporate minutes held at its headquarters, special stockholders' meeting on January 26, 1898.

[250]Copy of letter from Frederick A. "Fritz" Miller to Clara Miller, June 24, 1930.

[251]"Fred Miller, Chairman of Brewery, Dies," *Milwaukee Sentinel,* December 20, 1943, 1.

[252]Gunnar Mickelsen, When Milwaukee Meant 'Beer' – Magic of Milwaukee's Art Led Frederick Miller to Menomonee Valley," *Milwaukee Sentinel,* section D, January 24, 1932, 6-1.

Frederick A. Miller's financial account for the year 1917. (MBCo archives.)

[253]Frederick A. Miller's 1918 U.S. Tax Return, (author's collection.)

Frederick A. Miller's personal 1919 balance sheet compiled by his bookkeeper, (author's collection.)

[254]Ibid.

[255]Copy of Frederick A. Miller's letter to Clara Miller, June 24, 1930.

[256]Wright City of Milwaukee Directories kept at the Milwaukee County Historical Society.

[257]1930 U.S. Census kept at the Milwaukee County Historical Society.

[258]City of Milwaukee Directories, 1896-1928.

[259]1919 balance sheet of Emil P. Miller prepared by his bookkeeper, (author's collection).

Letter to Louis Quarles c/o Line, Spooner & Quarels, February 3, 1930, (MBCo archives).

[260]Series of notes from Ernest Miller to his siblings regarding Lisette Miller's Will's proceeds, September 29, 1921.

[261]"Emil Miller's Estate Fights $37,000 Claims – Refuses to Pay Associates on Pleasure Trips," *Milwaukee Sentinel,* October 17, 1935, 1-1.

"Night Life Costs Came to $100,000 a Year," *Milwaukee Journal,* October 16, 1935, 1-6.

[262]Ibid.

[263]"Emil Miller's Estate Fights $37,000 Claims – Refuses to Pay Associates on Pleasure Trips," *Milwaukee Sentinel,* October 17, 1935, 1-1.

[264]Emil Miller's financial papers, (author's collection.)

"Nigh Life Costs Came to $100,000 a Year," *Milwaukee Journal,* October 16, 1935, 1-6.

[265]"Maker of 'High Life' Tries It in Chicago," *Wisconsin News,* December 12, 1928 1-1.

"Maker of 'High Life' Brew Has Three Days of It," *Chicago Tribune,* December 12, 1928.

"Police Put Mr. Miller and Party in Drydock," *Milwaukee Journal,* December 12, 1928.

[266]Ibid.

[267]"Maker of 'High Life' Brew Has Three Days of It", *Chicago Tribune,* December 12, 1928.

[268]Emil Miller's papers collected by his personal assistant, which are in the author's possession.

[269]Papers from Emil Miller's personal assistant, which are in the author's possession.

[270]Ibid.

[271]George E. Hargrave, copy of letter to Oscar Treichler, March 12, 1929. (MBCo archives.)

[272]Papers from Emil's personal assistant, (author's collection.)

[273]*Milwaukee Journal,* obituary of Charles H. John, June 18, 1950.

[274]Harry G. John Sr. and Elise John's municipal, state, and federal income tax returns from 1913-1933. (These returns, in the author's possession, often have substantial supporting documents as their bookkeeper and lawyer skirmished with tax officials.)

Ernest Miller 1913 to 1924 municipal, State, and federal tax returns, (MBCo archives.)

[275]Harry G. John, Sr. and Elise John's municipal, state, and federal income tax returns from 1913-1933, & 1941, (author's collection).

.[276]Ibid.

Elise John 1919 balance sheet compiled by her bookkeeper, (author's collection.)

[277]Harry and Elise John's municipal, state, and federal income tax returns from 1913-1933.

[278]Consumer Price Index 1913-2003, Federal Reserve Bank of Minneapolis, Accessed at http://minneapolisfed.org/research/data/us/calc/hist1913.cfm on February 20, 2003.

[279]Harry and Elise John's municipal, state, and federal income tax returns from 1913-1933.

[280]Consumer Price Index 1913-2003, Federal Reserve Bank of Minneapolis.

[281]Harry and Elise John's municipal, state, and federal income tax returns from 1913-1933.

[282]Ibid.

[283]Consumer Price Index 1913-2003, Federal Reserve Bank of Minneapolis.

[284]Harry and Elise John's municipal, state, and federal income tax returns from 1913-1933.

[285]Oliver P. Kuechle, "Notre Dame's Milwaukee Captain Put Himself in Shape Up North," *Milwaukee Journal,* October 4, 1928, 6-3.

[286]Ibid.

[287]"Capt. Miller Rookie Again," *Milwaukee Journal,* June 16, 1929, 6-1.

[288]1930 United States Census, Milwaukee County Historical Society.

[289]Oscar Treichler letter to Clara Miller, June 10, 1930, (author's collection).

[290]Papers from Emil Miller's personal assistant, (author's collection).

Oscar Treichler letter to Clara Miller, June 10, 1930, (author's collection).

[291]Frederick A. Miller letter to Emil Miller, May 31, 1930, (author's collection).

[292]Oscar Treichler letter to Clara Miller, June 10, 1930, (author's collection).

[293]Frederick A. Miller letter to Emil Miller, undated, c June 1930, (author's collection).

[294]Ibid., June 13, 1930.

[295]Emil Miller letter to Frederick A. Miller, June 14, 1930, (author's collection).

[296]Emil Miller letter to Frederick A. Miller and Elise John, July 9, 1930, (author's collection).

Oscar Treichler, copy of a sketchy time line of the house and content disposition from 1927 to 1935, (author's collection).

Frederick A. Miller letter to his family and friends, June 2, 1888, nine days before his death, (MBCo Archives).

[297]Frederick A. Miller letter to Clara Miller, June 24, 1930, (author's collection).

[298]Cochran, 361, 364, 365.

[299]MBCo Time Line.

Behling.

Cochran, 352.

[300]Claire Miller McCahey, "The Miller Family and Their Brewery, A Granddaughter Remembers", 39. (This document was derived from a series of interviews conducted by Professor John Neuenschwander of Wisconsin's Carthage College during the 1970s.)

[301]Robert W. Wells, *Yesterday's Milwaukee,* (Miami, E. A. Seemann Publishing, 1976), 120.

John Gurda, *The Making of Milwaukee,* (Milwaukee County Historical Society, 1999), 297.

Julius J. Schwarz, "Continuous Improvement Features Miller Brewery," *Brewery Age,* May 1, 1935.

"Brewers Face Higher Taxes," *Milwaukee Journal,* section II, August 20, 1933, 6-6.

[302]"Miller Plant Is Still Run By Family," *Milwaukee Sentinel,* April 7, 1933, 8-1.

[303]"Yeast Is Yeast, and Yet Brewer's Yeast Is Fussy," *Milwaukee Journal,* sports/market section, February 5, 1933, 5-3.

Schwarz.

[304]"Miller Plant Is Still Run By Family," *Milwaukee Sentinel,* April 7, 1933, 8-1.

[305]Schwarz.

Edward H. Vogel, Jr. et al. *The Practical Brewer: A Manual for the Brewing Industry,* (St. Louis, Master Brewers Association of America, 1946), 62.

[306]Ibid.

[307]Schwarz.

[308]Ibid.

David S. Ryder, Ph.D., M.I.Biol., C.Biol., F.I. Brew, Miller Brewing Company's brewmaster, personal interview in November 2003.

[309]Schwarz.

[310]Ibid.

[311]Dr. William J. Murphy report on Emil Miller's mental state, April 24, 1935, (MBCo Archives).

[312]"Miller Writes More Checks," *Milwaukee Journal,* November 14, 1933.

[313]Ibid.

"Emil Miller Drops his Check Suit," *Milwaukee Journal,* November 15, 1933.

[314]"Emil Miller's Estate Fights $37,000 Claims," *Milwaukee Sentinel,* 2nd section, October 17, 1935, 1-1.

[315]"E.P. Miller's Estate Now Over 4 Million," *Milwaukee Sentinel,* 2nd section, November 22, 1935, 1-3.

[316]"Fix $604,626 Tax on Miller Estate," *Milwaukee Journal,* local, February 19, 1937, 1-5.

[317]"Miller Estate Three Million," *Milwaukee Journal,* December 3, 1934, 1-7.

"$500,000 Tax Tenders for E. Miller Estate," *Milwaukee Journal,* November 5, 1935.

"Miller's Estate Four Millions," *Milwaukee Journal,* section 2, November 22, 1935, 1-3.

"$186,438 Refunded to Estate of Miller," *Milwaukee Journal,* December 26, 1942, 14-2.

[318]"Emil P. Miller Estate Fights $65,000 Claims," *Milwaukee Journal,* final edition, August 9, 1935, 1-6.

[319]"Demand Jury in Miller Case," *Milwaukee Journal,* local news, August 18, 1935, 1-7.

"Night Life Costs Came to $100,000 a Year," *Milwaukee Journal,* October 16, 1935, 1-6.

[320]Frederick M. Bransfield, (Marguerite Miller Bransfield's son) telephone interview with the author on January 20, 2004.

[321]Elizabeth Blommer and Marguerite Saule, (Charlotte Miller's children) telephonic and personal interviews done in 2002 and 2003.

[322]Ibid.

[323]Ibid.

Gunnar Mickelsen, "When Milwaukee Meant 'Beer' – Magic of Milwaukee's Art Led Frederick Miller to Menomonee Valley," *Milwaukee Sentinel*, section D, January 24, 1932, 6-1.

[324]Schwarz.

Miller Brewery Company Time Line. (This undated document, without an author noted, was compiled, over many years, by various individuals including Jeffrey T. Waalkes in the MBCo communications department. The information was culled from articles, company documents, and articles from internal publications.)

[325]Miller Brewing Co. Will Add Can Line," *Milwaukee Journal*, section 2, February 2, 1936, 7-7.

Herb A. and Helen I. Haydock, *The World of Beer Memorabilia*, (Collector Books, Paducah, KY, 1997), 170.

[326]"New Buildings Are Scheduled," *Milwaukee Journal*, October 4, 1936.

[327]MBCo Minutes.

[328]Ibid.

[329]"Tax is Upheld on 1937 Gifts," *Milwaukee Journal*, local, April 13, 1941, 1-5.

[330]Charles Bransfield telephonic interview with the author on November 20, 2003.

[331]"Tax Is Upheld on 1937 Gifts," *Milwaukee Journal*, local, April 13, 1941, 1-5.

Clara A. Miller 1958 U.S. Estate Tax Return.

[332]MBCo listing of presidents. (MBCo. corporate records.)

[333]MBCo corporate records and minutes.

[334]"Tell Brewery Opposition to AFL," *Wisconsin News*, August 2, 1937, 8-1.

"Seek to Link Union to Firm," *Milwaukee Journal*, local, August 2, 1937, 1-4.

[335]"Tell Brewery Opposition to AFL," *Wisconsin News*, August 2, 1937, 8-1.

"Seek to Link Union to Firm," *Milwaukee Journal*, local, August 2, 1937, 1-4.

[336]"Tell Brewery Opposition to AFL," *Wisconsin News*, August 2, 1937, 8-1.

"Seek to Link Union to Firm," *Milwaukee Journal*, local, August 2, 1937, 1-4.

[337]Elise K. John Balance Sheet January 1, 1934, (author's personal collection).

[338]Elise K. John 1934 Federal and State Tax Returns, (author's personal collection).

[339]Harry G. John, Jr. story to the author, c. 1976.

[340]Elise K. John 1934 Federal and State Tax Returns, (author's personal

collection).

[341]Elise K. John 1934 Gift Tax Return, (author's personal collection).

Elise K. John Expenses Paid 1926-1943, (author's personal collection).

[342]Armin C. Frank correspondence in 1935 to Harry G. John, Sr, (author's personal collection).

Elise K. John letter to the Internal Revenue Service, October 31, 1949, (author's personal collection).

[343]Elise K. John letter to Treichler, Oscar F., August 31, 1936, (author's personal collection).

[344]Elise K. John 1934 Gift Tax Return, (author's personal collection).

Elise K. John Expenses Paid 1926-1943, (author's personal collection).

[345]Joe Navarro, "Mulberger's Vision Paved the Way For Today's Electronics' Giants," *Colorado Springs Gazette Telegraph,* section E, February 11, 1979.

[346]Frances Flower, "Lorraine John to Be Bride of H. Mulberger, Jr.," *Chicago Daily Tribune,* December 26, 1935.

[347]Elise K. John, Expenses Paid 1926-1943, (author's personal collection).

[348]Elise K. John, Expenses Paid 1926-1943, (author's personal collection).

[349]Elise K. John, 1942 Wisconsin Gift Tax Report, (author's personal collection).

[350]"Milwaukee Aviator Uninjured in Crash," *Milwaukee Sentinel,* final edition, October 10, 1935, 1-5.

"Three on Lake Saved by Plane," *Milwaukee Journal,* May 7, 1939, 1-7.

[351]Harry G. John Family Trust, December 30, 1937, (author's personal collection).

[352]Harry G. John, Jr. General Trust, December 30, 1937, (author's personal collection).

[353]Elise K. John, 1938 Wisconsin Gift Tax Return, (author's personal collection).

Elise K. John, 1941 Wisconsin Income Tax Return, (author's personal collection).

[354]Elise K. John, Expenses Paid, 1926-1934, (author's personal collection).

[355]Ibid.

[356]Harry G. John, Jr. General Trust 1940 and 1941 Balance Sheets, (author's personal collection).

Elise K. John, Expenses Paid, 1926-1934, (author's personal collection).

Harry G. John, Jr. Trust 1942 Balance Sheet, (author's personal collection).

[357]James Ewens & Erica P. John, *The Story of de Rancé, Inc.,* (unpublished) chapt. 2, 2004, 9.

[358]Ewens, 14.

[359]Harry G. John, John, Jr., series of letters to Mr. B.H. Protzmann and the Equitable Life Insurance Society from March 20 - April 9, 1945, (author's personal collection).

Rev. Albert J. Beston, O.C.S.O., letter to B.H. Protzmann, April 17, 1945, (author's personal collection).

[360]B.H. Protzmann, office memorandum to himself, April 19, 1945, (author's personal collection).

[361]Ibid.

[362]B.H. Protzmann, letter to the Equitable Life Insurance Society, April 20, 1945, (author's personal collection).

[363]Assets Owned by Harry G. John, Jr., Direct as of March 1, 1946, (author's personal collection).

[364]Rev. John A. Devers, C.S.C., correspondence to Harry G. John, Jr. May 4, 1946, (author's personal collection).

[365]Elise K. John, 1941 Auditor's Report compiled by the CPA firm of John G. Conley & Company, November 4, 1947, (author's personal collection).

[366]Elise K. John December 31, 1945 Auditor's Report compiled by the CPA firm of John G. Conley & Company, October 27, 1947, (author's personal collection).

[367]"Fire in Beer Storehouse Draws a Big Audience," *Milwaukee Journal*, April 10, 1938, 1-2.

[368]Ibid.

[369]"Fire Rages in Miller Brewery," *Milwaukee Journal*, final edition, April 9, 1938, 1-1.

[370]"Cholera Plague Failed to Stop Miller From Starting His Brewery in 1855," *Milwaukee Journal*, March 3, 1940.

"5,000 Beer Cases Burned—Oh, Yes, They Were Empty," *Milwaukee Journal*, June 30, 1940, 1-3.

[371]"Miller Brewing Firm Denies State Charges," *Milwaukee Journal*, section II, January 8, 1939, 8-4.

"'Kept Tavern' Cases Thrown Out by Neelen," *Milwaukee Journal*, section M, April 12, 1939, 1-1.

[372]"Nation-Wide Plan for Miller's Beer," *Milwaukee Journal*, section L, March 16, 1939, 13-2.

MBCo Time Line.

[373]Four-page MBCo pamphlet describing some Interesting Facts, March 10, 1941. (MBCo archives)

[374]"Miller Brewing Co. Plans Big Building," *Milwaukee Journal*, section L, October 12, 1945, 15-3.

[375]MBCo minutes.

[376]MBCo minutes.

[377]"End Marriage of Mulbergers," *Milwaukee Journal*, local, January 9, 1947, 1-1.

[378]Newspaper clippings from Frederick McCahey, (Claire Miller

McCahey's son.)

[379]*Chicago Tribune*, September 14, 1945.

[380]Newspaper clippings from Frederick McCahey, *Chicago Tribune*, September 14, 1945.

Charles "Chuck" Bransfield, telephone interview with the author in 2003.

[381]Charles Bransfield telegram from Western Union, March 7, 1945. (This telegram was written by Lerch Provost Marshal General, which included Bransfield's words.)

[382]Frederick McCahey news clippings.

[383]MBCo Time Line.

MBCo minutes.

[384]"Fred Miller, Brewer, Dead," *Milwaukee Journal*, December 20, 1943, 1.

[385]"Miller Estate Is $7,151,527," *Milwaukee Journal*, local, March 13, 1945, 3-5.

"Fred Miller Estate Placed at $6,905,749," *Milwaukee Journal*, final edition, April 13, 1945, 1-4.

[386]Frederick A. Miller, Last Will and Testament, December 30, 1938, 1, 2, (author's personal collection).

[387]"Gift Is $25,000 and Tax Stands," *Milwaukee Journal*, November 16, 1941, 10-5.

[388]Harry G. John, Jr., Last Will and Testament, December 27, 1943, (author's personal collection).

Fred A. Miller Last Will and Testament.

Harry G. John, Jr. Testamentary Trust 1944 Fiduciary Income Tax Return, (author's personal collection).

[389]Harry G. John, Jr. discussion with the author c. 1974.

[390]MBCo minutes.

[391]Ibid.

[392]Photo and caption, *Milwaukee Journal*, section II, March 17, 1946, 3.

"Miller Brewing Expansion Means Gain in Output, Staff and Property," August 24, 1947, newspaper unknown, (author's clipping file).

[393]MBCo minutes.

[394]Ibid.

[395]Ibid

[396]MBCo. April 30, 1946 Financial Statement, Statement of Profit and Loss., (author's personal collection).

[397]MBCo. minutes.

[398]MBCo. Financial Statement, December 31, 1946, (author's personal collection).

[399]Circuit court complaint of Harry G. John, Jr., Plaintiff, versus Elise K. John, and Lorraine John Mulberger, and Norman R. Klug, and Michael T. Stoiber, and Miller Brewing Company, a corporation, Defendants, January 26, 1948, (author's personal collection).

[400]John F. Savage, (John Savage worked at the MBCo from 1946 until the 1972. At first he was MBCo in-house attorney and eventually became the corporate vice-president) personal interview with the author in 2003.

Thomas Cannon, (Tom Cannon was the lead attorney of de Rancé, Inc. during a extensive court battle in which Erica P. John and Donald A. Gallagher had Harry G. John, Jr. removed as trustee and director of the corporation.) The information came from a telephonic interview with the author on January 26, 2004. Tom suggested that Lorraine likely was the impetus behind her father's inclusion as a brewery director.

[401]MBCo minutes.

[402]Ibid.

[403]Ibid.

[404]Ibid.

[405]"Employees Given Party by Miller Brewing Co.," *Milwaukee Journal,* August 3, 1947, local, 1-4.

[406]Charles Bransfield telephonic interview with the author in 2003.

[407]MBCo minutes.

[408]Harry G. John, Jr. 1946 Gift Tax Return Data, (author's personal collection).

[409]B.H. Protzmann letter to Harry G. John, Jr., September 9, 1946, (author's personal collection).

[410]Elise K. John telephone conversation with J. Peter Grace of the W.R. Grace Corporation, August 7, 1946, (author's personal collection).

[411]Ibid.

[412]Harry G. John, Jr., general letter to the Harry G. John, Jr. General Trust trustees explaining his motivation for creating de Rancé, Inc., December 27, 1954, (author's personal collection).

[413]James Ewens & Erica P. John, *The Story of the de Rancé foundation,* (unpublished) chapter 2, 2004, 9.

Dorothy Lechtenberg, (a sister of the Wittig brothers), telephonic interview with the author on April 3, 2004.

Paul Wilkes, "Saint and Scoundrel," *Milwaukee Magazine,* October 1993, 33.

[414]Richard H. Teschner, attorney at Line, Spooner & Quarles letter to de Rancé, Inc., June 4, 1952, (author's personal collection).

[415]*South Bend Tribune,* South Bend, Indiana, September 9, 1946.

MBCo minutes.

[416]Elise K. John December 31, 1946 Auditor's Report compiled by the CPA firm of John G. Conley & Company, (October 27, 1947), (author's personal collection).

[417]*Milwaukee Journal,* local, January 9, 1947, 1-1.

[418]"Vision of Former City Resident Paved Way for Today's Electronics' Giants," *Watertown Times,* Watertown, Wisconsin, April 23, 1979.

[419]"Sale of Miller Firm Possible," *Milwaukee Journal,* local, March 10, 1947, 1-4.

[420]"Names Mother in Fraud Suit," *Milwaukee Journal*, January 28, 1948, 1-5.

[421]MBCo Minutes.
"Deny Plan to Sell Miller Brewery," *Milwaukee Journal*, May 2, 1947, 22-4.

[422]"Father Carroll at M.U. Was the Answer Man," *Milwaukee Journal*, May 7, 1947, 3-1.

[423]MBCo minutes.

[424]Michael T. Stoiber, Untitled narrative of his experiences with Norman Klug, Elise John, and Lorraine Mulberger that he wrote in August 1949, (author's personal collection).

[425]Testimony by Frank Huber and Edward T. Donohue about their experiences with Elise John and Miller Brewery between January 1, 1946 and January 1, 1949, (author's personal collection).

Michael T. Stoiber letter to the MBCo, December 28, 1945, (author's personal collection).

[426]Frank Huber notes on January 28, 1948, (author's personal collection).

[427]Michael T. Stoiber untitled narrative of his experiences.

[428]Memoranda On Harry John Matter prepared by Harry G. John, Jr.'s attorneys, February 27, 1948, (author's personal collection).

[429]Michael T. Stoiber, Untitled narrative of his experiences.

[430]Elise K. John proxy, May 14, 1947, written on the letterhead of the law firm Timlin, Dean & Klug, (author's personal collection).

[431]"Dispute Value of Stock Gift," *Milwaukee Journal*, July 24, 1949.

[432]Information gleaned from a meeting with Frank Huber, Edward Donohue, Urban R. Wittig, and John A. Wittig on January 29, 1948, (author's personal collection).

[433]MBCo minutes.

[434]Ibid.

[435]Ibid.

[436]Ibid.

[437]Ibid.

[438]Ibid.

[439]"Miller Facing Auto Charges," *Milwaukee Journal*, July 7, 1954.

[440]Information gleaned from a meeting with Frank Huber, Edward Donohue, Urban R. Wittig, and John A. Wittig on January 29, 1948, author unknown, (author's personal collection).

[441]Testimony by Frank Huber and Edward T. Donohue about their experiences with Elise John and the MBC between January 1, 1946 and January 1, 1949, (author's personal collection).

[442]Norman Klug minutes of a Meeting in Mr. [Louis] Quarles' Office, January 24, 1962, (author's personal collection).

Charles S. Quarles notes of a phone conference on December 18, 1947, (author's personal collection).

Testimony by Frank Huber and Edward T. Donohue about their experiences with Elise John and Miller Brewery between January 1, 1946 and January 1, 1949, (author's personal collection).

Invoices from the Austen Riggs Foundation in Stockbridge, Massachusetts, September 8 and 26, 1947, (author's personal collection).

[443]Michael T. Stoiber untitled narrative of his experiences.

[444]Ibid.

[445]"F. C. Miller Elected Brewery President," *Milwaukee Journal,* local, May 29, 1947, 4-7.

"Employees Given Party by Miller Brewing Co.," *Milwaukee Journal,* local 1-4, August 3, 1947.

[446]"Huber Resigns Post at Miller," *Milwaukee Journal,* local, June 5, 1947, 5-3.

[447]MBCo Stockholder Agreement July 15, 1947, (author's personal collection).

[448]MBCo minutes.

[449]Testimony by Frank Huber and Edward T. Donohue about their experiences with Elise John and Miller Brewery between January 1, 1946 and January 1, 1949, (author's personal collection).

Typewritten notes of interviews with various people explaining events concerning Elise K. John between August 1 & August 11, 1947, (author's personal collection).

[450]Testimony by Frank Huber and Edward T. Donohue about their experiences.

[451]Typewritten notes of interviews with various people explaining events concerning Elise K. John between August 1 & August 11, 1947, (author's personal collection).

[452]"Dispute Value of Stock Gift," *Milwaukee Journal,* July 24, 1949.

[453]Joyce Meinicke personal interview with the author on April 8, 2004. (She was an employee of the trust funds of Frederick A. Miller and Elise K. John, knowing them both personally.)

[454]Walter C. Lemke, (long-time employee of Elise K. John), Four-page handwritten personal history of his employment in Elise John's office, June 27, 1952, (author's personal collection).

Meinicke.

B.H. Protzmann letter to Elise K. John, August 15, 1947, (author's personal collection).

[455]Lemke.

Meinicke.

[456]"Miller Brewing Expansion Means Gain in Output, Staff and Property," *Milwaukee Journal,* sect. II, August 24, 1947, 7-6.

[457]Ibid.

MBCo Time Line. (This undated document, without an author noted, was compiled, over many years, by various individuals including Jeffrey T. Waalkes in the Miller Brewing Company's communications department.

The information was culled from articles, company documents, and articles from internal publications.)

[458]"Another Fire Hits Brewery," December 23, 1947, newspaper unknown, (author's clipping file).

[459]MBCo minutes.

[460]"Names Mother in Fraud Suit," *Milwaukee Journal,* January 28, 1948, 1-5.

[461]MBCo minutes.

[462]Ibid.

[463]Ibid.

[464]Letter from the law firm of Line, Spooner & Quarles to Harry G. John, Jr., December 30, 1947, (author's personal collection).

[465]Attorneys Wittig & Wittig to the law firm of Line, Spooner & Quarles, January 12, 1948, (author's personal collection).

[466]"Names Mother in Fraud Suit," *Milwaukee Journal,* January 28, 1948, 1-5.

Elise K. John note to Harry G. John, Jr., January 27, 1948, (author's personal collection).

[467]"Names Mother in Fraud Suit," *Milwaukee Journal,* January 28, 1948, 1-5.

[468]"Post Dropped by Mrs. John," *Milwaukee Journal,* section L, April 7, 1948.

[469]Elise K. John letter never mailed but found beside her bed at the Sacred Heart Sanitarium to Harry G. John, Jr., March 23, 1948, (author's personal collection).

[470]Harry G, John, Jr. handwritten draft of a letter to Frederick C. Miller, undated, likely March 25, 1948, (author's personal collection).

[471]Frederick C. Miller letter on his personal letterhead to Harry G. John, Jr., April 13, 1948, (author's personal collection).

[472]"Open Building, Honor Miller," *Milwaukee Journal,* September 16, 1948.

[473]"Five Year Expansion Trail Near End, Miller Brewery to Celebrate," *Milwaukee Sentinel,* October 7, 1951.

"Cathedral Window in Brewery Building? It's a Symbol of Beauty for Brewhouse," *Milwaukee Journal,* special insert, July 19, 1949.

[474]Ibid.

[475]"Carl A. Miller Is Dead at 86," *Milwaukee Journal,* February 28, 1949.

"Carl A. Miller Funeral Set for Tomorrow," March 1, 1949, newspaper unknown, (author's clipping file).

[476]Stipulation of facts regarding the Marine Nation Exchange Bank of Milwaukee vs. Lorraine J. Mulberger, 1955, (author's personal collection).

Transcript of a MBCo meeting called by Frederick C. Miller, February 21, 1949, (author's personal collection).

[477]Ibid.

[478]"Ousted' Aid Sues Brewery," *Milwaukee Journal,* page L, July 29, 1949.

[479]"Brewery Wins $204,500 Suit Over Contract," *Milwaukee Journal,* final edition, November 28, 1949, 1-8.

"Brewery Suit Trial Ordered," *Milwaukee Journal,* April 5, 1950.

"John Estate Is $2,372,334," *Milwaukee Journal,* local, October 21, 1953, 1-5.

[480]"Miller Brewery Studies New Plant Expansion," *Milwaukee Journal,* July 21, 1949.

[481]MBCo timeline.

"Five Year Expansion Trail Near End, Miller Brewery to Celebrate," *Milwaukee Sentinel,* October 7, 1951.

"Miller Brewing Expansion Means Gain in Output, Staff and Property," August 24, 1947, newspaper unknown, (author's clipping file).

[482]Answers by the MBCo board of directors to questions asked by John A. Wittig, who represented Harry G. John, Jr. at a May 26, 1954 MBCo stockholders' meeting, (author's personal collection).

[483]"N. J. Kopmeier Is Dead at 26," *Milwaukee Journal,* section m, May 23, 1951, 25-1.

[484]Dr. H. H. Blanchard, M. D. letter to Harry G. John, Jr., December 14, 1950, (author's personal collection).

[485]Robert J. Riordan, "Group to Photograph Europe's Church Art," *Milwaukee Sentinel,* section 1, May 4, 1952, 1-6.

[486]Ibid.

[487]Ibid.

[488]Ibid.

[489]Ibid.

[490]Milwaukee County Circuit Court Order for Hearing and Notice in the Matter of the Guardianship of Elise K. John June 16, 1952, (author's personal collection).

[491]"Mrs. Elise Miller John Dead," *Miller High Life News Flash,* September 1952.

[492]"Elise K. John Estate Tops One Million," *Milwaukee Sentinel,* August 8, 1952, 1.

[493]Summary of Benefits from Elise K. John to Harry G. John, Sr., Lorraine Mulberger, and Harry G. John, Jr. compiled by Michael Stoiber in 1952, (author's personal collection).

[494]"Contest Will of Mrs. John," *Milwaukee Journal,* August 8, 1952, 1-7.

[495]"Court Hearing Seeks to Learn if $31,817 Was a Gift or Loan," *Milwaukee Journal,* final edition, October 22, 1953, 1-3.

[496]Frederick C. Miller letter to John A. Wittig, June 25, 1954, (author's personal collection).

[497]John A. Wittig letter to Harry G. John, Jr. November 19, 1953, (author's personal collection).

[498]Ibid.

[499]"Five Year Expansion Trail Near End, Miller Brewery to Celebrate," *Milwaukee Sentinel,* October 7, 1951.

[500]"Norman Klug Is Picked to Head Miller Brewery," *Milwaukee Journal,* December 21, 1954.

[501]John Pomfret, "Brewers and Strike Chiefs Agree on Terms," *Milwaukee Journal,* July 27, 1953, 1-1.

[502]Ibid.

Miller High Life News Flash, Vol. 7, Number 8, August 1953, (MBCo Archives).

[503]John A. Wittig letter to Harry G. John, Jr. November 19, 1953, (author's personal collection).

[504]Frederick C. Miller letter to John A. Wittig, June 25, 1954, (author's personal collection).

[505]Harry G. John, Jr., letter to Frederick C. Miller, May 22, 1953, (author's personal collection).

[506]John A. Wittig letter to Harry G. John, Jr. May 27, 1954, (author's personal collection).

[507]Ibid.

[508]"Illness Fatal to Kopmeier," *Milwaukee Journal,* local, June 4, 1954, 1-1.

[509]"Two Men Who Found Miller Beat Out Fire With Jacket," December 18, 1954, newspaper unknown, (author's clipping file).

[510]Ibid.

[511]"Norman Klug Is Picked to Head Miller Brewery," *Milwaukee Journal,* December 21, 1954.

[512]"Klug Had Varied Career," *Milwaukee Journal,* special insert, July 19, 1949.

[513]"Norman Klug, Miller President, Dies," *Milwaukee Sentinel,* October 25, 1966, 1.

[514]"Norman Klug Is Picked to Head Miller Brewery," *Milwaukee Journal,* December 21, 1954.

[515]Ibid.

"Her 'Outside Interest' Is Job as Executive," December 22, 1954, newspaper unknown, (author's clipping file).

[516]"Estate Now Is $2 Million," *Milwaukee Journal,* March 30, 1961.

[517]"Miller Brewery to Stage Centennial Celebration," *Milwaukee Journal,* part 2, January 12, 1955.

[518]"H. G. John, Sr. Dies, Former Miller Chief," *Milwaukee Sentinel,* January 9, 1956.

[519]"List Charities in Miller Will," *Milwaukee Journal,* March 30, 1957.

"Mrs. Clara Miller Leaves $2 Million," *Milwaukee Sentinel,* May 29, 1958.

Clara A. Miller 1958 U.S. Estate Tax Return, (author's personal file).

[520]"Miller Picks Board Chief," *Milwaukee Journal,* part II, May 24, 1956,

19-6.

[521]Harry G. John, Jr., general letter to the Harry G. John, Jr. General Trust trustees explaining his motivation for creating de Rancé, Inc., December 27, 1954, (author's personal file).

[522]Ibid.

[523]"450 Poor Children Enjoy Free Summer Camp in Milwaukee," *Catholic Herald Citizen,* July 18, 1959, 7.

"Bus Mishap Hurts Four," August 12, 1957, newspaper unknown, (author's clipping file).

[524]James B. McCahey, Sr., MBCo special stockholders' meeting of July 12, 1957, (author's personal file).

[525]Ibid.

[526]John Savage, memo on meeting in Mr. Quarles' Office, December 20, 1961, (author's personal file).

de Rancé, Inc. and Lorraine Mulberger July 15, 1957 MBCo stockholder voting agreement, (author's personal file).

[527]MBCo stockholders' Memorandum of Immediate Procedure, July 1, 1957, (author's personal file).

[528]McCahey.

[529]Harry G. John, Jr. letter to Norman Klug, July 8, 1957, (author's personal file).

MBCo October 4, 1957 Voting Trust Agreement, (author's personal file).

[530]de Rancé, Inc. versus W. R. Grace & Co. and J. Peter Grace, Affidavit from the lawsuit filed in the Supreme Court of New York, March 27th, 1973, 5, (author's personal file).

[531]de Rancé, Inc. Deferred Annual Meeting of the Trustees, April 21, 1958, (author's personal file).

[532]MBCo Voting Trust Agreement on May 28, 1958, (author's personal file).

[533]MBCo Introductory Statement To Brewery Acquisition Report, May 11, 1960, (author's personal file).

[534]Louis Quarles letter to Norman Klug, November 7, 1961, (author's personal file).

Hebert C. Hirschboeck letter to the East-Side Millers regarding their MBCo stock, October 18, 1961, (author's personal file).

[535]Louis Quarles letter to Norman Klug, November 7, 1961, (author's personal file).

[536]Ibid.

Hirschboeck.

[537]de Rancé, Inc. against W. R. Grace & Co. and J. Peter Grace, Affidavit from the lawsuit filed in the Supreme Court of New York, March 27th, 1973, 5, (author's personal collection).

[538]January 29, 1960 MBCo Voting Trust Agreement, (author's personal file).

[539]Norman Klug memo to MBCo management, December 28, 1961, (author's personal file).

de Rancé, Inc. against W. R. Grace & Co. and J. Peter Grace, Affidavit from the lawsuit filed in the Supreme Court of New York, March 27th, 1973, 7, (author's personal file).

[540]Norman Klug memo to MBCo management, December 28, 1961, (author's personal file).

de Rancé, Inc. against W. R. Grace & Co. and J. Peter Grace, Affidavit from the lawsuit filed in the Supreme Court of New York, March 27th, 1973, 7, (author's personal collection).

[541]Ibid., 9.

[542]Norman Klug minutes of a meeting in Louis Quarles' Office, January 24, 1962, (author's personal collection).

Herbert C. Hirschboeck letter to the East-Side Millers regarding their MBCo stock, October 18, 1961, (author's personal collection).

[543]Norman R. Klug memo to E. W. Huber and Charles W. Miller, March 29, 1961, (author's personal collection).

[544]Louis Quarles letter to Norman Klug, November 7, 1961, (author's personal collection).

[545]Herbert C. Hirschboeck letter to the East-Side Millers on their MBCo stock, October 18, 1961, (author's personal collection).

[546]John Savage memo of meeting in Louis Quarles' Office, December 19, 1961, (MBCo Archives).

[547]Norman Klug memo to MBCo management, December 18, 1961, (MBCo Archives).

[548]de Rancé, Inc. Annual Meeting of the Trustees, January 25, 1962, (author's personal collection).

[549]Norman Klug minutes of a meeting in Louis Quarles' office, January 24, 1962, (author's personal collection).

Norman Klug memo to MBCo management, December 14, 1961, (author's personal collection).

Ibid., December 28.

[550]Ibid., December 14, 1961.

[551]Harry G. John, Jr., & Donald Gallagher letter to Kenneth K. Luce, January 24, 1967, (author's personal collection).

[552]John Savage memo of meeting in Louis Quarles' Office, December 19, 1961, (author's personal collection).

[553]Ibid., December 20, 1961.

[554]Harry G. John, Jr., contemporaneous handwritten notes on MBCo stock redemption, undated.

Norman Klug memo to MBCo management, December 18, 1961, (author's personal collection).

[555]Ibid., January 25, 1962.

[556]Harry G. John, Jr., letter to J. Peter Grace, Jr., February 1, 1962, (author's personal collection).

436 *John*

[557]Kenneth K. Luce October 1963 Memorandum in re Proposed Acquisition by Miller Brewing Company of de Rancé Stock, (author's personal collection).

[558]Norman Klug notes from a February 20, 1965 telephone conference with Harry G. John, Jr., (author's personal collection).

[559]J. Peter Grace letter to Harry G. John, Jr. March 5, 1965, (author's personal collection).

[560]Norman Klug letter to Louis Quarles, April 8, 1965, (author's personal collection).

[561]Norman Klug notes of phone conversation with J. Peter Grace, June 18, 1965, (author's personal collection).

[562]Norman Klug notes on MBCo May 26, 1965 informal stockholder meeting, (author's personal collection).

[563]Ibid.

[564]Charles Miller notes of Harry John, Jr.'s visit on June 22, 1965, (author's personal collection).

[565]Ibid.

[566]Norman Klug memo on June 25, 1965 meeting with Lorraine Mulberger, (author's personal collection).

[567]Ibid., September 1.

[568]"Azusa Plant Shipping Set for November 1," *Miller High-Lites*, October 1966, 5, (MBCo Archives).

[569]de Rancé, Inc. against W. R. Grace & Co. and J. Peter Grace, 30.

[570]"Miller Brewery Sold to Grace Company," *Milwaukee Journal*, September 20, 1966.

[571]"Report Says W. R. Grace May Get Control of Miller," *Milwaukee Sentinel*, August 24, 1966.

[572]"Miller Stock Sale Related to Religion," *Milwaukee Sentinel*, September 21, 1966.

[573]Ibid.

Milo D. Bergo, "Religion, Aversion to Alcohol Led to Sale of Miller Brewery," *Milwaukee Journal*, September 21, 1966.

[574]"Miller Buys Brewery In Texas from Carling," *Miller High-Lites*, Vol. 4, No. 9, October 1966.

[575]"Norman R. Klug-1905-1966," *Miller High-Lites*, vol. 4, no. 9, October 1966, 1.

[576]"A Way of Life: A Will to Serve," *Miller High-Lites*, Vol. 4, No. 9, October 1966.

[577]Ibid.

[578]Ibid.

[579]"Pick Chief Executive For Miller," *Milwaukee Sentinel*, October 29, 1966.

"Charles W. Miller Named Chief Company Executive," *Miller High-Lites*, vol. 4, no. 10, November 1966, 1.

[580]"The Future Looks Good," *Miller High-Lites*, vol. 5, no. 1, January

1967.

[581]MBCo Report to Stockholders, March 22, 1967, (author's personal collection).

[582]Report to the MBCo Board of Directors, April 26, 1967, (author's personal collection).

[583]Ray Kenney, "Miller, Pepsi Deal Fizzles," *Milwaukee Sentinel,* December 1, 1969.

[584]Ross M. Dick, "Grace President Expands Views on Sale of Miller," *Milwaukee Journal,* May 14, 1969.

[585]"Miller Brewing Co. Sold to Philip Morris," *Milwaukee Journal,* June 13, 1969.

"Philip Morris to Obtain 100% Miller Ownership," *Milwaukee Sentinel,* July 30, 1970.

[586]"Miller Brewing Co. Sold to Philip Morris," *Milwaukee Journal,* June 13, 1969.

Joseph F. Cullman III, I'm a Lucky Guy, self published, 1998.

[587]de Rancé, Inc. against W. R. Grace & Co. and J. Peter Grace, 60.

[588]Laurence Eklund, "Foundation Owning Miller Stock Is Named in Report on Holdings," *Milwaukee Journal,* July 20, 1969.

[589]Ibid.

[590]"Philip Morris Net Up 33.1% to High In Second Period," *The Wall Street Journal,* July 30, 1970.

"Philip Morris Agrees to Buy Rest of Miller Brewing Stock," *Milwaukee Journal,* part 2, July 30, 1970, 18-6.

[591]"Philip Morris Net Up 33.1% to High In Second Period," *The Wall Street Journal.*

"Philip Morris Agrees to Buy Rest of Miller Brewing Stock," *Milwaukee Journal.*

INDEX

Miller Family Tree ∼ 1st, 2nd, 3rd Generations

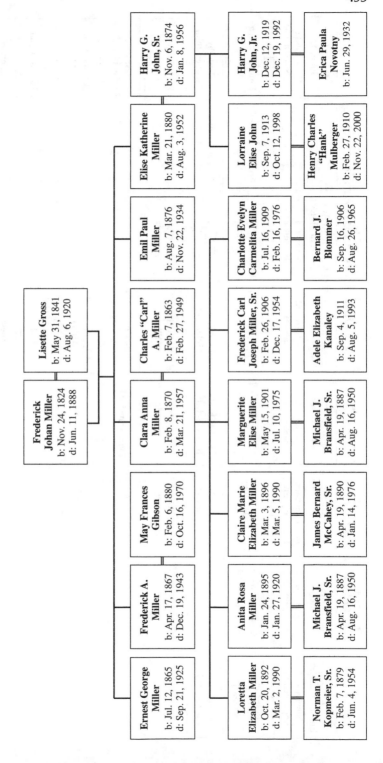

Miller Family Tree ～ 3rd and 4th Generations

Loretta Elizabeth Miller / Norman T. Kopmeier, Sr.	Anita Rosa Miller / Michael J. Bransfield, Sr.	Claire Marie Elizabeth Miller / James Bernard McCahey, Sr.	Marguerite Elise Miller / Michael J. Bransfield, Sr.	Frederick Carl Joseph Miller, Sr. / Adele Elizabeth Kanaley	Charlotte Evelyn Carmelita Miller / Bernard J. Blommer	Lorraine Elise John / Henry Charles "Hank" Mulberger	Harry G. John, Jr. / Erica Paula Novotny
Rose Mary "Rosie" Kopmeier	Charles "Chuck" Miller Bransfield	Claire McCahey	Marguerite Bransfield	Clair Miller	Elizabeth "Elise" Blommer	Lorraine "Karen" Mulberger	Emily Rebecca John
Norman J. Kopmeier, Jr.		James Brady McCahey, Jr.	Fr. Michael Bransfield, Jr.	Fred Carl Joseph Miller, Jr.	Marguerite "Margo" Blommer	Michael Henry Mulberger	Timothy Stephen John
		Anita Rose McCahey	Frederick Miller Bransfield	Elizabeth "Loret" Miller	Mary Claire Blommer		Paula Novotny John
		Frederick McCahey	Joan Bransfield	Kate Kanaley Miller			Henry Christopher John
		Carol McCahey		Marguerite "Gail" Miller			Bruno David John
				Carlotta "Robin" Miller			Gregory Theodore John
				Adele Kanaley Miller			Michael Theodore John
				Carl Anthony Miller			Elise Katherine John
							Jessica Marie John